The Language of Sophocles

This book is a wide-ranging study of Sophoclean language. From a detailed analysis of sentence-structure in the first chapter, it moves on to discuss in subsequent chapters how language shapes the perception of characters, of myths, of gods and of choruses. All chapters are united by a shared concern: how does Sophoclean language engage readers and spectators? In answering this question, *The Language of Sophocles* avoids the current emphasis on cultural specificity. Instead, it concentrates on those aspects of Sophoclean language which can engage a large number of different spectators and readers. With this change in emphasis, this study is able to offer various fresh observations about the workings of Sophoclean language. Although the book focuses on the original Greek, translations make it accessible to anybody interested in Greek tragedy.

FELIX BUDELMANN is Lecturer in Greek at the University of Manchester.

CAMBRIDGE CLASSICAL STUDIES

General Editors
P. E. EASTERLING, M. K. HOPKINS,
M. D. REEVE, A. M. SNODGRASS, G. STRIKER

THE LANGUAGE OF SOPHOCLES
Communality, Communication and Involvement

FELIX BUDELMANN
University of Manchester

PUBLISHED BY THE PRESS SYNDICATE OF THE UNIVERSITY OF CAMBRIDGE
The Pitt Building, Trumpington Street, Cambridge, United Kingdom

CAMBRIDGE UNIVERSITY PRESS
The Edinburgh Building, Cambridge CB2 2RU, UK   http://www.cup.cam.ac.uk
40 West 20th Street, New York NY 10011-4211, USA   http://www.cup.org
10 Stamford Road, Oakleigh, Melbourne 3166, Australia

First published 2000

Printed in the United Kingdom at the University Press, Cambridge

Typeset in Times New Roman   [AO]

A catalogue record for this book is available from the British Library

Library of Congress cataloguing in publication data
Budelmann, Felix.
The language of Sophocles: communality, communication and
involvement / Felix Budelmann.
p.   cm.
Enlargement of author's thesis (Ph.D.) – Cambridge University.
Includes bibliographical references and index.
ISBN 0 521 66040 8 (hardback)
1. Sophocles – Language. 2. Mythology, Greek, in literature. 3. Oral
communication – Greece. 4. Community in literature. 5. Greek language – Style.
6. Tragedy. I. Title.
PA4432.B86   1999
882'.01 – dc21   99-13645 CIP

ISBN 0 521 66040 8 hardback

CONTENTS

Acknowledgements   *page* ix

Introduction   1
1 Sentences: a shared world   19
2 Characters: a shared perspective   61
3 Myth and prophecy: shared order   92
4 Gods: a shared future   133
5 The chorus: shared survival   195

Short titles of editions and works of reference   273
Bibliography   275
General Index   289
Index of passages discussed   292

ACKNOWLEDGEMENTS

A great number of people have helped me in writing this book and the Ph.D. thesis on which it is based.

Dr Johannes Haubold and Professor Geoffrey Horrocks read, and generously commented on, drafts of individual chapters. Dr Tim Shields and Dr Bruce Fraser gave me valuable bibliographical information. Dr Simon Goldhill and Professor Oliver Taplin kindly showed me unpublished work. As my examiners, they read my Ph.D. thesis with much care and pointed me to the areas in which revision was needed most. Professor Michael Reeve read a draft of the whole book as an Editor of the *Cambridge Classical Studies* series. His comments were both precise and sympathetic. It is a pleasure to thank all these scholars for giving up their time to help me.

Dr Richard Hunter was the Director of Studies for Classics in my College. I am most grateful both for his acute observations on a draft of the entire thesis and for his support in other matters. I also wish to thank Dr Torsten Meißner, who was generous with his linguistic advice as well as his friendship. Dr Ellen Makinson corrected more than one draft and helped wherever help was needed. For both I am extremely grateful to her.

The greatest debt, however, I owe to Professor Pat Easterling, who taught me as an undergraduate in London and as a graduate student in Cambridge. I benefited immensely from her careful scholarship, her perceptive criticism and her unfailing support.

In the final stages of preparing this book I benefited greatly from the expertise of Pauline Hire and Jan Chapman of Cambridge University Press. They spared me a large number of infelicities and errors.

ACKNOWLEDGEMENTS

Finally I would like to express my gratitude to the Studienstiftung des deutschen Volkes, Pembroke College Cambridge and the British Academy. Without their financial support I would not have undertaken graduate work.

INTRODUCTION

This is a study of Sophoclean language. As such it stands in a long tradition of scholarship, which begins already in antiquity. Most famously Plutarch reports[1] that Sophocles himself traced a development in his style (λέξις). From Aeschylean grandeur (ὄγκος) he passed on to a pungent and artificial style (τὸ πικρὸν καὶ κατάτεχνον τῆς αὑτοῦ κατασκευῆς) and finally to the best kind of writing, that which is most expressive of character (ἠθικώτατον). Plutarch is not alone: a substantial number of scattered remarks by various authors[2] suggest that the language of Sophocles has interested spectators and readers from the very beginning.

This ancient interest was taken up by modern scholarship. In particular the end of the nineteenth century and the beginning of the twentieth saw a great number of works on various aspects of Sophoclean language. Titles like *De assimilatione syntactica apud Sophoclem*, *De figurae quae vocatur etymologica usu Sophocleo* or *De Sophoclis quae vocantur abusionibus*[3] are representative of the aims and scope of many such treatises. Some of them are still widely used today. Lewis Campbell's 'Introductory essay on the language of Sophocles' at the beginning of his edition, Ewald Bruhn's *Anhang* to the edition by Friedrich Schneidewin and August Nauck, and Wilhelm Schmid's article on Sophocles in the *Geschichte der griechischen Literatur*[4] contain highly valuable collections of

---

[1] *De profectibus in virtute* 7.79b. The most recent discussion, with previous literature, is Pinnoy (1984).

[2] Collected by Radt under T II.

[3] Åzelius (1897), Haberlandt (1897), Kugler (1905). For some further titles see Goheen (1951) 160–1. For a very early modern treatise on Sophoclean language see Stephanus (1568).

[4] Campbell (1871), Bruhn (1899), Schmid (1934) 485–99. Note also the index to Pearson's edition of the fragments.

material. All of them share an emphasis on syntactic, grammatical and linguistic features. What they are often less interested in is the context in which these features occur. They usually confine themselves to individual words and sentences, leaving discussion of the larger context to literary studies. This tradition continues today. The outstanding recent study is A. C. Moorhouse's *The syntax of Sophocles*,[5] which is the most thorough work on Sophoclean language of its kind. Its concerns, as Moorhouse says, are 'essentially syntactic and linguistic, not stylistic'.[6]

Between them, such studies have accumulated much valuable information about Sophoclean language, but in their stress on its formal aspects they fail (and often freely admit that they fail) to capture many of the things that Sophoclean words or sentences can do in their particular surroundings. Among the most successful attempts to go further are the books by Robert Goheen and A. A. Long. Long's subject in his 1968 monograph *Language and thought in Sophocles*[7] is abstract nouns, which he discusses in their context, thus distinguishing himself from the works I have mentioned so far. Although Long's book concentrates on abstract nouns, it throws much light on the passages in which the nouns occur as a whole, illustrating how certain choices of word have certain effects. As he puts it, 'one element of Sophocles' vocabulary is subjected to very close scrutiny, but this examination inevitably involves analysis of his language and thought in a wider sense'.[8]

Long regarded abstract nouns as just one of many 'aspects

---

[5] Moorhouse (1982). See also Webster (1969) 143–62, Earp (1944), Stevens (1945), Nuchelmans (1949), Tsitsoni (1963), pp. 263–80 of Stanford's edition of *Ajax* and pp. 12–17 of Kells's edition of *Electra*, all of which despite obvious differences are comparable. Many useful observations can also be found in commentaries, most of all those of Jebb, and the works of textual critics, especially Dawe (1973), Dawe (1978) and Lloyd-Jones and Wilson (1990). For more detailed reviews of work on Sophoclean language until the 1950s and 60s see Goheen (1951) 101–3 and Long (1968) 4–6.

[6] Moorhouse (1982) preface (no page number).

[7] Long (1968). For a further, less successful, study of certain words in their contexts see Coray (1993).

[8] Long (1968) ix.

of Sophocles' language and thought' which can be studied in this way.[9] Thirty years later his choice of single words, rather than clauses or sentences, can be seen as part of a larger pattern. Long, it turns out, is not alone in his choice. As early as 1951 Robert Goheen published a book entitled *The imagery of Sophocles' Antigone*,[10] in which he traces certain images and tropes throughout the play. Much of his study is concerned with suggesting a web of associations between related or repeated words.

Although Goheen is less interested than Long in the precise effects of an individual passage and concentrates instead on the significance certain images have in the play as a whole, he shares with Long lengthy discussion of individual words and their place in the play. This emphasis is central not just to Long and Goheen but to much twentieth-century criticism on tragedy and otherwise. The work of scholars influenced by Cambridge English and by New Criticism such as R. P. Winnington-Ingram, Gordon Kirkwood and Bernard Knox gains much of its force from close attention to language and in particular to recurrent words. Winnington-Ingram, in his study of Euripides' *Bacchae* (1948), was one of the first classicists who rigorously traced various verbal themes throughout a play, and his later work on Sophocles is characterised by similar methodology.[11] Gordon Kirkwood devotes a large part of the chapter on language in *A study of Sophoclean drama* to verbal 'themes'.[12] Finally, Bernard Knox has been greatly influential with his books about *Oedipus Rex* and about the 'Sophoclean hero', both of them works which study thematic words in great detail.[13]

Winnington-Ingram, Knox and Kirkwood, in turn, share their interest in thematic words with many later Sophoclean critics. One of the most prominent recent works that make recurring words one of their chief concerns is Charles Segal's

---

[9] Long (1968) 168.
[10] Goheen (1951).
[11] Winnington-Ingram (1948) index *s.v.* '*Bacchae*, words and themes'; Winnington-Ingram (1980), which is on Sophocles, dates back a long way.
[12] Kirkwood (1994a) 215–46.
[13] Knox (1957), e.g. 147–58 on *isos* ('equal'); Knox (1964), especially 1–61.

Tragedy and civilization (1981).[14] This wide-ranging discussion of Sophoclean drama shows that verbal themes can also be studied to great effect from a more structuralist perspective. More than once, concentration on thematic words has proved a point of contact between critics of rather different critical persuasions.

The study of verbal themes still continues. What has changed is the approach. Literary theory and criticism in the last twenty or thirty years have increasingly come to stress the spectator's and reader's roles in the construction of meaning. As it is widely emphasised that all writing may mean different things to different people, the study of tragic language has also taken a new direction. Thematic words are now often looked at for their ambiguity. Again Winnington-Ingram is an early example. All his writing on Aeschylus, Sophocles and Euripides investigates the ambiguity of tragedy and tragic language. Yet the scholar who has been most influential in making ambiguity a buzzword of recent criticism on Greek tragedy is probably Jean-Pierre Vernant, who in a 1969 article with the title 'Tensions and ambiguities in Greek tragedy' pointed to the different ways in which different characters use terms such as *dikē* ('justice', 'right') and *kratos* ('authority', 'force'). Vernant concludes that 'it is only for the spectator that the language of the text can be transparent at every level in all its polyvalence and with all its ambiguities. Between the author and the spectator the language thus recuperates the full function of communication that it has lost on the stage between the protagonists in the drama.'[15] With a less strong emphasis on the certainty of the spectators, Vernant's suggestions have become highly influential. Simon Goldhill has the backing of numerous scholars when he concludes his chapter on 'The language of tragedy: rhetoric and communication' in the recent *Cambridge companion to Greek tragedy* by saying that 'tragedy puts language itself *es meson*, on display and at risk in the glare of democratic scrutiny'.[16]

---

[14] Segal (1981).   [15] Vernant (1988b) 43.
[16] Goldhill (1997a) 149–50, who cites further literature.

The word 'democratic' in Goldhill's sentence points to a second and related recent critical development. As Edith Hall puts it, 'the greatest innovation in the study of Greek tragedy over the last thirty years has been the excavation of its historical and topographical specificity'. Universalist approaches, like those of Aristotle and many nineteenth-century scholars, are now avoided. 'A scholarly project of the last three decades has been to undermine such universalising readings and to locate the plays within the historical conditions of their production.'[17] A brief glance at the titles of influential collections published in the last fifteen years is enough to show what Hall means: *Greek tragedy and political theory*; *Nothing to do with Dionysos?: Athenian drama in its social context*; *Tragedy, comedy and the polis*; *Theater and society in the classical world*; *History, tragedy, theory: dialogues on Athenian drama*; *Tragedy and the historian*.[18]

Along with much else, the language of tragedy has been put into its historical context. Rather than trying to determine what is special about Sophocles, scholars have come to look for the connotations that Sophocles', as well as Aeschylus' and Euripides', language may have had for fifth-century spectators. In the article from which I have just quoted, Goldhill stresses that 'the language of tragedy is public, democratic, male talk . . .: that is, the language of tragedy is in all senses of the term *political*'.[19] Long, too, had a historical interest and traced the rise of abstract nouns during the fifth century. But for him this historical development was the background against which he investigated 'certain highly individual

---

[17] Hall (1997) 94. A scholar who is more interested than most not only in what is culturally specific but also in what is universal in Greek tragedy is Oliver Taplin. See, for instance, Taplin (1978) 5–8, with the criticism in Wiles (1997) 5–14, and Taplin (forthcoming). Note also discussions of Greek tragedy from the viewpoint of the modern philosopher: Nussbaum (1986) and, especially, Williams (1993).

[18] Euben (1986), Winkler and Zeitlin (1990), Sommerstein *et al.* (1993), Scodel (1993), Goff (1995), Pelling (ed.) (1997). More varied approaches in Silk (1996) and Easterling (ed.) (1997); perhaps the fact that they are among the most recent collections suggests a change in scholarly preoccupations?

[19] Goldhill (1997a) 128, his italics. See Knox (1957) for an early sustained study of Sophoclean drama and language in its historical context.

ways'[20] in which Sophocles used these nouns. Goldhill and other recent scholars, by contrast, place their emphasis on the historical frame. They are interested in the 'political' meaning that is shared by *all* tragedy.

No outline in five or six pages can convey the full breadth of work that has been carried out on the language of Sophocles in the last two centuries. At the risk of making a somewhat simplifying generalisation and of doing injustice to the specific interests of individual scholars, I none the less draw attention to a development that can be traced in this selective history of Sophoclean scholarship. It concerns the different places at which different scholars have been prepared to accept limits to their investigations. While formalist studies tend to give a panoramic view of all kinds of linguistic details, they often fail to take the context into account. Long, by contrast, who makes a point of contextualising the passages he discusses, confines himself to abstract words. Similarly, Winnington-Ingram, Knox, Segal and others have much to say about certain words in certain contexts, but have abandoned many of the more grammatical and linguistic interests of earlier scholars. Critics like Vernant and Goldhill distance themselves still further from formalism in two ways. Firstly, their analysis of tragic language is often dominated by their concern with ambiguity. Sentence structure, thematic words and other such areas of long-standing interest are now frequently studied in the first place for the polyvalent meaning that they yield. Ambiguity was already at the heart of Winnington-Ingram's work, but only Vernant and later scholars repeatedly make it their declared object of investigation. Secondly, by stressing the context that is provided by history and society in addition to that provided by the play, they focus not only on thematic words but, more particularly, on words that yield especially well to historical investigation. For these scholars Sophoclean language is no longer itself an object of study, but is subordinated to tragic language, which in turn is one aspect of the historically contingent nature of

---

[20] Long (1968) 26.

Greek tragedy. To put it briefly, work which examines various linguistic phenomena, but is not interested in the context or in the different ways in which different spectators might react, and approaches which centre on ambiguity and politics all have their limits. There is still much work to be done on the way Sophoclean language works.

My aim in this book is to do some of this work by learning from as many as possible of the varied observations that scholars have made over the years. In particular I will try to combine an awareness of the spectators' and readers' role in the production of meaning with a concern for the uniqueness of Sophocles and of each Sophoclean play. I will therefore give due weight to the differences between different spectators and readers, and still make room for aspects of Sophoclean language other than its ambiguity and its political nature. In other words, I will neither take it for granted that all spectators and readers of all time are the same, and thus produce a formalist study, nor place all my emphasis on the differences between different spectators and readers, and thus concentrate on historical context and indeterminacy. Rather, I am interested in those aspects of Sophoclean language that may be shared by different spectators and readers, whether at different times and in different places or at the same time in the same theatre. For want of a better term, I will call this kind of shared response 'communality among the different', giving the term both a diachronic (various times and places) and a synchronic (one theatre at one time) meaning.

As the starting-point for my discussion I will use the observation that I made at the outset: Sophoclean language has produced an impressive tradition of scholarship. There are, of course, few classical authors whose language has not been scrutinised in great detail over the years. But even against this backgound, the amount of work carried out on Sophoclean language is remarkable. Clearly, it has been fascinating critics for a long time. Sophocles' continuous success as a playwright both in antiquity and in the modern world, moreover, suggests also that various generations of spectators have not, to say the least, found his language off-putting. One of my guiding questions, therefore, in my search for communality among the different will be what there is that may make many different spectators and readers of many times and places engage with Sophoclean language.

Before I begin to answer this question, it is necessary to stress that, like all the earlier scholars whose work I have reviewed, I have to accept various limitations. The most important of them is the inevitably tentative nature of any answer that I will give. Differences between different spectators and readers are overwhelming. At a very basic level there is the difference of language. Most spectators today see, and readers read, Sophoclean tragedies in translation, rather than in the original Greek as in antiquity. A study like mine, which is based on the Greek text, is applicable to users of translations only to a degree, lesser or higher depending on the aims and the success of the translator.[21] And even spectators and readers who are confronted with the Greek original, or with the same translation, may describe Sophoclean language in differing terminology. Many will speak, say, of the 'Sophoclean hero', others will not, and those who do may mean a wide variety of things. Much that I will say would therefore have to be rephrased in order to be even comprehensible to many given spectators and readers. Most important, even if one sets all such problems of translation and terminology aside, one comes back again and again to the fundamental truth that everybody who watches or reads Sophoclean plays watches or reads them with different expectations and assumptions, in different states of mind, under different conditions and so on. Strictly speaking, one might be tempted to say, there is no communality but only difference.

And yet, I repeat, Sophoclean language has the power to engage all these different spectators and readers. To put it very crudely, different spectators and readers can have very different views of *what* Sophocles means, but none the less, to some degree, they will be affected by *how* he means; they differ

---

[21] This is not to say that it can only be read by those who know Greek. Almost all of the Greek is translated. See below, p. 18.

over *what* Sophoclean language communicates but they all react to *how* it communicates. This is a distinction which ought not to be pressed too hard, since it would ultimately become hard to sustain. 'How' and 'what' are reminiscent of 'form' and 'content', and this is a notoriously difficult pair. It would be a great mistake to assume that 'how' a passage communicates is nothing whatsoever to do with the individual spectator or reader. However, if they are not made to carry this kind of weight, 'how' and 'what' are useful terms which (if nothing else) can help to give an impression of what I try to do in this book. At its very heart is the desire to describe how Sophoclean language communicates.[22] For all the differences between the various ways in which spectators and readers understand a passage, there is still often something in the way the passage is written, in 'how it means', how it communicates, to which many of them are responsive. In this respect there is not only difference but also communality.

In order to talk about this communality, of course, it will be necessary to allow for a wide margin of variation. Even *how* Sophocles means is after all not the kind of absolute that allows sweeping formalist statements. Here, too, differences between different spectators and between different readers make a certain difference. Nothing, therefore, that I say about communality in the perception of how Sophoclean language means will be meant to suggest identity. Nothing I say will be meant to be true for all spectators and readers in the same way. I am interested in communality *among the different*. With these provisos I ask again: what is there in Sophoclean language, in the way Sophoclean language communicates, that can engage different spectators and readers?

The path that I will pursue in order to answer this question is by no means untrodden, but it has not, as far as I am aware, previously been used for an investigation into Sophoclean language, and it will let me arrive at new insights (I hope) into

---

[22] This kind of project is by no means unparalleled. A recent book on 'Greek literature in its linguistic context' begins by invoking a recent 'shift in interest from the "what" to the "how" in the production of meaning': Bakker (1997) 1.

how it functions. Sophoclean language, I suggest, can engage different spectators and readers of different times because, repeatedly, it makes them both know and not know something. As I will argue in detail, it often gives them a degree of information, and at the same time withholds full knowledge. There is much that spectators and readers do not know, but they still know enough to escape utter bafflement. They are given some understanding and can try to push forward its limits. There are many moments when spectators and readers are busy negotiating and re-negotiating certainty with uncertainty, moments when they engage with Sophoclean language as they know (or think they know) some things and do not know (or think they do not know) others.

These are moments of what I call communality among the different. People are different. Not everybody has the same kind of knowledge. Different people are certain or uncertain about different things when they see and read Sophocles. But allowing, as I said I would, for a large margin of variation, I will have enough space to think about the spectators' and readers' shared involvement. As I hope to bring out in this book, Sophoclean language is such that they all, again and again, find themselves having something to start from and yet struggling to get a full grasp, and that again and again such moments of being certain about some things and uncertain about others are shared by many spectators and readers, different though their reactions are in detail. To look at communality as I understand it is to try to see both what is different and what is similar.

Stepping back a little, I wish to draw attention to the way this concern with both what is different and what is similar informs also my assumption that simultaneous knowing and not knowing, or being certain and being uncertain, may prompt involvement. Knowledge was not conceptualised in the same way by the ancient Greeks as it is today, and there is no *a priori* reason for believing that fascination with the half-known is identical in all cultures. I do not therefore try to develop a detailed and universally valid psychological, behavioural or other kind of model of audience or reader response, as, in their different ways, narratologists following Gérard Genette, reception theorists like Wolfgang Iser or Hans Robert Jauss, students of semiotics like Umberto Eco, anthropologists like Victor Turner, scholars interested in the semiotics of theatre or psychoanalytic critics have done.[23] Although I have learned from such models as well as from the criticism that has been levelled against them, my emphasis throughout the book will be on Sophoclean language and kinds of possible response, rather than on detailed accounts of the spectators' and readers' precise reactions. There is too much that is different from one spectator or reader to the next to make the latter a worthwhile project.

Yet at the same time there is much that different spectators and readers have in common. The twentieth century's fascination with the half-known and the ambiguous does not need elaborating. A few pointers will be enough. This is a century in which novelty has been a central category by which art works are judged, in which the concept of defamiliarisation has been at the heart of much aesthetic theorising, in which a term like 'absent presence' has widely gained currency, and in which critics from Roman Ingarden ('places of indeterminacy'), via Wolfgang Iser ('blanks', 'Leerstellen') to Anne Ubersfeld ('le texte troué')[24] construct aesthetic theories around gaps.

While 'absent presences', 'places of indeterminacy' and other such details are distinctly modern, there can be no doubt that also fifth-century Athens liked to juxtapose knowledge and ignorance. Not only is the ambiguity of language thematised in tragedy and the limits of human knowledge a concern of Sophoclean plays like *Oedipus Rex* and *Trachiniae*, but other genres display similar interests. Most famously, Socrates is reported to have proclaimed that he, unlike others, knows that he does not know,[25] and in Plato's early dialogues he is portrayed as somebody who makes others, who believe that

---

[23] For a review of recent theories of the theatre see Carlson (1993) 505–40.

[24] Ingarden (1973), especially 50–5, Iser (1976) 257–355, Ubersfeld (1978) 13–25 and Ubersfeld (1996) 10–18.

[25] Plato *Apol.* 21d.

they know, realise that they do not know. From smug certainty Socrates' interlocutors are thrown into *aporia*.

Socrates shares his paradoxical phrasing and his concern with the possibility of knowledge with intellectual figures such as Parmenides, Heraclitus, Democritus, Protagoras and Gorgias. The last is the one most immediately relevant for my present purposes. Gorgias came to Athens in 427 and instantly made a great impact. In various fragments he engages with epistemological problems, often putting them into the context of communication. In his work *On what is not* he says 'Nothing is. And if it is, it is not knowable. And if it is and is knowable, it cannot be communicated to others.'[26] Closely related is Gorgias' interest in the interaction between being and seeming and the combined strength of the two: 'Being is invisible if it does not attain seeming, and seeming has no strength if it does not attain being.'[27] Most immediately relevant, however, to the project of this book is a passage in the *Encomium of Helen*. Here Gorgias uses knowledge and ignorance for a model of audience response: 'To tell those who know what they know is persuasive, but does not please.'[28]

Even without the discussion that these quotations deserve,[29] it should be clear that fifth-century-BC Athens, like the twentieth-century Western world and like no doubt many other periods and cultures, was fascinated by questions of knowledge and ignorance, and in particular by the grey area that there is between the two. Details inevitably vary. Arguably, discussions of knowledge in the fifth century were more intricately bound up with the question of what it is to be human than they are today. Be that as it may, what matters here is that, allowing for a certain degree of difference, there are enough parallels between fifth- and twentieth-century concerns to justify the assumption that Sophoclean tragedy

---

[26] Fr. 3.1 Buchheim. Cf. frs. 1 and 28.

[27] Fr. 26 Buchheim.

[28] *Hel.* 5; cf. fr. 23 Buchheim. Compare also Aristotle, *Poetics* 1460a11–12 'one should in tragedies use what is amazing (τὸ θαυμαστόν)' and 1460a17 'amazement is enjoyable' (τὸ δὲ θαυμαστὸν ἡδύ), as well as Eur. *Ba.* 474–5.

[29] For a recent discussion that is relevant to the questions that I am pursuing, see Wardy (1996) 6–51.

engaged spectators then, as it engages them now, through simultaneous certainty and uncertainty. There is much room for communality among the different.

Before I finally start looking at the texts, a few more words are in order about the term 'communality' which I have been using repeatedly in the last few pages. To apply it, as I do, to reactions that are shared by spectators of different times is to stretch its ordinary meaning. If I have none the less chosen 'communality' as a central term in my discussion, then this is because the word describes so well the situation that, as it were, crystallises such shared reactions: spectators gathering in the theatre and, different as they all are, forming a group that watches a play.

Performance criticism, like literary criticism, has come to stress different spectators' different responses. The same play is perceived in different ways not only because the shape of the theatre, the sets, the costumes, the directing and the acting vary from one performance to the next,[30] but also because of differences between spectators at each one performance. Performance critics have discussed generally how each individual spectator will inevitably respond individually, and more specifically how certain sub-groups in the audience, such as women or spectators of a specific cultural origin, react differently to the same performance.[31] Yet for all this variety, going to the theatre, sitting in a crowd, watching a play together, laughing and clapping together remains also a communal act. As Oliver Taplin puts it, 'the experience of gathering at a special place and of participating communally ... is the crucial difference between going to the theatre and listening to a

---

[30] The various elements that make up a performance are discussed in semiotic studies such as Elam (1980) and Fischer-Lichte (1992).

[31] For two books reflecting the move away from universality in recent performance criticism see Bennett (1990) and Bulman (1996). See also Blau (1983), Carlson (1990b) and, for a more psychoanalytical approach, Blau (1990). On women see e.g. Dolan (1988), esp. 1–3, and, for a brief overview of feminism and theatre, Carlson (1993) 527–40. On cultural origin see e.g. Hodgdon (1996) and Pavis (1996). A similar trend away from universality can be observed in the related field of media studies. See Hay et al. (1996) for a large collection of recent essays with extensive bibliography.

recording or watching television'.[32] To be a spectator is not only to be an idiosyncratic and isolated individual but it is also to be a member of a group.

A number of factors suggest that this was perceived similarly in ancient Athens. Already then, of course, different spectators reacted in different ways. They too had differing political and moral views, differing social, political and geographical origins (some of which were perhaps even represented in the seating arrangements), were perhaps not all men, and so on.[33] But none the less there is much that points towards communality. In Athens, tragedies were performed in a large open theatre. At least the first performance of any tragedy was part of communal celebrations at the Great Dionysia.[34] The presiding god, Dionysus, was a god who broke down the boundaries of individuality. His worshippers were often perceived as losing their ordinary selves, participating in communal activities of various sorts.[35] More specifically, the sense that theatre-going is a communal activity already pervades Plato's writings. Much of the anxiety he voices in the *Republic* about the effects of theatre on its audience stems from his disapproval of the spectators' emotional and non-rational reaction to what they see and hear. To weep or laugh at a character, he stresses, is to do damage to oneself.[36] How much this emotional reaction to which Plato objects is a communal reaction is noticeable when he complains in the *Laws* about noisy audiences (*ta theatra*), which have created what he calls a *theatrokratia* ('rule of the audience').[37] Communal involvement was a central aspect of theatre-going

---

[32] Taplin (1995) 115.

[33] On the composition and seating of the Athenian audience see most recently Goldhill (1997b). The case for simultaneous consensus and conflict is argued by Lada (1996) 102–10. On political aspects see also ch. 5.

[34] On this context see especially Goldhill (1990a), Csapo and Slater (1994) 103–85 and Sourvinou-Inwood (1994).

[35] Henrichs (1984), esp. 223–32, charts the place of 'loss of self' in modern scholarship on Dionysus. As he points out, this is an important, but not the only, aspect of Dionysiac worship and myth.

[36] X 606b.

[37] III 700c–701b; the context is a discussion of musical performances.

in antiquity as it is today.[38] It is in reference to this experience of almost physically shared engagement with a play that I speak of 'communality'.

In order to avoid raising false expectations, however, I wish to emphasise that this reference to the communality of theatre-going is not part of a larger concern for what makes live theatre special. Much that I say in this book will be phrased in terms of theatrical performance rather than of the printed book. Most important, I will from now on speak of 'spectators' and 'watching', rather than 'readers' and 'reading'. But what I will not do is put much weight on the specifics of theatrical performance. The reader should not expect any detailed discussion of acting, of costumes and masks, of theatrical space, of self-referential language, of the spectators' seating or of their behaviour. All of these are topics of immense interest, but they are not the subject of this book.

Despite my use of theatrical terminology, in other words, my aim is to be as inclusive as possible. This is a book about Sophoclean language, about how it communicates and about why it is as engaging as it is. It is not a book about theatrical performance. When I choose the term 'spectators' rather than 'readers', I do so not in order to exclude readers, critics or anybody else; if indeed there were a word meaning 'spectators (and readers)', I would use it in preference to 'spectators'.

---

[38] On *theatrokratia* and on ancient audience response in general, see most recently Wallace (1997). More generally, on dramatic performance in classical Athens as breaking down the boundaries of individuality, see Lada (1997) 90–7. Interest in communality has often centred on comedy; e.g. Reckford (1987) 301–11. For discussion of the relation between communality and individuality in the *modern* theatre, see Turner (1982), who speaks of 'communitas', Ubersfeld (1996) 273–87, Beckerman (1970) 130–7, Bennett (1990) 163–7 and, for cinema, Ellis (1992) 87–9. See also works such as De Marinis (1987), Carlson (1990) and De Marinis (1993) 158–88, which try to do justice to the individuality of each spectator's reaction, while discussing aspects of the performance that influence this reaction. Note further that a central concern of many artists and theorists occupied with intercultural performance is the relation of the culturally specific with the universal: see Pavis (1996) for a recent collection of essays. Similarly, critics writing on television watching are increasingly interested in the kind of communality that is created by the global availability of certain programmes: Morley (1996) with further bibliography.

There can be no doubt that reading a play in one's room is a very different experience from watching it in the theatre. Most of all, it is a more solitary experience. Much, therefore, that I will say about 'spectators' would need a great deal of adaptation before it could be applied to readers or critics. But this is not to say that it could not be applied to them at all. They, too, are not just lonely individuals but also part of a tradition of engaging with Sophoclean tragedy which began a long time ago and will continue, I hope, for a long time to come. And, they, too, are responsive to the characteristics of Sophoclean language which I study in this book. Communality in the narrow sense of shared watching, listening and clapping at the same time in the same place is confined to the theatre. But as I noted earlier, I am interested not only in synchronic but also in diachronic communality. Communality in this sense, the communality of involvement shared by people at different times in different places, is less restricted. Readers, as much as spectators, can engage with Sophoclean language. Readers, as much as spectators, are affected by how Sophoclean language communicates. My choice of 'spectators' over 'readers', then, is meant to point to theatre-going as the most obvious form of shared engagement with Sophoclean tragedy. It is not meant to distract from the fact that the aspects of Sophoclean language which will be discussed in this study also have an effect, often a similar effect, on readers.

Now the programme is clear. My subject is the language of Sophocles. Between them, the three nouns in the subtitle bring it into closer focus: *communality, communication and involvement.* Throughout this book I will discuss how Sophoclean language communicates (*communication*). By concentrating on this 'how', rather than asking 'what' meaning it communicates, I will try to move away from the current emphasis on each individual spectator's (and reader's) individual creation of meaning, and to stress shared reactions instead. The ways in which Sophoclean language communicates, I will suggest, can often engage many spectators (and readers), different as they all are (*communality*). In particular, I will argue, Sophoclean language can get different spectators (and readers) involved because it does not communicate a straightforward message in a straightforward way but rather gives them a degree of understanding and lets them struggle for more (*involvement*).

As my examples I have chosen five aspects of Sophoclean tragedy which have all proved engaging already by becoming topics of long-standing scholarly interest, and I have arranged them so as to form a movement from small to large. I begin in chapter 1 with a discussion of individual sentences and their structure. In chapters 2 to 4, I look at longer stretches of text, analysing how the way Sophoclean language communicates affects the understanding of characters (2), of myths and prophecies (3) and of gods (4). Finally, in chapter 5, I chart the language used by and of the chorus through three whole plays.

Between them, I hope, the five chapters will bring out much that is characteristic of Sophoclean language. However, I should come clean at the outset and declare that I will rarely corroborate my case by contrasting the language of Sophocles with that of Aeschylus or Euripides. I have little doubt that the linguistic features which I am going to present are both more frequent and more elaborate in Sophocles than in Aeschylus or Euripides. Sophoclean language fascinates different critics and engages different spectators through its intricate blend of saying one thing and at the same time pointing to another thing it does not say, and it does so, I believe, to a degree that Aeschylean and Euripidean language does not. The problem is that the aspects of tragic language that I shall be talking about are neither black-and-white enough nor quantifiable enough to permit negative proofs. This is why I just said 'I have no doubt' and 'I believe'. It would be easy to find a plethora of passages in Aeschylus and Euripides which *do not* exhibit the features that I discuss in Sophocles. However, it would also be possible to find passages which *resemble closely* those which I discuss in Sophocles. The language of Aeschylus and the language of Euripides deserve studies in their own right. They cannot be used successfully as mere foils. I shall, therefore, be content with establishing

17

that Sophoclean language does what I say it does, and shall leave unproved the more ambitious claim that Aeschylean or Euripidean language does so to a lesser extent.

Finally a note on translations. In a study devoted to language it is perhaps inevitable that certain aspects are difficult to convey to readers without Greek. It is especially in chapter I that these readers may find themselves concentrating on the general argument rather than the details. I hope that they persevere none the less. Throughout I have tried to keep my discussion accessible by providing translations wherever it seemed sensible. Most of the book should therefore be accessible to any reader with an interest in Sophoclean tragedy. Quotations of Sophocles are taken from the Oxford Classical Text, eds. H. Lloyd-Jones and N. G. Wilson. Translations are taken from the Loeb by H. Lloyd-Jones.[39] I have silently adapted the translations wherever a more literal rendering helps to bring out matters of interest.

[39] Reprinted by permission of the publishers and the Loeb Classical Library from Sophocles, translated by H. Lloyd-Jones, 2 vols., Cambridge, Mass.: Harvard University Press, 1994.

CHAPTER I

SENTENCES: A SHARED WORLD

INTRODUCTION

At the heart of this book is an interest in how Sophoclean language communicates. In particular, I am interested in how Sophoclean language can engage many different spectators[1] by giving them a degree of information but no complete knowledge, prompting them to use what they know for struggling with what they do not know. In later chapters the spotlight will be on the effects language has on the way characters are perceived, on language about myth and prophecies, on language about gods, language used by the chorus and on many other aspects of Sophocles' language. In those chapters it will be necessary to discuss the language of continuous passages, scenes and even plays. Before opening out the view on such lengthier stretches of text, I will look in this chapter at a number of individual sentences, at their structure and their word order.

By discussing unconnected sentences, this chapter adopts the preferred format of scholars such as Campbell, Long and Moorhouse, who are interested mainly in the formal aspects of Sophoclean language,[2] and much indeed that I will say is based on their work. Yet at the same time this chapter is designed in various ways to go beyond the scope of Campbell, Long and Moorhouse, and will eventually lead into the increasingly wide-ranging discussion of the following chapters, which are more in the style of most of the recent work on Sophocles. A central tenet of my book is that such continuity

---

[1] As I have said in the Introduction (pp. 15–16), I speak of 'spectators' throughout this book, but I do not mean to exclude readers, critics or anybody else.

[2] For a brief overview of work on Sophoclean language see the Introduction, pp. 1–7.

19

between small-scale and large-scale approaches is possible. There are many different aspects of Sophoclean language, I claim, which keep spectators busy, prompting them to put together what they are certain about and what they are uncertain about. There is scope for involvement at all levels.

Here is an example which will help to set the scene (*OT* 339–41):

> Οι. τίς γὰρ τοιαῦτ' ἂν οὐκ ἂν ὀργίζοιτ' ἔπη
> κλύων, ἃ νῦν σὺ τήνδ' ἀτιμάζεις πόλιν;
>
> Τε. ἥξει γὰρ αὐτά, κἂν ἐγὼ σιγῇ στέγω.

Oed. Why, who would not be angry, hearing such words as those with which you now show disrespect for this city?
Teir. Yes, they will come of themselves, even if I veil them in silence.

I am interested here in the last of the three lines. Tiresias' reply is by no means the most obvious of Greek sentences. What makes it remarkable is its lack of explicit grammatical subject. What does αὐτά refer to? Who are 'they'? These are difficult questions. For the time being I shall content myself with quoting some commentators who address them in their different ways. First, Campbell speaks of 'the vague subject, which ... assists the effect of mystery'. Next, Jebb says that 'the subject to ἥξει is designedly left indeterminate: "(the things of which I wot) will come of themselves." The seer is communing with his own thought, which dwells darkly on the κακά of v. 328.' Similarly, Kamerbeek regards the sentence as 'vaguely referring to the matter he is unwilling to disclose'. Finally, Dawe comments that 'Sophocles has glided imperceptibly from ἔπη, words, to the events denoted by those words, as the subject of ἥξει.'

I have quoted Tiresias' lines and these four scholars because together they provide a first glimpse of the blend of uncertainty and certainty which is, as I suggest, conveyed by Sophoclean language: 'the vague subject', 'indeterminate', 'darkly' and 'has glided imperceptibly', on the one hand, go together with 'assists the effect' and 'designedly', on the other. The commentators I quoted seem to perceive both elusiveness

and purpose in Tiresias' sentence. Much more of course will
have to be said about the sentence later. What exactly is uncertain about it, and what certain? In exactly what way is this
engaging? Even so, I hope, the passage has already provided a
first impression of the kind of sentence and the kind of phenomenon that will be the subject of this chapter.

I will return to Tiresias' sentence at the end of the chapter,
having, by then, accumulated information about many comparable sentences. However, before I start to accumulate this
information, I need to set out clearly how I will go about
analysing Sophoclean sentences and the kind of involvement
they make possible. In the long run, quoting other critics will
not be enough. Let me start by pointing to three major difficulties inherent in any such project. Firstly, it is important
to realise that no answer can be more than partial. As my
choice of quotations may already have suggested ('left indeterminate', 'has glided imperceptibly'), mine will concentrate
on the ways in which sentences like Tiresias' communicate
information, giving priority to one item over another, letting
spectators know *this* before letting them know *that*. Many
other aspects of these sentences will remain undiscussed. I
will have hardly anything to say, for instance, about sound
and hardly anything about metre, although both acoustic
and rhythmical patterning do much to determine the way
sentence-structure and word order are perceived by spectators.
The discussion of this chapter is therefore intended not as a
comprehensive treatment of Sophoclean sentences and their
effects but only as an illustration of *some* of the ways in which
these sentences may engage spectators.

Secondly, there is the question of how best to speak about
the ways in which sentences are processed. The way language is understood has been the object of research by, among
others, experimental psychologists and linguists, and no comprehensive theory is readily available to the non-specialist.[3]
What I will say here is therefore by no means designed to

---

[3] Pinker (1995) 437, n. on p. 197, gives some relevant items.

account for the processes in spectators' brains. Rather, I will use a very simple model as a way of speaking about some effects of Sophoclean sentences.

Thirdly, as I stressed in the Introduction, all spectators are different and react in different ways. I am interested in the communality of shared engagement, but this is a communality not among identical people but a communality among the different. I will therefore refrain not only from trying to account for the processes in the spectators' brains, but also from claiming that anything I say is true for all spectators in the same way. When I speak, for instance, as I will, about spectators 'being surprised by' or 'wondering about' certain features of a sentence, I do not suggest that each of them is in a state of shock or that they all have the mentality of crossword-solvers. Rather, I will use expressions like these – and some such expressions are unavoidable – in order to draw attention to particular characteristics of Sophoclean sentence-structure and to the *kind of* reaction Sophoclean sentence-structure may prompt. Everything I say about the spectators' possible reactions, both in this chapter and elsewhere in the book, should be understood as tentative and should be granted a certain margin of variation. With these *caveats* I can begin to explain more positively how I will go about analysing Sophoclean sentences.

My starting-point is the simple observation that every word in a sentence conveys information, and that the information is released in the order in which the words of the sentence are arranged. As a result, every reader, and in the theatre every spectator, relies on the sentence to continue for finding out what it says. They do not know what comes next.

Yet this observation is not just simple, but too simple. To say that spectators are at the mercy of a sentence for the staggered release of information gives them too passive a role. While not knowing how the sentence will continue, they still have certain expectations: the next word will be a noun, the sentence will end soon, there will be a sub-clause with a certain meaning, and so on. How many such expectations spectators may have, how concrete they may be, and how justified, depends partly (if not exclusively) on the individual sentence. Some sentences prompt more numerous and more precise expectations than others, some sentences fulfil expectations they prompt more quickly and more exactly than others. Sentences, to put it simply, are not all equally predictable. Some, in fact, are distinctly unpredictable.

It is this unpredictability that I am interested in here. Unpredictability can be involving. As spectators wait for their expectations to be fulfilled or as they are surprised by having them thwarted, the sentence seizes their attention. Rather than fully knowing what happens next or having no expectations whatsoever, spectators are busy following the sentence to have their expectations at last fulfilled or adjusting their expectations to the unexpected course the sentence has taken. This is the basic linguistic model (if it deserves this term) which I will use.

In order to avoid possible misunderstandings I should stress that this model is not designed to advance linguistic theory. In this book I will analyse ways in which *Sophoclean* language communicates, not ways in which language in general communicates. For this purpose I will draw repeatedly on the methods and terminologies of linguists in order to bring out certain characteristics of Sophoclean language. I will not try to add to our understanding of language as such. My model of spectators' expectations and involvement would need extensive elaboration and refinement before it could stand up as a valid theory of how language communicates.

Even without this elaboration and refinement, however, crude as it is, the model will help me to throw light on Sophoclean sentences. In what follows I will investigate how sentences like the one I quoted at the start raise, fulfil and thwart expectations, and I will suggest that one of their chief characteristics is exactly this: they keep spectators in suspense or surprise them, by creating strong expectations but fulfilling them late or not at all. They are in various ways unpredictable.

In order to describe this unpredictability, it will from time to time be convenient to have an object of comparison. A case could be made for sentences from Homer, Pindar, Euripides,

Aristophanes, Herodotus and various others. None of these authors, however, would be as helpful for my specific purposes as Gorgias. Gorgias is one of the syntactically most predictable Greek writers.[4] It is therefore perhaps not a particularly interesting thing to say that he is more predictable than Sophocles. What *is* interesting (I hope) is to look at some of the ways in which Sophoclean unpredictability engages spectators; and the glaring contrast that Gorgias presents will make it easier to talk about them.

Here, then, are two examples of Gorgianic sentences, both taken from the *Encomium of Helen*:

(A) δῆλον γὰρ ὡς μητρὸς μὲν Λήδας ⟨sc. Helen⟩, πατρὸς δὲ τοῦ μὲν γενομένου θεοῦ, λεγομένου δὲ θνητοῦ, Τυνδάρεω καὶ Διός, ὧν ὁ μὲν διὰ τὸ εἶναι ἔδοξεν, ὁ δὲ διὰ τὸ φάναι ἠλέγχθη,[5] καὶ ἦν ὁ μὲν ἀνδρῶν κράτιστος, ὁ δὲ πάντων τύραννος (3).

It is obvious that Helen's mother was Leda, her father actually a god but nominally a mortal, Tyndareus and Zeus. One of them was famed for what he was, the other refuted for what he claimed to be, and one was the best of men, the other the ruler of all.

(B) ἐπειράθην καταλῦσαι μώμου ἀδικίαν καὶ δόξης ἀμαθίαν, ἐβουλήθην γράψαι τὸν λόγον Ἑλένης μὲν ἐγκώμιον, ἐμὸν δὲ παίγνιον (the last sentence: 21).

I tried to do away with the injustice of the reproach and the nonsense of the reputation; I wanted to write the speech as praise for Helen and as entertainment for myself.

Like all sentences, these two release information as they proceed. What distinguishes them is the ways in which they create and fulfil expectations. This is where the pragmatic terms 'head', 'specifier' and 'complement' prove useful. I will speak of the 'head' as the governing element, and the specifier and complement as the governed elements.[6] In the phrase *Peter's field*, for instance, *field* is the governing head of the specifier

---

[4] For remarks about the style of Gorgias see Norden (1898) 1.63–71, Denniston (1952) 9–12 and Dover (1997) index *s.v.* 'Gorgias'.

[5] The precise text and translation are uncertain here.

[6] This definition begs some questions, but it will be sufficient for my purposes. Linguists widely use the terms 'head' and 'complement', but disagree over their exact definition. See for instance Matthews (1981) 160–7 and, for a classical language, Bauer (1995) 18–46.

Peter's, and in the phrase *in school*, *in* is the governing head of the complement *school*. The difference between a specifier and a complement is that the first is optional (*field* can stand without *Peter's*) while the second is obligatory (*in* cannot stand alone). The interdependency of governing heads, specifiers and complements is one of the most obvious ways in which sentences raise and fulfil expectations. Specifiers and complements preceding their governing heads usually make the listener expect the head, and, inversely, governing heads preceding their complement create the expectation of a complement. By contrast, specifiers following their governing heads, since they are optional, are not usually to be anticipated by spectators. A word such as *books* is expected as a complement after *she likes* but not in the same way as a specifier after *she reads*.

The first thing to note about (B) is that wherever rules of dependency demand a certain kind of word and form, listeners do not have to wait for long. ἐπειράθην receives its expected complement (καταλῦσαι) in the next word, καταλῦσαι its complement (μώμου ἀδικίαν, expanded by καὶ δόξης ἀμαθίαν) in the next but one, μώμου its governing head (ἀδικίαν) in the next, and so on. At no point is the sentence under much tension. More notorious is a second characteristic of Gorgias' language. While almost every Greek sentence raises expectations through the mutual dependency of governing heads, complements and specifiers, (B) also guides its listeners by various kinds of parallelism. Ἑλένης μὲν ἐγκώμιον makes it likely that a similar phrase with δέ instead of μέν will come later, as indeed it does with ἐμὸν δὲ παίγνιον. Even without the marker μέν the sentence raises the expectation of balanced phrasing when ἐβουλήθην at the beginning of its clause imitates the form and position of ἐπειράθην in the preceding clause. The correspondence of the sentence heads anticipates parallel structures of the complements (καταλῦσαι with accusative object – γράψαι with accusative object). With hindsight, many words refer back to earlier ones. Some, in fact, do so even where there is no syntactic guidance. Rhythm and rhyme make ἀμαθίαν point back to ἀδικίαν, and παίγνιον back to ἐγκώμιον. The second word in each pair matches the first, so that the sentence appears to be a unified and almost static whole in which there is little disruption once it has begun.

Sentence (A) is similar. Here, too, listeners do not have to wait a long time for governing heads and complements, here, too, the particle μέν makes balanced structures predictable (μητρὸς μέν – πατρὸς δέ; τοῦ μὲν γενομένου θεοῦ – λεγομένου δὲ θνητοῦ; ὁ μὲν διὰ τὸ εἶναι ἔδοξεν – ὁ δὲ διὰ τὸ φάναι ἠλέγχθη), and here, too, acoustic patterning evokes one expression when one hears another (γενομένου θεοῦ – λεγομένου ... θνητοῦ; ἀνδρῶν κράτιστος – πάντων τύραννος). In addition (A) does something that (B) does not, or at least does much less clearly: a number of words give indications not only of the syntactical function of words to follow, but also of their content. μητρὸς μέν creates an expectation of πατρὸς δέ, as θνητοῦ is predictable after θεοῦ, and a word with a meaning like φάναι after εἶναι.

The typical Gorgianic sentence, then, like all sentences, reveals itself only piecemeal. But unlike many other sentences, it gives spectators considerable power of anticipating some of the revelations. At many points in the sentence, listeners can predict what kind of meaning, sound or grammatical form the next word will have, whether because it is an expected head or complement, because it has been advertised by parallel clause-structures, or for some other reason. Almost needless to say, the sentence fulfils the expectations it raises. In fact expectations are more than fulfilled. When this sentence has arrived at its end, it has created a whole network of structures in which words point at one another or, to put it differently, the sentence points at itself.

Of course, Gorgias' sentences also have surprises in store. Not all his sentences are as predictable as (A) and (B), and even (A) and (B) are not entirely predictable. The phrases Ἑλένης μὲν ἐγκώμιον and ἐμὸν δὲ παίγνιον in (B), for instance, are similar in both function and rhythm, but not identical in all other respects. While Ἑλένης is objective, ἐμόν is possessive and thus, in effect, subjective. At times, Gorgias uses the generally high level of predictability as a means of surprising his listeners with intruding elements of unpredictability. But this twist in the tail ought not to detract from the fact that flaunted predictability is a hallmark of Gorgianic sentence-structure, responsible for much of its power.

As Gorgias' sentences (A) and (B) represent extremes of syntactical predictability even within Gorgias' writings, so there are of course various levels of unpredictability in Sophocles. Many of his sentences are no more unpredictable than *I saw a woman with a bunch of flowers in her hand* (C). Even sentences like this are of course more unpredictable than (A) and (B), making virtually all Sophoclean sentences very different indeed from the Gorgianic ones I have discussed, but both in order to lend clarity to my argument and because they are characteristic of Sophocles, I will here discuss sentences which betray a rather high level of unpredictability. To stay with English examples for a moment, the following sentence will serve as an illustration of the kind of thing I am interested in: *That man – who is he?* (D). This sentence is more obviously unpredictable than (C) in that (and I am deliberately vague) its flow is interrupted after *that man*. In English, very few noun phrases at the beginning of a sentence are followed by an interrogative particle. It is unpredictable sentences like (D) which I will discuss in the following pages.

At this point I wish to stress an essential distinction. The observation that Sophoclean sentences do not always run as one might predict is not new. Campbell's, Jebb's, Kamerbeek's and Dawe's comments about the 'vagueness', 'indeterminacy' and 'imperceptible gliding' of Tiresias' sentence all point to something remarkable in its structure. More generally, critics have often observed that Sophocles' language is particularly complex. In the words of A. A. Long,[7] 'Sophocles is more difficult to analyse than either of his fellow tragedians. He is more original and complex than Euripides, but less obtrusive than Aeschylus.' This complexity has prompted scholars such as Campbell, Bruhn and Moorhouse[8] to draw up

[7] Long (1968) 3.
[8] Campbell (1871), Bruhn (1899) and Moorhouse (1982).

catalogues of grammatical peculiarities. Like these scholars, I am concerned with the complexity of Sophoclean sentences, but my aims are different from theirs. Rather than wishing to catalogue deviations from the grammatical norm, I am interested in the ways Sophocles' complex sentences engage spectators.

At one level my dissatisfaction with Campbell, Bruhn and Moorhouse turns on a question of norms. What do we call grammatical? What norms should we use for classifying Sophoclean Greek?[9] But behind this, perhaps rather limited, question of norms, there is a crucial question about the effect of Sophoclean sentences. Sophocles, I would argue, is remarkably lucid in all kinds of ways, and J. W. Mackail,[10] for one, speaks of 'the clarity of his language' in particular. Tiresias' sentence is again a case in point. Jebb calls it '*designedly indeterminate*' and Campbell feels that the 'vague subject *assists the effect* of mystery'. Like almost all Sophoclean sentences, this one is perfectly lucid. A catalogue of grammatical peculiarities, useful as it is in many ways, does little to explain this lucidity. On the contrary, it may even suggest the opposite: a grammatically unusual sentence, one might be forgiven for thinking, is hard to understand and may somehow appear awkward. Since this does not seem to be the case for most Sophoclean sentences, the question arises how one should reconcile their complexity with their clarity. This question is at the heart of my project. If Sophoclean sentences were unclear and awkward they would be less engaging. To say (as I do) that they are unpredictable and keep spectators in suspense is one thing. To say that there is something odd about them is quite another. For this reason it is important to me to suggest reasons why the complex sentences which I will discuss are often challenging, surprising or tantalising, but never confusing.

---

[9] Cf. West (1990) 10–12, who argues that much of what we may regard as ungrammatical in Aeschylean Greek was perceived as normal at a time when grammatical analysis was still in its early stages (e.g. *nominativus pendens* and sliding between direct and indirect expression).

[10] Mackail (1910) 156.

The answer will lie in the detail but, roughly, it is this: to think of Sophocles' complex sentences as grammatically peculiar leads one in the wrong direction. Sophocles' sentences are not complex for complexity's sake but because they express complex information in a complex context. Looked at in this way, they are not so much grammatically peculiar as appropriate, and thus clear. This is why there is (typically) nothing awkward or confusing about them.

The complex or, as I look at it in order to express one of its chief effects, unpredictable sentence (D) will illustrate what I mean. I have said rather vaguely that its flow is interrupted after *that man*. One way of putting this more precisely would be to say that the sentence is ungrammatical, classifying it as a case of anacoluthon. Valid as such an analysis might be, it would miss much of the effect of the sentence. What the sentence does is emphasise the words *that man*, and then ask a question about them. In a certain context the emphasis may help to introduce *that man* as a new topic of conversation. It may also draw attention to the fact that the man has just surprisingly appeared on the scene or that he looks in some way conspicuous. The complex and unpredictable sentence (D) is not only easily comprehensible but in its context may also seem both most effective and appropriate. In this sentence unpredictability and clarity are closely linked.[11]

Something like this, I will argue, is usually the case with Sophoclean sentences. Details vary greatly, but the basic argument remains the same. No matter how unpredictable a sentence is, it is not baffling. There is much both in the sentence itself and in its context that helps spectators to make sense of the sentence. Sophocles' unpredictable sentences may be perceived as complex, but they need not be perceived as unnecessarily complex. Again and again their complexity

---

[11] Cf. Slings (1997), who argues that certain phenomena such as antithesis or ana-coluthon ought to be looked at as strategies for conveying complex information in the pragmatically most effective way. Slings, however, goes further than I do in that he criticises concepts such as 'emphasis' as too vague. Where I have stressed that (D) may introduce a new topic of discussion *and* that it may draw attention to a man who is for whatever reason noteworthy, Slings would concentrate on the former.

appears as the appropriate way of saying certain things in a certain context.

Sophoclean sentences, to sum up my suggestions, can engage many different spectators through a complex interaction of knowledge and ignorance (and more will have to be said in the end about the communality of their shared engagement). They keep spectators busy as they fail to fulfil the expectations they raise. Spectators are given some knowledge with which to predict the run of a sentence but often this knowledge turns out to be only partial. Yet at the same time many Sophoclean sentences make sure that the balance does not tilt too much towards ignorance, potentially alienating spectators and losing their attention. They are not just challenging instances of grammatical peculiarities, but always allow spectators to make sense of their unpredictable structure. Rarely do they appear odd or unclear.

In what follows I will illustrate these suggestions by playing out, in slow motion as it were, the ways in which some Sophoclean sentences, both Tiresias' and others, raise and thwart expectations, and by tracing some of the ways in which it is possible to make sense of their unpredictable movements. Since my aim in this chapter, as in the rest of the book, is not to advance linguistic theory but to describe Sophoclean language, I will give considerable space to these illustrations. The proof of the pudding is in the eating, as it were, rather than the recipe. The examples are organised in three sections: the first is concerned with 'intervention'. It contains sentences which raise certain expectations but, before fulfilling them, are temporarily thrown off course by words which are unexpected. Next, I will speak about 'change of direction': sentences continue although all expectations have already been fulfilled, or continue in ways that conflict with the expectations they have raised earlier. A third section, entitled 'ambiguity', will cover sentences that stop without either fulfilling all expectations they have raised or conflicting with them. In that section I will finally return to Tiresias' sentence, with which I began.

INTERVENTION

Like the two Gorgianic examples, many Sophoclean sentences use a variety of ways to set up expectations. Often such expectations are fulfilled; often fulfilment does not come exactly as anticipated. In this section I want to look at some sentences where it does come, but is delayed by a group of words that intervene. Where Gorgias' sentences (A) and (B) were notable for their quick fulfilment of expectations, the Sophoclean sentences in this section make spectators wait.

A second sentence from *Oedipus Rex* makes a good starting-point (*OT* 739–41):

> Ιο. τὶ δ' ἐστί σοι τοῦτ', Οἰδίπους, ἐνθύμιον;
> Οι. μήπω μ' ἐρώτα· τὸν δὲ Λάϊον φύσιν
>   τίν' εἷρπε[12] φράζε, τίνα δ' ἀκμὴν ἥβης ἔχων.

Joc. What is this, Oedipus, that weighs upon your mind?
Oed. Do not ask me yet; but tell me about Laius, what appearance (*phusis*) he had and what stage in manhood he had reached.

There are no less than two cases of intervention in Oedipus' second sentence. φύσιν τίνα intervenes after Λάϊον, and εἷρπε, if the text is correct, after φύσιν τίνα, letting spectators wait for the expected governing heads of both τόν ... Λάϊον and φύσιν τίνα. Scholars speak of prolepsis, which 'is usually described in syntactic terms as a construction whereby the subject of a subordinate clause occurs by anticipation as an object in the main clause'.[13] In this case the imaginary subject of εἷρπε (*ὁ Λάϊος) has been anticipated as the object of φράζε (τόν ... Λάϊον).

Prolepsis can be looked at in many ways. The most helpful

---

[12] εἷρπε is Schneidewin's conjecture for the MSS' εἷχε, adopted by Pearson and Lloyd-Jones and Wilson. See Lloyd-Jones and Wilson (1990) 97. The constellation of εἷχε and ἔχων in parallel expressions is unlikely to be correct. Schneidewin's conjecture is only one of many which have been put forward. My discussion of the intervention is valid for all those that replace εἷχε with an intransitive verb (apart from εἷρπε, for instance Hartung's ἔτυχε). This way of tackling the problem seems more promising to me than proposals which break up the parallel τίνα – τίνα (cf. Dawe *ad loc.*).

[13] Panhuis (1984) 26.

one in the present context turns on pragmatic roles such as topic and focus. Different theorists use these terms in different ways. For the purposes of this chapter I will adopt the definitions of Bernard Comrie, which have gained widespread acceptance.[14] Comrie applies 'focus' to 'the essential piece of new information that is carried by a sentence' and 'topic' to 'what the sentence is about'. Unlike the focus, the topic is therefore usually a piece of information that is assumed to be known; it is 'given'. Although in many sentences there is room for disagreement over precisely which words form the topic and which words form the focus, these terms are extremely useful tools for analysing how a sentence communicates, and will therefore recur in my discussion.

Analysed in these terms, prolepsis is a means of releasing information in the pragmatically most effective order.[15] Since the topic is what a sentence is about, it often comes early in its sentence. When Oedipus begins his sentence with τὸν δὲ Λάϊον, spectators have every reason to guess that this phrase may be the topic. Jocasta has asked Oedipus about his thoughts (σοι τοῦτο ... ἐνθύμιον); Oedipus now, on this assumption, changes the topic from his own thoughts to 'Laius'. At that moment a second noun (φύσιν) intervenes. Now, spectators can speculate, the topic is specified further: not just Laius but also his *phusis* (here: 'appearance'). The advantage for the spectators of having the topic introduced in two steps becomes clear if one imagines the alternative: why does the Greek not begin *τὴν δὲ Λαΐου φύσιν ... ? Why two cases of intervention for a straightforward enquiry? Because, as a look at the pragmatics of the question shows, the transition from the previous sentence would be too abrupt otherwise. Neither Laius nor his appearance has been talked about in the immediately preceding lines. Both are new information, and thus more suitable for the focus than for the topic of Oedipus' sentence. Oedipus makes them none the less acceptable as the topic by introducing them individually, first Laius, then his appearance.

---

[14] Comrie (1989) 62–5; the quotations are from pp. 63 and 64.
[15] On prolepsis see Slings (1992) 105–9 with further literature cited on p. 105, n. 46, including Panhuis (1984).

Hearers have to process only one piece of new information at a time.[16] Intervention, it appears, produces a sentence which is less unified and more dynamic than Gorgias' (A) and (B), modifying its structure as it goes on, and which at the same time perfectly serves its pragmatic function in the context.

This observation can be taken further by a closer look at the way intervention emphasises certain words. Instances of prolepsis in Greek literature, both in Sophocles[17] and elsewhere, are numerous. It is possible, therefore, that they place only little emphasis on the anticipated object. The present sentence, however, is not an ordinary case of prolepsis. It is distinguished from a sentence such as *τὴν δὲ φύσιν φράζε τίνα ἔχων ὁ Λάϊος εἶρπε ... in that it places *two* objects, τόν ... Λάϊος ('Laius') and φύσιν (*phusis*), next to one another, leaving both without construction for a while. As a result, it seems fair to say that considerable emphasis falls on both Λάϊον and φύσιν. This emphasis is another factor that makes the unpredictability seem appropriate in the context. The sentence is the last of Oedipus' questions about the killing (726ff.). Before, he has asked about the place where three roads meet, about its precise location, and about the time of the killing, leaving the central point to the end: the victim and his *phusis*. The two instances of intervention mark this climax.

In a different way they also mark a theme of the play: *phusis*. In the present context it means something like 'appearance', but elsewhere its wide semantic range includes 'nature' and 'origin'. In all these different meanings, Oedipus' *phusis* is under examination throughout the play.[18] Who is his father? Who is his mother? Is he as intelligent as he believes he is? Is he too quick-tempered? When the sentence which I am discussing gives much prominence to the word *phusis*, it recalls a

[16] Slings (1992) 106 distinguishes topic and theme, and says that prolepsis (he prefers the word 'displacement') in Greek marks a theme rather than a topic because it introduces new information, but new information which the sentence is about. As an English example of a theme construction he gives *The American universities are great institutions; as for the students, they work extremely hard.*

[17] Collections in Azelius (1897) 13–15 and Bruhn (1899) 18–19.

[18] See 262, 436, 437, 438, 440, 458, 674, 822, 827, 1015, 1017, 1019, 1082, 1084, 1184, 1359, 1364 and 1404.

question that is a constant of the play: who is Oedipus? Oedipus is asking a question about the *phusis* of Laius. But ultimately it is his own *phusis* that will need investigation. For various reasons, therefore, the emphasis that falls on Λάϊον ('Laius') and φύσιν (*phusis*) is anything other than awkward. More could be said about these lines, but even in this brief discussion it ought to have become obvious that unpredictable as it is, or rather because it is unpredictable, Oedipus' sentence is both clear and appropriate in both the narrower and the wider context.

Oedipus' sentence is rather short. In order to gain a broader view of the kind of effects intervention can have, I turn to one that is longer. After telling Teucer and his men what to do after his death, Ajax addresses his son (*Aj.* 574–6):

> ἀλλ' αὐτό μοι σύ, παῖ, λαβὼν ἐπώνυμον,[19]
> Εὐρύσακες, ἴσχε διὰ πολυρράφου στρέφων
> πόρπακος ἑπτάβοιον ἄρρηκτον σάκος.

But do you, boy, take the thing from which you take your name and carry it, wielding it by means of its well-sewn thong, the shield unbreakable, made of seven hides.

Again it is worth briefly following the course of the sentence. αὐτό is left without construction for a while when the words μοι σύ, παῖ intervene. The temporary lack of construction is all the more notable since forms of αὐτός have little meaning by themselves. It is of course open to the actor playing Ajax to make a gesture which points to the shield, but linguistically αὐτό is much in need of its head and thus gains considerable prominence.[20]

Both need and prominence are diminished nearer the end of

[19] Lloyd-Jones and Wilson, as well as Garvie, adopt Fraenkel's τοὐπώνυμον. For two other passages in which words that have to wait for a construction and that therefore gain prominence in their sentences are sometimes emended, see *Aj.* 331–2 (δεινά) and *Aj.* 770–3 (δίας Ἀθάνας). My discussion is intended to provide a certain degree of support for ἐπώνυμον. In an English translation it is difficult to express the difference between ἐπώνυμον and τοὐπώνυμον, since something like 'the thing' has to be supplied in any case.

[20] It is true that enclitics such as μοι (the first of the intervening words) have a tendency to appear early in the sentence. There is however no syntactical reason why μοι follows αὐτό rather than ἀλλά or λαβών. As much as σύ and παῖ, therefore, μοι is felt to intervene.

the line. First λαβών provides a governing head for the noun phrase that will include αὐτό, and then ἐπώνυμον ('the thing from which you take your name') not the head itself of that noun phrase, but some indication of what it might be. Even now, however, the sentence is still under tension, and it will remain so until the end: further words intervene, deferring σάκος ('shield'), the governing head of αὐτό ... ἐπώνυμον, by almost another two lines. ἐπώνυμον now takes over much of the attention that αὐτό had before.

Yet while intervention keeps the sentence under tension and gives prominence to αὐτό ... ἐπώνυμον, it does not risk leaving spectators behind. The reference to 'the thing from which you take your name' is followed by the name itself; Εὐρύσακες (Eurysakes = 'Broad-Shield') leaves little doubt about the kind of thing Ajax is referring to. Spectators now have good linguistic grounds on which to predict σάκος ('shield'). The syntactic marking of αὐτό ... ἐπώνυμον does not make the sentence difficult to follow. What is more, it makes good sense in the context. Not only does the stress on naming evoke Ajax's earlier interpretation of his own name (430–3), but ἐπώνυμον also draws attention to Eurysakes' connection with the shield, which he will hold on to towards the end and for which he is known. By stressing that it is Eurysakes' eponymous weapon, Ajax insists on the propriety of his arrangements, even as he invoked earlier in the same speech the 'justness' (δικαίως 547, cf. ἐν νόμοις πατρός 548) with which Eurysakes is his son. Again a sentence keeps spectators busy by separating a number of specifiers from their heads, but is unlikely to make them feel that they are busy for nothing.

Intervention can help the temporarily isolated words to spread their influence while they are without construction. Potentially this tactic puts comprehensibility at risk, and with it much of the meaning that is gained. Oedipus' request for information is short enough to be understood easily, and Ajax's sentence makes every effort to counterbalance the gap between αὐτό ... ἐπώνυμον and σάκος by making the latter predictable. So what about a lengthy sentence which does not reveal what will happen after the intervention?

35

Here is one such case (*Ant.* 458–60):

> τούτων ἐγὼ οὐκ ἔμελλον, ἀνδρὸς οὐδενὸς
> φρόνημα δείσασ᾽, ἐν θεοῖσι τὴν δίκην
> δώσειν.

For this I was not going to pay the penalty among the gods for fear of any man's pride.

In the immediately preceding sentence Antigone has described the eternity of the unwritten laws. After taking up that theme with τούτων, she interposes herself (ἐγὼ οὐκ ἔμελλον) and then moves on again, now to men (ἀνδρὸς οὐδενός), who in turn are contrasted with gods (ἐν θεοῖσι). The result of this series of intervening words is that, almost two lines into the sentence, spectators still do not have a governing head for τούτων, which was the first word.

What is more, τούτων is not only separated from its governing head, but is marked also by its case. Genitives are usually integrated in a clearly identifiable construction, either forming together with another word a genitive absolute or being governed by one particular word, sometimes a verb, sometimes a noun, very often a preposition.[21] Seldom is their construction as indeterminate as that of many datives (such as the so-called ethical dative) and accusatives (such as the accusative of limitation). A free-standing genitive therefore raises more specific expectations and is in greater need of a governing head than a dative or accusative without construction. The question arises therefore to what degree the long intervention endangers the comprehensibility of the sentence. How much meaning is there to be gleaned from a word whose syntactic function is unclear for a long time?

The first answer turns on the context. The laws are not only the subject matter of the previous sentence, but have domi-

---

[21] In the rare exceptions the genitive usually expresses a cause (see below) or a point in time (examples for Sophocles at Campbell (1871) § 10.γ.5 and Bruhn (1899) 29). Fraenkel on Aesch. *Ag.* 950 discusses a 'genitive of respect'. In nearly all his instances (Renehan (1992) 350–1 adds *Aj.* 770) the genitive strongly marks what is arguably the topic or part of the topic, as, I go on to suggest, it may be taken to do in the case of τούτων. Compare also Moorhouse (1982) 72–5 on the 'genitive of relation'.

nated Antigone's speech from the very beginning (450ff.). Many critics have indeed seen Antigone's statements about the laws as crucial to the understanding of the whole play. When, therefore, the long separation of τούτων from its governing head makes the laws hang over the lines that I have quoted, this emphasis is entirely in keeping with the surroundings in which the lines occur. Spectators can, all in their different ways, fit the intervention into a larger frame.

The second answer concerns the internal pragmatics of the sentence. There is some room for discussion in identifying topic and focus. Concentrating on the first words, one can argue that τούτων is the topic; it takes up information that is given after the preceding lines, which had much to say about the laws. On this account, ἐγώ, emphatic like most instances of personal pronouns in classical Greek, bursts in as new information after a general and impersonally phrased sentence (456–7). What matters now is Antigone's position towards the laws. ἐγώ is therefore an important part of the focus. Alternatively, Antigone's regard for the gods and her defiance of Creon may be regarded as a given after the prologue. The news this sentence brings, then, is that the laws are the cause of her stance. No matter which of these two analyses is more persuasive, the first two words, one of which is marked as a free-standing genitive and one as the beginning of the phrase that makes the genitive free-standing, are substantial parts of topic and focus. In this respect the intervention of ἐγώ after τούτων (and arguably also that of ἀνδρὸς οὐδενὸς φρόνημα and of ἐν θεοῖσι) is pragmatically effective because it provides straightaway information that is not only prominent in the context but also crucial to the understanding of the sentence.

A third answer draws on an alternative construction. While waiting for τούτων to receive a construction, spectators can make sense of the pronoun by provisionally interpreting it as what is sometimes called a genitive of cause.[22] They can

---

[22] Campbell (1871) § 10.γ.1.d and Moorhouse (1982) 70–1 give instances for Sophocles, including *Aj.* 41 χόλῳ βαρυνθεὶς τῶν Ἀχιλλείων ὅπλων ('stung by anger on account of the arms of Achilles'); *El.* 1027 ζηλῶ σε τοῦ νοῦ, τῆς δὲ δειλίας στυγῶ ('I envy you for your good sense, but I hate you for your cowardice'); and

understand it as meaning 'because of this', that is in the context, 'because of the laws', while its dependence on the governing head τὴν δίκην ('the penalty for this') is not yet known. With hindsight this is not too far off. The laws are indeed the cause for Antigone's defiance of 'any man's pride'. Again an intervention can engage spectators in a number of ways, producing a sentence which is both complex and clear.

A final example will illustrate further how both an alternative, or at least provisional, construction and the context may help spectators to sustain the delay that intervention causes to the fulfilment of their expectations (*El.* 1260–1):

> τίς οὖν²³ ἀξίαν σοῦ γε πεφηνότος
> μεταβάλοιτ' ἂν ὧδε σιγᾶν λόγων;

Who could exchange speech for a silence worthy (*axian*) of your appearance?

The specifier ἀξίαν (*axian*, 'worthy') is separated from its governing head σιγᾶν by more than a line, and the phrase μεταβάλλειν ... σιγᾶν λόγων is unusual and rather abstract. Yet these potential difficulties are not as grave as they may first appear. ἀξίαν (*axian*), free of syntactical bonds as it is for a while and helped along by its morphological identity with the accusative of the noun ἀξία ('worth'), looms large over the sentence as a whole rather than describing a specific noun. Electra, it becomes clear, is asking something about worth. The scholiast captures the effect when he separates the adjective ἀξίαν (*axian*) from its noun, glossing it with an adverb: 'Who could *justly* be silent rather than speak now that you have appeared?' What the scholiast does *not* capture is the

---

especially *Ant.* 1074–5 τούτων σε λωβητῆρες ὑστεροφθόροι | λοχῶσιν Ἅιδου καὶ θεῶν Ἐρινύες ('*On account of this* there lie in wait for you the doers of outrage who in the end destroy, the Erinyes of Hades and the gods'). Interpretation of a genitive as causal helps spectators to make sense of a sentence before the construction is complete also at *El.* 1153–6, *OT* 857–8, *Tr.* 1122–3, *Ph.* 618–19, *OC* 1173–4. Provisional constructions also help with isolated genitives at *Aj.* 946–7 (link ὤμοι ἀναλγήτων δισσῶν) and *Aj.* 1266–7 (link φεῦ τοῦ θανόντος).

23 Lloyd-Jones and Wilson (1990) 69 take οὖν ἂν ἀξίαν in HADXr as support for Arndt's ἀντάξιαν. They may be right, but the insertion by a scribe of οὖν is no likelier than that of ἂν (perhaps under the influence of ἂν in the following line). For what it is worth, ἀντάξιος does not occur in surviving tragedy.

way in which ἀξίαν gives a construction to σοῦ γε πεφηνότος. Electra is asking not just anything about worth, but something about worth in connection with Orestes' appearing. With hindsight the genitive can be taken as absolute, but while much is uncertain, spectators will be grateful for being able to give the first line a meaning like 'who does justice to your coming, if he ...?' By the time they get to hear the second line, they can already speculate what the sentence will eventually say.

And they can do something else, too: put ἀξίαν into context. As in the previous examples, not only is intervention a powerful tool within the framework of the sentence itself but it also makes good sense in its wider surroundings. Electra's emphasis on what is worthy is both pragmatically effective and continues her insistence that she is justified in being jubilant. ἀξίαν takes up ἀξιώσω (1240), πρέποι (1254) and δίκᾳ (1255). For various reasons her sentence is as lucid as it is unpredictable.

Many Sophoclean sentences, then, unlike my examples from Gorgias, postpone through intervention the fulfilment of expectations they themselves create. Such sentences can engage spectators by making them listen carefully until their expectations are eventually fulfilled. The potential danger of lengthy intervention is that spectators find a sentence too difficult to make it worth their attention and thus lose interest. In the sentences that I have discussed, and they are by no means exceptional in Sophocles,[24] this risk is minimal. There is nothing unclear or inappropriate about these instances of intervention. Spectators can get a purchase on the sentence long before grammatical expectations are finally fulfilled. They are given crucial information right at the beginning of the sentence, and sometimes alternative constructions help to bridge

---

[24] Some comparable passages: *Aj.* 25–7, *Aj.* 334–5, *Aj.* 541–2, *Aj.* 556–7, *Aj.* 738–9, *Aj.* 1266–70, *El.* 78–9, *El.* 153–63, *El.* 303–4, *El.* 431–2, *El.* 525–6, *El.* 709–11, *El.* 809–12, *El.* 954–7, *El.* 1015–16, *El.* 1253–5, *El.* 1372–5, *El.* 1505–7, *OT* 800–4, *Ant.* 594–5, *Ant.* 1199–1202, *Ant.* 1312–13, *Tr.* 49–51, *Tr.* 507–13, *Tr.* 1222–4, *Ph.* 192–200, *Ph.* 236–7, *Ph.* 343–7, *Ph.* 380–1, *OC* 101–5, *OC* 440–4, *OC* 1161–2, *OC* 1540–1, *OC* 1615–16. See also Campbell (1871) § 41 and Bruhn (1899) 90–100.

the gap between heads and complements or specifiers that are separated from each other. Often, moreover, intervention highlights words or ideas that are also prominent in the immediate or in the wider context. To put it briefly, intervention engages spectators, as it keeps them busy following the run of the sentence and at the same time allows them to make sense of the sentence and its run. It now remains to be seen in what way these conclusions can be confirmed for other kinds of unpredictable sentences.

CHANGE OF DIRECTION

Intervention is only one way in which a sentence can behave unpredictably. Another is what may be called change of direction. Under this heading I will first discuss sentences that continue unexpectedly when no expectations are left unfulfilled, and when the continuation therefore seems tacked on, surprising or superfluous. Secondly, I will speak of direction change when sentences militate against expectations. Moving off on a different course, they never come back to fulfil what they have promised. In both cases the sentence is thrown off course permanently, rather than temporarily as those discussed in the previous section. The following examples therefore differ even more clearly from my two Gorgianic sentences (A) and (B) than instances of intervention.

The first is taken from the end of the short speech with which Odysseus supports Teucer's wish to bury Ajax against the resistance of Agamemnon. After calling Ajax the best of the Argives apart from Achilles, he sums up (*Aj.* 1342–5):

> ὥστ' οὐκ ἂν ἐνδίκως γ' ἀτιμάζοιτό σοι·
> οὐ γάρ τι τοῦτον, ἀλλὰ τοὺς θεῶν νόμους
> φθείροις ἄν. ἄνδρα δ' οὐ δίκαιον, εἰ θάνοι,
> βλάπτειν <u>τὸν ἐσθλόν</u>, οὐδ' ἐὰν μισῶν κυρῇς.

And so you cannot dishonour him without injustice; for you would be destroying not him, but the laws of the gods. It is unjust to injure a noble (*ton esthlon*) man (*andra*), if he is dead, even if it happens that you hate him.

In the last sentence τὸν ἐσθλόν (*ton esthlon*, 'noble') brings a change of direction. The sentence could have ended after βλάπτειν, so as to translate 'it is unjust to injure a man if he is dead'. Nothing more is expected. In particular a continuation that qualifies ἄνδρα (*andra*, 'man') comes as a surprise. From its beginning, the sentence is a general statement. ἄνδρα (*andra*) does not have an article and the optative removes εἰ θάνοι from any particular death. The shift to the gnomic has been prepared already in the previous sentence, which turned attention away from Ajax (τοῦτον) to the laws of the gods (τοὺς θεῶν νόμους). Treatment of the dead is the subject of many funerary customs, laws and sayings, including Solon's law that prohibited verbal abuse of the dead (Plut. *Sol.* 21.1) and Semonides' couplet τοῦ μὲν θανόντος οὐκ ἂν ἐνθυμοίμεθα, | εἴ τι φρονοῖμεν, πλεῖον ἡμέρης μιῆς ('our concern for a dead man would not, if we had any sense, outlast one day'; fr. 2 W). Earlier in *Ajax* (988–9) Teucer remarked that τοῖς θανοῦσί τοι | φιλοῦσι πάντες κειμένοις ἐπεγγελᾶν ('all men like to mock the dead as they lie low'). Another generalisation on such a subject, especially one rounding off a speech, would therefore have been nothing out of the ordinary.[25]

Those spectators who expect such a general reflection are forced to think again at the end of the clause. Because of εἰ θάνοι the statement is still general, but ἄνδρα (*andra*) now has two qualifications, εἰ θάνοι and ἐσθλόν (and thirdly, as the sentence continues further, οὐδ' ἐὰν μισῶν κυρῇς). These definitions produce problems. Would it, by implication, be just to injure a noble man while alive? Or a bad man when dead?[26] The reason why such questions are rarely asked is that ἐσθλόν (*esthlon*) takes up something that is prominent in the context. Problematic as the sentence is as a general maxim, it is applicable specifically to Ajax:[27] he is dead, and ἐσθλόν takes up ἄριστον in v. 1340. A central thrust of Odysseus' speech is to re-evaluate Ajax. He was Odysseus' greatest enemy, but what counts now is that he is the best of the Argives. When τὸν ἐσθλόν (*ton esthlon*) emphatically alters the course of the

---

[25] Compare also 1348–9 and Aesch. *Ag.* 884–5 with Fraenkel's note on 885.
[26] Perhaps this is why some critics, with reference to 1352, make τὸν ἐσθλόν the subject, rather than the object, of βλάπτειν. See Stanford *ad loc.*
[27] Cf. Garvie *ad loc.*

sentence, it also underlines Ajax's new position. He is no longer the enemy of the army but is singled out as 'noble'.[28] Like intervention, it seems, change of direction may involve the spectators, by surprising them and at the same time allowing them to put the surprise into a larger frame. The sentence suits its context.

A rather different kind of unpredictable addition, which makes, however, a comparable contribution to the meaning of the sentence, occurs at the end of one of Theseus' last sentences in *Oedipus at Colonus* (1760–3):

> ὦ παῖδες, ἀπεῖπεν ἐμοὶ κεῖνος
> μήτε πελάζειν ἐς τούσδε τόπους
> μήτ' ἐπιφωνεῖν μηδένα θνητῶν
> θήκην ἱεράν, ἣν κεῖνος ἔχει.

Girls, that man (*keinos*) instructed me that no mortal should go near to those regions or address the sacred tomb which that man occupies (*hēn keinos echei*).

In the previous example the words τὸν ἐσθλόν (*ton esthlon*) came as a surprise when they were tacked on to a sentence that seemed finished. Similarly, Theseus' sentence could have ended after ἱεράν. The relative clause ἣν κεῖνος ἔχει (*hēn keinos echei*, 'which that man occupies') is as unpredictable as τὸν ἐσθλόν was before. Where the addition in Ajax's sentence was surprising because it gave a general statement a personal thrust, this time the surprise is caused by logical redundancy. Theseus first introduces Oedipus as the grammatical subject of the sentence by means of κεῖνος (*keinos*, 'that man') in 1760. Why does he then repeat κεῖνος in the relative clause at the end of the sentence? Again spectators are given something to think about.

One effect, I suggest, of the repeated κεῖνος in particular and the relative clause in general is to hint at Oedipus' changed role after death. Much is extraordinary about the end of Oedipus' life. The claps of thunder (1447ff.), the way in which the blind man leads Theseus and his daughters off stage (1540–55) and the divine voice reported by the Messenger

---

[28] On the changing evaluation of Ajax see further ch. 5, pp. 233–8.

(1621–8) are only the most obvious of many indications that point at supernatural participation in Oedipus' death. One of the less obvious signs is the absence of the name 'Oedipus' from the last scenes of the play. Oedipus is last named at 1638, around 150 lines before the end. After that he continues to be prominent, but is now either the zero-represented subject or is referred to by pronouns and periphrastic expressions. This avoidance of the proper name is particularly noticeable when there is emphasis on the word replacing it, as there is in the sentence I have quoted. Oedipus is not Οἰδίπους but κεῖνος, and that not just once but twice. If names are anything to go by, he is no longer the man he used to be. By failing to name him, Theseus makes Oedipus a rather numinous kind of figure.[29]

And there is more. The verb ἔχει (*echei*, 'occupies') adds to the effect of the double κεῖνος. Albert Henrichs argues (in a different context) that the notion of somebody 'holding' or 'occupying' a tomb (rather than the other way round) serves as a 'signal ... of the special power of the cultic hero, which resides with him in his tomb'.[30] Oedipus is not an ordinary dead man. Both κεῖνος (*keinos*) and ἔχει (*echei*), like so much else in the play, suggest that his death is more than just the end of his life.

With this premise let me look at the rest of the sentence. The relative clause comes as the climax of a set of lines in which the dead Oedipus is looked at from two perspectives. On the one hand he has been transformed. Theseus speaks of χάρις ἡ χθονία (1752), νέμεσις (1753) and θεμιτόν (1758). Oedipus' death has brought non-human standards into the play. At the same time, it is still possible for characters to look back at Oedipus the man. Antigone still calls him father at 1757, and in the present sentence Theseus, too, speaks of Oedipus as he knew him when he begins with a past tense: ἀπεῖπεν ἐμοὶ κεῖνος. While alive, Oedipus banned him from letting anybody come 'near to those regions'. The further the

---

[29] Cf. ch. 4, pp. 139–68, on the difficulty of naming gods in Sophocles.
[30] Henrichs (1993) 171 on καθέξει at *Aj.* 1167.

sentence proceeds, the more Oedipus the man loses in prominence. When Theseus goes on to speak of the θήκη ἱερά, he leaves behind the man he met and begins to look at a transformed Oedipus. It is not clear whether Theseus is quoting Oedipus' own words, put into indirect speech, or whether he is interpreting them.[31] But what is clear is the fact that nobody, neither Oedipus nor Theseus, had much to say about Oedipus' 'tomb' while he was alive, and that certainly nobody called it 'sacred'.[32] Oedipus' status changes as the sentence goes on.

Finally, at the end of the sentence, the relative clause trumpets Oedipus' enhanced presence. ἔχει opposes the past ἀπεῖπεν, the repetition of κεῖνος highlighting the contrast. Oedipus is now seen as the non-human being who occupies a sacred grave at Colonus. Again there is no way of establishing who exactly is speaking. The repetition of κεῖνος and the indicative ἔχει (as opposed to the infinitives πελάζειν and ἐπιφωνεῖν) connect the relative clause with ἀπεῖπεν ἐμοὶ κεῖνος at the beginning of the sentence. This connection suggests that ἥν κεῖνος ἔχει (*hēn keinos echei*) is Theseus' own description of the grave. But at the same time the relative clause comes at the end of a sentence reporting Oedipus' commands and therefore has a certain claim to reporting something that Oedipus has said, even if Theseus is putting his own interpretation onto it. The result of this vagueness is that the sentence does not break after ἱεράν. Different views on Oedipus blend into one another. Oedipus the man shades slowly into Oedipus the mysterious figure who still has power after his death,

---

[31] Narratologists like Gérard Genette speak of 'transposed' speech, standing in the middle between 'narrated' speech ('Oedipus ordered his burial') and 'reported' speech ('Oedipus said: "…"'). Genette (1980) 171 says about it: 'Although a little more mimetic than narrated speech, and in principle capable of exhaustiveness, this form never gives the reader any guarantee – or above all any feeling – of literal fidelity to the words "really" uttered: the narrator's presence is still too perceptible in the very syntax of the sentence for the speech to impose itself with the documentary autonomy of a quotation.'

[32] In his first encounter with Theseus Oedipus calls him his future ταφεύς (582). Ismene, reporting an oracle, speaks of σοῖς … τάφοις (411). In Oedipus' last speech on stage, when he stops relying on his daughters' guidance and declares that he will find his tomb with divine help, he refers to it as τὸν ἱερὸν τύμβον (1545).

and, at a different level, the voice of Oedipus and the voice of Theseus are hard to separate at many points of the sentence. The sentence is not static like Gorgias' (A) and (B), but neither is it abrupt or jerky in its movements. The surprising relative clause at the end is in various ways tied into the context of both its sentence and the play as a whole.

Both Odysseus' and Theseus' sentences revoke what they promise only in so far as they go on where they might be expected to stop. Other sentences, by contrast, change direction before fulfilling all expectations that they have created. The opening line of the first stasimon in *Trachiniae* is a case in point (*Tr.* 497):

μέγα τι σθένος ἁ Κύπρις ἐκφέρεται νίκας ἀεί.

In great strength, Cypris always carries off victories.

Short though it is, this sentence defies analysis; some critics, like Dawe, even regard it as corrupt. Possibly they are right, but the least that can be said in defence of the manuscript reading is that spectators can make sense of the sentence as it has been transmitted. In order to describe how it raises, fulfils and thwarts expectations, I will briefly trace its structure, starting at the beginning. The phrase μέγα τι σθένος does not call for a specific kind of continuation; none the less it may cause certain vague expectations. Neuter adjectives with τι are often used predicatively,[33] and, in most occurrences of σθένος, the context makes it clear whose strength is referred to. The Chorus's sentence would go with both trends if it added a genitive and, less crucially, a copula: 'great is the strength of …' Genitives with σθένος are greatly varied, including χερῶν (fr. 939 Radt), ἀληθείας (*OT* 369), χώρας (*OC* 727), ἀγγέλων (Aesch. *Ch.* 849), τῆς θεοῦ (Eur. fr. 898.6 N) and proper names like Ὠκεανοῖο (sometimes even with the same adjective: μέγα σθένος Ὠκεανοῖο: *Il.* 18.606, 21.195), so that many kinds of continuation would have been possible, but instead there follows the nominative ἁ Κύπρις.

Some scholars propose, with various degrees of confidence,

---

[33] Ferrari (1983) 43.

that the sentence ends here.[34] This is just about possible since σθένος has the quality of an adjective in a great number of periphrastic expressions. The phrase ζεῦξον ἤ|δη μοι σθένος ἡμιόνων (Pind. *Ol.* 6.22–3), to give just one example, translates 'yoke now the *strong* mules for me'. In the sentence that I have quoted from *Trachiniae* μέγα ... σθένος might therefore be taken as the equivalent of μεγασθενής: 'Cypris is very strong.' A powerful objection, however, is the lack of passages in which σθένος does not belong to somebody: one *has* σθένος; σθένος is not what one *is*. Strictly speaking, σθένος ἡμιόνων is the 'strength *of* mules' rather than 'the *strong* mules'. A break after Κύπρις is therefore conceivable, but spectators are likely to expect the sentence to continue. I will carry on by describing the continuation they are presented with.

With the nominative Κύπρις in addition to the nominative or accusative σθένος, there are now two words that need a construction. The most obvious solution would be a transitive verb, for instance ἔχει, 'Cypris has some kind of great strength.'[35] This expectation, too, is then severely threatened by ἐκφέρεται (a difficult verb for the object μέγα τι σθένος), and finally thwarted when νίκας provides a semantically ideal object for ἐκφέρεται. With hindsight, a perfect sentence begins at ἁ Κύπρις, which has the phrase μέγα τι σθένος added on at the front. Spectators are kept busy as they constantly have to rearrange the parts of the sentence.

As they have arrived at the end, they may try to come to an overall understanding. As Franco Ferrari[36] points out, the sentence supports such efforts by evoking various possible constructions. I noted, for instance, that μέγα ... σθένος alludes to μεγασθενής. This allusion makes it slightly easier to take this expression as a description of Cypris' action: she carries away victory in great strength. Alternatively μέγα τι

---

[34] Wakefield's punctuation after Κύπρις is adopted in the OCT and advocated by Stinton (1990b) 221–3, who discusses and dismisses various approaches and tries to refute objections to Wakefield (for further objections, raised after Stinton's original article was published, see Davidson (1987) 290).

[35] Cf. Eur. *El.* 958 ἔχει γὰρ ἡ Δίκη μέγα σθένος.

[36] Ferrari (1983) 43–4, from where some of the above references are taken.

σθένος ... νίκας may be taken as a close unit equalling μεγα-σθενῆ τινα νίκην and may be translated as 'great and mighty victory'.[37] Finally, in view of the many periphrastic expressions with σθένος plus genitive, it is also possible to say that the sentence points to an imaginary sentence *μέγα τι σθένος τᾶς Κυπρίδος ἐκφέρεται νίκας ἀεί, a sentence, however, which remains imaginary because of the intruding nominative ἁ Κύπρις (as well as, perhaps, the qualifying pronoun τι, which would be unusual in a perphrastic expression of this type).

All such attempts vary in detail, but they have one thing in common: the words ἁ Κύπρις are given prominence at the heart of a sentence that changes direction.[38] As Oedipus, lifted out of the ordinary at his death, changes the course of Theseus' sentence, and the 'nobility' of Ajax, discussed in many previous lines, brings surprising continuation to Odysseus' sentence, so Cypris puts her stamp on this sentence. What is more, she does so in a stasimon that speaks about exactly that: her power to dominate. Evocation of various possible constructions and the context of the ode join forces to produce a sentence which is both unpredictable and, at least in some ways, strikingly clear in its meaning.

Change of direction gives emphasis to words, such as ἐσθλόν ('noble'), ἥν κεῖνος ἔχει ('which that man occupies') and, in a more complex way, Κύπρις ('Cypris'), which introduce it. Like intervention, it can also give room, and hence influence, to the phrase that precedes it, as it does in my next example. Theseus refuses Oedipus' praise for rescuing Antigone and Ismene, and then changes tack (OC 1150–2):

> λόγος δ᾽ ὃς ἐμπέπτωκεν ἀρτίως ἐμοὶ
> στείχοντι δεῦρο, συμβαλοῦ γνώμην, ἐπεὶ
> σμικρὸς μὲν εἰπεῖν, ἄξιος δὲ θαυμάσαι.

But contribute your opinion regarding a *logos* that has lately come to my ears on my way here, a thing one can relate briefly, but one that occasions surprise.

[37] This is the solution adopted by Jebb and recently advocated by Davidson (1987). Davidson also stresses the 'subtle combination of ideas' (p. 289) in the phrasing.
[38] '... ἁ Κύπρις su cui cade incisivamente l'accento ...', Ferrari (1983) 44.

47

Expectations are thwarted by συμβαλοῦ, which prevents there ever being a third person singular verb for λόγος (*logos*, 'report', 'speech', 'word'). At the end of the sentence λόγος is still the supplied subject of the sub-clause ἐπεὶ | σμικρὸς μὲν εἰπεῖν, ἄξιος δὲ θαυμάσαι, but the run of the main-clause is irreversibly altered by the imperative. Grammar books speak of *nominativus pendens*.[39] Theseus forces spectators to adjust their expectations as he changes the direction and breaks the construction, leaving the nominative λόγος 'hanging'. In this respect his sentence resembles that about Cypris, in which the phrase μέγα τι σθένος remains without clear construction. Yet the word that triggers the change of direction is rather different. In *Trachiniae* it was a noun, and what is more, a noun in the nominative. Nominatives are often subjects of the sentence, and subjects, in turn, are often topics. συμβαλοῦ, by contrast, is a verb, and the noun in the nominative precedes it. No rivalry about the role of topic here.

The verb in fact *helps* to make the opening phrase the topic. Rather than *following* the imperative, λόγος (*logos*) and its relative clause are moved forward. By means of this movement Theseus makes the first line and a half acceptable as the topic of his sentence, although they contain new information. Looked at with hindsight, an expression in the nominative, a case that is often used for the topic, rather than one that grammatically depends on συμβαλοῦ γνώμην, is put first, and the construction then altered for the enquiry. Again the dynamics of a Sophoclean sentence vary greatly from the unified and static Gorgianic examples (A) and (B).

In Oedipus' questions about Laius (above, pp. 31–4), as well as in some of the other examples, I suggested, intervention does not just help to make the preceding phrase the topic but also gives it room to spread its influence. The same effect is possible in the case of direction change. Here certain words are left without their governing head or complement, or some

---

[39] Slings (1992) 96–9 discusses *nominativus pendens* in pragmatic terms. A very similar structure to that in the present passage is to be found in Eur. *El.* 1072–3; see Diggle (1981) 40–1. Cf. also τὸ δ᾽ ἔπος οὐξερῶ at *OT* 936, a phrase which in its sentence can be analysed as nominative or accusative.

other kind of expected continuation, not only while other words intervene, but they are left without a construction even at the end of the sentence. As in the case of prolepsis, it is difficult to know just how much emphasis the unpredictable sentence-structure puts on λόγος (*logos*) δ' ὅς ..., but it seems possible, to say the least, that 'the word that has lately come to my ears' receives enough prominence to distinguish it from other kinds of words. This helps comprehension, since Theseus has spoken of λόγοι (plural of *logos*) and ἔπη (also 'speeches', 'words') three times already in the same speech (1139, 1141 and 1143). More generally, some spectators may find that the lack of construction highlights this 'word' as one of many words that are prominent in the play. Small words that have great effect, words that 'can see', words that 'do good', words that 'do bad' and many other kinds of words are a theme that goes through the whole of *Oedipus at Colonus*.[40] The present passage can be placed in this wider net of associations.

Direction change can produce various kinds of sentences,[41]

---

[40] For words in *OC* see especially 66, 74, 443, 569, 624, 721, 1116, 1187 and 1616.

[41] Many of the various kinds of complexity for which Sophocles' language is known could have been discussed under this heading. Here I list some instances of direction change resembling those quoted in the main text. The arrangement in categories is meant to provide some orientation rather than a consistent taxonomy. *Non-clausal complement following its head (including cases of hyperbaton)*: *Aj.* 988–9, *Aj.* 1244–5, *Aj.* 1363, *El.* 417–19, *OT* 6–8, *Ant.* 298–9, *Ant.* 891–4, *Tr.* 786–7, *Ph.* 8–11, *Ph.* 391–402, *Ph.* 1016–18, *OC* 555–9, *OC* 944–6 (reading ἀνόσιοι τέκνων), *OC* 1360–1, *OC* 1526–7; *non-clausal apposition, not clearly attached to particular words*: *Aj.* 454–5, *El.* 1136–7, *OT* 56–7, *Ph.* 1395–6; *unexpected subclause* (some of which can be taken as new sentences): *Aj.* 1040–1, *Tr.* 1–3, *Ph.* 271–5, *OC* 84–93, *OC* 978–80; *complement transferred from one head to another or subject transferred from one verb to another* (cf. the provisional constructions cited in the previous section): *El.* 153–63 (Χρυσόθεμις from supplied ἔστι to ζώει), *El.* 743–8 (παίσας weakens the connection λύων ... λανθάνει), *OT* 35–9, *OT* 93–4, *OT* 1329–30 (see Dawe *ad loc.*), *Ant.* 450–5 (*Dikē* first subject of ἦν ὁ κηρύξας, then of ὥρισεν), *OC* 47–8, *OC* 939–43; *new, instead of expected parallel, construction* (incl. main- instead of sub-clause): *El.* 881–2, *OT* 310–13, *Ph.* 1128–39; cf. Friis Johansen (1954) 8–18 (on Aeschylus); *one or more words left without construction* (incl. anacoluthon): *OT* 60–1, *OT* 159–63 (not accepting Blaydes's αἰτῶ), *OT* 758–62 (see Dawe *ad loc.*), *Ant.* 1–3 (on Jebb's analysis *ad* 2f.), *Tr.* 1233–6, *Tr.* 1238–9, *Ph.* 497–9 (see Lloyd-Jones and Wilson (1990) 190–1 for the different ways of interpreting the syntax), *Ph.* 547–52 (reading πλέων ... ὡς); see further Bruhn (1899) 100–11, Campbell (1871) § 36.B.6–7, Moorhouse (1982), index *s.v.* 'blending' (with the remarks on p. XIII) and 'anacoluthon', Reinhard

different from each other and different from those caused by intervention. But despite differences in detail, intervention and change of direction have much in common. Both produce sentences that can engage spectators as they move unpredictably. And both appear not disruptive but well suited to their context, communicating what they communicate in a clear and appropriate way. Spectators can in various ways make sense of the sentences for what they are. With these observations I move on to my last group of examples.

AMBIGUITY

This last section will be concerned with sentences that, like some of those which change direction, stop without fulfilling all expectations they raise but, unlike those which change direction, do not clash with the expectations. Rather than filling the space of an expected word with one that is unexpected (such as συμβαλοῦ instead of a verb in the third person after λόγος, *logos*), they leave the space unfilled.

Ambiguity, as the word is generally used, is not always reflected in the syntax, and the unfulfilled expectations can be more or less concrete.[42] When oracles tell Croesus that, attacking the Persians, he will destroy a great empire (Hdt. 1.53), they speak ambiguously. The ambiguity would be removed by specifying the potentially doomed empire. But not everybody – and Croesus is a case in point – perceives the need for this kind of clarification. The oracle is ambiguous without flaunting its ambiguity at everybody who hears it. Since sentences are often ambiguous in this way, not raising

(1920), who focuses on anacoluthon in Plato but adduces material also from other authors, including Sophocles, West (1990) 5–10, who discusses for Aeschylus anacoluthon and other phenomena which he regards as typical of a time without grammatical analysis, and Slings (1997) 192–213, who challenges the interpretation of anacoluthon as a figure of speech.

[42] But note that many linguists, like for instance Kempson (1977) 123–38, would speak of 'vagueness', reserving the term 'ambiguity' for sentences such as *Flying planes can be dangerous*. I use it here in the less technical meaning that is current among literary scholars.

precise expectations for a particular kind of supplement that would clarify them, the emphasis of my discussion will shift slightly. In comparison with the previous two sections, in which expectations and surprises were often discussed primarily in syntactic terms, and only in the second instance semantically, the balance will tilt in the following examples. Yet, in line with the rest of the chapter the syntactic side will not disappear. In all my instances of ambiguity there is one particular place where a particular kind of word, which would resolve the ambiguity, may be perceived as missing. Although ambiguity expresses itself in the first place semantically, I will discuss sentences in which it is clear what kind of syntactic function the clarifying word would have.

Like intervention and change of direction, ambiguity can engage. But where intervention and change of direction may make spectators closely follow the movements of the sentence, ambiguity is likely to involve them in thinking about the gap. *Ajax* 263–4 gives a first impression:

> ἀλλ' εἰ πέπαυται, κάρτ' ἂν εὐτυχεῖν δοκῶ.
> φρούδου γὰρ ἤδη τοῦ κακοῦ μείων λόγος.

Why, if it has ceased, I think he may indeed enjoy good fortune; for if the trouble is now departed, it counts for less.

The Chorus of Ajax's men are criticising Tecmessa's statement that Ajax, now that he is sane again, suffers from seeing what he has done. Their reply is somewhat imprecise, leaving εὐτυχεῖν ('enjoy good fortune') without a subject. Any expectation that they will clarify whom they expect to enjoy good fortune is disappointed when the sentence ends soon after.

There are two *bona fide* candidates: Ajax, the subject of parts of Tecmessa's little speech, and the Chorus's first person implied in δοκῶ. Most translators inevitably opt for either one or the other candidate ('he', in Lloyd-Jones's translation which I print), and so also will some spectators. Others will find this a hard choice to make. For them the lack of subject with εὐτυχεῖν puts much emphasis on the verb as all there is. The Chorus's ambiguity elides all agents and evokes instead a situation of being fortunate. Jebb has the courage to supply a different subject altogether and, as so often, captures the effect: 'I have good hope that all may yet be well.' This kind of weighting makes the sentence a suitable introduction to the dialogue that follows (down to 281). In this dialogue Tecmessa maintains her original analysis and convinces the Chorus that, in consequence of Ajax's madness, they all suffer, no matter whether he is still mad or not. By describing a state of good fortune, the Chorus's initial statement prepares for this emphasis on general suffering.

The Chorus also prepare for something that is characteristic of my other examples in this section: they all evoke general situations at the expense of individual agents. Ambiguity, as I discuss it here, may frustrate some spectators' attempts to fill the gap with certainty, but it gives them something else instead. A sentence by the Stranger in *Oedipus at Colonus* will help to flesh this out. He ends his account of the place Colonus with the words (62–3):

> τοιαῦτά σοι ταῦτ' ἐστίν, ὦ ξέν', οὐ λόγοις
> τιμώμεν', ἀλλὰ τῇ ξυνουσίᾳ πλέον.

Such are these things, stranger; they are not honoured in words, but rather by the *xunousia*.

By whose *xunousia*, literally 'being-with', is τοιαῦτα ... ταῦτα, that is, Colonus, its gods, heroes and features, honoured? The sentence fails to provide a genitive or adjective with τῇ ξυνουσίᾳ ('the *xunousia*') and thus an answer to this question. Most commentators bring in the men of Colonus, who are the subject of the preceding sentence. Their 'being with' or 'dwelling with' these things is a way of bestowing honour. This supplement produces a rhetorically effective contrast between honour in words (no matter whether they are boasts or poetic traditions, both of which have been suggested) and actual life in a place.

None the less it is not the only possible supplement. The men of Colonus are not necessarily alone in honouring the place in which they live. In a different way, the local deities may be said to honour it too. Like the men of Colonus, Poseidon, Prometheus and the eponymous 'horseman Colonus' were mentioned in the previous lines, and even the Erinyes, who were said to 'hold' the place at 39–40, may be used to fill the gap. Understood as the claim that all (or some) of these deities confer honour on 'these things' by being with them,[43] the present sentence takes up both the sentence that opened the Stranger's account, χῶρος μὲν ἱερὸς πᾶς ὅδ' ἐστί (54), and the statement that the region (οἱ ... πλησίοι γύαι) boasts that it has (σφίσιν .... εἶναι) the horseman Colonus as its first leader (58–60). Finally, λόγοις again provides a marked contrast with ξυνουσίᾳ since the Stranger's words are set off against the deities' presence: 'these things' are honoured not just by empty claims, but actually receive honour from the gods' 'being with' them.

Spectators are not given either of those supplements. Instead they are presented with a situation which is characterised by a general sense of 'being-with': deities with the place, locals with the place, and even deities with locals. As a result, the lines are not only packed with meaning in their own right but also deserve their place in the play as a whole. A vague sense of being-with suffuses the whole of *Oedipus at Colonus*. Most specifically, the situation of *xunousia* will receive a further half-human and half-divine connotation when the word returns at 647. In that line Theseus says to Oedipus μέγ' ἂν λέγοις δώρημα τῆς ξυνουσίας, 'the gift of your *xunousia* that you speak of is a great one'. Once Oedipus is dead he, too, will honour 'these things' by 'being' or 'dwelling with' them. More generally, Colonus as a place, as well as both the locals' and Oedipus' attachment to it, is repeatedly prominent, the being-with of the daughters, but not the sons, with Oedipus is frequently emphasised, and divine forces are close at many points in the play, while often, as in the present passage, details are left vague. The absence of a genitive with τῇ

---

[43] For gods as subject of συνεῖναι see *Aj.* 702–5 and *Tr.* 515–16; compare also *OT* 863–71 and Ellendt *s.v. ad fin.*

ξυνουσίᾳ contributes to a situation that fits its surroundings perfectly. Again ambiguity may engage both for what is certain and for what is uncertain.[44]

Not deities but another group far removed from the events on stage is one of the possible supplements in the following ambiguous sentence (*Ph.* 126–9):

> καὶ δεῦρ᾽, ἐάν μοι τοῦ χρόνου δοκῆτέ τι
> κατασχολάζειν, αὖθις ἐκπέμψω πάλιν
> τοῦτον τὸν αὐτὸν ἄνδρα, ναυκλήρου τρόποις
> μορφὴν δολώσας, ὡς ἂν ἀγνοίᾳ προσῇ.

And if you seem to me to be taking too long, I will send back that same man, disguising him as a sea captain, so that *agnoia* may attend.

Odysseus leaves Neoptolemus to his task, announcing that he will send one of his men if Neoptolemus and the Chorus should take too long. He adds that he will dress him up as a captain, 'so that *agnoia* may attend'. Less explicitly perhaps than the previous sentences, this one calls for a supplement of a particular kind. Yet glosses of *agnoia*, such as Jebb's 'ignorance, on the part of Philoctetes' and Webster's ' "unrecognisability", which will "attend" him' (i.e. 'the scout') suggest that a supplement, whether a dative or a prepositional phrase, would be needed to determine an unequivocal meaning for the expression. As it is, it is unclear whether *agnoia* means 'unrecognisability' and attends the False Merchant or whether it means 'ignorance' and attends Philoctetes (or even something different altogether).

The result is a rather general kind of meaning: there will be a situation of ignorance and lack of recognition. In the immediate context most spectators are likely to feel more or less strongly that what Odysseus is talking about is the effect of the dressed-up scout on Philoctetes. But once the False Mer-

---

[44] Non-human forces may also be supplied as agents at *Tr.* 786–7 (it is not clear who or what dragged Heracles to the ground) and *Tr.* 896–7 (the Erinys of 895). σύν-compounds contribute to ambiguity also at *Aj.* 361 (συνδάιξον), *Aj.* 1316–17 (ξυνάψων and συλλύσων), *OT* 220–1 (σύμβολον; on the interpretation of Lloyd-Jones and Wilson (1990) 84–5), *Ant.* 523 (συνέχθειν and συμφιλεῖν), *Ph.* 519–21 (συνουσία; only a dative, not a genitive, is missing) and *OC* 410 (συναλλαγῆς).

54

chant has appeared, the word *agnoia* justifies all the space that Odysseus gave it. That scene[45] is extremely complex in a number of ways. The False Merchant's words, for instance, cannot all be explained on the basis of the instructions which Odysseus gave Neoptolemus in the prologue, and many of Neoptolemus' statements can be taken at various levels. The deception is no longer under control. The situation is indeed one of general ignorance and lack of recognition. Many spectators may feel that they too fall victim to *agnoia* in the sense of 'ignorance' and that *agnoia* in the sense of 'unrecognisability' attends Neoptolemus as much as the False Merchant. Odysseus' ambiguous sentence prepares for the later scene.

Of the sentences discussed in this section Odysseus' is the one in which the semantic need can be phrased least precisely as a syntactic one ('a dative or a prepositional phrase', as I have just put it). I will finish with a case of ambiguity which is at the opposite end of the scale, and this brings me back to where I started. When Oedipus and Tiresias in *Oedipus Rex* begin to level accusations at each other, an exchange occurs which I have quoted already (339–41):

> Οι. τίς γὰρ τοιαῦτ᾽ ἂν οὐκ ἂν ὀργίζοιτ᾽ ἔπη
> κλύων, ἃ νῦν σὺ τήνδ᾽ ἀτιμάζεις πόλιν;
> Τε. ἥξει γὰρ αὐτά, κἂν ἐγὼ σιγῇ στέγω.

Oed. Why, who would not be angry, hearing such words as those with which you now show disrespect for this city?
Teir. Yes, they will come (*hēxei*) of themselves, even if I veil them in silence.

At the beginning of the chapter I quoted various commentators as evidence for Tiresias' sentence having the effect of a blend of certainty and uncertainty. In the light of all the other sentences in this chapter, it is now possible to be more precise. Like many of those sentences, that of Tiresias does not fulfil the expectations it raises. Grammatically, αὐτά can take up ἔπη, but the resulting sense is difficult; the words that Tiresias has already spoken can no longer 'come' nor is he able to

---

[45] On the False Merchant scene, see further ch. 3, pp. 113–23.

'shroud them in silence'. αὐτά therefore has all the appearance of being used adjectivally and in need of a governing head in the neuter plural. When no such word follows, spectators can correct their grammatical interpretation and take αὐτά substantivally.

Yet no matter whether or not they adopt such a syntactic cure, it does not entirely meet the semantic need.[46] Spectators are left to speculate about the kind of word that would make sense here, and the context is less forthcoming than in any of the sentences I have discussed before. As Jebb points out, Tiresias spoke of κακά ('sufferings') which he will reveal (329). However, this was more than ten lines earlier, so that κακά is no more than a remote possibility. There is, in other words, no obvious supplement. Much of Tiresias' prophecy is left unsaid. Certainty is only in ἥξει (hēxei, 'will come'), which becomes all-dominant: all that can be said about αὐτά is that it 'will come'. Oedipus adds to the effect when he repeats ἥξει in his reply: οὔκουν ἅ γ' ἥξει καὶ σὲ χρὴ λέγειν ἐμοί; The less help an ambiguous sentence gives with supplements and the more the need for supplements is syntactic, the more power is given to the remaining words. Ambiguity again vaguely evokes a situation, so vaguely in fact that little is known beyond the fact that a situation will arise (ἥξει, hēxei).

And yet, there is, as I put it earlier, not only uncertainty but also certainty. For all that is uncertain about Tiresias' sentence, spectators can place the ambiguity in a wider frame. The second half ('even if I veil them in silence') is only one aspect of Tiresias' insistent refusal to say all he knows (cf. 328–9, 332–3, 343–4). Moreover, by suggesting that something will happen but not saying clearly what, Tiresias fits a pattern. As Campbell's 'the vague subject, which ... assists the effect of mystery' and some of the other comments that I quoted in the beginning suggest, he is adopting a stance that is

---

[46] The need may be softened somewhat by a vague similarity to the saying αὐτὸ δείξει ('it will become clear by itself'). This saying is quoted by Sophocles in fr. 388 R. See schol. vet. Pl. *Hipp. Mai.* 288b, p. 175 Greene (our source for the fragment).

characteristic of prophetic speech in tragedy and elsewhere.[47]
This ambiguous sentence, like so many others in Sophocles,[48]
suits both its context and its speaker.

CONCLUSION

Different spectators, I have noted repeatedly, have different
expectations when they listen to a sentence. They do not perceive the same gaps and are not surprised in the same way.
When I have none the less spoken about their reactions to a
sentence, I have done so using a model which was not intended to express the exact processes in the brain of any individual spectator who listens to a sentence. Rather, I have tried
to give an impression of the *kinds* of reaction that Sophoclean
sentences may prompt. Allowing for a large margin of variation, I hope therefore that what I have said in these pages is in
one way or another applicable to many different spectators. I
hope, in other words, that I am justified in concluding that
Sophoclean sentences can engage many spectators because of
the discrepancy between the expectations they raise on the one
hand, and the fulfilment of these expectations on the other.
Sophoclean sentences, I have argued, involve spectators in a
constant re-adjustment of their expectations.

---

[47] Tiresias uses the future in this play at 373, 425, 428, 438, 448, 453, 456, 457. For
language in prophetic contexts which hints at matters that it does not spell out, see
87–8, 110–11 (both Creon on returning from Delphi), 325, 328–9, 362, 366–7,
372–3, 379, 412–25 and 438 (all Tiresias). Words of 'coming' and 'going' occur in
comparable contexts at 88, 711, 713, 953, 1011 and 1084.

[48] Further sentences that could have been discussed in this section include (in
brackets the word or words gaining most space): *El.* 171–2 (ποθεῖ), *El.* 947 (τελεῖν),
El. 1063–5 (ἀπόνητοι), *El.* 1251–2 (παρουσία; not all critics accept the ellipse: see
Kells), *El.* 1344 (τελουμένων), *El.* 1467 (ἔπεστι νέμεσις), *Ant.* 570 (ἦν ἡρμοσμένα),
Ant. 799–800 (ἐμπαίζει θεὸς Ἀφροδίτα), *Tr.* 653–4 (ἐξέλυσε), *Ph.* 50–3 (ὑπουργεῖν),
Ph. 106 (θρασύ), *Ph.* 352–3 (λόγος καλὸς προσῆν), *Ph.* 1270 (μεταγνῶναι), *OC*
1448–50 (μοῖρα ... κιγχάνει). Instances are particularly frequent in *OT*: 9–11
(δείσαντες ἢ στέρξαντες; the exact text is uncertain), 408–9 (ἐξισωτέον), 676–7
(ἴσος, if not corrupt), 786 (ὑφεῖρπε), 906–9 (ἐξαιροῦσιν). For 906–9 compare a
series of further passages in which the Chorus fail to make it clear who they are
speaking about (especially where a reference to Oedipus is expected): 523–4, 527,
681–2 and 897–902; note also the lack of objects in Oedipus' questions at 1173,
1175 and 1177. Further instances in Campbell's section on 'ellipse': Campbell
(1871) § 39.C.3.a. Long (1968) 140–7 speaks about some related aspects of
Sophocles' language under the heading 'Alternatives to a personal construction'.

Despite their unpredictability, I suggested further, these sentences do much to make sure that what spectators do *not* know does not outweigh what they do know and thus threaten to alienate the spectators. Sophoclean sentences rarely risk the breakdown of communication. For a number of reasons, which vary from sentence to sentence, unpredictability is not something that makes a sentence obscure or difficult to follow, but something that spectators can make sense of. Unpredictable sentences are in fact designed to communicate what they communicate as clearly as possible. Often they give spectators information in the pragmatically most effective order, and often they emphasise or evoke particular words or ideas which are also prominent otherwise. For all the surprise they may cause, Sophocles' unpredictable sentences do not leave spectators perplexed and do not stand out as inappropriate. They are always lucid in their context.

In order to describe these characteristics of the way Sophoclean sentences communicate I introduced, near the beginning of my discussion, two sentences from Gorgias' *Helen*. As I have arrived at the end, I will now turn to them once more. Along with guiding and quickly fulfilling expectations, I noted, these two sentences point at themselves. Later words refer back to earlier ones, setting up a network of correspondences. This kind of prose style quickly went out of fashion. In Lysias, Isocrates and Demosthenes highly self-referential sentences are the exception rather than the rule. Geoffrey Horrocks, commenting on Lysias, concludes that 'a "colloquial" directness and simplicity of diction apparently gave a better impression of honesty in a court of law'.[49] Tragedy and forensic oratory differ in many ways, and the term 'simplicity' would need precise definition before it could be applied to Sophocles; none the less, Horrocks's comment is suggestive also for Sophoclean sentences, which, like Lysias', use modes of communication that are distinctly different from those of Gorgias' (A) and (B).

I suggest that Sophoclean sentences create, as Horrocks

---

[49] Horrocks (1997) 25.

puts it, 'an impression of honesty' by failing to point at themselves in the way that Gorgianic sentences do. They become, to use a different phrase, trustworthy. The risk of sentences that point at themselves is that they appear not to point at anything else. They are in danger of suggesting that there is nothing apart from the words of the sentence; that is why their rhetoric is often called empty. Sophocles' sentences, whose beginnings so often give wrong clues about their continuation, make it easy to believe that they react to something in the world. Like the world itself, they provide material for much speculation but remain ultimately unpredictable. By not pointing at themselves to the degree that Gorgias' sentences do, they may seem to point at something that there is beyond their words.

Spectators have all the more reason for faith in something that there is beyond the mere words when a sentence and its context provide, as in Sophocles they often do, good grounds for making sense of the unpredictability. To put it strongly, they can account for the unpredictability. Theseus may be seen as adding a relative clause because of Oedipus' presence, which is so strongly noticeable in the last scenes of the play. Laius and *phusis*, also both dominant elsewhere in the play, may be intervening in Oedipus' question. Cypris, all-powerful goddess that she is in *Trachiniae*, may be confusing the Chorus, and so on. In each case an outside force, the dead Oedipus, the dead Laius, *phusis* or Cypris may be invading the mind of the character who speaks the sentence, producing the unpredictability.

Few spectators would probably regard themselves as 'accounting for unpredictability'. This is only one way, my way, of speaking and thinking about Sophoclean unpredictability, but it is a way that expresses just how much these sentences do in order to suggest that they point at something outside their words. They go out of their way to make sure that spectators understand them and, at the same time, suggest that there is still more to be understood. In various ways they have the potential of making spectators sense that the world does not end with the words of the sentence. There always seems to be

59

something that is hinted at, but is not said. Spectators who find themselves understanding much but wanting to understand more as they listen to Sophoclean sentences are given a world that goes beyond the sound of the words they hear. They are given, in other words, something they can share with one another. All spectators live in their individual worlds, but Sophoclean sentences offer them in addition a world they can all share. All spectators look from different directions, but Sophoclean sentences try to involve all of them by making them believe in something that is there but will never be fully known, something around which to gather and something at which to look in communality.

CHAPTER 2

CHARACTERS: A SHARED PERSPECTIVE

INTRODUCTION

By being unpredictable, I have argued at the end of the previous chapter, many Sophoclean sentences inspire trust and appear to point at a world beyond their own words. In the rest of this book I want to explore this world in more detail. I will begin in this chapter with its most visible aspect: the characters. They are most obviously part of the world that spectators get to share, appearing, as they do, on stage for all to see. Much can be said, and has been said, about the ways in which spectators can engage with the things they see the characters do.[1] What I am interested in here, however, is not so much what they do as what they say. Throughout this book I trace the ways in which Sophoclean language communicates and the ways in which it gets many different spectators involved in a play. In this particular chapter, therefore, I will ask how the ways in which Sophoclean language communicates affect the characters and their interaction with the spectators. How can spectators engage with the way the characters speak? How do the characters fit into the shared world that I talked about at the end of chapter 1? What scope is there for what I call communality among the different?

Discussion of characters in tragedy tends to focus on the singular 'character' and the 'presentation' or 'portrayal' of 'character'.[2] The term is an inheritance from Aristotle and

---

[1] On stage action see, for Sophocles, Seale (1982) and Taplin (1983), and, for tragedy in general, Taplin (1978) and Wiles (1997).

[2] For recent discussions of character in Greek tragedy, see Easterling (1977), Gould (1978), Gill (1986), Podlecki (1989) (on Sophocles in particular), Gill (1990), Goldhill (1990b), Easterling (1990) and Seidensticker (1994) (on Sophocles in particular).

over the years has been interpreted in many ways. Different writers have argued for different nuances in describing roughly what a person in a play is like, accounting in particular for the motivation of the person's acts and thoughts. Additionally 'character' can mean a personage in a work of fiction, a *dramatis persona*. Sharing features of both, there are less technical usages which speak of a person as a 'shady' character, or of somebody's 'good' character. Since the term is so ill defined, I will use it in this chapter exclusively as a synonym for 'dramatic personage' (except where I refer to other critics' phrasing). My concern here is neither to define nor to discuss any less concrete notion of 'character'.

This is of course not to say that observations by scholars whose questions are different from mine, or who use the term 'character' differently from me, will not be extremely useful at various points in this chapter. One of these scholars is P. E. Easterling. In her most recent article on character-portrayal in Greek tragedy[3] she suggests that a character does not as such exist, but is 'constructed' by the audience. 'All the time we are led to make new constructions, and the constructions always lead to larger questions, ensuring that character and action can never be kept tidily separate. And the desire to construct is perfectly compatible with the knowledge that strictly speaking there is nothing there at all. It is the very elusiveness of the "inwardness" of other people, real or fictive, let alone of ourselves, that gives drama its extraordinary appeal.' The suggestion Easterling makes in the last sentence will be at the centre of this chapter: it is the 'elusiveness' of their 'inwardness' that makes characters fascinating. To understand better what gives a character 'inwardness' or, as I will say, 'depth'[4] is to understand better one of the things that make the character engaging.

---

[3] Easterling (1990). The quotation is taken from p. 99.
[4] Also a word Easterling uses: 'this impression of depth, of a solid individual consciousness behind the words' (Easterling (1977) 125). Attempts to express this kind of effect go back a long time. Note especially E. M. Forster's distinction between 'round' and 'flat' characters: Forster (1993) 46–54.

Easterling links the 'elusiveness' of the characters' 'inward-ness' to the spectators' 'knowledge that strictly speaking there is nothing there at all' when they make constructions about characters. What is implicit in this remark, and what I want to stress strongly as the starting-point for further exploration, is the fact that the constructions spectators make vary in the degree to which the spectators notice them as constructions. Spectators may either make rather confident constructions which they only faintly qualify as constructions, or they may have a distinct sense that what they think about a character is nothing but a construction, or again they may find themselves at some point on the sliding scale between the two extremes. It is the more qualified, the more self-conscious and the more hesitant constructions that produce the impression of a char-acter's inwardness or depth. They are an acknowledgement that the character is no less elusive than a real person. To say that he or she is (for instance) 'happy' or 'confused' or 'insin-cere' is felt to be a possibly valid, but ultimately insufficient description of what he or she is really like. Like a real person, the character is perceived as not fully accessible. What, then, produces a hesitant construction?

There are many ways in which this question can be ap-proached. As I noted already, the one I will explore in this chapter stems from the overriding concern of this book with how Sophoclean language communicates. Spectators may feel more or less on top of a statement characters make. They may be sure about it, have a sense of understanding it well, judge it in one way or another. Or they may be hesitant, feel that it is less easy to understand, less easy to judge, not in every way accessible. The different ways of responding to the things characters say lead to different ways of making constructions about the characters. Often when spectators feel more on top of characters' statements, they will also feel more on top of the characters themselves and make confident constructions. 'This is a stupid man, otherwise he wouldn't have said that.' If a character's statement seems straightforward, the character, too, becomes simple and transparent. On the other hand, when spectators feel that statements are in some way out of their reach, they are likely to be more hesitant in making constructions about the characters themselves or to be more aware that these constructions are only that: constructions. 'What an odd thing to say. I wonder why she said it and what exactly she meant.'

My object of study in this chapter begins to come into focus. I will argue that it is characteristic of Sophoclean characters to say things that prompt all kinds of judgements, thoughts and opinions, but judgements, thoughts and opinions which leave room for further judgements, thoughts and opinions; judgements, thoughts and opinions which are in some way felt to be limited or incomplete. The brief detour *via* the characters' depth and the spectators' awareness 'that strictly speaking there is nothing there at all' has brought me back to the fascination about which Easterling speaks. One of the things that make Sophoclean characters engaging, I suggest, is that they give spectators much to think about in their statements, and think about without feeling that they have exhausted the matter. Here, then, is the theme of knowledge and ignorance that runs through this book. Characters are fascinating because they make spectators feel that there is much they know, but much as well that they do not know.

At this point it is essential to stress once more that different people react in different ways. Athenian spectators of the fifth century BC differ from American spectators of the twentieth century, and both are different from European spectators of the eighteenth century. Equally important are differences between individual spectators. Even people living in the same kind of society are bound to see many matters differently. Here as elsewhere, I neither wish to exclude any specific era or any specific spectator nor do I claim to speak for all of them. Rather, I suggest that Sophoclean characters give spectators various reasons for thinking that they are not in every way on top of a statement. Some reasons apply more to an ancient audience, some more to a modern one, some to this spectator, some to that, some apply exactly as I describe them, others would need to be adapted to apply to certain spectators. As in the previous chapter, the generalisations I will make about the ways in which 'the spectators react' will inevitably suffer from a measure of inaccuracy and artificiality. Yet I hope that if they are granted a suitable margin of flexibility, they will help to bring out some typical features of Sophoclean characters and their language.

With this programme it is now possible to look at examples. The claim that spectators will have views and make judgements on the characters' statements is probably a more obvious one to make than that they will often perceive limitations in their views and judgements. I have therefore chosen as my examples what might be called hard cases: three types of passage which very obviously ask for the spectators' agreement or disagreement, perhaps even strong agreement or disagreement. I will try to show that even in such passages spectators may feel, at the same time as agreeing or disagreeing with some of the things the characters say, that there are other things that remain more inaccessible.

The three types of passages fall under the headings 'agōn scenes', 'general statements' and 'dramatic irony'. Agōn scenes often invite the spectators' agreement or disagreement by presenting them with overtly logical argument. In these scenes, characters tend to make speeches which can be judged for, among other criteria, the soundness of their reasoning. Discussion of two such speeches will then lead to the more particular case of general statements, which in their universality reach out to the world of the audience and can therefore be measured against that world: many people have a view on whether it is true that 'never to be born is best'. Finally, dramatic irony is a set-up in which speakers know markedly more than certain characters about the events of the play. As a result, they are almost forced to realise that the characters are clearly wrong in some of the things they say. Discussion of all three types of passage will broaden the view from that of chapter 1. All the passages I look at will run over a number of lines. The unit of analysis will cease to be the individual sentence.

AGŌN SCENES

The most obvious aspect of Greek tragedy to choose for a discussion of the kinds of opinions spectators form and the kinds of judgements they pass on the things characters say is perhaps the *agōn*. The word *agōn* can refer to a wide variety of competitions in Greek life, including law-suits and athletic contests. In tragedy, critics[5] use it to describe a particular form of verbal competition enacted by two characters which, like all competitions, invites the audience to pass some kind of judgement. Critics point in particular to parallels with law-court speeches.[6] In both cases the audience, whether spectators or jurors, hear a pair of speakers state their cases, and may compare and assess their arguments. *Potentially*, therefore, the interest of *agōn* speeches lies in the quality of the argument rather than in the character who delivers it. As spectators find themselves in agreement with one piece of reasoning and in disagreement with another, there may well be little that makes them think of the character as a person. The character becomes just 'a clever' or 'a bad arguer' or 'a vehicle for the playwright's technical brilliance'. He or she has little depth.

However, as far as Sophocles is concerned (and arguably some *agōn* scenes in Euripides are rather different) this is not what happens. I turn to Clytemnestra's speech in the *agōn* of *Electra* (516–51) as my first example, in order to suggest that there is not only much for spectators to judge but much also that may prompt them to qualify their judgement. Clytemnestra is not somebody who comes on stage just in order to display her or Sophocles' rhetorical power, but she is a fascinatingly multi-layered character at the same time as being a powerful speaker.

---

[5] The word *agōn* also occurs in Greek tragedy itself in the context of verbal competition: *Aj.* 1163 (at the end of Teucer's exchange with Menelaus); cf. *El.* 1492.

[6] For instance Duchemin (1945) 12–14, 192–216. Most recently, comparing law courts to theatre rather than theatre to law courts, see Hall (1995). On *agōn* scenes in general, see also Lloyd (1992), and on links between theatre and oratory, Ober and Strauss (1990) and Bers (1994).

Clytemnestra begins her speech by levelling accusations at Electra. I take it up at the point at which she turns to Agamemnon's killing of Iphigenia, the central topic of the *agōn*, and adopts a less accusatory and more reasoned style of exposition (528–33).

ἡ γὰρ Δίκη νιν εἷλεν, οὐκ ἐγὼ μόνη,
ᾗ χρῆν σ' ἀρήγειν, εἰ φρονοῦσ' ἐτύγχανες.
ἐπεὶ πατὴρ οὗτος σός, ὃν θρηνεῖς ἀεί,
τὴν σὴν ὅμαιμον μοῦνος Ἑλλήνων ἔτλη
θῦσαι θεοῖσιν, οὐκ ἴσον καμὼν ἐμοὶ
λύπης, ὅτ' ἔσπειρ', ὥσπερ ἡ τίκτουσ' ἐγώ.

Yes, Justice was his killer, not I alone, and you would take her side, if you happened to have sense. For, that father of yours, whom you are always lamenting, alone among the Greeks brought himself to sacrifice your sister to the gods; he who felt less pain when he begot her than I did who bore her.

Clytemnestra claims that she had Justice (or justice) on her side when she killed Agamemnon, since Agamemnon himself had killed Iphigenia. She adds (532–3) that Agamemnon, 'when he begot' Iphigneia (ὅτ' ἔσπειρε), felt less pain than she did 'who bore' her (ἡ τίκτουσα). These lines are an implicit appeal to a general sentiment, or rather it would be more correct to say that they *might* have been phrased as an appeal to a general sentiment: 'I was justified in killing Agamemnon for killing Iphigenia not least because he suffered less for her than I did. For giving birth is more painful than begetting.' Phrased like that, Clytemnestra's lines would invite the spectators' judgement: is this a valid argument or not? As the passage is phrased, however, the effect is different. The participle καμών leaves open the precise logic behind the addition of the last line and a half ('he who ...'; no 'not least because' as in my hypothetical phrasing), and the general statement never appears: the first-person pronouns ἐμοί and ἐγώ are mixed in with what is potentially a logical argument and thus turn this argument into a personal perception, as is particularly obvious in the last line when ἐγώ follows the general ἡ τίκτουσα. Jebb puts this very clearly when he comments that 'the regular mode of expression would be, οὐκ ἴσον λύπης καμὼν ἐμοί, ὁ σπείρας τῇ τίκτουσῃ ["he who felt less pain than I, the man who begot than the woman who gave birth"]. But, having written ὅτ' ἔσπειρε, the poet explains ἐμοί by repeating the comparison in a new form, ὥσπερ ἡ τίκτουσ' ἐγώ.[7] There is still room for judgement, but it is reduced considerably. As Clytemnestra hints at a logical argument but makes a personal lament, she stays clear of the openly accessible and remains in her own private world.

Personal phrasing in this speech is not restricted to ἐμοί and ἡ τίκτουσ' ἐγώ; it pervades every sentence Clytemnestra speaks: ἔοικας 516, στρέφῃ 516, σε 517, ἐντρέπῃ | ἐμοῦ 519–20, ἐξεῖπας 521, ἐγώ ... ἔχω 523, σε | λέγω 523–4, πρὸς σέθεν 524, σοί 525, ἐξ ἐμοῦ 526, ἔξοιδα 527, μοι 527, οὐκ ἐγὼ μόνη 528, σε 529, ἐτύγχανες 529, σός 530, θρηνεῖς 530, τὴν σὴν ὅμαιμον 531, ἐμοί 532, ἐγώ 533, δίδαξον 534, ἐρεῖς 535, ἐμήν 536, μοι 538, ἐξ ἐμοῦ 544, δοκῶ 547, σῆς δίχα γνώμης 547, ἐγώ 549, σοὶ δοκῶ 550, ψέγε 551. Clytemnestra speaks much more about herself and addresses Electra much more frequently than, for instance, her counterpart in the *agōn* of Euripides' *Electra* (1011–50) and, in consequence, puts the audience in a rather different kind of position. The context of these first- and second-person expressions varies. Some form part of the opening statements in which Clytemnestra accuses Electra of treating her unfairly; others come from Clytemnestra's defence of what she has done herself, and others again highlight what Agamemnon's killing of Iphigenia meant to her. The effects of these different passages cannot easily be generalised, but what can be said is that, again in contrast to Euripides' play, few of Clytemnestra's lines can be assessed as arguments appealing to universal truths or generally accepted evidence. Spectators' reactions are likely to be more complex than 'yes, that's right', or 'no that's wrong'.[8]

After pointing to the difference between begetting and giv-

---

[7] In his note on 532f.
[8] The different effects of personal and general phrasing on the perception of a character are stressed by Gould (1978) 52–8.

ing birth, Clytemnestra comes to the core of her justification in ll. 534–48:

> εῖέν· δίδαξον δή με ⟨τοῦτο⟩· τοῦ χάριν
> ἔθυσεν αὐτήν; πότερον Ἀργείων ἐρεῖς;
> ἀλλ' οὐ μετῆν αὐτοῖσι τήν γ' ἐμὴν κτανεῖν.
> ἀλλ' ἀντ' ἀδελφοῦ δῆτα Μενέλεω κτανὼν
> τἄμ' οὐκ ἔμελλε τῶνδέ μοι δώσειν δίκην;
> πότερον ἐκείνῳ παῖδες οὐκ ἦσαν διπλοῖ,
> οὓς τῆσδε μᾶλλον εἰκὸς ἦν θνῄσκειν, πατρὸς
> καὶ μητρὸς ὄντας, ἧς ὁ πλοῦς ὅδ' ἦν χάριν;
> ἢ τῶν ἐμῶν Ἅιδης τιν' ἵμερον τέκνων
> ἢ τῶν ἐκείνης ἔσχε δαίσασθαι πλέον;
> ἢ τῷ πανώλει πατρὶ τῶν μὲν ἐξ ἐμοῦ
> παίδων πόθος παρεῖτο, Μενέλεω δ' ἐνῆν;
> οὐ ταῦτ' ἀβούλου καὶ κακοῦ γνώμην πατρός;
> δοκῶ μέν, εἰ καὶ σῆς δίχα γνώμης λέγω.
> φαίη δ' ἂν ἡ θανοῦσά γ', εἰ φωνὴν λάβοι.

So, explain this! For whose sake did he sacrifice her? Will you say for that of the Argives? But they had no right to kill her, who was mine. But if he killed her who was mine for his brother Menelaus, was he not to pay the penalty to me? Had not Menelaus two children, who ought to have died in preference to her, since it was for the sake of their father and mother that the voyage took place? Or had Hades a desire to feast on my children rather than on hers? Or did your accursed father feel sorrow for the children of Menelaus, but none for mine? Is that not like a father who was foolish and lacked judgement? I think so, even if I contradict your view. She who died would agree, if she could acquire a voice.

Clytemnestra argues first that the sacrifice of Iphigenia was not demanded by the Argives, and secondly that, if a sacrifice was needed, Menelaus' children would have been a more obvious choice than her daughter. Here spectators are presented, as is to be expected in an *agōn* speech, with the kind of logical argument which asks for judgement of its cogency.

However, they may not find this judgement straightforward. First of all there is a preliminary consideration concerning the literary and iconographic traditions behind this scene. Spectators will inevitably, as far as they are able to, draw on earlier representations of Iphigenia's sacrifice as a basis for the appreciation of Clytemnestra's lines. This basis, however, is far from secure. Not only is there variation between previous versions,[9] but there is also the added complication that *Electra* does not necessarily have to follow *any* of these versions. Spectators have no way of telling precisely what off-stage Agamemnon, precisely what off-stage Iphigenia and precisely what off-stage army they should be thinking of, and may therefore be unwilling to decide whether Clytemnestra's account is true or false.[10]

The flexibility of Greek myth, of course, makes drawing a clear line between what is 'true' and what is 'false' a pointless undertaking in many arguments, both in *agōn* speeches and elsewhere. In order to say something more specific, therefore, about Sophocles and about Clytemnestra, I turn to the *phrasing* of the passage I have quoted. The paraphrase I gave is misleadingly imprecise in one important respect. In the better part of the passage Clytemnestra asks questions rather than makes assertive statements. 'For whose sake did he sacrifice her? Will you say for that of the Argives?', she begins, and soon lets a number of further questions follow. To a degree this is of course well-established oratorical practice. 'Why should one spare this man? Because...? But...' However, Clytemnestra's questions do not just lead up to a quick and final 'but'. Rather, the 'but' ('But they had no right to kill her, who was mine') is immediately followed by a long sequence of further questions. By asking these questions rather than making statements, Clytemnestra does not commit herself to any particular sentiment. There can be little doubt that, in their context, her questions will be treated as rhetorical, and that they come, therefore, close to assertive statements. But to come close to is not to be identical with. Rhetorical as they are, Clytemnestra's questions are not just emphatic statements.

Most important, by virtue of being questions they draw attention to the fact that it is difficult to supply a motive for

---

[9] Iphigenia sometimes did and sometimes did not agree to be sacrificed. Sometimes Artemis whisks her away before her death. See L. Kahil in *LIMC* v 1, pp. 706–19, with bibliography on p. 708.

[10] More on the importance of the mythical tradition for the appreciation of a play in ch. 3.

Agamemnon's killing of Iphigenia. Clytemnestra ends the string of questions by asking 'Is that not like a father who was foolish and lacked judgement?' (546). According to the next line ('I think so. . .'), she does indeed believe that it was; but does the choice of seven questions perhaps also express her difficulty in finding a more comprehensive explanation? Perhaps. Perhaps not. Perhaps she is content with calling Agamemnon foolish, perhaps she would like to understand better what exactly it was that drove him to kill Iphigenia. There is, and this is my point, no way of telling what is behind Clytemnestra's question. Clearly, her questions are rhetorical and give spectators much to agree or disagree with, but they are still questions, to a degree even real questions, and thus not fully accessible to the spectators' probing.

Clytemnestra's argument about Agamemnon's sacrifice of Iphigenia ends at this point. She emerges as a thought-provoking character who, in the midst of a rhetorical argument, has the depth of a real-life person. Rather than continuing the analysis until the end of her speech or extending it to that of Electra, I wish to look, again briefly, at a different speech from a different play: Creon's defence against the charge of plotting Oedipus' overthrow, *OT* 583–615. It is the centrepiece of a dispute between Creon and Oedipus which, although it does not take the shape of a formal *agōn*, shares many of its characteristics.[11] Most important, Creon's reasoning invites the listener's evaluation. Critics use the ancient critical term *eikos*:[12] Creon makes an appeal to likelihood. He presents a case which demands to be assessed on the basis of what spectators regard as likely or unlikely. The question is therefore again with what degrees of certainty spectators may form an opinion of the speaker's reasoning. As might be expected, some aspects are familiar from Clytemnestra's speech and need only a cursory glance, but there will also be something new.

---

[11] Cf. Duchemin (1945) 60.

[12] Duchemin (1945) 202–4, Kennedy (1994) 24–5; see Kennedy's index *s.v.* 'probability' for the term *eikos* in ancient rhetorical theory. To judge from Pl. *Phaedr.* 266e2, it was established early on.

To begin with, the familiar. Creon starts off with what is not quite a general argument. 'Consider first this, whether you think (σκέψαι δὲ τοῦτο πρῶτον εἰ ... δοκεῖς) anyone would choose to rule in terror rather than to rule while sleeping unafraid, if the power he has will be the same', he asks Oedipus (584–6), rather than saying outright that 'nobody would desire ...' Some spectators may not feel that the imperative and the second person make any difference and that Creon, despite these details of phrasing, commits himself to the general sentiment that 'nobody would choose ...'; others may be more hesitant. Be that as it may, as Creon goes on everybody will perceive that he too, like Clytemnestra in *Electra*, withdraws into the personal (587–8):

> ἐγὼ μὲν οὖν οὔτ' αὐτὸς ἱμείρων ἔφυν
> τύραννος εἶναι μᾶλλον ἢ τύραννα δρᾶν, ...

Well, I am not the man to wish to be a king (*turannos*) rather than to have royal (*turanna*) power, ...

Whatever one thinks about the more general beginning of the speech, at this point Creon is talking emphatically about himself, and later in the speech he continues to be concerned as much with his own specific preferences and situations as with the general advantages and disadvantages of being a *turannos*:[13] ἦρχον, ἔδρων 591, ἐμοί 592, κυρῶ 594, χαίρω, με 596, με 597, ἐγώ ... λάβοιμι 599, ἔφυν 601, τλαίην 602.

More immediately, however, he adds (589):

> ... οὔτ' ἄλλος ὅστις σωφρονεῖν ἐπίσταται.

... nor is any man who knows how to be in his right mind (*sōphronein*).

Here there can be no doubt that the phrasing is aggressively general and likely to provoke some kind of judgement. Is it right or wrong that nobody in his right mind will prefer being a *turannos* to having the power of a *turannos*? Spectators are likely to have views on this. But even here, I suggest, they have a very good reason for avoiding views which are all black and white: the complexity of *sōphronein*, a word which

---

[13] Roughly 'king'; for the precise meaning of this word see ch. 5, pp. 214–19.

is formed from roots meaning roughly 'healthy' (*sō-*) and 'mind' (*-phron-*), and which translates therefore, again roughly, as 'to be in one's right mind'.

At this point it is useful to remember something Simon Goldhill has to say in his most recent article about 'character'.[14] One of his central arguments is that it would be restrictive to look at a dramatic character in isolation from the context of the society, the literary tradition and the language of the play in question. I have already said something about the literary tradition and will come back to it later. For the moment I wish to concentrate on Goldhill's other two points. Different societies have different notions of what 'to be in one's right mind' means, but at least in some of them the notion is not monolithic. In ancient Greece, at least, *sōphronein* was used in a wide variety of ways.[15] Also in today's Europe it is unlikely that all spectators in any given audience would agree on what kind of activities 'to be in one's right mind' involves. All spectators, ancient and modern, will bring their individual views to bear on Creon's statement. At the same time, however, they may be aware of the multiple associations of the word *sōphronein* and, rather than vehemently agreeing or disagreeing with Creon's statement, say: 'it depends'. Before giving their verdict they may wish to know what Creon means by *sōphronein* – and that, of course, they are not told.

Many spectators may also take account of Goldhill's third category, the language of the play.[16] Not only do words of disease (as in the *sō-* part of *sōphronein*) as well as mind (as in the *-phron-* part) abound in *Oedipus Rex*, but, more specifically, Oedipus' mind (*-phron-*) is frequently under discussion.[17] *Sōphronein*, therefore, adds to a theme of the play. To put it in terms of the present discussion: on the one hand, the preceding and, later, the following scenes give spectators something with which to connect Creon's statement, and

[14] Goldhill (1990b). One of Goldhill's examples is *sōphronein*.
[15] North (1966) and North (1979).
[16] On verbal themes in general and on their prominent place in recent scholarship on tragic language, see the Introduction, pp. 3–4; in the context of a discussion of 'character', apart from Goldhill, especially Gill (1996) 154–74.
[17] *Phron-* words in such contexts at 316, 328, 528, 550, 617 and 649.

hence something which may help them to form a view of it. On the other hand those scenes complicate matters because they underline, rather than answer, the question of how a man acts 'who is in his right mind'. Does he, like Oedipus, risk his life as a ruler, or does he, as Creon claims to do, avoid this? The rest of the play provides spectators with plenty of relevant material, but this material may only make them aware of just how charged a statement Creon has made.[18]

My discussion of Creon's speech has been even shorter than that of Clytemnestra's. None the less, I hope the central point has become clear. Creon, like Clytemnestra, makes a speech which invites spectators to agree or disagree, to judge the quality of the argument and, to put it most generally, to think about it. However, in the case of Creon as of Clytemnestra, many spectators may find that, for one reason or another, such judgements and thoughts are not a straightforward affair. Both Creon's and Clytemnestra's speeches do much to make spectators feel that there are things they do not fully know or do not fully understand – both about the speeches themselves and about the characters who speak them.

GENERAL STATEMENTS

Both *agōn* speeches which I discussed in the previous section make some use of general statements. Following on from there, I will now look at passages in which general statements, more or less recognisable as such, do not occupy short phrases or clauses in longer sentences, but carry on over a number of lines, so as to form considerable stretches of general argument. Are these passages, too, likely to meet with a rather hesitant or nuanced kind of response? Or will they prompt something like a clear 'yes, that's right' or a clear 'no, that's wrong'? In some ways the second alternative might seem the more obvious. General and gnomic statements[19] can after all

---

[18] A second general statement in Creon's speech, in which *phronein* is an important word, is deleted by Dawe and Lloyd-Jones and Wilson in v. 600.

[19] For my purposes exact definitions are not needed. For possible classifications see De Grouchy (1985) 32–46, Lardinois (1997) 214–15 and Russo (1997).

easily be referred to the world outside the play and therefore tend to be rather accessible. Many people have a view on whether life is miserable and whether good deeds bring their own reward. Some statements characters make even recall *gnōmai* that are also found elsewhere. In those cases spectators can (or could) draw not only on the world at large, but also on a gnomic tradition which offers relevant information for forming a view on the line in question. No matter whether recognised as *gnōmai* or not, general statements have the potential to provoke strong views. It therefore seems worth looking at such phrases in more detail.

Creon's first speech in *Antigone* contains one of the lengthiest series of general statements in Sophocles (175–84):

> ἀμήχανον δὲ παντὸς ἀνδρὸς ἐκμαθεῖν
> ψυχήν τε καὶ φρόνημα καὶ γνώμην, πρὶν ἂν
> ἀρχαῖς τε καὶ νόμοισιν ἐντριβὴς φανῇ.
> ἐμοὶ γὰρ ὅστις πᾶσαν εὐθύνων πόλιν
> μὴ τῶν ἀρίστων ἅπτεται βουλευμάτων,
> ἀλλ' ἐκ φόβου του γλῶσσαν ἐγκλήσας ἔχει,
> κάκιστος εἶναι νῦν τε καὶ πάλαι δοκεῖ·
> καὶ μείζον' ὅστις ἀντὶ τῆς αὑτοῦ πάτρας
> φίλον νομίζει, τοῦτον οὐδαμοῦ λέγω.
> ἐγὼ γάρ . . .

There is no way of getting to know a man's spirit and thought and judgement, until he has been seen to be versed in government and in the laws (*nomoisin*). Yes, to me anyone who while guiding the whole city fails to set his hand to the best counsels, but keeps his mouth shut by reason of some fear, seems now and has always seemed the worst of men; and him who rates a dear one higher than his native land, him I put nowhere. I would . . .

Creon speaks about the right way of governing a city, arguing that a good leader will put the common good before the advantage of his dear ones. Again spectators may for all kinds of reasons be unsure whether or not to agree with Creon. But what is notable about this passage is that some of these reasons are much weaker than in the previous passages. I give two examples. First, spectators may be wondering how precisely to take words like *nomos*, 'law' (177), just as I suggested they may be uncertain about the meaning of *sōphronein* in the context of Creon's speech in *Oedipus Rex*. 'Law' is a watchword of the play. Most famously, Antigone claims that respect for the eternal laws made her bury Polyneices (450–60). For spectators who are familiar with the *nomos* theme, Creon's *nomoisin* will have a special ring. Compared, however, to the passage about *sōphronein*, these lines are remarkably clear in their meaning. In the immediate context (ἀρχαῖς τε καὶ νόμοισιν ἐντριβής), and long before Antigone speaks about the eternal laws, it is difficult to understand the *nomoi* as anything other than the laws of the city.

A second potential difficulty for spectators who try to take a position on these lines is the personal phrasing with which Creon insists on his own opinion (ἐμοί 178, λέγω 183, ἐγώ 184), and this reason, too, is not as strong as elsewhere. In comparison with the speeches of Clytemnestra and the other Creon which I have just discussed, the first-person language is rather inconspicuous. The emphasis of the passage is on *what* Creon believes, rather than *that* he believes it; it does not point at Creon as a person. Clytemnestra and the Creon of *Oedipus Rex* were talking about their own actions and feelings; the Creon of *Antigone* speaks, most of all, about generic men. This speech, therefore, much more than the previous ones, invites clear-cut responses – whether positive or negative.

Some such responses are on record. I will give two examples, the first of which is by Demosthenes. For reasons that are irrelevant here, he speaks approvingly about the passage. He calls the lines 'beautifully and instructively composed'[20] and holds it against Aeschines that he fails to act in accordance with Creon's sentiments, although he often acted that role himself. Demosthenes' treatment of the speech is interesting not only as an example of a clear-cut (positive) response to Creon's string of *gnōmai*, but also because of what he has to say about Creon himself: next to nothing. Demosthenes does not worry about Creon, and does not want to know why Creon says what he says. He is happy to quote the passage in complete abstraction from its play and its speaker.

Quotation out of context, of course, has always been com-

---

[20] Dem. 19.246.

mon. There are many other passages from Greek tragedy that have suffered a similar fate, and many factors influencing the selection of these passages. These passages and the criteria for their selection would deserve detailed study.[21] What I want to suggest here is that one reason (and it is easy to think of others, such as Aeschines' association with the role of Creon) for quoting this particular passage with little regard for its context and for the character who speaks it is that Demosthenes felt on top of it. There is nothing in the passage that made him feel it necessary to speak in any detail about its place in the play or about Creon as the person who speaks it. A central assumption of this chapter is that a character whose lines are not unequivocally judged can keep something like inwardness or depth. Here we have the other side of the coin. Demosthenes does not hesitate in giving his unequivocal evaluation of Creon's speech – and at the same time strips Creon of every kind of depth. Creon almost vanishes altogether as his lines are treated as an outline of model behaviour.

My second example of a clear-cut response is complementary to the first. Where Demosthenes is all approving of Creon's sentiments, Anthony Podlecki is all disapproving. Both kinds of unequivocal evaluation, the positive and the negative, have the same effect. They deprive the speaker of any inaccessibility or depth that might be attributed to him. Unlike Demosthenes' Creon, Podlecki's does not altogether disappear, but little survives: 'He is a weak man, used to taking second place in Thebes. His new power rests uneasily upon him. He must cover up his insecurity with well-sounding, if somewhat muddled, political platitudes.'[22] Podlecki knows what to make of Creon's general statements ('somewhat muddled political platitudes') and is in consequence in a position to make a confident construction about Creon himself ('a weak man ...'). On top of the general statements, he is also on top of Creon.

---

[21] The following, in their different ways, have made a start: Perlman (1964), Lanza and Fort (1991) and Wilson (1996).

[22] Podlecki (1966a) 362.

Creon, then, seems to pose a challenge to my thesis that spectators often have good reason to hesitate before coming down heavily on the things Sophoclean characters say. He does indeed show that there is great variation between the ways in which different characters speak. It is not least, I suggest, because of the aspects of Creon's language which I have analysed that many spectators and critics have found Antigone in some way the dominating character of the play. What I want to stress, however, is that Creon is exceptional in his use of *gnōmai*.[23] I have discussed him because of the contrast he provides with most other characters. That he is indeed exceptional is perhaps suggested by the fact that equally long stretches of generalising statements are exceedingly rare in Sophocles' surviving plays, and that scholars sometimes go so far as to attribute gnomic fragments that are transmitted under Sophocles' name to Euripides.[24] It is suggested also, and more significantly, by the fact that the other generalising passages that there are can be looked at in a rather different way. As far as I am aware, few (if any) of them have provoked the same kind of reactions as Creon's speech, and there are good reasons.

As an example I will discuss Oedipus' comments on time and change (*OC* 607–15):

> ὦ φίλτατ' Αἰγέως ταῖ, μόνοις οὐ γίγνεται
> θεοῖσι γῆρας οὐδὲ κατθανεῖν ποτε,
> τὰ δ' ἄλλα συγχεῖ πάνθ' ὁ πακρατὴς χρόνος.
> φθίνει μὲν ἰσχὺς γῆς, φθίνει δὲ σώματος,
> θνήσκει δὲ πίστις, βλαστάνει δ' ἀπιστία,
> καὶ πνεῦμα ταὐτὸν οὔποτ' οὔτ' ἐν ἀνδράσιν
> φίλοις βέβηκεν οὔτε πρὸς πόλιν πόλει.
> τοῖς μὲν γὰρ ἤδη, τοῖς δ' ἐν ὑστέρῳ χρόνῳ
> τὰ τερπνὰ πικρὰ γίγνεται καὖθις φίλα.

Dearest son of Aegeus, for the gods alone there is no old age and no death ever, but all other things are confounded by all-powerful time (*chronos*). The strength of the country perishes, so does the strength of the body, loyalty dies and disloyalty comes into being, and the same spirit never remains

---

[23] Menelaus in *Ajax* comes closest. See especially 1071–83.
[24] See for instance Pearson on frs. 354 and 583.

between friends or between cities, since for some people now and for others in the future happy relations turn bitter, and again friendship is restored.

In a string of general statements, Oedipus argues that there is nothing that, in the course of time, is not affected by change. Why should any spectators hesitate in their response? Not, as so often elsewhere, because of personal phrasing. Apart from the address to Theseus at the beginning ('dearest son of Aegeus'), nothing shifts the argument into the realm of the personal. Oedipus does not even use phrases like 'I think', as Creon did in the previous passage.

Yet in other respects, Oedipus' general statements are considerably less straightforward. The first is one that is familiar already from Creon's remark about *sōphronein* in *Oedipus Rex*. The relevant word in Oedipus' speech is *chronos*, 'time'. Time, and especially its role in Oedipus' life, has been focused on repeatedly ever since the short first speech of the play, in which Oedipus spoke of himself as an 'old man' (1), described his day-by-day mode of life (3), and said that he has learned from 'the time that has long been my companion', ὁ χρόνος ξυνών | μακρός (7–8). Already before he grew old, when he was still king of Thebes in *Oedipus Rex*, time was a key player (especially 1213). Even though each spectator may have strong views as to what kind of things in his or her own world change through time, and may judge Oedipus' statements accordingly, these passages create a second frame of reference.

The second difference between Oedipus' and Creon's general statements is a matter not so much of verbal themes as of the phrasing of whole clauses. Time is 'all-powerful' (παγκρατής) and 'confounds' (συγχεῖ) all things,[25] as the land has 'strength' (ἰσχὺς γῆς), which in turn 'perishes' (φθίνει), while loyalty 'dies' (θνῄσκει) and disloyalty 'comes into being' (βλαστάνει). Even spectators who have much to say about time in general may not necessarily hold strong views on expressions like this. There is much that is predictable about the

---

[25] The phenomenon is usually referred to as 'personification'. De Romilly (1968) 33–58 discusses these lines and other instances of 'personification' of time. See also her pp. 87–111 for time in Sophocles.

effects of time, but time itself cannot be observed. It is considerably easier to say that something is happening *over* time than that it is happening *because of* time. Spectators may find an (imaginary) sentence like 'everything changes in the course of time' considerably closer to home than the sentence 'but all other things are confounded by all-powerful time'.

Thirdly, there is a more general consideration. Time is prominent in *Oedipus at Colonus* in a number of ways, but is associated most of all with Oedipus himself. When he speaks about time, therefore, he speaks with the authority of a man who, one might say, has lived through more time and has experienced more change than many others. Immediately after this passage he even begins to make prophecies about future events. Time for Oedipus is not what it is for everybody else, and the present passage is a reminder of his special relation with it. Oedipus speaks at some length about time, and speaks about it in a way not everybody else does, making time an agent. Far from just inviting the spectators' agreement or disagreement (as Creon's speech in *Antigone* does to a remarkably high degree), these general statements mark out Oedipus as a man who is in some ways beyond the spectators' understanding.

DRAMATIC IRONY

Discussion of *agōn* scenes and general statements has already suggested many ways in which the things Sophoclean characters say may engage many spectators by giving them much to be certain and as much to be uncertain about. Before using this discussion as a basis for drawing some conclusions, I will turn to a last set of statements which invite the spectators' agreement – or rather disagreement.

This set of statements is defined by the term 'dramatic irony'. The concept of dramatic irony has been much discussed and has been used in many ways.[26] I am here inter-

---

[26] See Rosenmeyer (1996) for the most recent discussion of irony in tragedy. He also gives guidance on the critical literature.

ested only in one of its aspects, an aspect, however, which has often been seen as central, namely the marked difference in knowledge between the audience and a character. As D. C. Muecke puts it, an important characteristic of dramatic irony is that the 'observer already knows what the victim has yet to find out'.[27] When Oedipus, to give a well-known example, declares his will to investigate the murder of Laius as though he was his father (*OT* 264–8), spectators familiar with the story are able to understand the words in a more informed way than Oedipus. The point of interest for my discussion of characters is that on this basis the spectators can make constructions about Oedipus, saying that he is a man who, despite his surpassing intelligence, is not aware of the full implications of a simple statement, that he is too sure of himself, and so on.

I will here concentrate not on *Oedipus Rex* but on *Electra*, because in this play there are not just one but two characters who are both for a considerable time put into the position of knowing markedly less than the audience. Both Clytemnestra and Electra are taken in by Orestes' pretended death. As a consequence, there is much scope for dramatic irony. Many statements Clytemnestra and Electra make are based on false assumptions. For many lines spectators can watch them being mistaken about what is going on. This set-up is potentially damaging to Clytemnestra and Electra as objects of interest. They are in danger of no longer being taken seriously since all that needs to be known about them seems to be known: they are being deceived. The only question now might be when and how Orestes will reveal his identity. Clytemnestra and Electra thus threaten to become mere props in Orestes' drama. However, as is obvious to anybody who knows the play, this is not the case. Both Clytemnestra and Electra remain fascinating until the end. Few will be tempted not to take them very seriously indeed. In this section I will discuss how this is possible.

Sophocles' Electra recognises her brother much later in the play than do her Aeschylean and Euripidean counterparts, and is not made party to his plan of announcing his own

[27] Muecke (1969) 104.

death until long after it has been put into practice. As a result she is hit as much as Clytemnestra by the Paedagogus's speech and can be observed for over 500 lines speaking and acting under the illusion that Orestes is dead. Rachel Kitzinger is not alone when she stresses in a recent article[28] the blow that this set-up deals to Electra's credibility. 'The distance ... created between the audience's knowledge and Elektra's deprives her speech of its power to reflect reality and makes her an object of pity rather than the persuasive interpreter she has been [earlier in the play].'

What Kitzinger means becomes clear in Electra's first words after the Paedagogus's speech (788–96):

Ηλ. οἴμοι τάλαινα· νῦν γὰρ οἰμῶξαι πάρα,
    Ὀρέστα, τὴν σὴν ξυμφοράν, ὅθ' ὧδ' ἔχων
    πρὸς τῆσδ' ὑβρίζῃ μητρός. ἆρ' ἔχω[29] καλῶς;
Κλ. οὔτοι σύ· κεῖνος δ' ὡς ἔχει καλῶς ἔχει.
Ηλ. ἄκουε, Νέμεσι τοῦ θανόντος ἀρτίως.
Κλ. ἤκουσεν ὧν δεῖ κἀπεκύρωσεν καλῶς.
Ηλ. ὕβριζε· νῦν γὰρ εὐτυχοῦσα τυγχάνεις.
Κλ. οὔκουν Ὀρέστης καὶ σὺ παύσετον τάδε;
Ηλ. πεπαύμεθ' ἡμεῖς, οὐχ ὅπως σὲ παύσομεν.

El. Ah, miserable me! Now I can lament your disaster, Orestes, when in this plight you are insulted by this mother of yours! Am I not well off?
Cl. Not so; but as he is he is well off.
El. Hear this, Nemesis of the one who lately died!
Cl. Nemesis has heard what she needed to hear and has decided well.
El. Insult me! Now is your moment of good fortune.
Cl. Then will not Orestes and you stop this?
El. We are finished, far from stopping you!

Electra laments here, as she will do frequently afterwards,[30] the death of Orestes, whom the audience knows to be alive. In this respect her speech has indeed lost the 'power to reflect reality'. Everybody notices that Electra's assumptions are mistaken. But this is far from all that one can say about her.

---

[28] Kitzinger (1991); the quotation is taken from p. 319. It represents only one strand of Kitzinger's argument, since she is otherwise interested in the way not only the characters, but also the spectators, are affected by the Paedagogus's speech.
[29] F. W. Schmidt's emendation of the MSS' ἔχει, accepted by Lloyd-Jones and Wilson.
[30] In this episode compare 674, 677 and 804ff.

To begin with, there is once again personal phrasing. Electra has as much to say about herself, and in particular about her feelings, as about Orestes' death. She sighs (οἴμοι) and calls herself wretched. She speaks of her lament (οἰμῶξαι) and finally says that 'we', that is, she and Orestes, 'are finished'. This emphasis on her emotions is important. Emotions are something very different from facts such as the death of Orestes. There can be no doubt that Electra's assumptions are false. Her emotions, by contrast, while no doubt real, are ultimately inaccessible. Nobody can know what somebody else feels, how somebody else perceives loss. One can (and does) try to imagine, but one never really knows. By giving much room to what she feels, Electra points to herself as an ultimately inaccessible person. There is much spectators know about her statements, in some regards more than she does herself, but there is also much they cannot know (in passing it is worth pointing out that spectators have not been warned: when Orestes and the Paedagogus plotted the deception in the prologue, they did not waste any thought on the effects it might have on Electra). Electra's personal phrasing, therefore, is a major reason why she remains interesting despite the great weight of dramatic irony that is poised against her.

This prompts the question of whether the same is true for Clytemnestra. The whole of this scene invites comparison between her and Electra's different reactions to Orestes' death. Electra's πεπαύμεθα (796), which means both 'we are finished' and 'we have been stopped', is prompted by παύσετον, another form of the same verb, in Clytemnestra's preceding 'then will not Orestes and you stop this?' (795). Like Electra, Clytemnestra has no doubt about Orestes' death, but unlike Electra, she does not point to herself and her feelings in this passage.[31] At least in the first instance, she is alluding to *Electra's* and *Orestes'* inability to carry out their revenge when she asks 'will you not put an end to this?' Electra, by contrast, also expresses what Orestes' death means to *herself* when she replies 'we are finished' / 'we have been stopped'. In

---

[31] She does so immediately before: 766–87.

83

this respect, Clytemnestra suffers more from dramatic irony than Electra does: the prologue allows spectators to regard it at least as very likely that she is wrong. Is she, then, a completely different case from Electra?

I think not. For a variety of reasons most of her statements are vulnerable to a lesser degree than that of line 795. When Electra invokes Nemesis to hear her (ἄκουε Νέμεσι), Clytemnestra replies that Nemesis has heard (ἤκουσεν) what she needed to hear and has decided well. Here, too, the repetition of a word (ἄκουε – ἤκουσεν prompts a comparison between Electra and Clytemnestra.[32] For different reasons, different spectators may find it difficult to arrive at a simple verdict. I will give three of these reasons.

The first is familiar from the previous sections and needs little discussion: Nemesis, like time in Oedipus' lines, is the kind of force whose movements cannot be predicted with any certainty. Was the death of Agamemnon the act of Nemesis? Will Nemesis act again? What does it mean to say that 'Nemesis hears' something? Clytemnestra's statement is worth contemplating. The second reason (and this, too, is familiar) concerns the literary traditions. Like the prologue, previous treatments of the story may suggest that Nemesis will later (cf. Electra's νῦν in 794) punish Clytemnestra. Electra, on this assumption, seems right to call Clytemnestra hubristic (ὕβριζε in 794 means both 'insult me' and 'be hubristic'). And yet, the literary tradition has more to say about punishment. In many versions of the myth it is Orestes who is persecuted, by the Furies who are goddesses of revenge like Nemesis. The knowledge spectators have about Nemesis may therefore not be unproblematic. Thirdly, there is a temporal dimension to the assessment of these lines. Whatever spectators think about this scene at the time of watching it, almost everything becomes more complex (rather than, as one might hope, easier) as the play goes on. In the final scene, as has often been observed, there is no Nemesis. Nor is there the kind of trial of

---

[32] Note also the repetition of καλῶς: 790, 791, 793. On verbal repetition in stichomythia in general see Hancock (1917) 35–9.

Orestes that *Eumenides* dramatised.[33] Are spectators who invoke the literary tradition in the present scene right to do so? After many invitations throughout the play to think about the justice as well as the outcome of Electra's and Orestes' revenge ploy, there is little help in the end. The help there is, moreover, is unsatisfactory. Most famously Orestes says (1424–5) 'in the house all is well, if Apollo prophesied well (Ἀπόλλων εἰ καλῶς ἐθέσπισεν)', attaching an unverifiable condition to the hoped-for final verdict. Spectators who wonder how justified Clytemnestra was in describing Nemesis' action with the adverb 'well' (καλῶς) in the present passage (793) may wonder even more when they hear Orestes' conditional clause near the end of the play. There is much more to this couple of lines about Nemesis than the irony that revenge is closer than Clytemnestra and Electra expect.

The following scenes up to the entry of Orestes are dominated by Electra, who voices her distress both in trimeters and in a kommos with the Chorus, and then convinces Chrysothemis that the grave offerings she has seen cannot have been made by Orestes. Again everything she says is based on the false assumption that Orestes is dead, and again she remains interesting. I want to emphasise one point in particular. To put it briefly, Electra retains considerable control over the action of the play despite being taken in by the Paedagogus's false report. One example will be enough to illustrate this (817–22):

> ἀλλ' οὔ τι μὴν ἔγωγε τοῦ λοιποῦ χρόνου
> ξύνοικος εἴσειμ',[34] ἀλλὰ τῆδε πρὸς πύλῃ
> παρεῖσ' ἐμαυτὴν ἄφιλος αὐανῶ βίον.
> πρὸς ταῦτα καινέτω τις, εἰ βαρύνεται,
> τῶν ἔνδον ὄντων· ὡς χάρις μέν, ἢν κτάνῃ,
> λύπη δ', ἐὰν ζῶ· τοῦ βίου δ' οὐδεὶς πόθος.

But in the future I shall not enter the house to live with them, but by this gate I shall let myself go and without a friend waste away my life. In face of

---

[33] More on the end of *Electra* in chs. 4 (pp. 180–2) and 5 (pp. 256–68).

[34] This is Hermann's emendation, adopted by Dawe and others, of ξύνοικος ἔσσομ' *vel sim.* It provides a slightly better contrast with the following phrase than Dawes's ἔσομαι ξύνοικος, which Lloyd-Jones and Wilson print.

that let any of those inside kill me, if he resents me; to die will be a pleasure, to survive will be a pain, and I have no desire for life.

Electra does not just express her grief but also says something new in these lines. She will not, so she announces, enter the house again. No longer does she wish to live, and therefore she challenges those indoors to kill her. Obviously all this will not happen, since Orestes is about to arrive and change everything. But who can be sure? Will he arrive immediately? Will he arrive later? Will Electra have time to start acting on her plans?

For the time being it is indeed for Electra to determine the course of events, as becomes clear when Chrysothemis (rather than Orestes) enters. At first Electra crushes all her hopes for a return of Orestes, and then (938ff.) goes on to try to persuade her to act and take revenge without Orestes. Once more spectators have it driven home to them that Electra is deceived about Orestes' death, but at the same time they have every reason to be impressed by several lines of imperatives and futures in which there is nothing to be known for certain and much to be wondered about. Will Electra launch a single-handed attack on the palace before Orestes makes his presence known?

Oedipus in *Oedipus Rex* is the paradigm of a character trapped in dramatic irony, but still the play depends on his actions. Only if he carries his investigation through will the trap close. Similarly, Electra is on the one hand enfeebled by the ironical set-up. 'The distance', to quote Kitzinger again, 'created between the audience's knowledge and Elektra's deprives her speech of its power to reflect reality and makes her an object of pity.' But at the same time it is clear that there is much, for instance the acts of Nemesis, about which the audience knows no more than Electra does, and much in fact, about which the audience knows a good deal less than Electra. Only Electra knows what she feels and only Electra knows what she will do next. As much as any Sophoclean character, she is attractive as a person who has what Easterling calls inwardness and what I have been calling depth. There are many more passages to be discussed. In particular the recognition scene would no doubt yield a number of new insights. But I trust that the central point has become clear from what I have said about Clytemnestra and Electra so far. If it is characteristic of dramatic irony that the 'observer already knows what the victim has yet to find out' (as Muecke and others assume it is), the term 'dramatic irony' catches only one aspect of the relevant passages in Sophocles.[35]

CONCLUSION

It is time to come to an end. The ways in which spectators react to the things characters say are influenced by a vast number of factors which cannot all be accounted for at the same time. Any discussion which, like mine, is concerned with audience response is therefore inevitably imprecise and partial. This is, to be sure, a high price to pay. The pay-off, however, is that such a discussion, imprecise and partial as it is, can bring out something that is characteristic of how Sophoclean language communicates. This is what I have tried to do in the preceding pages. As in chapter 1, I have stressed that Sophoclean language is often complex and anything other than straightforward. But while the focus in that chapter was on the ways in which sentences conflict with the spectators' expectations, I have argued in this chapter that the language characters use produces statements which spectators may find in some way difficult and out of their reach.

Sometimes, for instance, statements turn on words which have complex connotations in the play; sometimes their language points to matters (like the acts of time and Nemesis) that some spectators may find difficult to grasp; often they are phrased personally and thus put the emphasis on the characters' intentions, feelings or other matters on which nobody knows as much as the speaker. Statements like this make

---

[35] For remarks on the shortcomings of 'tragic irony' (dramatic irony's sister) as an adequate tool for describing many effects in *OT*, see Pucci (1988) 132–44 and Pucci (1992) 80–1. Compare also Heiden (1989) 13–14 and Williams (1993) 148–9.

Sophoclean characters engaging. Even when spectators might have every reason to react with a quick 'yes, that's right' or 'no that's wrong' to something a character says, there is often something in the phrasing that may make them realise that there is much more to be said and more to be known. Few of the things Sophoclean characters say are quickly dismissed as obviously true or obviously false.

As a result, I suggested further in the wake of Easterling, Sophoclean characters have to a remarkable degree what may be called inwardness or depth. They seem to be only partially accessible and seem to reveal themselves only partially in their speeches. All the sources of difficulty and complexity that I have discussed can contribute to this effect of depth. The effect is perhaps most distinct where the phrasing points at a character as a person spectators do not fully know. Only Creon knows what being second in government means to him. Only Oedipus knows what time means to him at the end of a long life. Only Electra knows what Orestes' death means to her. Watching Sophoclean tragedy, spectators come to confront characters who seem to extend beyond their words and their bodies.

Over the years, these characters have attracted a great deal of comment. From antiquity onwards, many critics have found Sophoclean characters remarkable. A few highlights will have to do. Aristotle attributed to Sophocles himself reflections about his characters: 'if ⟨a poet⟩ is criticised for representing something that is not true, perhaps what he represents is as it ought to be; just as Sophocles himself said that he created people as they ought to be while Euripides created them as they are...'[36] Centuries later Goethe, according to Eckermann, talked as follows about Sophoclean characters: ' "That is the very thing", said Goethe, "in which Sophocles is a master; and in which consists the very life of the dramatic in general. His characters all possess this gift of eloquence and know how to explain the motives for their action so convin-

---

[36] *Poet.* 1460b32–5. For further statements made in antiquity about Sophocles' characters, see *Vita Sophoclea* 21 and Plutarch, *De profectibus in virtute* 7.79b.

cingly that the hearer is almost always on the side of the last speaker.'[37] In this century Gordon Kirkwood wrote that 'in Sophocles to a degree greater than in Aeschylus or Euripides the development of a tragic action depends on the interplay of characters',[38] and H. D. F. Kitto concludes an essay as follows:[39] 'if a dramatist is one who portrays recognizable human characters in action and in passion, grappling with each other with all their strength over matters of importance and significance, then surely Sophocles is a dramatist of great stature'.

The differences between these critics (and many others might be added) are obvious. Sophoclean characters are idealistic rather than realistic, they bring hearers over to their side, they are central to the action, they are recognisable. Unsurprisingly, critics vary as to the place where they put their emphasis. Sophoclean characters are interesting in more than one way. Yet there is something on which critics all appear to agree: Sophoclean characters are significantly 'there'. They are not easily overlooked or dismissed. This sense of their presence, more than anything else, is what I want to express by 'depth'. Sophoclean characters are somehow substantial, they are, to put it in the language of this book, something around which different spectators can gather in communality. I will conclude by illustrating further what this means.

In an article on 'The question of character and personality in Greek tragedy'[40] Christopher Gill distinguishes between two ways of looking at people in fiction, calling these ways the character-viewpoint and the personality-viewpoint. The first is 'the kind of perspective on character in which our primary

---

[37] Eckermann (1971) 178, reporting the conversation of 28 March 1827.

[38] Kirkwood (1994a) 99. For a recent brief treatment of differences between Sophoclean and Euripidean characters, see Gould (1978) 52–4.

[39] Kitto (1958) 20. Note also his pp. 14–18 on the scene between Electra and Clytemnestra, discussed above, pp. 80–7.

[40] Gill (1986). All the following quotations in this paragraph are taken from pages 252 and 253. He modifies his terms slightly in Gill (1990) and again in Gill (1996) 116–17. Gill (1996) is chiefly concerned with *ethical* judgement and has therefore, despite many points of contact, a different thrust from the present discussion.

concern is with placing or locating the person in an evaluative schema or framework. This concern typically expresses itself in giving descriptive accounts, in which the person concerned appears as the proper noun to whom we attach evaluative adjectives: "Charles is warm and kind but sometimes weak and self-indulgent." ' 'The primary concern' of the personality-viewpoint, by contrast, is 'to explore, or respond to, the person "as he really is" (as we loosely but significantly put it), to his distinctive psychological being, his unique "personality" '. Descriptive statements are rare. 'More typical of the personality-viewpoint are statements of this kind, "don't you see what he's going through now?"; that is, statements which invite us to share the person's own point of view (or to try to understand it), and to recognise with some exactness a particular, transient psychological state.' Gill suggests that Greek tragedy is responsive to both kinds of perspectives. Most scholars would probably agree with Gill, and indeed my discussion in this chapter could easily be adapted to support his thesis. What I want to point out here is that some similarities move the kind of response to Sophoclean characters which I have been discussing in this chapter close to Gill's personality-viewpoint in particular: the avoidance of simple evaluations which Gill associates with the personality-viewpoint has been central to the whole of my discussion, and to respond, as Gill suggests one does when one adopts the personality-viewpoint, to a person 'as he really is' and to speak of his or her 'personality' attributes something like 'depth' to this person.

It is because of these overlaps that I will now conclude by borrowing one of the metaphors that Gill uses in the description of the personality-viewpoint which I have quoted: 'to share the person's own point of view', or as I will call it in order to avoid confusion with the character- or personality-'viewpoint', 'to share the person's perspective'. The expression 'to share a character's perspective' is reminiscent of my suggestion at the end of the previous chapter that Sophoclean sentences are formed in a way that gives spectators a world to share. Thus it brings out the importance characters have for what I call communality among the different: many different spectators all get a perspective to share. What, I ask therefore, does it mean to say that spectators share a character's perspective?

It can mean many things. It can mean, for instance, to *think with* the character. While Creon does not challenge the assumptions that Demosthenes or Podlecki have about right government and does not stop them making their respective quick judgements, Oedipus can (arguably) prompt contemplation on time and change. Similarly, spectators can *wonder with* Clytemnestra about the sacrifice of Iphigenia and Agamemnon's motives for going ahead with it. Or they can *suffer with* Electra when they try to imagine what she might be feeling. They can, moreover, *fear with* her that her future in the palace will be unbearable, and can therefore *anticipate* a single-handed attack on the rulers *with* her, when they know her situation but do not know whether she will ever have the chance or need to put her plans into action.

Not every spectator thinks, fears and suffers in the same way, since they all keep their own perspectives, which colour their responses, while sharing the character's. Yet whatever 'think', 'fear' and 'suffer' may mean for each of them, there is a common element. Spectators who share a character's perspective all bring in their own views, but allow the character's statement to interact with these views. They can all get involved in struggling with the same words, even if this involvement may take rather different shapes for each of them. They all get involved in making sense of Agamemnon's killing of Iphigenia; they all get involved in reflecting on time and change; they all get involved in coming to terms with the death of Orestes. By inviting spectators to share a character's perspective, Sophoclean language invites spectators to share something with one another.

CHAPTER 3

MYTH AND PROPHECY: SHARED ORDER

INTRODUCTION

Sophoclean sentences, I suggested in chapter 1, can create trust in a world that exists beyond their words. Rather than pointing at themselves as some Gorgianic sentences do, they are unpredictable and therefore often appear to reflect the equally unpredictable world beyond them. In chapter 2 I looked at characters as one important part of this world. I argued that the language they use gives them the depth and elusiveness that is an attribute of real people, inviting spectators to share their perspective. In this chapter I will continue exploring how Sophoclean language evokes a world that seems almost palpably real although it goes beyond what can be seen and heard. Moving on from the characters (whose bodies and words, at least, are manifest on stage), I turn to entities which (like Cypris, *phusis* or the dead Oedipus of chapter 1) are entirely invisible and inaudible.

For this purpose I will continue to scrutinise individual sentences, as in chapter 1, and individual passages, as in chapter 2. But since part of my project is to suggest that Sophoclean language repays study on both a small and a large scale, in chapters 3 and 4 I will broaden the outlook further and trace certain invisible entities through whole plays. Locally observable linguistic detail will remain in the foreground, but for as full an appreciation as possible I will look for connections between the individual passages that I consider, will study these passages as part of a larger whole, and will also draw on non-linguistic aspects of Sophocles' writing. Where Sophoclean language is concerned, to contain would be to curtail.

There are many different invisible entities that play significant roles in Sophoclean tragedy and therefore offer themselves as suitable objects of study. The most prominent among them are perhaps the gods. I will look at them in the next chapter. As examples of the other, more low-profile, invisible entities, I will discuss in this chapter myth and prophecy in *Philoctetes*. The central suggestion I want to make resembles those of the preceding chapters. The language of *Philoctetes*, I will argue, provides spectators with numerous cues for thinking about myth and prophecy. Since the cues are no more than cues, they are a starting-point for thought but give no definite answers. All answers have the potential of leading to new questions. Like the sentences of chapter 1 and the characters of chapter 2, myth and prophecy in *Philoctetes* gain much of their force from the peculiar blend of accessibility and complexity that is characteristic of the way Sophoclean language communicates. To put it simply: in their different ways, different spectators can share the sense that for everything they are able to grasp there is something else that eludes them – and vice versa. Few of them are likely to run out of either questions or answers. There is, therefore, much scope for involvement, and much scope for what I call communality among the different.

Before starting to ask some of those questions and to give some of those answers, I wish to stress straightaway something which I have said before, but which bears frequent repetition. What follows is a discussion of various questions spectators *may* ask and of answers they *may* give. No spectator is likely to engage with the play exactly as I suggest. Some of them will find none of the questions interesting, others will give different answers, others again will ask similar questions and give similar answers, but they will do so in a different way. What matters is the *kind* of involvement that Sophoclean language makes possible for many spectators, not any one variation. I am interested in communality among *the different*.

MYTH

The first thing to note in a discussion of myth is the fact that the word 'myth' (as well as 'tradition', the other word I will use) is only a convenient shorthand for something that can be rather unhomogeneous. Myth consists of a multitude of different strands with different degrees of authority in different kinds of context. More so perhaps than some other invisible constituents of Sophocles' world, therefore, myth is different for different spectators. Variations depend largely on the aspects of the tradition on which a spectator is able to draw. At least some, and possibly most, fifth-century spectators were familiar with far more mythical material than anybody is today. By contrast, many modern performances will be given to people with a knowledge of only the bare essentials of the legend. Building as it does on as much of the tradition as has lived on until today, the following discussion assumes spectators situated somewhere between those extremes, and therefore is not valid in the same way for all spectators of all times.[1] Yet this is not to say that myth, as I will speak about it, separates spectators. The different knowledge that they have does not so much provoke opposed reactions as allow some spectators to see more than others. Those who know more see more, and those who know less see less. Rarely in Sophocles does knowledge of myth make as great a difference as in the final scene of *Electra*, where the Furies' punishment of Orestes is not in the text but may be imported from earlier literary versions, thus making the play end in gloom.[2]

The mythical background of *Philoctetes*, the play that I have chosen as my example, has been much studied,[3] both in

[1] Spectators differ also in the kind of information they have about the play itself: they may have seen it before, heard or read about it, been present at the *proagōn* (see van Erp Taalman Kip (1990) 123–9 for the most recent discussion of the little evidence that there is for this event). It would be an interesting project to ask how knowledge about the play influences the way spectators watch it. In this chapter I will assume spectators who do not have such knowledge, but much of my discussion could be adapted to apply to those who do.

[2] But even here the difference is not *all*-important. Spectators who know the earlier versions of the myth may wonder what weight they ought to give them, and spectators who do not know them may find the ending disconcerting for other reasons. Cf. ch. 4, pp. 180–2.

[3] Stanford (1954) 1–117, Beye (1970), Fuqua (1976) 32–62, Hoppin (1981), Mandel (1981), Schnebele (1988), Garner (1990) 145–9, O'Higgins (1991), Perysinakis (1992), Perysinakis (1994–5), Davidson (1995), Kittmer (1995), esp. 24–9, Whitby (1996), Müller (1997) 211–57 and the introductions to the commentaries. Of these Kittmer and especially O'Higgins are closest to my approach here.

its own right and for its contribution to dramatic effect. To speak of 'myth', as I just noted, is a simplification. The Philoctetes legend was told, or told in part, in the *Iliad*, the cyclic epics, Pindar, several plays by all three major tragedians, pictorial representations and probably elsewhere. These works display many different versions, some of which are extremely powerful, so that it is for instance almost imperative that Philoctetes will eventually go to Troy, while others, such as the circumstances of Philoctetes' wounding by the snake, are more changeable.

All the known aspects of the Philoctetes myth, whether strong or weak, make their various demands on the action of Sophocles' play, and thus interact with the three main characters, Philoctetes, Neoptolemus and Odysseus, all of whom try at one point or another to steer the play in their preferred direction. In what follows I will look at moments when spectators can notice, primarily in the language but also otherwise, signs that the characters come into contact with what I will call the 'force of myth'. This expression, metaphorical as it is, will help me to describe some of the ways in which Sophoclean language communicates and some of the ways in which it makes *Philoctetes* an engaging play, and will, I hope, justify itself. Not everybody might think of myth as possessing force, but one of the aims of my discussion is to suggest that in *Philoctetes* at least this is a suggestive metaphor.

Odysseus and the False Merchant

To begin at the beginning. When Odysseus comes on stage, many spectators may recognise him from his costume, mask and accoutrements. Some, moreover, may expect him to play an important role because of what they know about Aeschylus' and Euripides' earlier *Philoctetes* plays. Yet even they may find it difficult to identify the young man who accompanies Odysseus. Never before (as far as we know) has Neoptolemus been involved in fetching Philoctetes from Lemnos. As Odysseus introduces him to the audience, he is changing myth. Not only has he brought Neoptolemus along, but he also has him do almost all the work: 'but from now on your task is to help me ...' (15). That was different in Euripides. According to Dio's paraphrase, Odysseus said (59.2) 'now I have come to Lemnos in a most precarious and difficult matter: in order to secure Philoctetes and the bow of Heracles for my allies'. No farming out of tasks there.

The first signs of tension appear almost straightaway. In verse 14 Odysseus says that he wants to capture Philoctetes by means of a 'trick' (*sophisma*) – after all, one might add, that is how he succeeded in Euripides' play and on many other occasions in his life –, but in verses 3–4 he addresses Neoptolemus (in accordance with myth) 'O son of the noblest father among the Greeks, son of Achilles, Neoptolemus' (ὦ κρατίστου πα-τρὸς Ἑλλήνων τραφεὶς | Ἀχιλλέως παῖ Νεοπτόλεμε). This is conspicuous phrasing for a conspicuous change of cast. Spectators may find it difficult to know what to think. They may know a tradition which has much to say about the son of Achilles but nothing to suggest that he is the kind of man who uses cunning, and may therefore find Neoptolemus one of the least promising changes of cast possible. The conspicuous phrasing draws attention to his pedigree. Neoptolemus is emphatically the son of Achilles: not a man known for his trickery. But what does that mean? Is the language of the address to Neoptolemus a first sign of trouble ahead, since Odysseus may be able to introduce Neoptolemus into the Philoctetes myth but only at the price of introducing his Achillean nature, too? Or does it only highlight just how far Odysseus can go in changing the tradition? Many variations as there are in the Philoctetes myth, Odysseus may well be able to add another. The members of the embassy, in particular, are anything but stable: it was only Aeschylus who made Odysseus himself, rather than Diomedes as in the *Little Iliad*,[4] go to Lemnos. And trickery, Odysseus' envisaged mode of operation, is in no way an innovation but was already an important part of both Aeschylus' and Euripides' *Philoctetes* plays.[5] All in all, spec-

---

[4] Proclus p. 106, 25 Allen.   [5] Dio Chrys. 52.9 and 59.3, respectively.

tators have reason both to trust and distrust Odysseus' outline of events. Will he get away with the changes he introduces, and if not, what will happen?

Neoptolemus' involvement in deceiving Philoctetes is perhaps easy to swallow compared to another manipulation of Odysseus', which comes right in the first two lines:

> ἀκτὴ μὲν ἥδε τῆς περιρρύτου χθονὸς
> Λήμνου, βροτοῖς ἄστιπτος οὐδ' οἰκουμένη.

This is the shore of the seagirt land of Lemnos, untrodden by mortals and not inhabited.

Lemnos was by no means uninhabited, either at any time the play was performed or, as far as we know, in any of the literature predating it. In the fifth century BC the Lemnian women were so famous (or rather infamous) that Herodotus (6.138) could tell a story about how all acts of cruelty in Greece came to be called 'Lemnian'. The *Iliad* knows of the Sinties (1.590–4) and Euneus (21.40ff.) living there, and in both Aeschylus' and Euripides' *Philoctetes* plays the Chorus consisted of Lemnians; Euripides' cast included additionally a Lemnian called Actor.[6] Finally Lemnian women attacked the Argonauts in Aeschylus' *Hypsipyle* and Sophocles' *Lemnian Women*.[7] Clearly, Odysseus' play has not only a surprising cast but also a novel setting, and this innovation is accompanied by conspicuous language. Rather than speaking nonchalantly of lonely Lemnos, Odysseus gives it a prominent place at the very beginning of the play, and with βροτοῖς ἄστιπτος οὐδ' οἰκουμένη (untrodden by mortals and not inhabited), he uses both an extremely rare word[8] and a striking pleonasm.[9]

At the same time the spectators depend on Odysseus' scene-

---

[6] Dio Chrys. 52.7–8.

[7] Schol. Ap. Rhod. 1.769–73. Some kind of Lemnians, whether men or women, gave the title to Aeschylus' *Lemnians or Lemnian Women*: see Radt's entry on the play (which also lists evidence for a number of comedies called *Lemnian Women*).

[8] For ἄστιπτος LSJ give only one further reference (an inscription from Syria).

[9] Cf. Schlesinger (1968) 147, 'macht uns Sophokles am Anfang des Prologs mit einem Hendiadyoin, das ... beinahe einen ganzen Vers füllt, auf seine ... Neuerung aufmerksam'.

setting and are, for the most part, likely to hesitate before rejecting it. Uninhabited Lemnos, moreover, does not just recall the starkness of tragic settings like that of *Prometheus Bound* but, to some degree, is a necessary aspect of Philoctetes' abandonment: according to Odysseus, the Greeks left him behind because of his ill-omened screaming (8–11). If Lemnos were inhabited, what would the inhabitants have said?

There is therefore a dilemma. On the one hand Lemnos is inhabited in both literature and reality. On the other hand, Odysseus has the authority of the prologue speaker, and an uninhabited Lemnos is an appropriate setting for the play. What should spectators think? As much as Odysseus they have to gauge what I call the force of myth. Twice in the opening speech Odysseus uses rather conspicuous language where he interferes with myth. Neither the change of cast nor the change of scene is introduced without linguistic and (Neoptolemus the trickster) logical repercussion. In one way or other, spectators may notice a pattern. The more clearly they do so, the closer they come to perceiving the force of myth. To perceive it is to see that myth is vital to many of the things the characters say and do in this play. But much remains unclear about this force. How strong is it? How much will it let Odysseus get away with? In what ways will other characters have to confront it?

At the end of the prologue Odysseus declares that he will send one of his men, should Neoptolemus linger too long.[10] Spectators therefore have reason to expect the character who eventually arrives (who is conventionally called the False Merchant) to be Odysseus' substitute. Indeed at least as far as his treatment of myth is concerned, he resembles his master. Like Odysseus, the False Merchant violates the mythological tradition. To say that Phoenix and the sons of Theseus are coming for Neoptolemus while Odysseus and Diomedes are allegedly chasing up Philoctetes (561ff.) is to deviate from all known variants. Also like Odysseus, the False Merchant makes up for his overall deviation by a subtle treatment of

---

[10] 126–9. See ch. 1, pp. 54–5, on these lines.

the detail. Rather than inventing a story out of nothing, he makes concessions to the tradition by combining elements from various existing versions. In the *Little Iliad* it was Diomedes, in Aeschylus Odysseus, and in Euripides Odysseus and Diomedes who went to fetch Philoctetes. Phoenix and Odysseus moreover may have fetched Neoptolemus in Sophocles' *Scyrians*.[11]

This is where the trouble starts. As Neoptolemus' Achillean descent jars with Odysseus' deception ploy, so the False Merchant's avoidance of violent innovation produces its own kind of discrepancy. Some of the details he gives are difficult to match with his purpose. On the one hand spectators know that Odysseus is already in Lemnos, so that the False Merchant is apparently telling a lie when he says that Odysseus is still on his way (cf. 620–1). On the other hand he comes close to the truth when he speaks of Odysseus, rather than anybody else, as one of the two people hoping to fetch Philoctetes. Why does he? It seems doubtful strategy to warn Philoctetes of Odysseus' coming. Myth, it may appear, shows its force again.

And it may appear to do so not just in questions of motivation, but, once again also in the language. The False Merchant is forced, as it were, into rather elaborate and almost pleonastic phrasing which is reminiscent of Odysseus' earlier stress on the lack of habitation on Lemnos: ... ἃ τοῖσιν Ἀργείοισιν ἀμφὶ σοῦ νέα | βουλεύματ᾽ ἐστί, κοὐ μόνον βουλεύματα, | ἀλλ᾽ ἔργα δρώμεν᾽, οὐκέτ᾽ ἐξαργούμενα ('... the new plans that the Argives have concerning you, and not only plans, but actions which are no longer being put off, but are in hand', 554–6), and ὡς ταῦτ᾽ ἐπίστω δρώμεν᾽, οὐ μέλλοντ᾽ ἔτι ('know that these things are in process, and are no longer in the future', 567). In the False Merchant scene, as in the prologue speech, there is a pattern: irregularities, both linguistic and otherwise, occur repeatedly at moments when characters

---

[11] *Little Iliad*: Proclus p. 106, 25 Allen. Aeschylus: Dio Chrys. 52.2 (and *passim*). Euripides: Dio Chrys. 52.14. *Scyrians*: Pearson's entry on the play. The sons of Theseus have been seen as an attempt to play to the Athenian audience (e.g. Fraenkel (1977) 60).

make mythological innovations. Spectators who, in one way or another, notice such a pattern, may wonder, in one way or another, about the force of myth and the way characters react to it. The force of myth gives them a new angle on the play,[12] but again it also raises questions. If the myth is strong enough to cause irregularities in the False Merchant's words, is it strong enough to overthrow the deception ploy altogether? And if it does, how will the play end? Myth in *Philoctetes* can engage spectators in many ways.

Neoptolemus

If not even Odysseus, the great manipulator, and his substitute escape the force of myth, what about the character who is for a long time the object of various manipulation attempts? How does Neoptolemus react to the force of myth? Neoptolemus stands between the opponents Odysseus and Philoctetes. Many critics have described how he begins the play under the influence of the former and moves increasingly towards the latter, a development that culminates when he gives in to Philoctetes' wish to be brought home to Malis. For watching Neoptolemus interact with the force of myth I choose a passage from the middle of the play (343–460), where he still implements the programme that Odysseus has set him, but is already exposed to Philoctetes' power. The passage begins with the long speech (343–90) in which Neoptolemus claims that the Greeks, and in particular Odysseus, denied him his father's weapons when he arrived at Troy, fetched by Odysseus and Phoenix. This is a flagrant innovation. In the *Little Iliad*, according to Proclus,[13] 'Odysseus fetches Neoptolemus from Scyros and gives him his father's weapons.' Neoptolemus, comparison with this summary suggests, not only introduces Phoenix into the story but also

---

[12] It may also draw their attention to the dramatic medium itself: see Easterling (1997b) 169–71.
[13] P. 106, 29–30 Allen.

substantially alters events at Troy. Since Odysseus invited Neoptolemus in the prologue (64–5) to slander him in whatever way he liked, and since Neoptolemus nowhere in the play betrays any signs of the resentment that would be expected towards the man who allegedly deprived him of his rightful property, spectators have every reason to assume that he is lying.

Yet they may come to a verdict on Neoptolemus' speech not quite as easily. Critics certainly find it hard to decide whether he is lying or telling the truth,[14] and there are good reasons. The first thing to note is that he uses one of the techniques that characterise Odysseus and the False Merchant. Rather than inventing his version from nothing, he makes careful use of known stories. In the *Little Iliad*, to quote Proclus again,[15] 'the contest for the arms takes place, and Odysseus gains them in accordance with Athena's will. Ajax goes mad, wreaks havoc on the flocks of the Achaeans and kills himself.' Neoptolemus adopts this version, substituting himself for Ajax and, for obvious reasons, leaving out Athena and the suicide.[16] Like Odysseus and the False Merchant, he avoids complete innovation.

But this is where the resemblance ends. Unlike Odysseus and the False Merchant, Neoptolemus does not seem to get into trouble. Near the end of the play (1362–6), Philoctetes reminds him of his story; he is surprised, he says, that Neoptolemus wants to go to Troy despite the disgrace Odysseus and the Atridae have inflicted on him. Neoptolemus' only comment is 'what you say is sensible' (1373). The scene which seemed designed to embarrass Neoptolemus passes without clearing up the truth about the version he gave of his past.

---

[14] For the extreme views of complete truth and complete lie, see Adams (1957) 142–3 on the one hand, and Knox (1964) 191 nn. 29–30, Calder (1971) 158–9 and Hamilton (1975) on the other. Most critics stress the intricate mixture of truth and falsehood, e.g. Schlesinger (1968) 124–33, Taplin (1987) 69–70 and Ringer (1998) 107–11. Zielinski (1924) 60–1 posits a previous treatment of the story that Neoptolemus is telling here in Sophocles' (doubtful) *Neoptolemus*.

[15] P. 106, 20–3 Allen.

[16] Whitby (1996) 32–3 additionally observes parallels between Neoptolemus' story and that of Telemachus in the *Odyssey*.

Equally, the speech itself in which he tells his story in the first place does not exhibit any signs of unease. Odysseus' and the False Merchant's struggle with myth were to be detected in their language, but if spectators look for similar traces in Neoptolemus' language they will be disappointed. If anything, Neoptolemus is *supported* by the phrasing of his speech. The longer he speaks, the more alive his past appears to become. 'And I, poor fellow, . . .', he exclaims (359), falls into direct speech not much later and begins to strew present tenses through the past narrative (ἐξανίσταμαι 367, λέγω 368 and κυρεῖ 371). It is as though Neoptolemus experienced his suffering for a second time.

These so-called historic presents, in which Neoptolemus brings his past to life, may be a clue to why much less resistance can be perceived when Neoptolemus, than when Odysseus or the False Merchant, makes mythological innovations. Both Odysseus and the False Merchant on the one hand and Neoptolemus on the other change the tradition that many spectators know, but while Odysseus and the False Merchant interfere with other men's stories, Neoptolemus is speaking about himself. It would, I think, be rewarding to investigate whether one's own life appears to be more readily written and rewritten than those of others elsewhere in Sophocles. No critic seems ever to have doubted, for instance, the veracity of Odysseus' statement (v. 6) that he exposed Philoctetes at the command of the Atridae, although the surviving sources are less specific;[17] and Ajax's good-will in the so-called deception speech, Deianira's intention not to fight the power of love (*Tr.* 490–6), and even the account of Orestes' death given by his substitute, the Paedagogus, have repeatedly been defended as credible both where they occur and with hindsight. Lichas' account of Heracles' campaigns, on the other hand, which, as Lichas says later (*Tr.* 479–83), was not ordered by Heracles, has often been scrutinised for irregularities.

---

[17] 'The sons of the Achaeans' at *Il.* 2.722 and a passive 'he was left behind' in Proclus' summary of the *Cypria* (p. 104, 23 Allen).

There is not the space here to give those speeches the specific discussion that they need, but perhaps the comparison of Neoptolemus and Odysseus in *Philoctetes* allows the suggestion that for the success of a speech which changes myth, and, more generally, of a speech which tries to convince its audience of something potentially unconvincing, it matters greatly whether characters speak about their own lives or about those of others. Neoptolemus uses himself, the man standing in front of the audience, in order to convince. He enacts visibly on stage the continuation of his past, which spectators know only from myth. As a result, he seems to have enough authority to change substantial aspects of the tradition without running into problems with the force of myth. His speech is both linguistically and logically smooth.

As Philoctetes enquires why nobody supported him (410–13), Neoptolemus cannot help speaking about others, and here he loses at last some of his smoothness.

> (Φι.)   ἀλλ᾽ οὔ τι τοῦτο θαῦμ᾽ ἔμοιγ᾽, ἀλλ᾽ εἰ παρὼν
>   Αἴας ὁ μείζων ταῦθ᾽ ὁρῶν ἠνείχετο.
> Νε.   οὐκ ἦν ἔτι ζῶν, ὦ ξέν᾽· οὐ γὰρ ἄν ποτε
>   ζῶντός γ᾽ ἐκείνου ταῦτ᾽ ἐσυλήθην ἐγώ.

(Phil.)   But it is not so much this that surprises me, as that the greater Ajax can have been there and put up with this.
Neopt.   He was no longer living, stranger; if he had been alive, I should never have been robbed of the arms.

As soon as Neoptolemus is no longer setting out a story of his own life but is engaged in a dialogue about another man, slight irregularities appear; the myth seems to recover its force. Neoptolemus now avoids further confrontation with the tradition, including recombination of known versions. Faced with Philoctetes' question, he cannot tell the story about Ajax's suicide over the judgement of the arms, which was well established from the *Little Iliad* onwards, because he has already left it out of the account of his arrival in Troy. What he could do instead is invent a tale in which Ajax supports Odysseus as the rightful owner of the arms or, better, is temporarily absent from the scene (compare παρών, 'have been

there') or ignored. Neoptolemus avoids this further innovation and settles for the half-truth that Ajax is dead, remaining
silent about his part in the story of the arms.

As he goes on to mention Diomedes, Odysseus, Nestor,
Antilochus and Patroclus in the following lines, he avoids
even half-lies and speaks in full accordance with myth. His
strategy here, as in the case of Ajax, is all the more remarkable for its possible consequences. Destroying Philoctetes'
ideas about Troy, Neoptolemus runs the risk that he will be
even less willing to go there since he now knows that he will
meet only the men that he loathes. When he speaks about
anybody other than himself, Neoptolemus is more compliant
with the mythological tradition than with what ought to be his
priority: his task on Lemnos. Again irregularity suggests the
force of myth, keeping alive the question of whether the force
which the myth is now displaying will later turn the action in a
new direction.

Neoptolemus' difficulty in satisfying the exigencies of both
myth and task is greatest when his catalogue of heroes is
interrupted by Philoctetes' laments (428–32):

> (Φι.) φεῦ φεῦ· τί δῆτα δεῖ σκοπεῖν, ὅθ' οἵδε μὲν
> τεθνᾶσ', 'Οδυσσεὺς δ' ἔστιν αὖ κἀνταῦθ' ἵνα
> χρῆν ἀντὶ τούτων αὐτὸν αὐδᾶσθαι νέκρον;
>
> Νε. σοφὸς παλαιστὴς κεῖνος, ἀλλὰ χαἰ σοφαὶ
> γνῶμαι, Φιλοκτῆτ', ἐμποδίζονται θαμά.

(Phil.) Ah, ah! Where must one look, when they are dead, and Odysseus is
alive, even when he ought to be pronounced dead instead of them?
Neopt.   That man is a clever (*sophos*) wrestler; but even clever (*sophai*)
plans are sometimes thwarted, Philoctetes.

Κεῖνος ('that man') refers to Odysseus as Philoctetes imagines
him: on his way from Troy to Lemnos. According to Neoptolemus, he is a clever wrestler; but, Neoptolemus goes on,
clever plans can fail. The general phrasing of the sentence
about clever plans makes it possible to refer Neoptolemus'
statement also to men other than the imaginary Odysseus,
who is reported to be on the way to Lemnos, and the repetition *sophos ... sophai*, harking back, as it does, to the *so-*

phisma that Odysseus set out in the prologue,[18] suggests in particular Neoptolemus himself and the actual Odysseus who is already on Lemnos. Neoptolemus' statement thus envisages the possibility that the deception ploy will fail.

Like so many irregularities before, this ambiguity or, as some critics would say, dramatic irony, may be said to be caused by the force of myth. Neoptolemus has made many clever statements already; but can he, the son of a father who hates as much as the gates of Hades a man who says something different from what he thinks, make a clever statement about cleverness failing without getting into trouble? Will the tradition that knows Neoptolemus as the son of this Achilles trip up clever wrestlers and plans, or will it be deflected as, it seems, the stories about life on Lemnos have been deflected before? The combined strength of Odysseus and the version that has Philoctetes fetched by trickery is poised against that of the entire Achilles and Neoptolemus tradition. Again the force of myth engages as it answers some questions and poses others.

Rarely can Neoptolemus be seen suffering from the force of myth as clearly as here. Leaving him while he is in danger of being tripped up would therefore do him an injustice. A little later Philoctetes enquires (438–42):

> (Φι.) καὶ κατ᾽ αὐτὸ τοῦτό γε
> ἀναξίου μὲν φωτὸς ἐξερήσομαι,
> γλώσσῃ δὲ δεινοῦ καὶ σοφοῦ, τί νῦν κυρεῖ.
> Νε. ποίου δὲ τούτου πλήν γ᾽ Ὀδυσσέως ἐρεῖς;
> Φι. οὐ τοῦτον εἶπον, ἀλλὰ Θερσίτης τις ἦν, ...

(Phil.) ... and under that very head I will ask about the fortunes of a man who is unworthy, but clever and skilled in speech.
Neopt.   About whom will you ask other than Odysseus?
Phil.   I did not mean him, but there was one Thersites, ...

As Philoctetes explains in 442, the man he has in mind in these lines is Thersites. Neoptolemus, however, replies as though

---

[18] Cited above, p. 96; cf. also 119: 'You would be called *sophos*, and at the same time valiant' (Odysseus speaking to Neoptolemus).

he thought Odysseus was meant. Should he be believed? One critic speaks of 'an air of naturalness about the words' and declares that 'surely we have here his true and unflattering view of Odysseus'.[19] Perhaps other responses would be equally confident, perhaps not. In any case, what is remarkable about the line is that many positions on Odysseus coincide; those of many spectators and readers of the play, of many myth variants and of Philoctetes. Neoptolemus is once again in harmony with myth. Only at the end of the play, when Philoctetes persuades him to take him home, does Neoptolemus openly defy the prescriptions of myth. And that is a tribute to Philoctetes' strength.

This scene, then, like those with Odysseus and the False Merchant which I have looked at before, displays a pattern. Again various irregularities, such as risky honesty and ambiguous language, surround allusions to myth, and again spectators can engage with them by attributing them in one way or another to the force of myth. Yet there are differences. First, Neoptolemus bends myth much more rarely than Odysseus and the False Merchant do. Secondly, much of the time that he does, it is his own story which he changes. From those passages irregularities are conspicuously absent. This last kind of pattern can be seen again in Philoctetes' speeches.

Philoctetes

It can in fact be seen even more distinctly here. Philoctetes is in many regards the dominant character of the play. One such regard is the way he treats myth. There are few irregularities that could be put down to a struggle with the force of myth, as was the case with the other characters. Hardly ever can Philoctetes be seen giving a version that is the result of careful negotiation with known myth variants; instead he appears constantly to put the power of his person behind his words. What Neoptolemus does in his speech about the judgement

---

[19] Kirkwood (1994a) 146 n. 35 and Kirkwood (1994b) 430.

of the arms of Achilles, Philoctetes does all the time: speak about himself. And in giving his version of his past and future, he challenges myth more seriously than any of the other characters.

If there was ever hope that Philoctetes would come to Troy voluntarily, it all but vanishes at the end of his first speech (314–16). He invokes the Olympian gods to make Odysseus and the Atridae experience themselves what they did to him, before Neoptolemus even mentions their names. They are the reason, so Philoctetes concludes, for all the suffering which he has expounded in the speech. Unsurprisingly after this speech, Philoctetes resists all of Neoptolemus', Odysseus' and the Chorus's attempts to make him go to Troy. Throughout he appears to be immune to any force there may be in a myth which unequivocally demands his participation when the Greeks take Troy. Philoctetes is indeed so strong that he has stirred up a critical debate over whether any ancient spectator might have believed that he can change the tradition that he will go to Troy.[20]

The journey home to Malis, rather than to Troy, is only the most prominent threat Philoctetes poses to this tradition. Long before he persuades Neoptolemus to take him home, he tries another innovation, and it is here that he may seem closest to Odysseus in his treatment of myth (799–803):

> ὦ τέκνον, ὦ γενναῖον, ἀλλὰ συλλαβὼν
> τῷ Λημνίῳ τῷδ' ἀνακαλουμένῳ[21] πυρὶ
> ἔμπρησον, ὦ γενναῖε· κἀγώ τοί ποτε
> τὸν τοῦ Διὸς παῖδ' ἀντὶ τῶνδε τῶν ὅπλων,
> ἃ νῦν σὺ σῴζεις, τοῦτ' ἐπηξίωσα δρᾶν.

O my son, O my noble son, take me and burn me with this fire that is invoked as Lemnian, noble one! I also once consented to do this to the son of Zeus in return for those weapons which you now are guarding!

Of course Philoctetes' death on Lemnos would be as unheard of as his journey to Malis. But Philoctetes supports it, as it were, with a parallel, when he says that he himself once did

---

[20] See Hoppin (1990) 149 n. 18 for discussion and references.
[21] Dawe, among others, emends.

for Heracles what he is now asking from Neoptolemus. There is a mythological precedent on which he can fall back. Philoctetes' strategy is comparable to the False Merchant's clever scrambling of variants as he spoke about the embassies sent for Philoctetes and Neoptolemus, to Odysseus' later suggestion that Philoctetes is not needed since Teucer is a good enough bowman to take Troy (1055-9), and also to Neoptolemus' use of models in his account of the judgement of arms. Now at least a glimpse of a struggle can be caught. Philoctetes appears to show himself aware of the demands the mythological tradition makes on him and to try to accommodate them. Notably, however, his wish to commit suicide comes at the moment when the onset of the disease culminates and makes this one of his most despairing moments in the play.[22] Only when Philoctetes is so enfeebled, it seems, can myth force him into this kind of manoeuvring.

This brings me to the end of my discussion of myth. At various moments, I have suggested, conspicuous pieces of phrasing, logical contradictions and other kinds of irregularity point at what I call the force of myth. Spectators who, in one way or another, perceive this force are offered a perspective for looking at the different characters. Differences appear between Philoctetes, who pits his own life against myth, Odysseus, who carefully recombines items of myth in ways that suit him, and Neoptolemus, who stands between the two and who often avoids conflict altogether. Yet for all that the force of myth may make spectators see, it creates questions at the same time, posing a challenge to spectators as it does to the characters. Spectators who perceive this force at work at many moments in the play are not at the same time told exactly how strong a force it is and whether it will eventually carry the day. And even if they are convinced that the play will in the end follow the prescriptions of myth, they may still be in doubt over the precise variant. With these conclusions I turn to my second example.

---

[22] Philoctetes threatens to kill himself again at 999-1002.

THE PROPHECY

Like myth, prophecies impose restrictions on the characters' freedom, and answer as well as pose questions for the audience. More concretely, there are overlaps between the two, because prophecies, the one in *Philoctetes* included, have a well-established place in the mythological tradition. Still, there are enough differences to make it worth looking at myth and prophecy separately. Most important, unlike myth as I talked about it, prophecies are often explicitly referred to by the characters themselves and, to that degree, provide a starting-point from which spectators can make further inferences. Moreover, prophecies in Greek tragedy (and by 'prophecy' I mean both oracles and predictions made by seers) almost always, in one way or another, come true in the end.[23] Spectators, therefore, who are familiar with this tendency may expect that a prophecy *must*, in some way, have an effect, while strands of the mythological tradition of which they are reminded *may* determine the outcome of the play, but will sometimes be unable to leave a mark.

In *Philoctetes* there is just one prophecy, that by the seer Helenus. Helenus is referred to twice, once by the False Merchant and once by Neoptolemus near the end of the play. Roughly speaking, his prophecy specifies that Troy will not fall until Philoctetes enters the fight. Later the precise phrasing will need to be discussed in more detail, but before embarking on such a discussion, I want to set the scene by looking at the prologue.

The prologue

In the prologue Odysseus gives Neoptolemus all kinds of detailed instructions about Philoctetes and about the way in which Neoptolemus should try to gain Philoctetes' trust, but

---

[23] Mikalson (1991) 90–1 (oracles) and 100 (seers).

he outlines only roughly what Neoptolemus has to do afterwards. The most precise lines about his task are these (68–9,
77–8):

> εἰ γὰρ τὰ τοῦδε τόξα μὴ ληφθήσεται,
> οὐκ ἔστι πέρσαι σοι τὸ Δαρδάνου πέδον.
> . . .
> ἀλλ' αὐτὸ τοῦτο δεῖ σοφισθῆναι, κλοπεὺς
> ὅπως γενήσῃ τῶν ἀνικήτων ὅπλων.

For if *this man's bow* is not captured, it is impossible for you to conquer the
land of Dardanus.
. . .
This is the thing that we must scheme for, for you to become the thief of *the
invincible weapon.*

To judge from these lines, the aim of Neoptolemus' mission is
to fetch Philoctetes' bow; Philoctetes himself appears to be at
best secondary. In fact if κλοπεύς ('thief') can be pressed,
Odysseus wants Philoctetes to stay behind. Many critics[24] have
seen that these instructions will be overturned by Heracles,
who, in line with Helenus' prophecy, demands at the end of
the play that Philoctetes himself go to Troy. C. M. Bowra[25]
and others advocated the interpretation that Odysseus here
misunderstands the prophecy: otherwise he would not have
misled Neoptolemus. Similarly, it might be argued that
Odysseus simply did not know the prophecy. Had he known
it, again, he would have given Neoptolemus different advice.
Neither solution is fully satisfactory, if only because nothing
is made of Odysseus' alleged misinterpretation or ignorance
either here or elsewhere in the play. I will come back to Bowra
shortly and will then also discuss alternative approaches to the
prophecy. For the moment, it is enough to stress that as long
as nobody has as much as mentioned a prophecy spectators
have little reason to worry about it.

The little reason there is turns again on myth: the prophecy
has been an important part of the tradition ever since the

---

[24] Segal (1995) 241 n. 22 and Kittmer (1995) 27 n. 60 give references to the most
important discussions of the prophecy. See also Thummer (1981) and Hoppin
(1981).
[25] Bowra (1944) 261–306.

Little Iliad,[26] demanding that Philoctetes should go to Troy. On the other hand, the tradition also makes the bow of Heracles[27] the sacker of Troy, and it came into prominence in both Aeschylus' and Euripides' plays, in which it may have been seized in order to make Philoctetes yield.[28] Few spectators who know these good precedents for both bow and man as primary focus are likely to ponder Odysseus' deviation from the stipulations of the prophecy before they have been referred to. Probably neither many of those who are familiar with previous variants, nor many of those who are not, will be made to pause by Odysseus' references to the bow.

The man, rather than the bow, makes his first appearance when Neoptolemus resists Odysseus' plan and voices disagreement (88–91).

> ἔφυν γὰρ οὐδὲν ἐκ τέχνης πράσσειν κακῆς,
> οὔτ' αὐτὸς οὔθ', ὥς φασιν, οὐκφύσας ἐμέ.
> ἀλλ' εἴμ' ἑτοῖμος πρὸς βίαν τὸν ἄνδρ' ἄγειν
> καὶ μὴ δόλοισιν.

It is my nature to do nothing by treacherous plotting; that is my nature, and it was also my father's nature. But I am ready to take *the man* by force and not by tricks.

Trickery, Neoptolemus says, is contrary to his nature, but he is prepared to capture Philoctetes by force. Underneath this pronounced opposition, it is hardly noticeable that Neoptolemus has silently replaced the bow of Odysseus' orders with 'the man' (τὸν ἄνδρα). Those spectators who are none the less alive to the change get something like a foretaste of Neoptolemus' success in escaping confrontation with the force of

---

[26] Proclus p. 106, 23–5 Allen.

[27] E.g. 'Philoctetes and the bow of Heracles' in Dio's version of Euripides' prologue (59.2).

[28] Dio Chrys. 52.2: 'All of ⟨the *Philoctetes* plays⟩ have the same subject matter: the theft of Philoctetes' bow – or perhaps I should say its seizure. Either way, deprived of his weapon, Philoctetes himself, too, was carried off to Troy by Odysseus, partly voluntarily, but largely giving in to necessity after he had lost the weapon which ...' Cf. Schnebele (1988) 134–8 and Hoppin (1981). Hoppin suggests further that spectators who know the earlier *Philoctetes* plays will assume at all stages of the tragedy that Odysseus, when he speaks of capturing the bow, implies that Philoctetes will follow. This seems to me to put too much trust in an argument from silence: Odysseus never says that this is his strategy.

myth in long stretches of the play. No matter what the details are, the tradition agrees that Philoctetes will go to Troy, and Neoptolemus follows it. Already at this early stage, spectators may see him avoid challenging myth. Nothing, however, I repeat, draws attention to the phrase 'the man'. There is still only little reason for wondering about Neoptolemus' precise task.

Rather, the main emphasis of the dialogue is on Neoptolemus' reluctance to use trickery, so that Odysseus has to insist (101–3):

> Οδ. λέγω σ' ἐγὼ δόλῳ Φιλοκτήτην λαβεῖν.
> Νε. τί δ' ἐν δόλῳ δεῖ μᾶλλον ἢ πείσαντ' ἄγειν;
> Οδ. οὐ μὴ πίθηται· πρὸς βίαν δ' οὐκ ἂν λάβοις.

Odys. I am telling you to take *Philoctetes* by a trick.
Neopt. But why must I take him by a trick rather than by persuasion?
Odys. He will never be persuaded, and you could not take him by force.

Odysseus comes over from bow to man ('Philoctetes'). This *may* be interpreted as an attempt to avoid all disagreement, until he has overcome Neoptolemus' growing resistance to trickery. Probably, however, Odysseus' change of phrasing, too, goes unnoticed by most spectators, for whom the prophecy is still rather distant. Be that as it may, as Odysseus finally persuades Neoptolemus he is back to the bow again (113–15).

> Οδ. αἱρεῖ τὰ τόξα ταῦτα τὴν Τροίαν μόνα.
> Νε. οὐκ ἄρ' ὁ πέρσων, ὡς ἐφάσκετ', εἴμ' ἐγώ;
> Οδ. οὔτ' ἂν σὺ κείνων χωρὶς οὔτ' ἐκεῖνα σοῦ.

Odys. *This bow* is the one thing that takes Troy.
Neopt. Then am I not the one who is to capture it, as you said?
Odys. *You* cannot capture it without *the bow*, nor *the bow* without *you*.

The language of Odysseus' last line joins Neoptolemus and the bow so emphatically and fails to mention Philoctetes so notably that, in view of the tradition which has Philoctetes destroy Troy, doubts about Odysseus' strategy may grow at last. Not even now, however, does he exclude Philoctetes. There are moreover no logical contradictions or any other kind of irregularity which would give further emphasis to the conspicuous language.

As Odysseus departs, he leaves Neoptolemus to instruct his men in the lyric dialogue of the parodos. Again spectators find him speaking about Philoctetes, and this time about the bow as well. He tells the Chorus in anapaests (191–200) that Philoctetes will not be cured until the time has come 'for him to direct against Troy the irresistible arrows of the gods' (τόνδ' ἐπὶ Τροίᾳ | τεῖναι τὰ θεῶν ἀμάχητα βέλη, 197–8). Again Neoptolemus does not adopt Odysseus' narrow focus on the bow and also pays attention to the man, and again he does so quietly.

In the early parts of the play, it seems, there is little emphasis, linguistic or otherwise, on the question of man or bow. Spectators who pose the question none the less may notice that Neoptolemus, more than Odysseus, is in agreement with the tradition, including the prophecy of Helenus, which has Philoctetes destroy Troy. With this conclusion I turn to the scene in which the prophecy is first explicitly referred to.

The False Merchant scene

This reference does not come until the False Merchant brings news from the Greek camp to Neoptolemus and Philoctetes (the latter being mostly a silent listener). His report about the two embassies, in which he struggles to transform known myth variants into something new, prompts Neoptolemus to ask why the Atridae have now taken an interest in Philoctetes, whom they had neglected for such a long time. The reason, the False Merchant replies, is a prophecy in which the Trojan seer Helenus, caught by Odysseus, predicted that the Greeks would never destroy Troy unless Philoctetes were persuaded to join them (610–13):

> ὃς δὴ τά τ' ἄλλ' αὐτοῖσι πάντ' ἐθέσπισεν
> καὶ τἀπὶ Τροίᾳ πέργαμ' ὡς οὐ μή ποτε
> πέρσοιεν, εἰ μὴ τόνδε πείσαντες λόγῳ
> ἄγοιντο νήσου τῆσδ' ἐφ' ἧς ναίει τὰ νῦν.

He prophesied all other events to them, and told them that they would never take the towers of Troy, unless by means of persuasion they brought this man from the island where he is now living.

The prologue may or may not have made a few spectators begin to wonder whether Philoctetes himself was needed in addition to the bow for taking Troy; this prophecy now makes it clear that he is, but at the same time it adds new uncertainties, surrounding in particular the word 'persuasion'. If the report of the prophecy can be taken literally, it appears to gloss the prologue to the effect that the bow without the man is not enough. Spectators, in fact, who contrast Odysseus' οὐ μὴ πίθηται ('he will never be persuaded') in the prologue (103) with the False Merchant's πείσαντες λόγῳ ('by means of persuasion', 612) will find that Odysseus is not just glossed but downright contradicted. But is that a relevant comparison to make? What counts as persuasion? How seriously can information be taken that comes from a bogus character? And whose words are 'by means of persuasion' anyway: Helenus', faithfully reported by the False Merchant, or the False Merchant's, an interpretation of Helenus?[29] Clearly, the report of the prophecy is problematic. In what follows I will describe ways in which spectators can engage with the report and the scene in general – problematic as they both are. For this purpose I will speak of the 'force of the prophecy' which both spectators and characters come to confront, just as I discussed in the previous section the 'force of myth'. This force, I will suggest, is felt throughout the False Merchant scene and gives it its particular character.

In the most general way the force of the prophecy expresses itself in the sheer complexity of the scene. Something baffling has arrived. Perhaps the question critics ask most frequently concerns the function of the scene. What does it do? Tycho von Wilamowitz's answer is telling.[30]

Surely one has to look at the scene first of all in the way it would have appeared to the spectators. One realises immediately that even the briefest thought about the situation Odysseus and Neoptolemus are in makes it unbearable.

[29] Narratologists speak of 'transposed speech'; see ch. 1, p. 44, n. 31.
[30] Wilamowitz-Moellendorff (1969) 282, my translation.

Wilamowitz goes on to explain why the scene would be 'unbearable' if spectators tried to work out its logic (which in his view they do not: see further pp. 119–23 below): the False Merchant does not say anything that could help Neoptolemus beguile Philoctetes, Neoptolemus' questions that bring the False Merchant to speak of Odysseus' arrival are unmotivated, the action resumes where it was left before the scene (note the repeated 'let us go': ἴωμεν at 533, and χωρῶμεν and ἴωμεν at 635 and 637) and so on. Not all of these arguments are equally convincing, but it is true that spectators are told neither why Odysseus should want to inform Neoptolemus of the prophecy nor indeed why he should have waited until now.[31] Hence it is perhaps not surprising that another critic[32] has concluded that 'the scene is entirely unnecessary to the plot'. As soon as the prophecy enters the play, interpretation becomes difficult. The prophecy, as I put it, shows its force:[33] it is almost impossible to reconcile the function that Odysseus intended for the False Merchant, when he announced him at the end of the prologue, with the kind of things that the False Merchant says when he eventually appears.

Adding some detail to this general picture will help to clarify why it is the prophecy that I say shows its force. The first

---

[31] Much else can be said about the function of the scene. Wilamowitz himself believes (Wilamowitz-Moellendorff (1969) 300–1) that it introduces the prophecy into the play in a way that motivates Philoctetes' later reluctance to come to Troy. Poe (1974) 19 argues for the view that 'the function of the merchant is to inform Philoctetes that Odysseus has sworn to return Philoctetes to the Greeks will he nill he like a piece of chattel goods, in order that Neoptolemus, and we, may see what this mission of his looks like from Philoctetes' perspective'. Østerud (1973) 24 thinks that 'the main objective of the episode with the false merchant is to imitate the bargaining about Philoctetes and to expose the underlying motives'. Buxton (1982) 217 n. 21 says 'that the episode with the "false merchant" diverts Philoktetes' attention towards the ideas of force and persuasion and away from that of deceit'. Recently the False Merchant scene has been looked at for its theatrical self-consciousness: Easterling (1997b) 169–71, Falkner (1998) 33–9 and Ringer (1998) 112–15. All these views and approaches contribute interesting observations, but do not make (and are often not designed to make) the appearance of the False Merchant any less puzzling.

[32] Podlecki (1966b) 239.

[33] Compare Buxton (1988), who argues that in Greek tragedy bafflement occurs particularly where human and divine come into contact with one another.

thing to note is how the entire scene leads up to the report of the prophecy at the end. 'Phoenix and the sons of Theseus are coming for Neoptolemus', the False Merchant begins. 'Why isn't Odysseus?', Neoptolemus wants to know. 'He is tracking down Philoctetes.' 'Why?' 'Because of a prophecy ...' The drive towards the prophecy is hard to miss.

The drive is even more noticeable for spectators who find some of the steps in the sequence of questions and answers trying. The last questions Neoptolemus asks before the False Merchant speaks about the prophecy are particularly difficult (598–602):

> τίνος δ' Ἀτρεῖδαι τοῦδ' ἄγαν οὕτω χρόνῳ
> τοσῷδ' ἐπεστρέφοντο πράγματος χάριν,
> ὃν γ' εἶχον ἤδη χρόνιον ἐκβεβληκότες;
> τίς ὁ πόθος αὐτοὺς ἵκετ'; ἢ θεῶν βία
> καὶ νέμεσις, οἵπερ[34] ἔργ' ἀμύνουσιν κακά;

But because of what circumstance have the sons of Atreus after so long a time taken so much trouble to secure one whom long ago they had thrown out? What yearning for him has come to them? Or is it the power and the just anger of the gods who punish wicked deeds?

It is hard to imagine lines more carefully designed to elicit exactly the speech that follows. The False Merchant has just said that Odysseus and Diomedes are on their way to fetch Philoctetes, but rather than concentrating on the threat that they pose to Philoctetes (compare Philoctetes' own reaction at 622ff.), Neoptolemus presses on to get more information. Not only does he ask what prompted the Atridae to launch this unexpected embassy, but he even brings the gods into play as if to prepare the way for the divine words of the prophecy (cf. 610 ἐθέσπισεν, 'he prophesied', literally 'he spoke divine words'). It is as though Neoptolemus wanted the False Merchant to speak about the prophecy. But why would he? Is this part of the deception ploy? The False Merchant does not help in deciding these questions when he begins his speech 'I shall explain all this to you, since *perhaps* (ἴσως) you have not heard

---

[34] The choice between the MSS' οἵπερ and Pallis's αἵπερ is difficult (see Dawe (1978) 126 and Lloyd-Jones and Wilson (1990) 193), and so is that between ἢ and ἥ in the previous line.

it' (603–4). Perhaps Neoptolemus knows the prophecy, but perhaps he does not. There is much here that is unclear. What *is* clear is the fact that there is also much that points to the prophecy. Is its force responsible for Neoptolemus' question?

And that is not all. Neoptolemus' questions are not only hard to account for, but they are also linguistically marked. Where a single line would have been enough, Neoptolemus gives the spectators five, and what is more, he chooses rather marked language. He begins with a hyperbaton that stretches over almost two lines (τίνος ... πράγματος χάριν, 'because of what circumstance') and follows it up with a series of three questions, the last being the longest. The False Merchant, too, in the preceding brief speech, uses some remarkable phrasing. After feigning reluctance to speak in front of Philoctetes for a while, he finally begins (591–7).

> λέγω. 'πὶ τοῦτον ἄνδρε τώδ' ὥπερ κλύεις,
> ὁ Τυδέως παῖς ἥ τ' Ὀδυσσέως βία,
> διώμοτοι πλέουσιν ἦ μὴν ἢ λόγῳ
> πείσαντες ἄξειν, ἢ πρὸς ἰσχύος κράτος.
> καὶ ταῦτ' Ἀχαιοὶ πάντες ἤκουον σαφῶς
> Ὀδυσσέως λέγοντος· οὗτος γὰρ πλέον
> τὸ θάρσος εἶχε θἀτέρου δράσειν τάδε.

I will speak! It is for him that the two men I spoke of, the son of Tydeus and the mighty Odysseus, are sailing, having sworn to bring him back, either by persuasion or by brute force. And all the Achaeans heard Odysseus saying this clearly; for he had more confidence than the other that he would accomplish this.

The False Merchant's sentences have become longer and more flowing than they were before, and for the first time since he began to deliver his news, he speaks more than two lines at a time, preparing the way for the even longer speech in which he will report the prophecy. As Neoptolemus and the False Merchant feed each other cues in the run-up to the prophecy, their language becomes increasingly elaborate and grand.

Apart from this general expansiveness there is some detail that makes the language of the False Merchant noteworthy. This detail concerns the leaders of the embassy that has been sent to Lemnos. Originally the False Merchant had spoken of Odysseus and Diomedes coming to fetch Philoctetes (570ff.), and he repeats their names in the second of the lines that I have just quoted. Yet it is remarkable that, after first introducing the pair by an expression in the dual (ἄνδρε τώδ' ὥπερ κλύεις, 'the two men I spoke of', 591), he then continues with an apposition and a verb in the plural (διώμοτοι πλέουσιν, 'are sailing, having sworn ...', 593). As a result of this change, attention is deflected from the precise number of men that are leading the embassy. In the next sentence Achaeans hear just 'Odysseus saying this' (ταῦτα ... | Ὀδυσσέως λέγοντος, 595–6) since he had more confidence than 'the other one'. Diomedes is still there but much reduced in stature.

Beginning to make Diomedes fade out like this, the False Merchant moves closer to the situation of the prologue, when the audience saw only Odysseus. This movement is completed after the report of the prophecy (614–19):

> καὶ ταῦθ' ὅπως ἤκουσ' ὁ Λαέρτου τόκος
> τὸν μάντιν εἰπόντ', εὐθέως ὑπέσχετο
> τὸν ἄνδρ' Ἀχαιοῖς τόνδε δηλώσειν ἄγων·
> οἴοιτο μὲν μάλισθ' ἑκούσιον λαβών,
> εἰ μὴ θέλοι δ', ἄκοντα· καὶ τούτων κάρα
> τέμνειν ἐφεῖτο τῷ θέλοντι μὴ τυχών.

And when the son of Laertes heard that the prophet had said this, at once he promised the Achaeans that he would bring this man and display him to them. He thought he would take him of his own free will and against it if he refused, and if he failed, he would allow anyone who wished to cut off his head.

Diomedes has disappeared altogether now, and Odysseus ('the son of Laertes') governs verbs that are all in the singular. Diomedes will never again be mentioned as Odysseus' imaginary companion. The force of the prophecy may be felt not only in the general difficulty of the scene, in the disconcertingly blatant cues the False Merchant is given by Neoptolemus and in the increasingly expansive language, but also in the elimination of a certain piece of fiction that the False Merchant had introduced only a few lines earlier.

As I said before, to speak of the 'force of the prophecy' is only one way of talking about this scene. Others use different language. What I have tried to suggest so far in invoking this force is the fact that there is much in the scene that points to the report of the prophecy as a key passage. Whether or not spectators would want to speak of the 'force of the prophecy' that makes itself felt, they are likely to notice, in their different ways, that the scene focuses on the False Merchant's report of the prophecy.

With this in mind, I return to the report and the questions which I said it raises. I quote again vv. 610–13:

> ὃς δὴ τά τ᾽ ἄλλ᾽ αὐτοῖσι πάντ᾽ ἐθέσπισεν
> καὶ τἀπὶ Τροίᾳ πέργαμ᾽ ὡς οὐ μή ποτε
> πέρσοιεν, εἰ μὴ τόνδε πείσαντες λόγῳ
> ἄγοιντο νήσου τῆσδ᾽ ἐφ᾽ ἧς ναίει τὰ νῦν.

He prophesied all other events to them, and told them that they would never take the towers of Troy, unless by means of persuasion they brought this man from the island where he is now living.

According to these lines, Helenus specified the persuasion of Philoctetes as a condition for the destruction of Troy. No question of the bow only, or of trickery. Again I ask how much weight ought to be put on these lines, reported as they are by the False Merchant.

I have already referred to the view, often connected with the name of C. M. Bowra, that the play turns on a misinterpretation of the prophecy by the characters, especially by Odysseus. Approaches like Bowra's have largely been abandoned, critics stressing instead the flexible shape of the prophecy and abandoning attempts to establish its exact phrasing. This stress essentially goes back all the way to Tycho von Wilamowitz. The central thesis of his *Die dramatische Technik des Sophokles* is that it is wrong to expect consistency throughout a play. If pressed for overall consistency, he argues, Sophocles' plays reveal great shortcomings. However, he continues, overall consistency is not what one should look for. Rather one should acknowledge that in the immediate context everything works well enough. 'It is only natural that a dramatist who still envisaged production on stage as the only purpose of his plays placed higher value on the effect of the individual scenes and the individual situations than on the unity and coherence of the whole ...'[35] Within this interpretative framework, Tycho von Wilamowitz suggests that the variation in the accounts of the prophecy is the result of Sophocles' interest in the dramatic effects of the individual scenes in which the prophecy is mentioned and that this variation would not be noticed by the spectators: Sophocles, he writes, 'designedly left the requirements [for sacking Troy], clearly defined in advance as they were by Helenus' prophecy, vague and ambiguous, and then made use of the ambiguity whenever it suited him'.[36]

Even though Tycho von Wilamowitz's uncompromising approach in general has been much criticised, his remarks about the prophecy are the origin of what today approaches the status of *communis opinio*: Sophocles treats the prophecy with too much flexibility to make a quest for the 'real' phrasing a sensible project.[37] There can be no doubt that some such corrective to Bowra's problematic position is both healthy and necessary. Tycho von Wilamowitz and his successors are certainly right in reacting against the idea that the various references to the prophecy can be put together like the pieces of a jigsaw puzzle. Yet in so far as they shift attention away from the prophecy itself, and especially from the phrasing of the prophecy, they are paying a rather high price. What I want to suggest here is that there are various good reasons why spectators might think about the precise phrasing of the prophecy as the False Merchant has reported it. While not adopting the jigsaw-puzzle approach, they may still take seriously what the False Merchant says.

The importance of the exact wording of prophecies in Greek literature (and indeed religion) is notorious. Heracles in *Trachiniae*, to give a Sophoclean example, realises only just

[35] Wilamowitz-Moellendorff (1969) 39, my translation.
[36] Wilamowitz-Moellendorff (1969) 304, my translation.
[37] Perhaps the most influential proponent of this view is Robinson (1969) 45–51. For a summary of the criticism levelled at Bowra, see Thummer (1981) 1–2 (with further references in n. 1 on p. 2) and Buxton (1982) 130.

before he dies that the 'release from labours' which Zeus's oak in the grove of the Selli had predicted means death rather than, as he thought, happiness (1164–73). Spectators familiar with such cases are likely to pay close attention to the prophecy here, even though it is only reported, and reported by a bogus character.

Apart from this general consideration there are more specific points, which once again turn on the force of the prophecy: various details, many of them linguistic, call attention to the phrasing of the False Merchant's report. First, as I have argued in detail, there is the emphasis which the whole scene puts on these lines. Spectators who, in one way or another, are aware of the preparation the prophecy has received are likely to listen very carefully when it is at last reported.

Secondly, the means by which Philoctetes ought to be brought to Troy are given much attention throughout the play. Already in the prologue Odysseus told Neoptolemus that he had to use deception, since force and persuasion would be pointless (101–3, quoted above). This is picked up by the False Merchant when, immediately after reporting the prophecy, he says that Odysseus is planning to take Philoctetes to Troy voluntarily (ἑκούσιον 617) or, failing that, against his will (ἄκοντα 618). The phrase πείσαντες λόγῳ ('by means of persuasion') in the report itself repeats almost exactly the earlier λόγῳ | πείσαντες (593–4). When the False Merchant reports that Helenus specified persuasion as a condition for destroying Troy, his words are therefore unlikely to pass unnoticed.

Thirdly, and following on from here, there is again a logical inconsistency. The references to violence, trickery and persuasion as the appropriate means of enlisting Philoctetes' support are not only numerous, but they are also contradictory. On the one hand, the False Merchant's report of Odysseus' intention to fetch Philoctetes ἑκούσιον ('of his own free will') or, if necessary, ἄκοντα ('against it'), seems to square with the instructions he gave Neoptolemus in the prologue. The terms are vague, but ἑκούσιον and ἄκοντα suggest persuasion and force, the two approaches Odysseus had ruled out before. Philoctetes, one may guess, will now become more vulnerable to deception, the approach that Odysseus, Neoptolemus and the False Merchant are currently putting into practice. But if this is the strategy, something has gone wrong. ἄκοντα ('against his will') and πείσαντες λόγῳ ('by means of persuasion'), the phrase the False Merchant used just six lines earlier, sit together uneasily. The False Merchant, it seems, is more inconsistent than should be expected from a smooth liar. Again, it may seem, the force of the prophecy has brought out a bit of the truth.

The 'force of the prophecy' thus proves a useful tool in describing some of the things that give the False Merchant scene its particular appeal. As many critics have noted, the scene is most complex. There is much that calls for attention. At the same time it has also been pointed out[38] that 'the most striking feature of *Philoctetes* ... is, paradoxically enough, its lucidity'. *Philoctetes* is a difficult and multi-layered play, but not one that leaves spectators bewildered. It is *not* a confusing jigsaw puzzle. In this respect Wilamowitz is no doubt right. The 'force of the prophecy' is one way of accounting for this paradox, of taking seriously details of phrasing without denying the play its obvious lucidity. This force may be seen to stand at the heart of all that is complex in the False Merchant scene: Neoptolemus' apparently unmotivated questions, the False Merchant's logical inconsistency and, repeatedly, language that is in various ways conspicuous may all be linked to the report of Helenus' prophecy. The prophecy intrudes, as it were, forcefully into Odysseus' carefully laid plot and, as it does, causes various kinds of turbulence. To put it less metaphorically, the False Merchant scene is complex but not unstructured: the complexity can be put into a pattern. This pattern of complexity gives the scene much of its 'lucidity' despite all the questions it raises.

A good number of these questions, it turned out, centre on the report of the prophecy itself. Although Helenus' prophecy is reported by a bogus character and although it is reported

[38] Easterling (1978) 29.

indirectly rather than in quotation, there are good reasons for spectators to give serious consideration to the exact phrasing of the report. The condition of persuasion seems not just part of Odysseus' deception ploy or the False Merchant's personal interpretation of Helenus. While being surrounded by uncertainty, the report of the prophecy lays claim to the spectators' attention as an important, if still uncertain, piece of information. The force of the prophecy, as I put it, not only creates a pattern of complexity but also secures attention for a certain piece of phrasing despite the most unpromising circumstances. The characters, if I may continue my metaphorical language, are not the only forces to reckon with in this scene. They are not alone in structuring or authorising what is said and done on stage. It is the perceptible presence of another force, the degree of structure and authority that may be noticed in between all complexity, that makes the False Merchant scene so engaging. Despite everything that spectators may be uncertain about, there is also some certainty to be attained.

After the False Merchant

The False Merchant's report of the prophecy creates a new situation. Spectators still do not know how and whether Philoctetes will be fetched, but, unless my discussion of the False Merchant scene has been misguided, they now have at least some reason for thinking that persuasion may be a necessary condition – uncertain as many of them are still likely to be. In the remainder of this chapter I will explore some of the consequences, both new questions and new answers, that result from this new situation.

I begin with a new question. Many prophecies in ancient Greece hinge on what seems to be an impossible scenario, an *adynaton*.[39] When Croesus is told in Delphi (Hdt. 1.55) that his rule is in danger only 'when a mule is lord of the Medes', he cannot imagine such a thing and expects never to lose his

[39] See for instance Gould (1985) 23–4.

empire. Needless to say, he does, the mule being the bastard Cyrus (Hdt. 1.91). The Athenians, to give an even more famous second example, have to find out not how to avert, but how to implement, the Pythia's prophecy, when they are told (Hdt. 7.141) that 'a wooden wall' would protect them against the Persians. This is a rather different kind of oracle, if only in that the Athenians meet with success as they take the phrase to refer to the navy. Even so it shares with the one Croesus received a seemingly impossible scenario: how can a mule be lord of the Medes, and how can a wooden wall protect the Athenians?

The mule and the wooden wall help in understanding Helenus' prophecy better. When the False Merchant reports that Philoctetes will have to be taken by persuasion in order for Troy to fall, he describes a similarly unlikely scenario. Odysseus has made it quite clear that persuasion is not an option, and when Philoctetes remains impervious even once Neoptolemus has returned the bow, spectators have plenty of opportunity to agree with this assessment. The *adynaton* in Helenus' prophecy introduces a new consideration. Before, myth and Odysseus agreed by and large that the goal of the play was to convey Philoctetes and his bow to Troy. Now that the prophecy enters the scene, everything becomes more complicated. Rather than predicting *that* Troy will fall (as myth does), the prophecy as the False Merchant reports it only says *how it is possible* that Troy falls: after persuading Philoctetes to come to Troy and curing him there. To the degree that spectators take the phrasing seriously, they are given a problem to solve that is not much easier than those faced by Croesus and by the Athenians.

At the same time they are given new ways of looking at the characters' actions. How do Neoptolemus, Philoctetes and Odysseus react to the report of the prophecy? Spectators who know other Greek prophecies will find in all characters' behaviour much that is familiar. 'In the early period', Walter Burkert writes, 'one can always try to make something even of unfavourable signs by waiting, circumvention, purification, repetition.'[40] This kind of manoeuvring is to be found also in Sophocles' play. None of the characters simply obey the conditions of the prophecy as stated by the False Merchant.

Philoctetes behaves towards the prophecy as he behaves towards myth, standing up against it without yielding any ground. He hardly acknowledges it, and when he does, he does so as follows (622–5; compare 628–30):

οἴμοι τάλας. ἦ κεῖνος, ἡ πᾶσα βλάβη,
ἔμ' εἰς Ἀχαιοὺς ὤμοσεν πείσας στελεῖν;
πεισθήσομαι γὰρ ὧδε κἀξ Ἅιδου θανὼν
πρὸς φῶς ἀνελθεῖν, ὥσπερ οὑκείνου πατήρ.

Alas for me! Did that man, that utter plague, swear that he would bring me to the Achaeans *by means of persuasion*? I shall as soon be *persuaded* to return from Hades to the world of light after my death, like his father!

Philoctetes concentrates on Odysseus' oath to persuade him to come to Troy. Whatever the reason for his failure to mention Odysseus' plan to use force in case he would not yield, it is clear that Philoctetes directly opposes himself to the terms of the prophecy (which he, for one, has no reason to distrust). For the time being, the prophecy, like myth, does not seem to have much power over him.

Odysseus is different. He is the character who is most immediately affected by the prophecy, since it enters the play through the mouth of his deputy and causes him, I suggested, considerable embarrassment. In the prologue he sets up the play in line with his ideas and then leaves it to be acted out by others. Just like the prophecy, he tries to determine the direction the action will take. Prophecies in tragedy have an enormous power to predict the outcome of events. In one way or another, I noted, they always come true. Odysseus and the prophecy are therefore in constant competition.

This becomes particularly obvious in the False Merchant scene when the prophecy (as far as it is given weight despite the circumstances of the report) asserts its direction against

---

[40] Burkert (1985b) 113. Compare Vernant (1991b) 310. On divination in tragedy see Mikalson (1991) 87–114, with further references on p. 263 n. 98.

the character who does most to challenge it. Before this scene, Odysseus seemed to rule supreme. In the prologue he instructed Neoptolemus what exactly was to be done, concentrating mostly on the bow rather than the man and advocating deception as the only approach that was possible by all reasonable calculations. But now that the prophecy shows its force, putting much emphasis on the condition of persuasion, he changes his tactic. If the False Merchant's phrasing is to be trusted, Odysseus' promise in response to Helenus' prophecy was to fetch 'this man' (τὸν ἄνδρα ... τόνδε 616), 'of his free will' or, failing that, 'against it'. For the time being, there is no more talk of either the bow or deception. Odysseus seems to comply at least partly with the prophecy.

As in the case of myth, however, Odysseus does not avoid all confrontation. According to the False Merchant, he envisages taking Philoctetes against his will, thus, as I noted, jarring with the prophecy, and towards the end of the play he tries indeed to put this plan into action, threatening to use violence.[41] Even the idea of taking only the bow returns, when Odysseus proposes to leave with the bow since Philoctetes is not the only able archer (1054–62). There is no way of telling whether he would have tried to go through with this proposal if Neoptolemus had not returned the bow to Philoctetes, but even if he is only trying a bluff, this is never made clear. The idea of fetching only the bow is not by any means treated as out of the question at this point. Nobody on stage knows how to interpret the prophecy, and Odysseus is the character who tries hardest to find out. He tries to fulfil his mission by hook or by crook, not knowing what exactly his mission is.

Spectators can watch him and compare his efforts to the stipulations that the False Merchant has reported. But even if they take a rather dim view of Odysseus' attempts, there is no certainty to be had for them either. Not only are doubts about the reliability of the False Merchant's report likely to persist, no matter how much emphasis is put on the condition of

---

[41] 983ff. and 1293ff. Cf. Garvie (1972) 220–1.

persuasion, but it is also unclear precisely how persuasion should work with a Philoctetes who seems impervious to all approaches. This imperviousness brings me to the final scenes and to Neoptolemus. For a long time Neoptolemus does not seem to take any notice of the prophecy. Although he, rather than Philoctetes, was speaking to the False Merchant throughout the scene, he is silent from the moment the prophecy has been reported until the False Merchant is gone. Later on, there are no signs of him trying either to enact or to resist the prophecy. It is as though he has not heard what the False Merchant said, or as though he does not realise that it needs acting upon.

This realisation comes (or is articulated) when he states most explicitly that 'the god' demanded the fetching of Philoctetes rather than just the bow, and it comes in a character- istically Neoptolemean fashion (839–42).

> ἀλλ' ὅδε μὲν κλύει οὐδέν, ἐγὼ δ' ὁρῶ οὕνεκα θήραν
> τήνδ' ἁλίως ἔχομεν τόξων, δίχα τοῦδε πλέοντες.
> τοῦδε γὰρ ὁ στέφανος, τοῦτον θεὸς εἶπε κομίζειν.
> κομπεῖν δ' ἔργ' ἀτελῆ σὺν ψεύδεσιν αἰσχρὸν ὄνειδος.

Why, this man can hear nothing, but I see that we capture the bow in vain if we sail without him! It is he who wins the garland, he whom the god told us to bring; and to boast of actions incomplete while uttering falsehoods is a shameful disgrace!

Whatever one thinks has happened to Neoptolemus, it is ob- vious that he is suddenly closer than either he himself or any other character has ever been to the False Merchant's report of Helenus' prophecy. Neoptolemus does not talk of persua- sion, but he makes it clear that he is now after Philoctetes himself. The bow alone, he says, is not enough. Like the False Merchant's report, moreover, Neoptolemus' lines are strongly marked: the prophecy expresses itself in hexameters, a favour- ite metre with oracles and one that is relatively rare in trag- edy.[42] The lines have an air of authority, even if (and partly perhaps *because*) it is unclear what Neoptolemus thinks.

---

[42] For hexameters as the metre of oracles see, for instance, the Delphic oracles collected from various sources, literary and otherwise, in Parke and Wormell (1956) vol. II. Note also the hexameter oracles in Old Comedy (see Wilamowitz-

In many respects, therefore, these passages are a more authoritative restatement of the False Merchant's report about Helenus. In *one* respect, however, there is a notable difference. The authoritative air of the passage fails to do any harm to Neoptolemus. There are none of the logical irregularities that appeared in the False Merchant scene. Compared to Odysseus and the False Merchant, Neoptolemus maintains what seems to be a rather struggle-free relationship with the prophecy.

This relationship is particularly obvious in Neoptolemus' last speech (1314–47). After criticising Philoctetes' intransigence as the cause of his suffering, he reports the prophecy in a new version. Already the phrasing of the introduction draws attention to what follows (1324–5):

> ὅμως δὲ λέξω· Ζῆνα δ' ὅρκιον καλῶ·
> καὶ ταῦτ' ἐπίστω, καὶ γράφου φρενῶν ἔσω.

But all the same I will speak, and I call on Zeus the guarantor of oaths! Know this, and write it down inside your mind!

The framing is no less elaborate after the report, when Neoptolemus insists that what he says is trustworthy, both because he himself knows (οἶδα, 1336) and because the prophecy comes from an excellent source, 'Helenus the best of seers' (Ἕλενος ἀριστόμαντις, 1338). This is the first time that anybody other than the False Merchant explicitly refers to Helenus. Again the phrasing gives much weight to the prophecy, most of it being cast in one long sentence (1329–35):

> καὶ παῦλαν ἴσθι τῆσδε μή ποτ' ἂν τυχεῖν
> νόσου βαρείας, ἕως ἂν αὐτὸς ἥλιος
> ταύτῃ μὲν αἴρῃ, τῇδε δ' αὖ δύνῃ πάλιν,
> πρὶν ἂν τὰ Τροίας πεδί' ἑκὼν αὐτὸς μόλῃς,
> καὶ τῶν παρ' ἡμῖν ἐντυχὼν Ἀσκληπιδῶν
> νόσου μαλαχθῇς τῆσδε, καὶ τὰ πέργαμα
> ξὺν τοῖσδε τόξοις ξύν τ' ἐμοὶ πέρσας φανῇς.

Moellendorff (1921) 347–9 with 349 n.1). Needless to say, the hexameters in the present passage have further associations. Winnington-Ingram (1969) 49 is reminded of epic and perceives 'a discord between the Homeric metre and the unheroic enterprise in which the son of Achilles has allowed himself to be engaged'. The only other hexameter passage in Sophocles' surviving plays is *Tr.* 1010–14, 1018–22 and 1031–40.

And know that you will *never* have respite from this grievous sickness, so long as the sun rises in one quarter and sets again in another, *before* you come of your own will to the land of Troy, and meeting the sons of Asclepius that are with us you are relieved of this sickness, and *with this bow and with me* you are revealed as the conqueror of the towers.

The phrasing not only gives the prophecy much weight, it also seems to leave little doubt about where exactly to place the weight. The pleonastic ἑκὼν αὐτός ('of your own will') re-emphasises the False Merchant's πείσαντες λόγῳ ('by means of persuasion'). Now it is finally clear that persuasion implies a voluntary decision, and that trickery or force are not the right means. A second conspicuous expression, ξὺν τοῖσδε τόξοις ξύν τ' ἐμοί ('with this bow and with me'), answers a second question: now spectators have a role for Neoptolemus. He will have a part in the destruction of Troy. Thirdly, Neoptolemus' speech is marked not only by its language but also by differing from the False Merchant's report. In the earlier version the destruction of Troy was predicated contingently. Only if the Greeks were to persuade Philoctetes would Troy fall. Now roughly the same condition, expressed by μή πότε ... πρίν ('never ... before'), is attached not to the destruction of Troy but to the healing of Philoctetes' wound.[43] The destruction of Troy comes a few lines later (1340–41):

⟨Helenus says⟩
ὡς ἔστ' ἀνάγκη τοῦ παρεστῶτος θέρους
Τροίαν ἁλῶναι πᾶσαν.

that it is fated that Troy will be entirely taken during this present summer.

Here all conditions have vanished; it is a certainty that Troy will fall, and fall this summer.

Again the prophecy shows its force without embarrassing Neoptolemus. The language of his speech is conspicuous in various ways, but there is nothing that contradicts Neoptolemus' declared aim. The prophecy fits in smoothly with other arguments designed to persuade Philoctetes. The whole speech has a certain clarity about it. Spectators who were

---

[43] Compare the anapaests 191–200, in which Neoptolemus says that the gods will not heal Philoctetes until it is time.

prepared to grant the False Merchant's report of Helenus' prophecy a degree of authority are likely to trust this speech even more.

And yet, all is still not clear. Neoptolemus says that he and Philoctetes will have to destroy Troy together. Does he know, or is this condition based on wishful thinking on the part of the man for whom the glory of sacking Troy was important as early as the prologue (111–20)? Philoctetes has to come voluntarily, and so indeed he will very soon. Reassuring as this prophecy is, it is at the moment anything but obvious that Philoctetes will follow it. Never before has the prophecy answered as many questions, but not even now has it stopped posing new ones. In the event Philoctetes will resist Neoptolemus' attempts to persuade him, and Neoptolemus, despite his knowledge of the prophecy, will give in, thus leaving spectators with a dilemma, which is solved only by the arrival of Heracles. The prophecy remains engaging.

CONCLUSION

To conclude: I have discussed, in this chapter, ways in which myth and prophecy, as two examples of the invisible entities that make up Sophocles' world, may engage spectators. As I stressed before, the discussion has been intended merely to provide characteristic examples of such engagement. The communality I am interested in is a communality among the different. Each spectator reacts in his or her own way. What I have tried to do, therefore, is not to describe the precise reactions of each individual spectator. Rather my aim was to give an impression of the *potential* which certain aspects of *Philoctetes*, and especially of its language, have to engage various spectators who try to understand the role of myth and prophecy.

In order to make this impression as vivid as possible, I introduced once again a metaphor. Throughout this chapter I have spoken of the 'force' of myth and the 'force' of the prophecy. *Philoctetes* contains much linguistic and other detail that stands out in some way from its context and thus calls for attention. Much of this detail, I suggested, points to myth and prophecy. This is where the term 'force' is suggestive: myth and prophecy show their 'force' by producing numerous irregularities. To recognise this force helps one to make sense of much that is conspicuous in the text of the play. The more spectators take this help, whether in the ways I described or in any other way, the more the text appears structured, rather than displaying confusing irregularities. The characters' words begin to fall into a pattern.

Yet this is the point at which it becomes clear that the force of myth and the force of prophecy are not just a means of getting a purchase on the text. They provoke as many questions as they answer. While the force of myth provides a way of looking at the characters' struggles, it does not give spectators any certainty about the outcome of the struggle. Which myth variants are relevant to the play? And to what degree can they be bent? The force of the prophecy is similarly problematic. While it can serve as a basis for assessing what the characters say and do, it is never a firm basis. The precise meaning of the prophecy is revealed only piecemeal. For a long time the wording is in doubt, and for a long time the condition the prophecy poses seems impossible to fulfil. The force of myth and, especially, the force of the prophecy, one might say, affect not just the characters, but also the spectators.

Once again Sophoclean language (supported this time by other aspects of the text) has shown its characteristic mode of communication: an intricate blend of speech and silence, of showing and hiding, of imparting information and pointing to the information that is missing. Spectators are never told 'This is the prevailing myth variant of the play and this is how it will be played out'; or 'This is the authorised phrasing of the prophecy and this is how it will come true.' Instead, they are given the sense that myth and prophecy are important for the understanding of the play but are left in doubt over the details. The characteristics of Sophoclean language (and, one might argue on the basis of this chapter, of Sophoclean tragedy more generally) invest myth and prophecy in *Philoctetes* with the power to involve spectators in a sequence of asking questions, giving answers, asking new questions and giving new answers which does not end until the end of the play. Myth and prophecy in *Philoctetes* are engaging because they can give spectators a sense of both certainty and uncertainty at the same time. In order to pay homage to this power I will end the chapter with yet another set of metaphors.

Myth and prophecy in *Philoctetes* are not just entities that can be pushed around, accessed or ignored as one pleases. They are not things. Rather, they have an influence on the action of the play. In their own ways they are themselves agents. They are somehow noticeable, they have depth, they have presence, they are real, they are 'there'. Although invisible, they are something around which spectators can gather. Different spectators have very different perceptions and will find different degrees of usefulness in such metaphors. What matters is the quality of Sophocles' writing which I have discussed in this chapter: the quality which makes his plays, for all their complexity, appear overwhelmingly simple. There is, somewhere, detectable in all kinds of ways and amenable to all kinds of terms – and here I change my metaphor for the last time – a hidden order. And this order, elusive but perceptible, is something that all spectators in their different ways are likely to perceive. It is an order for all to share.

CHAPTER 4

GODS: A SHARED FUTURE

INTRODUCTION

In the previous chapter I used the examples of myth and prophecy in *Philoctetes* in order to describe the contributions invisible entities make to the world of Sophoclean tragedy. Despite their invisibility, they can be traced throughout a play, involving spectators in endless sequences of asking questions and giving answers. They make a play, I suggested, appear both complex and structured, both challenging and lucid. As I said at the beginning of that chapter, the most prominent entities of this kind in Sophocles are the gods. It is to them that I now want to turn.

Gods are everywhere in tragedy. They are in fact not entirely invisible and occasionally appear as characters in the theatre. Much more frequently, however, they remain unseen. Sometimes they are explicitly referred to by their proper names, as 'gods', or otherwise. Sometimes they come into a play through their association with oracles (in the case of Apollo), with certain characters (like the Priest of Zeus in *Oedipus Rex*), through statues on stage, through descriptions of the scenery (like the grove of the Eumenides in *Oedipus at Colonus*) or, in Athenian performances, through the context of the Dionysia. Sometimes divine presence may be inferred where the gods are less explicitly evoked but, like myth and prophecy in the previous chapter, can be seen in gaps. This last way of perceiving gods has been seen as a typical response to Sophoclean tragedy. 'The gods of Sophocles are there, but remote, unattainable as the snows of Olympus; we can only see the effects, and are closer to the dark underpit', Richmond Lattimore says.[1] In

---

[1] Lattimore (1958) 102.

the surviving plays the most manifest kind of gods, those who are visible as characters, are indeed confined to Athena at the beginning of *Ajax* and, if he counts as a god, Heracles at the end of *Philoctetes*. Critics have therefore tried to grasp Sophocles' gods mostly where they see nothing but their traces.

George Steiner,[2] for instance, speaks of the impressive impact that the gods make when they assist the burial of Polynices in *Antigone*. In this context, he concentrates on the passage describing the dust-pillar that reaches from earth to sky, but also has much to say about various other kinds of detail which spectators may take as an indication of divine involvement. For *Oedipus Rex* Alister Cameron's book[3] is particularly useful. Cameron collects details which may make spectators sense that the gods guide the action from the beginning until the gruesome discovery near the end. There are not only the oracles themselves, but also a number of seeming coincidences. Oedipus appears after the Chorus's prayer to Apollo and other gods to show themselves, and the entry of the Corinthian herdsman follows Jocasta's prayer to Apollo, to mention just two of the mysterious turns of the action that Cameron points to. R. P. Winnington-Ingram, among others, writes about Aphrodite's power at various points in *Trachiniae*.[4] Already present at the duel between Achelous and Heracles which has given Deianira her husband, and noticeable at all decisive moments of her and Heracles' lives, Aphrodite may be perceived at work especially when Deianira sends the robe to Heracles. Although Deianira denies Aphrodite's influence, her jealousy of Iole and her sexually charged last words seem to tell otherwise. The main argument of Charles Segal's 1977 article on *Philoctetes*[5] is that there is also interest in gods as well as humans in a play in which little is said about divine action. Even here, he suggests, the charac-

---

[2] Steiner (1984) 221–31. See also Jordan (1979) 92–101.
[3] Cameron (1968) 63–95. The chapter is called 'The gods in the action'. On divine action in *OT* see further pp. 171–5 below.
[4] Winnington-Ingram (1980) 73–90.
[5] Segal (1977).

ters can be seen trying to find their place in the divine plan. Segal detects hints of the existence of this plan in, for instance, Philoctetes' wound and the bow, both of which implicate the gods in various ways. In *Oedipus at Colonus* the divine may be seen to abound even more than in Sophocles' other plays. The instructions for the purification ritual, a particularly impressive passage, and its reverberations in the remainder of the play have been analysed by Walter Burkert.[6] He sees in the pouring of the libation not merely an evocation of ritual practice but also a foreshadowing of Oedipus' mysterious death. In various ways Oedipus' arrival and eventual final rest at Colonus may appear to reflect divine guidance. H. D. F. Kitto[7] chose *Electra*, like *Philoctetes* a play in which gods are sometimes said to be of minor importance, to demonstrate divine presence. Most importantly, he points to Clytemnestra's and Electra's prayers to Apollo, to the oracle and to Clytemnestra's dream, but detects also various less explicit indications. Spectators may, for example, see in the Paedagogus's arrival as false messenger Apollo's answer to Clytemnestra's prayer. And when the Chorus pray to Zeus for the coming of Orestes, they know from the opening scene that the prayer is no longer needed, and may regard it, with Kitto, as already fulfilled by Zeus.

Much could be said about each of these observations and interpretations, and in some of them there is much to disagree with. But even without further discussion they suggest between them that Sophoclean tragedy offers many reasons for finding the gods at work in many places. It is therefore perhaps not surprising that numerous critics (and no doubt spectators) have formed the notion of a pious Sophocles. First traces of it are found in the ancient *Vita*, according to which 'Sophocles was friends with the gods (θεοφιλής) more than anybody else.'[8] The most prominent modern advocate of

---

[6] Burkert (1985a) 8–14.

[7] Kitto (1958) 21–41.

[8] *Vita* 12. Possibly such views are based not only on interpretation of the plays. A number of ancient sources link Sophocles in some way to religious practice. For a sceptical recent assessment see Connolly (1998).

pious Sophocles was probably C. M. Bowra. He believed that 'the central idea of a Sophoclean tragedy is that through suffering a man learns to be modest before the gods'.[9] More moderately, Albin Lesky writes: 'The deep piety which has made Sophocles' tragedies moving ever since antiquity is nurtured by traditional religion and yet grows beyond it. It grows to the heights of a piety which is fully aware of the extent of human misery and vulnerability and which, despite this horror and in this horror, worships the divine.'[10] For all their differences, Lesky and Bowra – and more could be listed[11] – share one perception: they see the gods at the centre of Sophoclean tragedy.

Others, however, object. In an article entitled 'The gods in Sophocles', Richard Buxton[12] criticises Bowra and stresses that humans are much more important than gods and that the gods' involvement in the action is more complex than Bowra has suggested. How is such a divergence to be explained? In this chapter I want to suggest that both sides are justified. As Lattimore implies, much that has been said about Sophoclean gods has been inferred from gaps. Many of the inferences that I have outlined, Steiner's, Cameron's and the rest, are extremely fragile. Certainty about Sophoclean gods, as Buxton stresses, is unavailable. But this is not to say that they have only a small part in the play. The Judaeo-Christian God demands to be worshipped and to be recognised in His power and at the same time commands that no images be made of Him. Similarly, I will suggest that Sophoclean gods are noticeable in their impact and yet ultimately inscrutable.

This contrast has its effect. The uncertainty that enshrouds Sophocles' gods makes them mysterious and may attract the spectators' interest in a way that more accessible gods would not. In the previous chapter I suggested that myth and prophecy can engage spectators, as they 'show their force' and come

[9] Bowra (1944) 365.
[10] Lesky (1972) 270, my translation.
[11] See Friis Johansen (1962) 152–64. This article gave currency to the term 'pietists' which is now widely in use for critics like Bowra.
[12] Buxton (1987).

to be the focus of many questions and answers. A similar paradox will again be at the centre of the present chapter. Sophoclean gods, like myth and prophecy, can engage spectators by leaving enough traces of their working to be distinctly noticeable but eluding efforts to describe them with any degree of certainty. This is what gives them much of the special quality to which many critics and spectators have reacted.

The power inherent in the paradox of divine impact and inscrutability is brought out particularly well by John Peradotto in the speech with which he opened the 1990 APA conference.[13] Peradotto argues for the necessity of 'disauthorising' Apollo in *Oedipus Rex* as a form of 'unresponsive authority'. What happens to Oedipus in this play happens by a chain of coincidences which forces spectators, for the play to work, to assume Apollo's influence. 'If we are to *make sense* of the *OT*, we may (in fact, we must) assume the reality of Sophocles' Apollo.' Apollo, according to Peradotto, has the position of the author. He works directly on the plot of the play, and his actions cannot be motivated like those of the characters. By pointing out this effect, Peradotto hopes to 'disauthorise' the 'powerful paradigm of theocratic and prophetic rhetoric' that is the *Oedipus Rex*. What scandalised Peradotto, I believe, is the paradox that I have sketched. On the one hand, Apollo is somehow noticeable in his impact, on the other hand, he cannot be fully known.

Being scandalised, of course, is only one possible reaction. The precise reactions to Apollo, and to any other Sophoclean god, are bound to vary greatly from spectator to spectator and from one social and historical context to the next. In the cinematic terminology of Christiane Sourvinou-Inwood,[14] different spectators use different 'perceptual filters' for understanding gods (and anything else) in Greek tragedy. Spectators from a Christian background, for instance, will see Sophocles' gods differently from any Athenian spectator in the fifth century BC. None the less, a project, like Sourvinou-

[13] Peradotto (1992). The following quotations are from pp. 11 and 12 (Peradotto's italics).
[14] Particularly relevant is Sourvinou-Inwood (1997).

Inwood's, which tries to reconstruct the filters produced by fifth-century religious practice, is not the only one worth while. Any ancient spectator could have chosen from a variety of filters. These include, for instance, Homeric epic as much as lived religion. They could then use these filters for looking at tragedy, but also adapt them in accordance with what they see. Every Athenian spectator could to some degree choose whether to regard a Sophoclean tragedy as a continuation of, or an alternative to, his (or perhaps her) experience outside the theatre. No doubt both approaches coexisted. Most spectators are likely to have used various filters, Homeric, real-life and otherwise, to make sense of Sophoclean gods, and at the same time to have seen these gods as an exploration of what they did not know about the gods, adding to their understanding.[15] Since there are many different filters and since the filters can be used in many different ways, no one project can do justice to the experience of any spectator. Mine is therefore meant as a contribution from one particular angle, to be read in conjunction with many others.

What I am interested in is once again the communality of shared engagement, and this is once again communality among the different. Like Sourvinou-Inwood, I will therefore try to avoid distinctly modern filters, but unlike her I will not replace them with reconstructed ancient ones. Obviously a filter-free view is impossible and much that I will say is for different reasons invalid for ancient spectators or modern spectators without some knowledge of Greek literature and religion, but despite this inevitable lack of tidiness, I believe, it is worth making an attempt to describe divine inscrutability and impact without at least some of the culturally most specific filters. I will suggest that simultaneous inscrutability and impact is such a dominant characteristic of Sophoclean gods that it can be perceived, at least at times, even through rather strong filters. Many different spectators can engage with Sophoclean gods as they notice – each in his or her own way

---

[15] On tragedy as presenting 'credible representations' of the unknown world of the gods, see Parker (1997) 159.

– that these gods are at work but are not quite able to pin them down. It is this kind of engagement that I will try to describe in this chapter, allowing as ever for a large margin of variation.

At the heart of my discussion there will be, as ever, Sophocles' language. Unlike some of the critics mentioned above, therefore, I will look for the gods not so much in the events of a play (like the arrival of the Corinthian herdsman in *Oedipus Rex* or that of the Paedagogus in *Electra*), but rather pay close attention to how characters speak about the gods. The paradox of divine inscrutability and impact, it will turn out, can not only be observed in plot patterns, but it is also an immediate effect of the phrasing. Once again it will become obvious that Sophoclean language likes to communicate by giving spectators enough information to make them think but not so much that they stop thinking – thus keeping them constantly involved.

The chapter will fall into three sections. The first discusses the ways in which characters *name* gods and some of the ways in which spectators may react, while the second looks at moments when characters *blame* gods and, again, asks what spectators may make of these moments. These discussions will lead into a final section which is concerned more generally with the connections between gods and human action.

NAMING GODS

How do characters speak about Sophoclean gods? Once again I am concerned primarily not with *what* but with *how* Sophoclean language communicates. I will, therefore, not try to answer time-honoured questions such as 'Does Sophocles criticise the gods?' or 'Is Apollo responsible for Oedipus' downfall?' Rather, I will explore what there may be in the way Sophoclean language communicates that has often prompted such questions. To put it more generally, I am interested in how the language Sophoclean characters use when they speak about gods can have certain effects on spectators.

I will begin by looking at the names characters use. Names

do not express everything that can be known about a god, but for spectators familiar with some divine representations in literature, art, cult and elsewhere, they evoke a set of associations about the god's characteristic activities, regular haunts, favourite mortals and so on. To name a god is therefore to single him or her out of the indistinct mass of gods and other non-human forces as an identifiable personage. The associations different spectators have with a divine name will differ in detail, but for all of them to know the name of a deity makes a difference: it is to have knowledge about the deity itself.[16]

References to super-human forces are frequent in all of Sophocles' plays. Often characters identify them as particular named gods like Zeus, Apollo or Aphrodite. But no less often they fail to give them names, speaking instead of something like *theos* ('god'), or even to single them out as a personage, staying with words such as *nemesis* ('divine retribution') or *tuchē* ('fate'). The interplay between naming and not naming, singling out and not singling out, and its possible consequences for the spectators' understanding of the gods, is my chief interest in this section. The way characters refer to gods varies from character to character, from god to god and from situation to situation. Each case deserves separate treatment, and it would therefore be unwise to try to be comprehensive within the limits of one chapter. As a sample for discussion I have chosen references to *daimōn* (very roughly 'divine power'; detailed discussion of the term will follow shortly) and *Zeus* ('Zeus'), the first term failing to name, the second naming, a god.

Named gods other than Zeus

In order to give an impression of what makes *daimōn* and *Zeus* different from, and what makes them similar to, other

---

[16] For the importance of names in general see the Chorus's thoughts about the name of Helen at Aesch. *Ag.* 681–98 and Ajax's about his own at *Aj.* 430–40. Two examples of modern treatments are Zeitlin (1982) on *Septem* and Pucci (1992) 66–78 on *Oedipus Rex*.

terms that are used for gods, I will begin by glancing briefly at the kinds of thing that characters say about gods *other than* Zeus when they name them by their proper names.[17] What I want to suggest is that, to judge from their statements, characters know little about the part that the gods they name play in the action. After this brief detour of two or three pages it will be easier to get a firm grasp of the terms *daimōn* and *Zeus* themselves.

The first thing to notice is the large number of general statements characters make about named gods. Apollo (along with Zeus) knows everything about mortals (*OT* 498–9), Cypris is powerful and victorious (*Tr.* 497), both the Chorus of the Muses and Aphrodite of the golden reins like the pastures of Kephisos (*OC* 691–3), people coming to blows with Eros are out of their right mind (*Tr.* 441–2), and so on. Other statements are less general but still relate to the god's general characteristics. Apollo, Phoebus and Loxias are (or is) said to issue specific oracles or to want them to be fulfilled,[18] Hades wants the laws which demand burial of a blood relative to be obeyed (*Ant.* 519), Hades and the gods of the underworld know who buried Polynices (*Ant.* 542), and so on. Characters occasionally speak in this way about specific instances of something that is known to most spectators as a god's typical behaviour. Apollo, Phoebus and Loxias are gods (or different names for one god) of prophecy, just as Hades since Homer has ruled over the realm of the dead. These statements are more specific than those about Apollo's knowledge or Cypris' power, but they are still firmly anchored in general knowledge.

When characters go further away from what is generally known about the god whom they name, they tend to avoid assertive statements: sometimes they express themselves conditionally (like, for example, Orestes in the much-discussed 'in the house all is well, *if* Apollo prophesied well'),[19]

---

[17] For my purposes no precise definition of a proper name is necessary. I follow editors' capitalisation. So both *Apollo* and *Phoebus* are proper names, while *lukoktonos* is not.

[18] *El.* 32–5, *OT* 96–8, 133–4, 278–9, 851–4, 994–6, *OC* 84–93, 101–3, 791–3.

[19] *El.* 1424–5. Compare *El.* 472–6, *OC* 621–3, *OC* 664–5.

sometimes quote anonymous speakers,[20] and sometimes use vague phrasing.[21] Or they do not so much speak about the god's action as ask for it. Clytemnestra and Electra, for instance, pray to Phoebus, Apollo and Apollo Lykeios for fulfilment of their respective desires (*El.* 637–59 and 1376–83), the Chorus of *Oedipus Rex* invoke in the parodos (151–215) a whole range of gods over the plague that has fallen upon Thebes, and the Chorus of *Antigone* in the fourth stasimon (1115–54) ask Dionysus, whom they describe in various ways, to come to Thebes 'with a purifying foot'. Their prayers go beyond speaking of something that could be expected of the gods as an instance of their characteristic behaviour, and much could be said about the particular gods asked for particular actions. What I want to stress here is that the characters do not *attribute* a certain action to the god but *pray* that he or she act in a certain way.

On other occasions characters speak more assertively about a god they name, but speak about things the god has done a long time ago or things that have no direct impact on the play. The Chorus of *Trachiniae*, for instance, talk about Cypris refereeing the fight between Heracles and Achelous (515–16), that of *Antigone* allude to stories about Danae, Lycurgus and Cleopatra (944–87), Electra speaks about Artemis' wrath after Agamemnon killed her stag (*El.* 563–76), and there is much more.

Each of the passages I mentioned would reward further discussion, and the list is anything but complete. Yet even from this brief account it has perhaps become clear that Sophoclean characters have much to say about many gods other than Zeus but that most of their statements are in one way or another different from Oedipus' 'this was *Apollo*' (*OT* 1329) or Tecmessa's 'indeed the daughter of Zeus, the dread goddess *Pallas*, creates such woe for the sake of Odysseus' (*Aj.* 953–4). These two statements are highly exceptional in the assertive way they speak about Apollo's and Pallas' impact on the play (and will need discussion). Between them, the pas-

---

[20] *Ph.* 334–5, *OC* 414–15.   [21] *El.* 489–91.

sages to which I referred in the last few paragraphs allow the interpretation that characters have little knowledge about the part that named gods (so far, I repeat, except Zeus) have in the action. They can speculate, one might say, on the grounds of a god's province, they can quote other sources, they can pray, they can tell stories from the past, but they cannot say with any certainty what the gods they name are doing to them now. Their statements are in one way or another distanced.

Such an interpretation finds further support in the small number of statements that appear to resemble Oedipus' about Apollo and Tecmessa's about Pallas. Tiresias says that it is not at his hands that fate will make Oedipus fall, since Apollo, who is concerned to bring this about, is suitable himself (*OT* 376–7), and, in another play, he predicts that 'the Erinyes of Hades and the gods' lie in wait for Creon (*Ant.* 1074–6). Similarly, in *Ajax* Calchas is reported by the Messenger as saying that Athena will pursue Ajax in her wrath for one day and one day only (*Aj.* 756–7), and the Messenger in *Trachiniae* tells Deianira how Lichas declared (another reported statement) before many witnesses that 'Eros alone among the gods', rather than the labours or the death of Iphitus, bewitched Heracles (351–7). All these remarkably precise statements about a named god's involvement in the action have one thing in common: their speakers and reported speakers are not ordinary characters but messengers (or, in the case of Lichas, half-messengers) and seers. In Sophocles, to name a god (still other than Zeus) and at the same time to speak about his or her impact on the action seems usually to require a special status or a special skill in reading signs.

Making *daimōn* more specific: *Ajax*

With this general impression in mind I turn to the first of the two terms that I have proposed as my subject for discussion: *daimōn*. The word is more frequent in Sophocles than any divine name except for those of Zeus and Hades. Its etymology is unclear and it appears to display a perplexing breadth of usage.[22] Terms as different as 'god' and 'fate' are among its most common translations in tragedy and elsewhere. The frequent Homeric formula δαίμονι ἶσος ('like a *daimōn*'), for instance, is usually translated as 'like a god'. By contrast, when the Chorus of Aristophanes' *Birds* tell Pisthetaerus (544–5) that he has come as their saviour κατὰ δαίμονα καί ⟨τινα⟩ συντυχίαν ('by the grace of *daimōn* and some happy coincidence'), *daimōn* seems to be best translated as 'fortune', 'fate' or suchlike: the notion of a divine personage is absent from this and many other passages. None the less, there is at least some common denominator which can be agreed on: *daimōn* describes a non-human force, and a non-human force that is not named. Walter Burkert[23] goes further: '*Daimōn* is occult power, a force that drives man forward where no agent can be named.' According to Burkert, the word *daimōn* does not just refer to a force that is perceived yet not named but, more than that, implies that the force *cannot* be named. This is not the place for investigating just how valid his suggestion is for Sophocles and otherwise. What I will do instead is use the weak definition of *daimōn* as a non-human force that is not named, drawing from time to time on Burkert's stronger definition in order to suggest *possible* further connotations of a passage.

I begin with *Ajax*. Tecmessa, speaking about Ajax, says in the parodos (243–4):

> ... κακὰ δεννάζων ῥήμαθ', ἃ δαίμων
> κοὐδεὶς ἀνδρῶν ἐδίδαξεν.

... uttering evil imprecations, which a *daimōn* and none among men had taught him.

When characters name gods, I noted, they rarely speak about their part in the action. This passage (and more will follow) presents the reverse situation. Tecmessa tells what has been

---

[22] Schlesier (1983) gives accounts of the most important discussions of *daimōn*. See also De Jong (1987) 158, Mikalson (1991) 22–9, with literature 241 n. 23, and, on *daimōn* in Sophocles, Podlecki (1980) 64–7. Attempts to define *daimōn* were already made in antiquity: Sfameni Gasparro (1997).
[23] Burkert (1985b) 180.

done to Ajax but does not name an agent. The word *daimōn* offers characters a way of speaking about non-human action without putting a name to it. Yet there is a second level. So far I have concentrated on the characters. Now it is time to bring in the spectators too. Some may be content with noting that Tecmessa does not name the force that she perceives at work. Others, especially those who understand *daimōn* in the way Burkert does, may in addition wonder whether they themselves can do what Tecmessa does not do.[24] The obvious choice of name is 'Athena'. Athena was there visible as a character in the prologue, talking to Odysseus and Ajax, both of whom identified her by name (14, 91). Tecmessa, spectators may reason further, cannot name Athena because she was not yet on stage in the prologue and therefore does not know what Athena did to Ajax. Obvious as this interpretation is in many ways, it demands some inferences: Athena said in the prologue that she was the cause of the madness which made Ajax attack the cattle (51–65), while Tecmessa here speaks more specifically about the words Ajax utters while flogging the rams. Is it certain that they are Athena's teaching? Perhaps it is unsurprising that recent critics have rarely committed themselves to 'Athena'.[25]

Daimōn occurs again in verse 504. Tecmessa tries to persuade Ajax not to kill himself. Eurysakes and she herself would be enslaved and mocked, she argues, and adds: 'and *daimōn* will afflict me' (κἀμὲ μὲν δαίμων ἐλᾷ...). Not much later (534) Ajax uses the word. Speaking of the possibility that Eurysakes might die, he says, if the text is not corrupt,[26] 'that would have been appropriate to my *daimōn*' (πρέπον γέ τἂν ἦν δαίμονος τοὐμοῦ τόδε). Again characters use *daimōn* to make statements about the impact non-human forces have on the action without giving them a name. And again 'Athena', the name of the goddess who might well be thought to extend

---

[24] Variation in the ability to name is highlighted by *daimōn* in Homer. Here characters use the word more frequently than the Muse, and human characters use it more frequently than divine ones. See De Jong (1987) 239–40.

[25] One who has come close is Easterling (1993b) 83: 'does she [Tecmessa] mean Athena?'

[26] See West (1978) 110–11, and Lloyd-Jones and Wilson (1990) 20.

her anger from Ajax to Tecmessa and Eurysakes, would be a viable way of filling the gaps. Yet if translators are anything to go by, then few spectators are likely even to contemplate this way. In both instances they express their conviction that neither the Chorus nor anybody else can name an agent by using words such as 'fate', 'destiny' and 'fortune', while translating 'god' in the previous passage. Why this difference of reaction?

One difference between the passages is that neither the persecution of Tecmessa nor the killing of Eurysakes is deducible quite as easily from Athena's words in the prologue as is her authorship of Ajax's 'terrible words'. 'Athena' is therefore not a ready gloss in either of the passages commonly translated as 'fate'. I am interested here in a second difference, one that concerns the phrasing. The passages vary in the way they specify or do not specify what precisely is meant by *daimōn*. In her earlier statement Tecmessa glossed *daimōn* by κοὐδεὶς ἀνδρῶν. κοὐδεὶς ('and none') individualises *daimōn*, and ἀνδρῶν ('among men') contrasts it (or him) with humans.[27] Because of the frequent polarity between humans and gods translators may think that Tecmessa is looking at something like a god and translate accordingly. In verse 504 she adds no such gloss. *Daimōn*, force without name, drives her. Critics and spectators are given little help in naming. Ajax's phrasing is different again. He speaks of *daimōn* as something (or somebody) that belongs to him ('my *daimōn*'). More than in either of Tecmessa's instances, *daimōn* becomes distinguishable. Ajax implies that he recognises it (or him). Yet what Ajax does not do is say what kind of force the *daimōn* is in the way that Tecmessa did in the first passage. Small wonder, therefore, that critics postulate separate meanings for *daimōn*. Their translations 'god', 'fate' and 'my fate' reflect the different degrees and different kinds of specification that characters give when they speak of *daimōn*.

---

[27] This is not always the case. *Daimōn* is contrasted with gods rather than humans in fr. 555.2 Radt οὔτε δαίμων οὔτε τις θεῶν ('neither a *daimōn* nor one of the gods').

The word appears for a last time[28] in the third stasimon. The Chorus sing about the protection that Ajax used to give them and add 'but now he is made over to a hateful *daimōn*' (νῦν δ' οὗτος ἀνεῖται στυγερῷ δαί|μονι, 1214–15). The Chorus, like Ajax, mark out *daimōn* as distinguishable: *stugeros*, 'hateful'; but they do so in a way that leaves the *daimōn* still in many ways undefined. A great variety of both persons and things can be *stugeros*.[29] Perhaps because of this variety there has been more disagreement among critics than over the previous occurrences of the word. Should it be translated as 'fate' or does it stand for some god, and if so which?[30] Whether or not Burkert is right to say that *daimōn* reflects the speaker's inability to name a non-human agent, the Chorus's failure to do so can cause a considerable degree of uncertainty among critics and spectators.

This brief discussion of *daimōn* in *Ajax* has complemented what I said before about named gods other than Zeus. Where I noted earlier that characters make only limited statements about named gods, *daimōn* has shown them saying more specific things about non-human involvement in the action,[31] but not naming the force. Beyond this general pattern, I want to emphasise two ways in which the usage of *daimōn* itself can bring out the difficulty of naming Sophoclean gods. First there is a paradox. Although the word refers to a force that is not named, characters still specify in various ways what kind of force this is. *Daimōn*, one might say, building on Burkert's definition, is at the heart of the characters' efforts to say something about a force which is not easily named. In the words of Eduard Fraenkel, 'to know the name of the daemon

---

[28] I pass over Menelaus' δαιμόνων νόμους ('the laws of *daimones*', 1130). The lack of a proper name is demanded by the rhetoric of the question: 'are there *any* non-human forces whose laws...?'

[29] LSJ *s.v.* The adjective is also one of the (exceedingly few) specifying words that accompany *daimōn* in Homer: *Od.* 5.396.

[30] See Ellendt and the more recent commentaries.

[31] The quality of *daimōn* as an ill-defined force whose impact can be noticed may be one of the causes for the later understanding of *daimōn* as an intermediary between gods and humans. See Pl. *Symp.* 203a and, for further instances and discussion, Sfameni Gasparro (1997).

is to acquire power over him'.[32] Secondly, spectators can try to name where characters fail to do so. They are likely to name with much more confidence in some cases than in others. To a considerable degree their confidence will depend on the articles, adjectives and phrases characters use to make *daimōn* more specific. When Tecmessa specifies the force she does not name as something like a god, when she (to rephrase as an interpretation at character level) understands at least so much about the force she cannot name that spectators recognise something like a god in it, she provides a firmer base for choosing a name than she does when she merely speaks of *daimōn*. But even here certainty is hard to attain. In many of its instances, I suggest, *daimōn* can mark moments of divine impact and inscrutability for both characters and, in consequence, spectators.

Daimōn and Zeus

The term which I have proposed to explore along with *daimōn* is *Zeus*. I will begin with Philoctetes' last words of farewell before he leaves the stage (1464–8):

χαῖρ', ὦ Λήμνου πέδον ἀμφίαλον,
καί μ' εὐπλοίᾳ πέμψον ἀμέμπτως,
ἔνθ' ἡ μεγάλη Μοῖρα κομίζει,
γνώμη τε φίλων χὼ πανδαμάτωρ
δαίμων, ὃς ταῦτ' ἐπέκρανεν.

Farewell, seagirt land of Lemnos, and waft me on a peaceful voyage that I cannot complain of, to where mighty Fate is taking me, and the will of my friends and the all-subduing *daimōn* who has brought this to pass!

What distinguishes this passage from all previous ones is the certainty with which many editors gloss the word *daimōn*. Jebb ('clearly'), Webster, Kamerbeek and Ussher agree on 'Zeus', and with good reason. Their certainty reflects the great amount of specifying detail that helps in finding the proper name which the word *daimōn* fails to give. To begin with,

[32] Note on Aesch. *Ag.* 160.

daimōn has an article (ὁ): the *daimōn*. Then, there is the relative clause ὃς ταῦτ' ἐπέκρανεν ('who decreed this'). The most prominent god in the whole of *Philoctetes* is Zeus, and Heracles calls his orders explicitly 'plans of Zeus' (1415). Zeus might well be said, therefore, to have 'brought this to pass'. The epithet πανδαμάτωρ ('all-subduing') reminds commentators of a passage in the second stasimon of *Antigone* (604–5) in which the Chorus address Zeus, asking 'Zeus, what arrogance of men could restrict your power?' Between them, moreover, relative clause and epithet make Philoctetes' lines resemble the famous κοὐδὲν τούτων ὅ τι μὴ Ζεύς ('and none of this that (is) not Zeus', *Tr.* 1278). Both the *daimōn* at the end of *Philoctetes* and Zeus at the end of *Trachiniae* are linked to 'this' (ταῦτα, τούτων) and granted a kind of universality (παν-, κοὐδέν ... μή).

Yet the case for Zeus is not without flaws. Some critics,[33] for instance, point out that the word πανδαμάτωρ is not attested as an epithet of Zeus. Homer uses it for sleep, Simonides and Bacchylides for time.[34] A debate over the *daimōn* is reflected already in the scholion on 1468: 'some ⟨interpret *daimōn* as⟩ Heracles, others ⟨as⟩ fate', both glosses which could be supported with further argument. Once again, then, spectators may use the way in which *daimōn* is made more specific for naming a god that lurks behind the word. But even if they choose 'Zeus' as a particularly well-supported gloss, the elusiveness of the specifying epithet and relative clause may make at least some of them realise that no gloss can fully replace a name, even where the context seems to make *daimōn* as specific a force as it does here.

This conclusion can be rephrased to focus on Zeus: more clearly perhaps than any other named god encountered so far, Zeus can be seen to stand behind the word *daimōn* but still eludes unequivocal glossing. Zeus can be named by critics and spectators but not with certainty. In the next few paragraphs I wish to look at three passages from *Oedipus at Colonus* in order to suggest that this pattern is not restricted to the lines

---

[33] See Ellendt *s.v.* δαίμων and Podlecki (1980) 64–5.   [34] LSJ *s.v.*

at the end of *Philoctetes*. Most instances of *daimōn* give little help in identifying a named god, but those that do remarkably often point at Zeus – and that although Zeus, unlike for instance Athena, never appears on stage.

Terrified by repeated peals of thunder the Chorus exclaim (1480–5):

ἵλαος, ὦ δαίμων, ἵλαος, εἴ τι γᾷ
ματέρι τυγχάνεις ἀφεγγὲς φέρων.
ἐναισίου δὲ σοῦ τύχοι-
μι, μηδ' ἄλαστον ἄνδρ' ἰδὼν
ἀκερδῆ χάριν μετάσχοιμί πως.
Ζεῦ ἄνα, σοὶ φωνῶ.

O daimōn, kindly be your coming, if you are bringing something wrapped in darkness to the earth our mother! May I encounter you in auspicious mood, and may my seeing of an accursed man not bring me a return that is no gain. *Lord Zeus*, it is to you I speak.

Seeing, presumably, that the passage contains two addresses, one to *daimōn* and one to 'lord Zeus', Ellendt glosses the first by *Iupiter Fulgurator*, 'Zeus the Sender of Lightning'. This gloss is perhaps even more obvious than that in the previous passage. Yet a gloss it remains. There are more than four lines between the two addresses. It is as though the Chorus had to learn how to give a name to the force that they perceive when they exclaim 'O *daimōn*'. And when they have learned how, they do not repeat the entire prayer: while the *daimōn* is addressed as the cause of thunder and as determining the Chorus's fate, Zeus is invoked by name and title in a new sentence without connective. There is much in this passage that links the terms *daimōn* and *Zeus* but much also that separates them.

Zeus and *daimōn* appear again together when Antigone despairs after Oedipus' death (1748–50).

φεῦ, φεῦ· ποῖ μόλωμεν,
ὦ Ζεῦ; ἐλπίδων γὰρ ἐς τί⟨ν' ἔτι⟩ με
δαίμων τανῦν γ' ἐλαύνει;

Alas, alas! Where are we to go, O Zeus? To what expectations is *daimōn* now driving me?

In this passage, too, Zeus and *daimōn* have much in common. Antigone feels that both of them have power over her. Twice she asks questions about her destination. The first, 'where are we to go?', accompanies an invocation of Zeus, the second, 'to what expectations is *daimōn* now driving me?', has *daimōn* as its subject. But again common ground does not mean identity. Antigone appears to turn to Zeus for *help*, as she is *driven* by *daimōn*. Spectators are bound to vary in how much weight they give to each of these aspects of the phrasing, but what seems clear is that there are again points of both contact and difference between *Zeus* and *daimōn*.

My third passage from *Oedipus at Colonus* is the first half of Oedipus' curse on Polynices (1370–82):

> τοιγάρ σ' ὁ δαίμων εἰσορᾷ μὲν οὔ τί πω
> ὡς αὐτίκ' εἴπερ οἴδε κινοῦνται λόχοι
> πρὸς ἄστυ Θήβης. οὐ γὰρ ἔσθ' ὅπως πόλιν
> κείνην ἐρείψεις, ἀλλὰ πρόσθεν αἵματι
> πεσῇ μιανθεὶς χὠ ξύναιμος ἐξ ἴσου.
> τοιάσδ' ἀρὰς σφῷν πρόσθε τ' ἐξανῆκ' ἐγὼ
> νῦν τ' ἀνακαλοῦμαι ξυμμάχους ἐλθεῖν ἐμοί,
> ἵν' ἀξιῶτον τοὺς φυτεύσαντας σέβειν,
> καὶ μὴ 'ξατιμάζητον, εἰ τυφλοῦ πατρὸς
> τοιώδ' ἔφυτον. αἵδε γὰρ τάδ' οὐκ ἔδρων.
> τοιγὰρ τὸ σὸν θάκημα καὶ τοὺς σοὺς θρόνους
> κρατοῦσιν, εἴπερ ἐστὶν ἡ παλαίφατος
> Δίκη ξύνεδρος Ζηνὸς ἀρχαίοις νόμοις.

Therefore (*toigar*) does the *daimōn* look upon you, not yet as he soon shall, *if* (*eiper*) these squadrons are moving towards the city of Thebes; for you shall never destroy the city, but first you shall fall, polluted by bloodshed, and your brother also. Such are the curses which I pronounced upon you in the past and which I now call to come and fight beside me, so that you two may learn respect for your begetters, and not dishonour them, even if the father that begot such men is blind; for these girls did not do this! *Therefore* (*toigar*) these curses have control of your supplication and your thrones, *if* (*eiper*) *there is Justice, spoken of for a long time and sitting by the old laws of Zeus.*

In the preceding words Oedipus has compared his sons' negligence with his daughters' care for him, and has denied that he is their father. 'Therefore' (*toigar*, 1370), he says now, the *daimōn* looks upon Polynices' actions in a new kind of way 'if' (*eiper*, 1371) Polynices is leading the army against Thebes, and he goes on to prophesy what will happen at Thebes. Oedipus links the treatment he received from his sons, their mutually inflicted death, and the *daimōn*. Near the end of the passage he comes back to the daughters (1379). His sons were lacking in respect for their blind father, while his daughters were not. Therefore, he continues, the curses have control of his sons' thrones. Again *toigar* connects the difference between his sons' and daughters' behaviour to Polynices' future. But what was the *daimōn* in the beginning is now 'Justice spoken of for a long time and sitting by the old laws of Zeus'. Zeus's role is closely comparable to that of the *daimōn*. Both supervise Polynices' fall. The difference is once again that less is said of Zeus's action: he appears in the genitive as only one aspect of the non-human guarantors of Oedipus' curse and he appears, like some of the named gods that I briefly discussed near the beginning of this section, in a conditional clause (*eiper*, 'if', in 1381) which is unverifiable, while the action of the *daimōn* is conditional (*eiper* in 1371) only on Polynices' impending attack on Thebes. These variations tell against a straight gloss of *daimōn* with *Zeus*, but, discounting such a gloss, there remains a marked connection between the two.

I will round off my discussion of passages which allow the linking of *daimōn* to Zeus[35] by looking at one of those instances in which *daimōn* is clearly associated with a named god *other than* Zeus. Clytemnestra ends her prayer to Apollo as follows (*El.* 655–9):

> ταῦτ', ὦ Λύκει' Ἄπολλον, ἵλεως κλυὼν
> δὸς πᾶσιν ἡμῖν ὥσπερ ἐξαιτούμεθα.
> τὰ δ' ἄλλα πάντα καὶ σιωπώσης ἐμοῦ
> ἐπαξιῶ σε δαίμον' ὄντ' ἐξειδέναι·
> τοὺς ἐκ Διὸς γὰρ εἰκός ἐστι πάνθ' ὁρᾶν.

Hear this, Lycian Apollo, with kindness and grant to all of us that which we are praying for! The rest I think that you, who are a *daimōn*, know well, even if I say nothing; for the children of Zeus can surely see all things.

This, perhaps, is the instance of *daimōn* in Sophocles that poses the greatest challenge to the assumption that the word

---

[35] See also *OT* 1193–1201, *Tr.* 278–80, *OC* 1448–56 and *OC* 1766–7.

expresses a failure or (following Burkert) an inability to name.[36] Clytemnestra names 'Phoebus' (637), the 'Lycian lord' (645) and now 'Lycian Apollo' (655) in her prayer. When she says, therefore, 'you who are a *daimōn*' in 658, the obvious way of taking the address is to refer it to Apollo. Yet there is more to be seen. Firstly, it is noteworthy that the prayer Clytemnestra addresses to Apollo as a *daimōn*, rather than as 'Phoebus', 'Lycian lord' or 'Apollo', is silent. The wish for her son's death or whatever else she may be thinking of is too dreadful to pronounce. Is it perhaps too dreadful also to be addressed to a named god? Secondly, the last line is interesting. In it Clytemnestra makes it even clearer that the *daimōn* is Apollo, but she again avoids the name. It is not 'Apollo' who, she says, should see everything but 'the children of Zeus' (τοὺς ἐκ Διός), a periphrasis in the plural. Although there is no doubt that the prayer is addressed to Apollo, the only name appearing in Clytemnestra's gloss of *daimōn* is that of Zeus. Even in a passage which strongly suggests the gloss 'Apollo', Zeus appears to hide behind *daimōn*.[37]

In the majority of its instances, and especially where it appears in the plural, *daimōn* resists attempts to name the non-human force to which it refers. In the previous paragraphs I have suggested that there are none the less a considerable number of passages in which *daimōn* can be more or less strongly associated with Zeus. These passages produce a tension. On the one hand *daimōn* is likely to yield a name for many spectators; on the other hand no degree of certainty (and the precise degree varies from passage to passage and spectator to spectator) makes *daimōn* the same as *Zeus*. It (or he) is an unnamed non-human force and not Zeus. In some passages the terms *daimōn* and *Zeus* appear within a short space. Here glossing is particularly easy, but at the same time

---

[36] Note also *OT* 244–5. It is worth pointing out that in the surviving plays of Sophocles there is nothing to match the δαίμονα | Δαρεῖον ('*daimōn* Dareius') of Aesch. *Pers.* 620–1, or the Dionysus of Eur. *Ba.* 22 who says ἵν' εἴην ἐμφανὴς δαίμων βροτοῖς ('so that I am manifest to mortals as a *daimōn*').

[37] Compare *OC* 707–19, in which ὁ μέγας δαίμων ('the great *daimōn*') is first addressed 'O child of Kronos', which might be *either* Zeus *or* Poseidon, and is only then specified by 'Lord Poseidon'.

it is often possible to observe that statements about Zeus, as about the other named gods that I briefly discussed at the beginning of this section, are, in one way or another, un-assertive. Where he is named, often less is said about him than about *daimōn*: he appears in invocations, in the genitive, in conditions and so on. Zeus hides behind *daimōn*.

Making Zeus more specific: *Trachiniae*

His fondness for hiding behind *daimōn*, and still peeping out despite hiding, provides a starting-point for investigating Sophocles' Zeus. Zeus is by far the most frequently named god in Sophoclean tragedy. To see how characters speak about him is therefore to see some crucial aspects of how characters speak about Sophocles' gods in general. In the attempt to do so, I will use the associations *Zeus* seems to share with *daimōn*. What is it that these terms have in common although the first is a name, while the second refers to a non-human force without name, perhaps even marking the impossibility of naming? What is it that makes both of them appear more often than the names of Apollo, Aphrodite and Co.? And what effect does the way these terms are used have on spectators? In order to try to answer these questions, I turn to the play in which Zeus's name is more frequent than in any other:[38] *Trachiniae*.

Central to the way the word *daimōn* will be understood, I suggested, are the ways in which characters who use it make it more specific through articles, adjectives and longer phrases. Following on from this suggestion, I will now look at the various ways in which characters specify what or whom they mean when they use the word *Zeus*. To begin with, Zeus, like *daimōn*, is described by adjectives and even adjectival nouns (or, to use the common term for both when applied to a god, epithets) and by relative clauses. Zeus is not just *Zeus*. Made more specific, he can also be 'Olympian Zeus' or 'Zeus the

---

[38] In relation to its length, about twice as frequent as in any other play.

protector of suppliants'. Secondly, since *Zeus*, unlike *daimōn*, is a name which identifies a particular god who has particular associations, it can at times be replaced altogether by terms, like the patronym *Kronidēs*, which point at Zeus as a relation of somebody: Zeus is 'the son of Kronos'. Vice versa, there are expressions that make somebody the relation of Zeus. Hera, for instance, is the 'wife of Zeus' and Heracles the 'son of Zeus'. Such expressions, too, privilege certain associations that for many spectators are inherent in the name *Zeus*.

Looking at references to Zeus in *Trachiniae*, one notices that, until Heracles comes on stage after almost a thousand lines, no character except Lichas (whom I will discuss shortly) speaks of Zeus without some such specific elaboration. There is first of all Hyllus, Heracles' son. He speaks of Zeus only once in those lines. Heracles, he says, marked out an altar and precinct for πατρῴῳ Διί (Zeus *patrōos*, Zeus 'the father' or 'of the father', 750–4). The epithet points in various directions at the same time. But no matter whether it primarily describes Zeus as Heracles' father, as the Zeus of Hyllus' father, or as a father in a more general sense, it makes Zeus more specific.

The Chorus have more to say about Zeus than Hyllus does. Their least specific usage of *Zeus* occurs in the parodos when they try to allay Deianira's fears for her husband by asking (139–40) ἐπεὶ τίς ὧδε | τέκνοισι Ζῆν' ἄβουλον εἶδεν ('for who has seen Zeus so lacking in counsel for his children?'). The adjective ἄβουλος ('without *boulē*', that is, 'counsel') evokes both the Zeus whose *boulē* gives the *Iliad* its shape and the Zeus of many stories (such as Io's) in which his concern for others, or the lack of it, are at the heart of the narrative. τέκνοισι ('for his children') focuses on Zeus as father, in the context particularly as the father of Heracles. *Zeus*, therefore, is made more specific, if not as specific as elsewhere. Later the Chorus speak four times, with varying implications, of the son of Zeus ('son of Zeus', 513; 'the son of Zeus and Alcmene', 644; 'the true son of Zeus', 826; and 'the mighty son of Zeus', 956), thus privileging Zeus the father of Heracles even more clearly. Twice they talk of Zeus without connecting him with Heracles or any anonymous children, and both times they choose a name other than *Zeus*: *Kronidēs*, 'son of Kronos'. At 499 he is overpowered by Aphrodite, and at 127–8, made more specific by ὁ πάντα κραίνων βασιλεύς, 'the king who ordains all things', he fails to give mortals lives without pain.

Deianira makes *Zeus* more specific still. Twice she, too, speaks of Zeus as Heracles' father ('son of Zeus and Alcmene', 19; 'the son of Zeus', 566). Yet like Hyllus and unlike the Chorus, Deianira also uses epithets. *Zeus agōnios* ('the god of contests'), she says, brought to its end the fight between Heracles and Achelous (26–7):

> τέλος δ' ἔθηκε Ζεὺς ἀγώνιος καλῶς,
> εἰ δὴ καλῶς.

But Zeus *agōnios* brought about a good outcome, if it was good.

Not much later Deianira addresses Zeus out of gratitude for preserving Heracles (200–1):

> ὦ Ζεῦ, τὸν Οἴτης ἄτομον ὃς λειμῶν' ἔχεις,
> ἔδωκας ἡμῖν ἀλλὰ σὺν χρόνῳ χαράν.

O Zeus, to whom belongs the meadow of Oeta which is never cropped, at long last you have granted us delight!

It is Zeus of Mount Oeta whom she thanks, and ἄτομον ... λειμῶνα ('the meadow which is never cropped') may make him Zeus of the wild at the same time. In the next scene, taken by the fate of the captive women whom Lichas parades, Deianira prays to Zeus (303–5):

> ὦ Ζεῦ τροπαῖε, μή ποτ' εἰσίδοιμί σε
> πρὸς τοὐμὸν οὕτω σπέρμα χωρήσαντά ποι,
> μηδ', εἴ τι δράσεις, τῆσδέ γε ζώσης ἔτι.

Zeus, god of trophies (*tropaios*), may I never see you go against my offspring in this fashion; if you do so, may it not be while I still live!

Again Deianira addresses Zeus in a special function, this time that of *Zeus tropaios*. He it was who subjected the women of Oechalia to slavery.

There are many passages, then, in which the characters of *Trachiniae* privilege, in all kinds of ways, certain aspects of Zeus over others. Between them these passages raise a question: is there one Zeus in *Trachiniae* or are there many different ones? This question cannot be answered absolutely for all spectators alike. Zeus *patrōos* (Zeus 'the father' or 'of the father'), the Zeus Hyllus speaks about, illustrates why not. He was worshipped at various locations in Greece. By contrast he is not attested at Athens, where this place seems to have been filled by *Apollon patrōos*.[39] And modern spectators are in a different position from both Athenians and other Greeks. For most of them the epithet *patrōos* is unlikely to produce any particular resonance. Spectators, therefore, differ strongly in what they associate with *Zeus patrōos*. For some of them he is just some variety of Zeus, while others have (or, mostly, had) a very clear conception of him as a god whom they know.

Even for the last group, however, as an argument recently put forward by Christiane Sourvinou-Inwood suggests,[40] *Zeus patrōos* is unlikely to have been entirely divorced from, say, *Zeus tropaios* ('Zeus, god of trophies'). Drawing on evidence from a variety of sources, Sourvinou-Inwood suggests that for all the differences between the 'individual cultic *personae*' of a deity, there was enough common ground between them to create a 'semantic field' Athena, Artemis and so on. Different ways of referring to the deity in a play 'zoom' the spectators in, as Sourvinou-Inwood puts it, on particular aspects of the deity without ever replacing his or her core personality. Turning to tragedy, Sourvinou-Inwood discusses ways in which Euripides presents certain *personae* of a deity as on the one hand continuous with the deity familiar to the audience and on the other hand no more than a partial aspect of it. So she argues, for instance, that Artemis as worshipped by Hippolytus would be seen by an Athenian audience as an aspect of Artemis as they know her, but as missing crucial facets. Hippolytus, on this interpretation, has 'a one-sided perception of Artemis'.[41]

In the light of Sourvinou-Inwood's argument it seems a reasonable assumption that not only spectators who have little

---

[39] *Zeus patrōos*: see Cook (1914–40) indexes of vols. I and II *s.v.*; *Apollon patrōos*: *RE* II.1 63. Cf. Dover on Aristoph. *Nu.* 1468.

[40] Sourvinou-Inwood (1997) 164–70, responding to Mikalson (1991).

[41] Ibid. 182–3.

familiarity with any particular *persona* of Zeus but also those for whom *Zeus tropaios* had very different cultic connotations from *Zeus patrōos* might conceive of the two as one Zeus, but one Zeus in two *personae*. To pray to *Zeus tropaios* is in some ways to address *Zeus patrōos*, while in others it is not. Depending on their conception of these two manifestations, different spectators will privilege what both Zeuses have in common or what divides them but, at least to some degree, many spectators of many times can and could perceive both continuity and discontinuity between the different Zeuses.

With this assumption I return to the characters. How can their efforts to privilege certain aspects of Zeus over others be interpreted? One possibility, I suggest, is to say that they try to make Zeus more manageable by narrowing him down to certain aspects. 'Zeus, father of Heracles' or *Zeus agōnios* are certainly no less powerful and no less dangerous than Zeus bare and simple. But what they are is more specific and hence easier to imagine and easier to grasp. If Zeus is Heracles' father, he is immediately closer to the world that they know. If he is the son of Kronos, and in particular if he is elaborated as ὁ πάντα κραίνων βασιλεύς ('the king who ordains all things'), he is the king of gods and humans portrayed in the *Theogony* and elsewhere. If he is *Zeus agōnios*, he oversees competitions, and so on. The strategy of making gods more specific is especially familiar, at least to ancient spectators, from prayers. Greek prayers sometimes devote considerable time to the terms of address.[42] Apparently it was considered important to address the god by the appropriate name in order to increase one's hope of having the prayer fulfilled. Privileging certain aspects of Zeus, one might say, gives characters a purchase on him.

But the purchase comes at a price. As Euripides' Hippolytus may be said to have a one-sided perception of Artemis, so Sophocles' Deianira, Hyllus and the Chorus do not appear to see all there is to be seen about Zeus. *Zeus agōnios* may

---

[42] Usener (1896) 334–6, Norden (1913) 144–7 and, most recently, Pulleyn (1997) 96–115, who warns against attributing to the Greeks a belief in the magic power of names.

have brought about a good outcome in Heracles' fight with Achelous, but there are further manifestations of Zeus and further ends for Heracles. Zeus may be Heracles' father, but that is not to say that he acts only as his father. Zeus of Mount Oeta may have given Deianira joy, but what about Zeus of Mount Cenaeum? Finally, even if Deianira's prayer to *Zeus tropaios* is heard, there are other manifestations of Zeus that she does not invoke and does not try to influence. Whether or not spectators think of attempts to 'influence' and to 'get a purchase', they are able to think about the characters' successes and failures in privileging certain aspects of Zeus. Spectators can observe characters in their struggles.

But how much does this tell them about Zeus himself? Do they learn about him at the same time as they learn about the characters? Zeus is only one of many gods who are named in different ways. Apollo, for instance, is also referred to as Phoebus and Loxias and receives numerous epithets, and the Chorus of *Antigone* spend more than two stanzas (1115–39) addressing Dionysus before they state their wish. Yet Zeus is exceptional in the consistency with which he prompts characters to specify which of his *personae* and which of his aspects they invoke or refer to. In order to understand this exception better, I now turn to the final quarter of the play.

Although Heracles comes on stage less than 300 lines before the end, he refers to Zeus no less than eleven times. The other characters by contrast total three mentions between them in those scenes. Like Deianira, Hyllus and the Chorus before, Heracles speaks of Zeus's family. Crucially, Zeus is his father (πάτερ, 'father' at 1088; Διός τοῦ με φύσαντος, 'Zeus who begot me' at 1185), and Heracles himself 'the one who saluted as the son of Zeus among the stars' (ὁ τοῦ κατ' ἄστρα Ζηνὸς αὐδηθεὶς γόνος, 1106). Others too, both gods and humans, are for Heracles functions of Zeus: Hades is 'brother of Zeus' (1042), Hera 'wife of Zeus' (1048) and Alcmene 'bedfellow of Zeus' (1148–9). Finally, Heracles appeals to the 'lightning of Zeus' (Διὸς ἀκτίς) to kill him (1086).

For all the similarities with Hyllus, Deianira and the Chorus, there are marked differences. Heracles never gives Zeus an epithet[43] or replaces the name by a patronym like *Kronidēs*. He does not exclude any of Zeus's facets. Sometimes, moreover, he does what Deianira, Hyllus and the Chorus never do and makes the name *Zeus* a noun phrase by itself, happy apparently to do without adjectives, nouns or relative clauses. His first words on stage are ὦ Ζεῦ, | ποῖ γᾶς ἥκω ('*O Zeus*, where in the world have I come', 983–4). In no way does he specify a particular *persona*. A moment later he repeats this kind of invocation (993–9):[44]

> ὦ Κηναία κρηπὶς βωμῶν,
> ἱερῶν οἵαν οἵων ἐπί μοι
> μελέῳ χάριν ἠνύσω, ὦ Ζεῦ·
> οἵαν μ' ἄρ' ἔθου λώβαν, οἵαν·
> ἣν μήποτ' ἐγὼ προσιδεῖν ὁ τάλας
> ὤφελον ὄσσοις, τόδ' ἀκήλητον
> μανίας ἄνθος καταδερχθῆναι.

Rock of Cenaeum where the altars stand, such is the thanks you have rendered me wretched one for such sacrifices, *O Zeus*! What outrage have you done upon me, what outrage! I wish I had never set eyes on you, wretch that I am. Then I would not see this ever-growing madness, not to be appeased.

After this desperate and almost accusatory outcry, Heracles changes the mode (1000–3):

> τίς γὰρ ἀοιδός, τίς ὁ χειροτέχνας
> ἰατορίας, ὃς τάνδ' ἄταν
> χωρὶς Ζηνὸς κατακηλήσει;

Where is the charmer, where the surgeon, other than Zeus, that shall lull to sleep this plague?

Now Zeus is needed to heal Heracles. Heracles' question seems to specify a particular *persona*: that of Zeus the healer. In this respect the passage is therefore comparable to those from the first three quarters of the play. However, what is notably different is the language. In the passages discussed above, the Chorus, Hyllus and Deianira use specifying epi-

---

[43] 1191 is hardly an exception. Lloyd-Jones and Wilson, but not Easterling and Dawe, print Wakefield's ὑψίστου for the MSS' ὕψιστον in τὸν Οἴτης Ζηνὸς ὕψιστον πάγον. The emendation holds little attraction.

[44] This is the conservative text printed by Easterling. See her note on 994–5 and, *contra*, Lloyd-Jones and Wilson (1990) 173.

thets and clauses, and they invoke well-known stories about Zeus. Heracles does none of this. He *does* specify a particular aspect of Zeus but he does so much less clearly than the other characters. Heracles, then, both speaks of Zeus more frequently than other characters and, as he speaks about him, does not privilege certain aspects of Zeus over others to the same degree as Hyllus, the Chorus and especially Deianira do earlier on in the play.

As Heracles speaks more than once of an unspecific Zeus, the other characters begin, as it were, to copy him. Hyllus does not just swear the oath by Zeus but also, like Heracles, sees Zeus as the power that controls events: τοιαῦτα νέμει Ζεύς ('such is the lot that *Zeus* assigns', 1022). Similarly, the Chorus (or Hyllus)[45] close the play with the famous κοὐδὲν τούτων ὅ τι μὴ Ζεύς ('and none of this that is not *Zeus*', 1278). Zeus increasingly sheds his *personae*.

But what is left? This question, I believe, is crucial for understanding how Sophoclean characters speak about Zeus. The first answer is that characters often seem to say more about Zeus when they do not specify a *persona*. The references to Zeus in the first three quarters of the play, just like those to other named gods that I mentioned at the beginning of the section, are distanced in one way or another: the Chorus ask a general question about Zeus (139–40), they say they pass by a past story about him (497–502), or say, again in general, that Zeus does *not* give humans a painless life (126–8). Similarly, Deianira qualifies what she says by a conditional (26–7), and prays that Zeus do something, rather than saying that he does something (303–5). Only once (200–1) does she say what Zeus did, thanking him for the joy which (she thinks) he gave her and her nearest and dearest. Between them, these passages set standards by which Hyllus' and the Chorus's statements about Zeus and, to a lesser degree, also Heracles' vague accusatory outcry and his question about healing seem remarkable. It would be a mistake to look for clear-cut rules, but there is an

---

[45] This has been much debated. See most recently Lloyd-Jones and Wilson (1997) 102.

obvious tendency: many of the passages in which characters speak about an unspecific Zeus, have more to say about his involvement in the action than those in which characters specify particular *personae* of Zeus.

At the same time, however, as saying more, characters say less when they cease to concentrate on certain of Zeus's facets. This will become clear from a look at the character whom I have ignored so far: Lichas. Like Deianira, the Chorus and Hyllus, he uses epithets and other kinds of descriptive terms when he refers to Zeus (Zeus 'of Mount Cenaeum', 238; 'Olympian' Zeus, 'the father of all', 275; *Zeus patrōos*, 288; 'mighty' (μέγας) Zeus, 399). Yet he is the only character before Heracles' arrival who also speaks of an unspecific Zeus. At the beginning of his messenger speech to Deianira he says (250–1):

$$\text{τοῦ λόγου}^{46} \text{ δ' οὐ χρὴ φθόνον,}$$
$$\text{γύναι, προσεῖναι, Ζεύς ὅτου πράκτωρ φανῇ.}$$

There should be no resentment concerning the story, lady, where *Zeus* is known to be the one who has done it.

Lichas leaves Zeus again unspecific when he speaks about the killing of Iphitus nearer the end of the same speech (278–9):

$$\text{εἰ γὰρ ἐμφανῶς ἠμύνατο,}$$
$$\text{Ζεύς τἂν συνέγνω ξὺν δίκῃ χειρουμένῳ.}$$

If he had fought him openly, *Zeus* would have pardoned him, since he had worsted his enemy in just fashion.

I am especially interested here in the first of the two passages. It introduces Lichas' account of the events around Eurytus and Iphitus. Lichas appears to be saying that Zeus 'did' all that which follows in his report. Again a character who speaks about an unspecific Zeus has something to say about his involvement in the action (although it needs stressing that this passage, like so many before, is, strictly speaking, general: Lichas suggests, rather than says, that Zeus 'did' it).

---

[46] Lloyd-Jones and Wilson print Margoliouth's τῷ λόγῳ. In defence of προσεῖναι without a dative (such as τῷ λόγῳ), Dawe cites *Ant.* 1252 and *OC* 1198 in the apparatus of his third edition.

My starting-point is what is perhaps a rather personal impression. I find that there is something very unsatisfactory, even disturbing, about this passage. Tracing reasons for this impression will soon take me out of the personal and lead me to some general and less subjective observations. To begin with, one problem with Lichas' statement is the attempt to exculpate Heracles by blaming a god. His denial of all responsibility on Heracles' part is (I think) immensely unattractive. What kind of a world is it in which people do not have to stand up for their actions?[47] But there is a further point beyond this, and this point brings me back to the claim with which I came to Lichas in the first place.

While characters who do not try to make *Zeus* more specific sometimes say more about his involvement in the action, I maintained, they say less in other ways. Lichas' statement brings this out well. What does it mean to say (or to suggest) that Zeus 'did' certain things? Zeus has too many *personae* to make this a statement with a clear meaning. If Lichas said (or suggested) that, say, Eros or Apollo 'did this', his statement would still be an unattractive exculpation, but it would be clearer. In the case of Eros, spectators could think about the women Heracles might have been enchanted by, and how this enchantment might have led him to do what he did. For Apollo many spectators would probably have more options to consider. They might look for oracles, they might look for disease, for music or for something else that is associated with Apollo. As it happens, such a statement, suitable as it might seem at the end of *Oedipus Rex*, would be difficult to make sense of in the context, and this difficulty suggests a certain degree of specificity. Apollo has (perhaps) more *personae* than Eros, but not enough to fit every bill. Zeus, by contrast, has a whole host of *personae* to fit both this and almost any other bill. Zeus as Heracles' father? Zeus as ruler of all gods? *Zeus*

---

[47] Lichas has of course famous predecessors (and followers), most prominently Agamemnon at *Il.* 19.86–7: 'I am not responsible, but Zeus is, and Fate, and the mist-walking Erinys.' In Sophocles compare the Odysseus of *Philoctetes*, especially 989–90: 'It is Zeus, let me tell you, Zeus, the ruler of this land, Zeus who has decided this, and I will execute his will.'

xenios? The options are almost endless. *Zeus* in Lichas' sentence is little more specific than 'a god'. Effectively, Lichas is saying that 'resentment is out of place where a god is at work'. This, I believe, is unattractive not only because it is a denial of human responsibility but also because it is a refusal to look for precise explanations. For the Lichas of this statement things are as they are, and that is all there is to it. Such an attitude makes for an unbearably bleak world, so that it comes as a relief when the Messenger, uncovering Lichas' deception, quotes him somewhat later as saying that 'Eros alone of the gods' bewitched Heracles (351–8). There is more to it after all, and Lichas, too, is not always content with minimal explanation. Whether or not his statement about Zeus is unattractive is of course a matter of personal judgement, but the contrast with the correction brought by the Messenger highlights what is not, I think, an idiosyncratic observation: unless he is made more specific, Zeus is very hard to pin down.

What, then, I go on to ask, about the passages later in the play? Are all instances of an unspecific Zeus bleak? Do I find them all disturbing? Yes and no. There is a great difference between the statement by Lichas on the one hand, and, on the other, Heracles' 'where is the surgeon, other than Zeus, that shall lull to sleep this plague?', Hyllus' 'such is the lot that Zeus assigns', and the Chorus's (or Hyllus') 'none of this that (is) not Zeus'. The difference is not just one of exculpating or not, but also, and perhaps more important, one of beginning versus end. All three come at the end, both the end of the play and the end of Heracles' life, while Lichas' comes at the beginning, both of his speech and, relatively speaking, of the play. This difference has two important effects.

Firstly, there is the question of the characters' experience. For Heracles, Hyllus and the Chorus, Zeus is a god who brought suffering either upon them or upon those who are close to them.[48] Where Lichas poses as a dispassionate ob-

---

[48] Note Teucer's ὀδυνᾶν or ὀδύναν ('pain', 1021) and the Chorus's πήματα ... καινοπαθῆ ('new sufferings', 1277) in the lines before their respective statements about Zeus.

server, the Chorus, Hyllus and Heracles are involved in what they are talking about. There is of course no guarantee, but it is at least possible that they *may* have learned something about Zeus that spectators and Lichas do not know. The Chorus, Hyllus and Heracles have been more exposed to Zeus's power than ordinary men and women, including Lichas. As a result their statements have what one might call depth: there may be some further meaning lurking somewhere. The name *Zeus* may mean more to them than it does to other people. Secondly, behind these passages there is the full wealth of statements and events that have a bearing on divine causation in *Trachiniae*. Almost all of those statements and events can be fitted into the flexible *persona* of Zeus, who is not only Heracles' father, a god of contests and the local deity of various places crucial to the play, but who as ruler of gods and men, at one level, is behind everything that happens anywhere. Where Lichas resigns himself (at least temporarily) to statements about an unspecific Zeus before much else was known, for Heracles, Hyllus and the Chorus this resignation comes only after much has been said and done. They leave Zeus unspecific at a point when Deianira, Heracles, Nessus, Aphrodite and the various *personae* of Zeus have between them suggested too many specific explanations of what happened in the play to make any one of them satisfactory by itself. The sum total of these explanations does not make it clear what precisely *Zeus* means in any of the passages, but it gives at least some shape to this most shapeless of gods. For these two reasons I believe that the effect of what Heracles, Hyllus and the Chorus say and ask about an unspecific Zeus is quite different from that of Lichas' statement. Their passages are less brutal and less bleak.

Yet these differences only highlight something that emerges from the discussion of both Lichas' and Heracles', Hyllus' and the Chorus's passages: *Zeus* needs to be made more specific. The name has too many associations to yield a clear meaning by itself. Where *Zeus* is left unspecific near the end of the play, I have suggested, spectators find some help in all that has been said before, and some sense of there being a clearer meaning somewhere in the hope that the characters themselves have a more precise understanding of the name. Yet all this is not to say that *Zeus* becomes clearly defined. What, after all, does it mean that 'Zeus is the one who did it' or that 'none of this that (is) not Zeus'? Small wonder, perhaps, that for the better part of the play almost all characters use epithets and other means to make *Zeus* more specific. To leave him unspecific is to be reconciled, for whatever reason, to the fact that there is only so much sense that one can make of him.

This need for specific elaboration, I think, explains at last some of the affinity between Zeus and *daimōn*. Fundamentally different though Zeus is as a named god from an unnamed force such as *daimōn*, I have noted that he likes to hide behind this unnamed force. Both, moreover, are more frequent than Apollo, Aphrodite and Co., and both seem to allow characters reasonably detailed accounts of their part in the action. One reason for this affinity, it seems now, is the difficulty of pinning them down. Not only *daimōn*, but also *Zeus* is a very vague term when it stands alone. Like all words, these two have a certain meaning in their own right, but they become much more meaningful when they are made more specific in one way or another: one because it is overdetermined, the other because it tends towards the undetermined.

This brings me to the end of my discussion of the ways in which Sophoclean gods are named. A long time ago, Ove Jörgensen[49] pointed out that in the *Iliad* and the *Odyssey* there is a strong tendency for characters to speak of *theos* ('god', 'a god'), *theoi* ('gods'), *Zeus* and *daimōn*, leaving Apollo, Aphrodite and Co. largely to the narrative of the Muse. More recently, Jon Mikalson[50] observed that in popular religion it is common practice to use 'fate', 'the gods' in general or *daimōn*, rather than any named god, to explain events. The last twenty-five or so pages of my discussion suggest that Sophoclean characters resemble their Homeric and real-life counterparts in this respect.

---

[49] Jörgensen (1904).   [50] Mikalson (1983) 58–62.

I began by looking briefly at named gods other than Zeus, pointing out that most statements about their part in the action of a play are limited in various ways, and I suggested that these statements can therefore be interpreted as reflecting the difficulty characters have in speaking about named gods. I then went on to discuss *daimōn* as a word that points to this difficulty as it refers to a non-human force that is not, and perhaps cannot be, named. The ways in which characters none the less make *daimōn* more specific show their attempts to mark out a force which they do not, cannot or dare not name as distinct and perhaps even identifiable.

This observation about *daimōn* provided a starting-point for discussion of *Zeus*. It became increasingly clear that, although it is a divine name, *Zeus*, like *daimōn*, yields much more precise meaning when elaborated in some specific way than when not, whether in prayer, statements or otherwise. *Zeus* is not a name like *Erōs*.

Neither, however, is it identical with *daimōn*. At the same time as provoking characters to make him more specific, I argued, Zeus eludes their efforts. *Daimōn* changes as it (or he) is made more specific, but Zeus, to some degree, remains Zeus. *Trachiniae* suggests that characters who try to make him more specific risk missing some aspects of Zeus by specifying others. Sophoclean gods are not easy to speak about.

This is also true for spectators. They can of course themselves try to say more about the gods than the characters do. They can try, for instance, to gloss *daimōn* or compare various instances of Zeus with epithet. Thus they become able to understand more about the gods than any of the characters. Yet there are limits. To a certain degree spectators depend on the ways in which characters make *daimōn* or *Zeus* more specific, as is obvious from the different translations and glosses of *daimōn* in *Ajax*. An unspecific *daimōn* or an unspecific Zeus is difficult to make sense of. And where spectators gloss, their glosses, even the most certain ones, are merely glosses. In short, although spectators can always stand back and have a wider perspective on the gods than the characters, they are also bound to share, to different degrees, the characters' difficulty in determining the names of the forces to which they refer.

These conclusions can be weighed in different ways. Bernard Williams stresses[51] the 'supernatural power's lack of style' in Sophocles. This is, I think, a valid observation. Sophocles' gods are often rather numinous. Lack of names makes for lack of style. And yet, that is not all there is to be said. Even where names are missing, characters often speak of individual divine personages. Characters do not and, it might seem, cannot always put a name to them, but they often suggest that they perceive them as distinct entities. It is the large area between clearly identified deities and shapeless non-human 'force without style' that can engage spectators who try, at least partially, to convert the latter into the former. The language of Sophocles proves once more to adopt its characteristic mode of communication: letting spectators know enough to get involved but not so much that they would not wish to know more.

BLAMING GODS

The previous section suggested that references to named gods in Sophocles can be problematic in various ways, and that it is particularly difficult to speak about their part in the action. In such statements *daimōn* and *Zeus* are far more frequent than *Apollo*, *Aphrodite* and Co. I will now follow up these observations by looking at passages, and especially at the language of passages, in which characters do not just speak of the gods' part in the action, but hold gods responsible for what they themselves, or those close to them, have suffered; passages, in other words, in which characters blame gods. Since such passages are exceedingly rare, I extend the discussion from *daimōn* and *Zeus* to all gods, named and unnamed, at the same time.

Responsibility in tragedy has been a topic of long-standing interest. As scholars like Jean-Pierre Vernant have pointed

---

[51] Williams (1993) 165.

out,[52] responsibility was much discussed in the Athens of the fifth century BC. The most obvious area is probably the law-courts, in which citizens served as jurors, determining guilt and innocence. Works like Gorgias' *Helen*, which presents various differing models of responsibility for Helen's desertion of Menelaus, ranging from the power of the word to the power of Eros, suggest that both divine and human causes for action had their place in the discussion. In tragedy, *agōn* scenes, legal language and – my topic here – references to divine responsibility, can all be seen as expressions of this general interest.

Yet human and divine responsibility in tragedy has been studied not only for its historic specificity. Ever since Aristotle's influential remarks about ἁμαρτία ('error'), it has been a core topic of work on tragedy. So when I look now at moments when Sophoclean gods are held responsible, I am discussing one of those aspects of tragedy which have repeatedly offered spectators, readers and critics material for involvement. My aim, here as elsewhere, is to bring out some of the ways in which Sophoclean tragedy makes this involvement possible.

Trachiniae

I begin with what should by now have become familiar: the Chorus's (or Hyllus') 'none of this that (is) not Zeus' at the end of *Trachiniae*. In what is a highly unusual conclusion to a tragedy, Zeus is held responsible for everything that has happened. – But is he really? The Chorus (or Hyllus) could have been more explicit. 'None of this that (is) not Zeus', a literal translation would run; not (for instance) 'none of this that Zeus did not *do*'. This is a rather vague statement. Quite apart from the difficulties inherent in the name *Zeus*, it is far from clear what it means that Zeus 'is (the easiest verb to supply) all of this', let alone what it means, with a double negative, that

<hr>

[52] Especially Vernant (1988d).

'there is none of this that he is not'. There can be no doubt, the last line of *Trachiniae* is accusatory, but it is accusatory in a rather vague way.

What, then, about the preceding lines? When Heracles is carried off, Hyllus chants (1264-74):

> αἴρετ', ὀπαδοί, μεγάλην μὲν ἐμοὶ
> τούτων θέμενοι συγγνωμοσύνην,
> μεγάλην δὲ θεῶν ἀγνωμοσύνην
> εἰδότες ἔργων τῶν πρασσομένων,
> οἳ φύσαντες καὶ κληζόμενοι
> πατέρες τοιαῦτ' ἐφορῶσι πάθη.
> τὰ μὲν οὖν μέλλοντ' οὐδεὶς ἐφορᾷ,
> τὰ δὲ νῦν ἐστῶτ' οἰκτρὰ μὲν ἡμῖν,
> αἰσχρὰ δ' ἐκείνοις,
> χαλεπώτατα δ' οὖν ἀνδρῶν πάντων
> τῷ τήνδ' ἄτην ὑπέχοντι.

Lift him, companions, showing great sympathy with me in what has happened, and knowing of the great unkindness of the gods displayed in these events, gods who beget humans and are called their fathers but who look on such sufferings as these! The future none can see, and the present is pitiful for us and shameful for them, and harder than on any other man upon him who is enduring this calamity.

In various ways this passage is quite explicit in the way it holds the gods responsible, more so, one might say, than the 'None of this that (is) not Zeus' that follows almost immediately. The provocative phrasing μεγάλην ... ἐμοί ... συγγνω-μοσύνην – μεγάλην ... θεῶν ἀγνωμοσύνην ('great sympathy with me' – 'great unkindness of the gods', with a rhyme and a neologism in the Greek) puts the blame on the gods. The accusation is elaborated with κληζόμενοι πατέρες τοιαῦτ' ἐφορῶσι πάθη ('... who are called our fathers but who look on such sufferings as these') and finally driven home with the strongly condemnatory αἰσχρά ('shameful'): 'the present is pitiful for us and shameful for them'.

It might seem then that the lines preceding the somewhat vague 'none of this that (is) not Zeus' are much more explicitly accusatory. In some respects this is certainly the case, but even this passage – and it is probably the clearest condemnation of divine action in the whole of Sophocles – is not as explicit as it could be. First, there is once again a point about naming. The description of the gods as 'fathers' is a clear allusion to Zeus, but it is notable that Zeus is not named. 'Fathers', moreover, is a plural; part of the blame falls on 'the gods' in general.

Secondly the word ἐφορῶσι is worth a closer look: 'who are called fathers but who look on such sufferings as these'. 'The gods' (whoever they are) do not care to help humans in their need. This is a strong statement. But as though it was *too* strong the Chorus use the verb ἐφορᾶν again in the next sentence. 'The future none can see (ἐφορᾷ).' In between the various accusatory statements the Chorus point out that nobody knows what the future will bring, and in doing so, they use the same verb they used immediately before in calling the gods to account. For all the blame that undoubtedly falls on the gods, there is the sense that the case is not yet shut, and this sense will be all the stronger for spectators who are reminded of stories about Heracles' future deification on Mount Oeta.[53]

The Chorus's (or the Chorus's and Hyllus') statements at the end of *Trachiniae* are exceptional in the way they hold the gods responsible. Even so, it is notable that the accusations are in various ways left vague. It is as though the Chorus (and perhaps Hyllus) drew back from a full-scale accusation. A look at other passages will betray other characters drawing back much more clearly. What is only hinted at in *Trachiniae*, is quite obvious in some other plays.

Oedipus Rex

The first of these plays is *Oedipus Rex*. As I mentioned earlier, one of the rare statements in which a named god is said to

---

[53] Critics disagree over whether to take the Chorus's statement as an allusion to this event or not, and if so, what precise significance to attach to it. Most recently see Holt (1989) and Finkelberg (1996).

influence the action of the play is the one Oedipus makes in the *kommos* of *Oedipus Rex* (*OT* 1327–30):

Χο. ὦ δεινὰ δράσας, πῶς ἔτλης τοιαῦτα σὰς
ὄψεις μαρᾶναι; τίς σ' ἐπῆρε δαιμόνων;
[new stanza]
Οι. Ἀπόλλων τάδ' ἦν, Ἀπόλλων, φίλοι,
ὁ κακὰ κακὰ τελῶν ἐμὰ τάδ' ἐμὰ πάθεα.

Chorus   Doer of dreadful deeds, how did you bring yourself so to quench your sight? Which of the gods set you on?
Oed.   This (*tade*) was Apollo, Apollo, my friends, who accomplished these (*tade*) cruel, cruel sufferings of mine.

'None of *this* (*tauta*) that (is) not Zeus', the Chorus (or Hyllus) say in *Trachiniae*. Similarly, Oedipus holds Apollo responsible for '*this*' (*tade*), which he then specifies as τάδ' (again *tade*) ἐμὰ πάθεα ('*these* sufferings of mine'). What, then, is τάδε? Not least since the line opens a new stanza, spectators may make it refer to anything in the play, including Oedipus' parricide, his incest and the chain of oracles and events leading up to the present moment. With *tade*, however, Oedipus uses a pronoun which often points to something close by, while *tauta*, the word the Chorus use in *Trachiniae*, tends to suggest that the object that is referred to is more distant.[54] In the context, moreover, he is replying to the Chorus's question why he blinded himself. The exchanges that immediately follow are also restricted to Oedipus' motives in gouging his eyes out. In the first place, 'this' and 'these sufferings' refer to his self-mutilation. Whatever Oedipus' lines do, they are not an explicit statement of Apollo's responsibility for everything that has happened to Oedipus in the play.

So much for the question of what Oedipus is referring to. In continuation he says (1331–2):

ἔπαισε δ' αὐτόχειρ νιν οὔ-
τις, ἀλλ' ἐγὼ τλάμων.

But nobody else dealt the blow with their own hand (*autocheir*), but I (*egō*), poor wretch.

---

[54] This is not a strict rule: K–G I 641–3, Schwyzer II 209–10.

Rather than expanding on Apollo's role in his sufferings, Oedipus now speaks of himself, explicitly excluding all second-party involvement (*auto-*, *egō*). Moreover, and this is remarkable, he does not name a god ever again in the remaining 200 lines of the play, whether in accusation or otherwise. Even the old oracles have almost disappeared.[55] Oedipus curses the man who saved his life when he was exposed as a baby (1349–55), invokes Kithairon, Polybus, Corinth, his father's house, the place where three roads meet and his marriage (1391–408), but does not look for divine explanation. As Pietro Pucci says,[56] 'even if we assume that Oedipus' emphasis on the human initiator of his story does not efface its correlate divine agent, undoubtedly he puts the accent on the human side of his catastrophic life'. After Oedipus' strong exclamation, it seems, Apollo has withdrawn. As one aspect of his desperate situation, Oedipus bemoans the absence of gods: he is now ἄθεος, 'abandoned by the gods' (1360).

Oedipus has little more to say about divine responsibility. Have the spectators? As once or twice before, I will use critics as my guide. It has become a commonplace in the study of Greek literature that human and divine responsibility can co-exist. Sophoclean scholars are no exception. Albin Lesky, for instance, observes a 'tension between divine dispensation and liberty of action', referring to E. R. Dodds and R. P. Winnington-Ingram for support.[57] Of all Sophoclean plays *Oedipus Rex* has perhaps prompted most statements of this kind. Joel Schwartz,[58] to give a recent example, is not alone when he speaks about 'the dual agency or over-determination that appears to result from a careful reading of the play'. The notion of over-determination, or as it is also called, the double bind or dual motivation, is at the heart of much writing about *Oedipus Rex*. Yet Schwartz, Eckard Lefèvre, R. Drew

---

[55] There are references to θεός ('god') and θεοί ('gods'), on which see below pp. 193–4: 1432, 1438, 1445, 1472, 1518, 1519.
[56] Pucci (1991) 8, cf. Pucci (1992) 160–73.
[57] Lesky (1972) 273, my translation.
[58] Schwartz (1986) 188.

Griffith, Bernd Manuwald, William F. Zak and Arbogast Schmitt,[59] to name just a few of the recent participants in the debate over divine and human responsibility in *Oedipus Rex*, are none of them content to let matters rest here. In one way or another all these critics try to weigh up human against divine, or to combine the two sides in a new way.

One reason, I suggest, why there is so much disagreement over divine responsibility in *Oedipus Rex*, is the absence of Apollo's name from the end of the play. On the one hand there is much in the play that critics, and equally spectators who want to explain why Oedipus suffered what he suffered, may use for saying: 'because of Apollo'. But on the other hand nobody in the play, neither Oedipus himself nor anybody else, says so. The end of the play takes a different course and gives critics and spectators little material to confirm speculation about divine causation. Apollo is prominent throughout the play but not at the end. Earlier I cited John Peradotto's complaint about Apollo's 'unresponsive authority'. He, too, can be seen as reacting, among other things, to the lack of statements about Apollo's part in the action after Oedipus' 'This was Apollo', which itself, at least in the first place, is restricted to the blinding, and which is immediately qualified by emphasis on Oedipus' own action. If little is said about Apollo's responsibility in the play and if he is not even named near the end, it becomes difficult for critics and spectators to make him 'respond'. Of course, it is always possible to close the discussion by invoking 'dual agency' or suchlike. But as the reactions of Peradotto and others testify, this is to miss much of the dynamics of the play. Critics and spectators are first emphatically directed towards Apollo as a driving force of the play, but then do not get the confirmation they may desire.

Uncertainty over divine and human responsibility, including the sense of a divine authority that does not respond, cannot be discussed exhaustively in the context of the *kommos*

---

[59] Lefèvre (1987), Griffith (1992), Manuwald (1992), Griffith (1993), Zak (1995) 13–28 and 134–205, Schmitt (1997).

that follows Oedipus' blinding. Yet even this limited kind of discussion suggests that Oedipus is not alone in his despair at being 'abandoned by the gods'. Many critics, and in their own way no doubt many spectators, find it difficult to get the information they are looking for. Much in the play gives spectators knowledge about Apollo and his oracles, but in the end they need to infer many of the things they might want to know about him. At the end of *Trachiniae*, the Chorus (and perhaps Hyllus) accuse 'the gods' and Zeus, but leave their accusations vague. In *Oedipus Rex*, Oedipus accuses Apollo but then revokes his accusation immediately. Apollo, to put it metaphorically, is there to give his oracles but withdraws when he is blamed, placing responsibility all the more firmly with Oedipus.

Antigone

In order to see whether the Chorus (and perhaps Hyllus) in *Trachiniae* and Oedipus in *Oedipus Rex* are unusual in the way they speak about divine responsibility, I turn to *Antigone*, a play more of 'the gods' than of any one named god (apart, perhaps, from Hades). The character who has most to say about the gods is Antigone. Whenever she is on stage she talks about them with apparent ease. In the prologue, for instance, she gives various reasons for burying Polynices, including this one (74–7):

> ἐπεὶ πλείων χρόνος
> ὃν δεῖ μ' ἀρέσκειν τοῖς κάτω τῶν ἐνθάδε.
> ἐκεῖ γὰρ αἰεὶ κείσομαι. σὺ δ' εἰ δοκεῖ
> τὰ <u>τῶν θεῶν</u> ἔντιμ' ἀτιμάσασ' ἔχε.

... for there will be a longer span of time for me to please those below than there will be to please those here. As for you, if it is your pleasure, dishonour what *the gods* honour!

Whoever these gods are, Antigone speaks confidently about them. And later, questioned by Creon, she expounds the 'unwritten and unfailing ordinances of the gods' (454–5) in a passage that is too famous to require complete quotation.

Everything changes in the *kommos*, but it changes slowly. Near the beginning Antigone says (810–13):

ἀλλά μ' ὁ παγ-
κοίτας Ἅιδας ζῶσαν ἄγει
τὰν Ἀχέροντος
ἀκτάν,...

... Hades who lulls all to sleep is taking me, still living, to the shore of Acheron ...

For the first time Antigone speaks of herself as merely acted upon by a god, whereas before she presented herself as responding to divine laws. Her statement may not be as prominent as Oedipus' about Apollo, since Hades is in tragedy often almost indistinguishable from 'death', but, like Oedipus', it is corrected immediately. The Chorus rephrase (821–2):

... ἀλλ' αὐτόνομος ζῶσα μόνη δὴ
θνητῶν Ἀίδην καταβήσῃ.

... of your own will (*autonomos*) you alone of mortals while yet alive descend to Hades.

Antigone follows her own law, they stress, in going down to Hades. As in *Oedipus Rex*, *auto-* emphasises that there is no further participation, divine or otherwise, in the action.[60] This rephrasing is all the more remarkable for coming from a Chorus who have just been shedding tears at Antigone's impending death (801–5).

In the following stanza Antigone compares herself to Niobe, and then insists that she does not cause her own death (832–3):

ᾷ με δαί-
μων ὁμοιοτάταν κατευνάζει.

... very much like her am I, as *daimōn* sends me to sleep.

Antigone insists, but she does not insist on Hades, nor does she speak of Eros, Zeus or any other god one might think of. She does not name the force which she says kills her as it killed Niobe, and perhaps even points to the fact that she

---

[60] Cf. 875 *autognōtos* ('self-willed'); the speaker is again the Chorus.

cannot name it (*daimōn*). Yet vague as Antigone's statement is, it is left to stand no more than the one before. Without picking up on *daimōn*, the Chorus point out that Antigone, being mortal, should be content to have the fate of a demi-god (834–8).

Antigone feels derided. She invokes the ancestral gods, the city and its wealthy men as well as the fountains of Dirce and the grove of Thebes, and then exclaims (847–9):

> ... οἷα φίλων ἄκλαυτος, οἵοις νόμοις
> πρὸς ἔργμα⁶¹ τυμβόχωστον ἔρ-
> χομαι τάφου ποταινίου.

... how unwept by friends, under what laws I come to the heaped-up prison that is my strange tomb.

In the passage to which I referred earlier, the divine laws gave Antigone the reason to act as she did; now she laments laws that are bringing her to her grave. By now even *daimōn* has disappeared, and οἵοις ('what') makes her complaint an expostulation rather than a statement. All there is left is the faint allusion to divine participation in her death that may be detected in her reference to 'laws'. Finally, even this allusion, faint as it is, disappears in the Chorus's reply (856):

> πατρῷον δ' ἐκτίνεις τιν' ἆθλον.

And you are paying for some crime of your fathers.

Once again human responsibility follows a hint at divine involvement. For the time being, Antigone ceases to suggest non-human participation in her death. In the rest of the *kommos* there is nothing but humans.

Antigone's long trimeter speech after the *kommos* brings a condensed repetition of her preceding dialogue with the Chorus. Near its end Antigone levels the harshest of her attacks at the gods (919–24).

> ... ἀλλ' ὧδ' ἐρῆμος πρὸς φίλων ἡ δύσμορος
> ζῶσ' ἐς θανόντων ἔρχομαι κατασκαφάς·
> ποίαν παρεξελθοῦσα δαιμόνων δίκην;

---

⁶¹ The OCT has the less well-attested variant ἕρμα.

τί χρή με τὴν δύστηνον ἐς θεοὺς ἔτι
βλέπειν; τίν’ αὐδᾶν ξυμμάχων; ἐπεί γε δὴ
τὴν δυσσέβειαν εὐσεβοῦσ’ ἐκτησάμην.

... but thus deserted by friends I come living, poor creature, to the caverns
of the dead. What justice of the gods have I transgressed? Why must I still
look to the gods, unhappy one? Whom can I call on to protect me? For by
acting out of reverence I have been convicted of lack of reverence.

Again she does not name a god, and the three central sentences are questions rather than statements. But neither lack of names nor interrogative phrasing detracts from the doubts she voices about divine justice.

As ever, the accusation is not maintained. This time, correction comes not from the Chorus but from Antigone herself. She has begun retracting already with the word δυσσέβειαν ('lack of reverence'), and now goes much further as she continues (925–8):

ἀλλ’ εἰ μὲν οὖν τάδ’ ἐστὶν ἐν θεοῖς καλά,
παθόντες ἂν ξυγγνοῖμεν ἡμαρτηκότες·
εἰ δ’ οἵδ’ ἁμαρτάνουσι, μὴ πλείω κακὰ
πάθοιεν ἢ καὶ δρῶσιν ἐκδίκως ἐμέ.

Well, if this is approved among the gods, I should forgive them for what I have suffered, since I have done wrong; but if they are the wrongdoers, may they suffer no worse evils than those they are unjustly inflicting upon me.

This is in fact more than a retraction. Antigone speaks hypothetically (εἰ, 'if') and couples the hypothesis with a second one about 'these people' which is opposed to the first, but even so her sentence is remarkable.[62] Never before did she consider the possibility of being in the wrong as she does here (ἡμαρτηκότες, 'since I have done wrong'). Antigone's strongest accusation is followed immediately by the moment of her greatest self-doubt.

Antigone does not come back to the gods again in the few lines that remain to her. In her last words she insists on her εὐσεβία ('reverence'), but the context is a lament for the things

---

[62] Some critics, most recently Cropp (1997) 140–3, think that most of the weight ought to be put on the second hypothesis ('but if they are the wrongdoers'). Yet to deny *all* force to the first is to beg the question.

that humans, rather than gods, are doing to her (942-3):

> ... οἷα πρὸς οἵων ἀνδρῶν πάσχω,
> τὴν εὐσεβίαν σεβίσασα.

... what things I am suffering from what men, for having shown reverence for reverence!

Finally, even when the Messenger describes the scene of her death, there is no suggestion of divine involvement as there was at the burial.[63] The Olympian gods shun death,[64] and with it, it seems, at least in Sophocles, they shun blame.

Antigone, then, confirms what began to become obvious already in the brief discussion of the end of *Trachiniae*: Sophoclean characters do not blame gods unreservedly. More than that, however, there emerge close similarities with *Oedipus Rex*. Like Oedipus, Antigone is a character who has throughout the play more to say about the gods than many others; like Oedipus, she makes gods partially responsible for her situation and, like Oedipus, she does not maintain her accusations. Oedipus, moreover, is desperate and calls himself 'abandoned by the gods'. Similarly Antigone, to whom death was not a threat before,[65] laments her impending death in the *kommos* and asks in the trimeters 'Why should I still look to the gods, unhappy one?' (922-3). Reasons can be found for Antigone's despair as death approaches, as well as for her increasing self-doubt and for the Chorus's opposition.[66] What I want to stress here is that, as in *Oedipus Rex*, despair and the failure to speak about gods as confidently as before coincide.

Finally, and most importantly for the theme of this book, similarity between *Antigone* and *Oedipus Rex* extends to critics and spectators. Again there is the question of divine and

---

[63] Explicitly in the Chorus's θεήλατον ('prompted by the gods', 278) and implicitly, according to many critics, in the Guard's speeches: see above p. 134, n. 2.

[64] See *Il.* 20.64-5, Eur. *Hipp.* 1437-8 with Barrett *ad loc.* and *Alc.* 22-3; cf. Mikalson (1991) 27-8. Loraux (1986) 37 with n. 80 points out that Olympian gods are absent from funeral orations. It is notable that even at the end of *OC*, where the divine is omnipresent, the Olympian gods have no clear part in Oedipus' disappearance (they are suggested at 1653-5).

[65] 72, 95-7, 460-8.

[66] Critics often emphasise the Chorus's loyalty to, or fear of, Creon: see for instance McDevitt (1982) and Hester (1986).

human responsibility.[67] For giving any kind of answer, critics and spectators have to fall back on earlier passages, like Antigone's speech about the divine laws, and make them bear on the *kommos* and the following trimeter scene. The fluidity of references to divine involvement in the later scenes does not by itself provide a basis for discussion. Neither divine approval nor disapproval of Antigone's deed can readily be gleaned from the way Antigone and the Chorus speak, or fail to speak, about the gods. While in earlier scenes Antigone's pursuit of divine laws allows much thought about the rightness of both her and Creon's behaviour, now it is difficult even to find the right terms. What does 'responsibility', what does 'freedom' mean in this scene?

Electra and *Ajax*

It would be both possible and rewarding to go on looking at the same play and to ask what happens when Creon blames his earlier error on a 'god',[68] but what I want to do here is round off my discussion of the rare moments when characters hold gods responsible by looking very briefly at two further plays, *Electra* and *Ajax*. *Electra* differs from *Trachiniae*, *Antigone* and *Oedipus Rex*, in that Electra and Orestes, unlike Heracles, Deianira, Antigone and Oedipus, complete their project without suffering any visible harm. They avenge their father's death and regain control over the palace. There is therefore in this play no *kommos* or comparable scene in which characters lament what has happened in the play.

Despite these differences there are striking similarities. Throughout the play Apollo is prominent. Orestes acts on the stipulations of an oracle that is reported in the prologue (32–7) and, as I noted before, both Electra and Clytemnestra pray to Apollo. After the killing of Clytemnestra, Electra and

---

[67] The most recent lengthy treatments are Riemer (1991) and Zak (1995) 89–133.
[68] 1271–6. Note the Messenger at 1312–13 as well as Creon's threefold ἐγώ (1319–20) and reference to himself as 'useless' (μάταιος, 1339).

Orestes have a much-quoted exchange (1424–5):

Ηλ. 'Ορέστα, πῶς κυρεῖ τάδ';[69]   Ορ. ἐν δόμοισι μὲν
καλῶς, 'Απόλλων εἰ καλῶς ἐθέσπισεν.

El. Orestes, how is it with you? Or. In the house all is well, if Apollo prophesied well.

Orestes implies that Apollo is responsible for what has happened, but he does not go beyond implication. For some spectators this statement is likely to be elusive, for others affirmative of Apollo's control and even beneficial control. As before, I am interested in the context. It is striking that this is the only mention of Apollo after Clytemnestra's prayer. The absence of his name is particularly obvious when Orestes claims a function that overlaps with that of Apollo's oracle by speaking of himself as a μάντις ('seer', 1481, 1499). Similarly, Zeus, the other god prominent throughout the play,[70] is referred to only once in the last part of the play: Aegisthus invokes him (1466–7)

ὦ Ζεῦ, δέδορκα φάσμ' ἄνευ φθόνου μὲν οὐ
πεπτωκός·

O Zeus, I see a vision that has fallen not without the envy of the gods.

As Apollo and Zeus become rare, characters seize upon minor deities and anonymous necessity: Ares (1385, 1423), Hermes (1396), those long dead (1421), θεοί ('gods', 1484), μοῖρα ('fate', 1414). Even the few gods that are left vanish in the last lines, yielding completely to nameless compulsion: δεῖ ('there is need', 1494), ἀνάγκη ('necessity', 1497), -έον ('one must', 1502), χρῆν ('it is necessary', 1505), νόμοι ('laws', 1506). As in *Oedipus Rex*, characters do little to hold gods responsible. Again there is a strong reaction on the part of the critics. Few questions in Sophoclean tragedy have recently caused as much disagreement as those about the ending of *Electra*. As the gods are gone, I suggest, criteria have once again become difficult. In *Choephori* matricide is ordered by Apollo, as Pylades reminds Orestes, and is later punished by the Furies. In the

---

[69] The text is uncertain here.   [70] 149, 162, 175, 659, 766, 824, 1063, 1097.

final scene of *Electra* neither divine command nor divine punishment is prominent. Critics and spectators have to import both or either, and they are not told which. Preceding scenes and odes give them good reasons for doing so, but the difference between a god who is named and a god who is imported can make for uneasiness.

The last play in which I will discuss divine responsibility is *Ajax*. It begins with a deity visible to the audience.[71] Along with Odysseus, spectators learn from Athena that she saved the Atridae by disturbing Ajax's eyesight and deflecting his attack onto cattle. The prologue is anything but a simple piece of theatre, but so much at least is clear. What I want to examine briefly now are the ways in which characters in the rest of the play speak about this action of Athena's and its consequences. Is Athena held responsible for Ajax's madness, and is she held responsible for his eventual death?

In the previous section I discussed passages in *Ajax* in which characters speak of *daimōn* in contexts where 'Athena' might, along with other names, be thought to be a good alternative. These passages fit into a larger pattern. Surprisingly, it might seem, the name 'Athena', used by both Odysseus and Ajax in the prologue (14, 74, 91), does not return except for two instances in Calchas' speech as reported by the Messenger (757, 771); and Calchas is speaking about Athena's wrath, which will last only to the end of the day, rather than about her action in the past. The Chorus, replying to Ajax's dismay at Odysseus' supposed derision, says that everybody laughs and weeps ξὺν τῷ θεῷ ('according as the god gives', 383). Ajax, lamenting what has been and is being done to him, speaks of ἁ Διὸς | ἀλκίμα θεός ('the daughter of Zeus, the mighty goddess', 401–2) as well as ἡ Διὸς γοργῶπις ἀδάματος θεά ('the fierce-eyed, untamable goddess, daughter of Zeus', 450), and states that he will assuage the wrath of θεᾶς ('a / the goddess', 656). Tecmessa refers to a σκιᾷ τινι ('some shadow', 301) which Ajax talked to, and attributes her own and the

---

[71] There are various ways of staging her appearance: for discussion see Stanford on v. 15, Seale (1982) 176 n. 3 and Mastronarde (1990) 272–80 with nn. 76 and 96.

Chorus's suffering to Ζηνὸς ἡ δεινὴ θεὸς | Παλλάς ('the daughter of Zeus, the dread goddess Pallas', 953–4), while Menelaus perceives himself as rescued by θεῶν τις ('one of the gods', 1057) and θεός ('a god', 1060, 1128). All of these terms allow the more or less obvious gloss 'Athena'.

Between them, these passages suggest the interpretation that for most characters in *Ajax* it is not easy to speak of Athena after the prologue, but that Ajax and Tecmessa still hold her responsible in a way that is rare in other plays. Looking for an explanation of this exception, one can point to the fact that *Ajax* is the only extant Sophoclean play which opens with a scene in which a god appears as a character. Looking at the instances collected in the previous paragraph, one may note further that Ajax, who, together with Tecmessa, comes closest to naming her, twice refers to her as the daughter of Zeus. Zeus, of course, is not only his ancestor but also, as I suggested earlier, the god about whom characters speak particularly often and particularly freely. Although, in other words, using an expression that is most easily related to Athena, Ajax takes a first small step towards making divine causation more general and less clearly determined when he speaks of Zeus's daughter rather than Athena.

What then about Tecmessa (953–4)?

> τοιόνδε μέντοι Ζηνὸς ἡ δεινὴ θεὸς
> Παλλὰς φυτεύει πῆμ' Ὀδυσσέως χάριν.

Indeed the daughter of Zeus, the dread goddess Pallas, creates such woe for the sake of Odysseus.

When Tecmessa speaks of Pallas, she comes about as close as one can to saying 'Athena' without using that word, and she does so in a statement about the cause of her own and the Chorus's suffering.

In discussing this as a moment when a character holds a god responsible, the first thing to notice is that Tecmessa, not unlike Oedipus when he says 'this was Apollo', blames a deity only for one aspect of the disaster. She attributes the consequences of Ajax's death to Pallas, but does not speak about the death itself. More importantly, and again Oedipus is comparable, the lines that follow interfere with what she said. First, the Chorus concentrate entirely on Odysseus ('the much-enduring man', 956) and the Atridae (960), whom they imagine to exult in triumph. Tecmessa picks up the theme (οἱ δέ, 'they', 961). She then returns to Ajax's death but, while still bemoaning the bitter consequences for herself, she opens out a new perspective onto Ajax (966–8):

> ἐμοὶ πικρὸς τέθνηκεν ἢ⁷² κείνοις γλυκύς,
> αὑτῷ δὲ τερπνός· ὧν γὰρ ἠράσθη τυχεῖν
> ἐκτήσαθ᾽ αὑτῷ, θάνατον ὅνπερ ἤθελεν.

For me his death is bitter as it is sweet to them, but to him it brought pleasure; for he got for himself what he longed for, the death he wished for.

As with Oedipus and Antigone, Ajax's own motivation is stressed (αὑτῷ 'to him', 'for himself'; ἠράσθη, 'he longed for'; ἤθελεν, 'he wished for'). Finally the gods come back (970):

> θεοῖς τέθνηκεν οὗτος, οὐ κείνοισιν, οὔ.

He died at the hands of the gods, not theirs, no!

The dative θεοῖς can be read as either 'at the hand of the gods' (as in my translation) or 'for the gods'. The expression is vague and is one of the many steps that move Ajax closer to the gods after his death. What is more, not only does Tecmessa now associate him in some imprecise way with the divine, but she also switches from 'Athena' (or 'Pallas'), who is Ajax's enemy, to 'the gods', who provide a less clearly determined frame in which to place Ajax.

The partial disappearance of Athena after the prologue also has the potential to affect many spectators. On the one hand they know more than any character and are able to introduce Athena into the later events of the play, whether by glosses or otherwise. On the other hand various matters that may have seemed clear in the prologue become more uncertain as the play goes on. Athena leaves the stage with a general statement

---

⁷² ἢ is Eustathius' and Schneidewin's emendation of the MSS' ἤ. Since neither produces easy Greek, M. D. Reeve (Reeve (1973) 160–1) revived Nauck's deletion of 966–70. However, his suggestion has not been followed by recent editors. Dawe prints a lacuna before 966.

of divine love and hatred: 'gods love those who think sensibly and hate the bad' (132–3). Already here problems begin. The statement is not in any obvious way applicable to the prologue. For Ajax to be called 'bad' (κακός) the term needs to be understood in a rather particular sense.[73] Moreover it is unclear whether Athena 'hates' Ajax, and if so whether she is alone or whether she is joined by other gods. Many spectators are likely to hope for further explanation in order to know how to take this statement.

As the play goes on, such explanation does not come; rather problems are compounded. There is for instance the problem of Ajax's madness. In the prologue all the emphasis was on Athena as the cause of Ajax's disturbed eyesight. Now it becomes increasingly obvious that he has been mad in some sense already before – how otherwise should his night-time raid be explained?[74] – and moreover, at least according to Tecmessa, he is still abnormal once he sees clearly again (311–27). As Calchas speaks of Athena's one-day wrath, spectators may speculate about her involvement in his suicide, but no straightforward connection is suggested with the prologue. At the same time once again alternative explanations appear. Spectators hear the stories about the quarrel over the arms of Achilles and about the sword of Hector. They learn that Ajax is not a man who easily accommodates himself to change. Finally, they are told that he displayed hubris already in the past. The further the play moves on, the more difficult it becomes to take the prologue as the basis of an interpretation. Athena's involvement remains significant but becomes increasingly hazy.

The priest in the myth of Plato's *Republic* says to the souls who are about to choose their lots that 'responsibility lies with him who chooses. The god is not responsible' (αἰτία ἑλομένου· θεὸς ἀναίτιος, x 617e4–5), and Robert Parker begins an article on similarities and differences between tragic and civic religion with the observation that oratory and other genres fre-

---

[73] Winnington-Ingram (1980) 55–6.
[74] On the complexities of Ajax's madness see Winnington-Ingram (1980) 11–56.

quently stress that the *polis* enjoys divine benevolence and that humans alone are to be blamed for its misfortunes.[75] The *polis* will need more thought in the next chapter, but for now it is enough to say that the language characters use makes Sophocles' gods resemble that of the *Republic* myth as well as those of Athenian civic religion in that they appear ultimately difficult to blame. The characters themselves rarely hold them responsible, and where they do, they are vague, they qualify their statements or they are contradicted by the Chorus. Sophoclean gods, as I put it earlier, withdraw when accused.

Spectators can still think about divine causation by drawing on what has been said earlier in the play. Yet the text often fails to help them in deciding what weight to give to those earlier references to gods. In various plays one of the results is a critical debate about divine responsibility. Clear references to divine participation in some parts of the plays, combined with a distinct lack in others, are therefore one of the central aspects of the simultaneous impact and inscrutability of the divine that I have been trying to describe in this chapter. Enough is said about the gods to give them a significant role in the play, but at the moment that the role most needs defining much that previously appeared knowable becomes uncertain. In their different ways, spectators may engage in the attempt to uncover what characters leave unsaid. As they do, they struggle with gods that are difficult to ignore and difficult to grasp. Spectators can try to push forward the limits of their knowledge about them, yet they will never overcome them entirely. Once again, Sophocles' language communicates through a blend of what is said and what is not said.

Once again, the blend is both subtle and powerful. As characters and critics can say more about them at some points than at others, the gods become, as it were, alive. They seem to elude many efforts at holding them responsible and withdraw when criticised. Like the world behind the sentences and like myth and prophecy in *Philoctetes*, Sophocles' gods can be notably real, real enough to be a focus of many spectators'

---

[75] Parker (1997) 143–4 with n. 2.

attention. Whether they are the gods of a pious playwright or elusive forces whose part in the action is hard to determine, they can be real enough for all kinds of spectators to think about them, real enough to try to take guidance from them, real enough to despair at them and real enough to find them reassuring. Sophoclean gods are something around which to gather. Different spectators are bound to perceive them in different ways, and not all of them will use words like 'real', 'alive' and 'withdraw', or find them equally maddening or consoling. But many of them may still, I believe, engage with the Sophoclean gods' simultaneous inscrutability and impact. This is another instance of what I call communality among the different.

THE NEED FOR ACTION

I have suggested in the two previous sections that Sophoclean language makes the gods difficult to name and, even when they are not named, difficult to hold responsible for what has happened in a play. In order to set these observations in a wider frame, I will now conclude this chapter by broadening the perspective and asking in rather general terms how Sophoclean gods relate to human action. For this purpose, I will open out my discussion beyond the moments when characters name gods or when they blame gods, and range instead more widely over whole plays.

What one notices perhaps more than anything else when one tries to find a pattern in the divine–human relations that Sophocles presents, is the fact that again and again the gods initiate the events of the plays. They create the need for human action. In *Philoctetes*, for example, it becomes increasingly clear that the embassy that is trying to convey Philoctetes to Troy was sent out on the basis of a divinely inspired prophecy by the seer Helenus (note ἐθέσπισεν, lit. 'he spoke divine words', 610). Much of the action is taken up by various attempts to implement the prediction.[76] When all efforts fail

---

[76] On the prophecy in *Philoctetes* see ch. 3, pp. 109–30.

and the play seems to have arrived at a deadlock, it is again the gods that make action possible. Heracles comes as a *deus ex machina* and makes Philoctetes go to Troy to fulfil the plans of Zeus (τὰ Διός ... βουλεύματα, 1415) that he reports.

Also in other plays prophecies or, to be precise, oracles are involved in setting off events in the first place, most clearly perhaps in *Oedipus Rex* and *Oedipus at Colonus*. Much of the action in these plays is both initiated and taken up by Oedipus' attempts to make sense of various oracles and to bring them to fulfilment. In *Trachiniae*, too, an oracle makes the play start. Hyllus, urged by Deianira and the Nurse, leaves in order to look for Heracles when he learns about the oracle that Euboea, the place where Heracles is known to be on campaign, is also the place[77] where he will either meet his death or secure a forever happy life (73–93). The oracle does not have the same impact on the action as Helenus' prophecy in *Philoctetes* or the oracles from Delphi in *Oedipus Rex* and *Oedipus at Colonus*, but frequent allusions make it none the less clear just how important the oracle is to the characters' thinking and doing.[78]

The fifth play in which a prophecy or an oracle plays a significant role is different again. In *Electra*, too, much of the action is related to an oracle, but the relation is not strictly causal: in so far as it is reported at the beginning, Apollo's oracle sets the play going and gives spectators one criterion by which to judge what Orestes and Electra are doing, but its precise role is not easily identified. Electra learns about the oracle only late on and then only in a vague allusion (1264–70), and Orestes has been interpreted as having decided on revenge before consulting Apollo.[79] This lack of guidance from the oracle makes *Electra* problematic in a way that Sophocles' other surviving plays are not. The almost complete absence of Apollo and Zeus from the characters' statements in the end, which makes it so difficult to get a handle on that

---

[77] Reading χώρας in 77. See Davies *ad loc.*
[78] 44–5, 76–81, 155–74, 821–30, 1159–73.
[79] See 32–7. These lines have been much debated ever since Sheppard (1927).

scene, only takes to extremes what has been noticeable already from the beginning where the oracle is concerned.

In *Antigone* there are no prophecies or oracles, but here, too, the gods spark human action. Antigone buries Polynices in the conviction that she follows divine commands. Her memorable lines about the unwritten divine laws give much emphasis to the gods as a motivation for the deed that stands at the heart of the tragedy. Finally, the play in which the relation between gods and humans is least manifest is probably *Ajax*. As far as spectators are told, Ajax's decision to attack his fellow Greeks has no divine origin. None the less the gods are once again at least involved in initiating the action. Not only can Athena be interpreted as a *didaskalos* figure, because she appears at the beginning of the play, choreographing the action of the prologue,[80] but she also says that she has deflected Ajax's attack from the Greeks onto the cattle. Through this intervention she has set off a play taken up in good part by Ajax's reaction to the discovery of the Don-Quixotean nature of his campaign.

Divine commands, interventions and predictions play a role in all surviving Sophoclean tragedies. In some the role is smaller and in others larger, yet in all of them the gods initiate a significant part of the action. Correspondingly, those characters who act in response to the divine have the lion's share of the story. Oedipus dominates *Oedipus Rex*, leaving a smaller role and shorter story both to Jocasta, who recommends stopping the inquiry, and to Creon, who is not as immediately affected by oracles as Oedipus. Antigone, who hopes to follow divine laws, has more stage time than Ismene, who tries to dissuade her. When Electra plots revenge as Apollo had ordered (although she does not know), she outshines both Chrysothemis, who tries to dissuade her, and Clytemnestra, who tries to defend the *status quo*. Ajax, who acts (at least partly) in response to Athena, towers over a play that deservedly carries his name. Philoctetes, who according to the prophecy will go to Troy, and Neoptolemus, who tries

---

[80] Segal (1995) 18–19, Easterling (1993b) 80, Ringer (1998) 32–7.

to make him go (whether in conscious response to the prophecy or not),[81] have much more stage time than Odysseus, who does not want to get involved himself. Odysseus and Teucer, burying Ajax (not a god, but more than a human once he has died) as he wished, stay in the play longer than Menelaus and Agamemnon, who resist. And in certain ways, but this is where the limitations of generalisation become noticeable, Heracles and Antigone attract more attention than Deianira and Creon. Obviously, divine commands and predictions do not account for everything that happens in Sophoclean tragedy, but there is a strong tendency for characters who act them out, whether knowingly or not, to end up in the limelight. The gods initiate action and cause stories.

And yet, the reader might ask at this point, am I not presenting too optimistic a view of what can be known? Am I not, in fact, going back on my previous claim that Sophoclean gods surround themselves with uncertainty? How can I reconcile my earlier emphasis on divine inscrutability with the apparently problem-free narratological model of the last three or four pages?

The answer that I would give if questioned like this is the following: yes, it is often a rather certain and unproblematic thing to say that the gods *initiate* action and *cause* stories. Much less certain, however, and much more problematic, are the action and the stories themselves. It is difficult to know before the event exactly how divine commands and predictions will be translated into action. Characters have to learn what the consequences are of an action that gods demand or predict. The learning is often slow and the consequences disastrous. Ajax, Deianira, Heracles and Antigone die, Creon has his family destroyed, Oedipus blinds himself and is exiled, and so on.

And even when all is said and done, endless questions remain for spectators to wonder about. Does Oedipus in *Oedipus Rex*, trying to make sense of oracles, act for the best of the city? Should Antigone, hoping to respond to divine will by

---

[81] On Neoptolemus and the prophecy see ch. 3, pp. 127-30.

burying Polynices, yield to Creon? Is Electra, (unknowingly) enacting an oracle, justified in attacking Clytemnestra? Does Ajax, pursued by Athena's wrath, neglect Tecmessa's and the sailors' needs when he kills himself? Is Oedipus in *Oedipus at Colonus*, acting at the prompting of an oracle, wrong to ignore the claims that Thebes may have over him? What will happen to Philoctetes when, yielding to Heracles' command, he arrives at Troy and meets his old enemies? Do all these characters do exactly what the gods want them to do, and do they do what other humans want them to do? Sophoclean gods often demand or predict action. Doing so, they make plays happen and create a frame in which to ask questions. What they do not do is to say what shape the play will take, or to give answers to the questions that the play may pose.[82] What they fail to do is as characteristic of Sophoclean gods as what they do.

The difficulty of making statements about named gods' involvement in the action and of holding gods responsible for what has happened turns out to be complementary to the need for action that gods create. Sophoclean gods, as it were, look forward rather than backward. They can often rather easily be connected, causally or otherwise, with the beginning of an action, while their involvement in the details of the action itself and in the often disastrous consequences tends to be more difficult to grasp. They are there when humans set out to act, but do not stay to see what happens. Sophoclean gods are always on the move – whether humans like it or not.

For a final illustration of these suggestions I return to the moments when action has come to an end. What happens when there seems nothing to be done any more? One possibility, perhaps the most obvious, is that characters look back, trying to account for what has happened. Gods, forward-looking as I have described them, tend to withdraw at those moments. Yet other characters (and it is probably unhelpful to demand clear reasons for the variation) keep looking forward at the same time as they attempt to make sense of the

---

[82] Similar suggestions in Schein (1997).

past. These are the characters whom the gods do not desert completely. Let me explain.

As I noted, one of the characters who look back earlier is Antigone. She is desperate at her impending death and tries to understand what has happened to her and why it has happened. Opposed for a while by the Chorus, she ultimately ends with emphasis on her own doing rather than divine participation. A rather different kind of situation arises in *Ajax*. After Ajax discovers that he has attacked cattle rather than warriors, he spends much time looking back. Unlike Antigone, however, Ajax does not stay with the past. Although he does not do what Tecmessa and his men want him to do, that is, stay alive and protect them, he sees his death not as the end of a story. Rather he gives detailed instructions for his burial and the future of Eurysakes (545–82). Ajax envisages action again, not his own, but at least that of his family and friends, in particular of Eurysakes, who is to continue Ajax's own life. And as he envisages action again, the gods come in. Immediately before killing himself, Ajax prays to Zeus and Hermes *chthonios* (824, 831–2) that Teucer find his body, so that it will not be exposed to the enemies. Again the gods are at the beginning of a new story.

Ajax's death, moreover, is an action in its own right. Where Antigone kills herself only after she has been led away and shut in to die, Ajax commits suicide centre stage and, certainly as far as humans are concerned, without being forced to. Here, too, the gods play a part. The action that is Ajax's suicide responds, at least at one level, to divine will: Ajax describes it in the deception-speech, with whatever intention, as an act of atonement to the 'goddess' (656). Calchas speaks later of Athena's one-day wrath (756–7, 778–9) and Tecmessa of a death for the 'gods' (970). In whatever way these passages are put together, it is clear firstly that Ajax turns from looking at the past to looking at the future, envisaging action that is partly his own, partly that of his family and friends, and secondly that again a divine will or plan is suggested.

As Ajax comes in touch with the divine again, he sets off the action that produces what some critics have called a dip-

tych play. A similar extension of the action takes place in
Oedipus Rex. George Gellie[83] summarises many critics', and
presumably spectators', opinion as follows: 'When Oedipus
rushes into the palace at line 1185 of the *Oedipus Tyrannus* we
have a sense of dramatic fulfilment which, most people would
say, is about as much as one play can offer . . . We are tempted
to ask no more of the dramatist.'

Various responses are possible to such a view (and Gellie
himself goes on to give his). What I want to suggest here is
that Oedipus remains receptive to some kind of divine plan.
Not all, but much, of what follows centres on Oedipus' future.
When he comes on stage again, he first looks back, trying to
make sense of what has happened to him. In this context,
discussed above, he says 'this was Apollo'. But he does not
stop there. Like Ajax, Oedipus does not just look back. He,
too, begins to envisage future action again. When Creon
comes, Oedipus asks to be exiled. At the same moment as he
stops looking back at the past, the gods are back. Apollo is
never again named, but Oedipus introduces his wish with
the invocation πρὸς θεῶν ('by the gods', 1432). In the ensuing
dialogue, Oedipus' possible exile is then made dependent on
divine will. Before granting Oedipus' wish, Creon declares, he
will consult 'the god' again (1438–9, cf. 1518). As many critics
have noticed, the oracle that the man who brought pollution
on Thebes ought to be exiled is never fulfilled.[84] Instead,
Oedipus comes under the prospective sway of a new oracle.

Oedipus Rex, like *Ajax*, does not end where critics or spectators may perceive, as Gellie puts it, 'dramatic fulfilment'.
The gods come back, and in Sophocles, where there are gods,
action and story do not end. Once again it is not clear what
kind of story this will be. The play ends before the new oracle
arrives. Will Oedipus be exiled, opening out the view onto the
events that some (at least of the later) spectators may know

---

[83] Gellie (1986) 35. References in his note 1.

[84] At least not in the play as transmitted. The lack of references to Oedipus' exile is
central to arguments about the authenticity of the ending. See Hester (1984), with
further literature in n. 1, and Davies (1991). See also Pucci (1991), Foley (1993)
and Kitzinger (1993) for recent interpretations using this lack of references.

from *Oedipus at Colonus*? Will he remain locked up in the house for many years to come, as some (at least of the later) spectators know him from Euripides' *Phoenissae*?[85] And what will happen to Antigone and Ismene, what to Eteocles and Polynices? The gods are on the move again. They guarantee *that* there will be a story but do not let spectators know *what* story this will be.

So I have finally returned to the spectators, and to the simultaneous inscrutability and impact of Sophoclean gods. Gods are one of the things that make Sophoclean plays reassuring despite all disaster: there will be a story, and with the story there will be a future. To the degree that spectators notice the essentially forward-looking drive of Sophoclean gods that I have tried to describe in the preceding pages, they can share the consoling sense that where there are gods, there is always a next step. Yet the next step is never simple. Divine commands and predictions produce problems that can puzzle spectators in all kinds of ways, and the ends of plays open up hazy views on new stories without producing them. Such puzzles and haziness can be as intriguing as the sense that there is a future may be consoling. Sophocles' gods can engage spectators, both by offering a future and by offering a future that is uncertain. In their different ways different spectators may find the gods and the future they promise both reassuringly reliable and maddeningly mysterious. Again there is much scope for communality among the different.

In order to look more closely at the promised future, I leave the gods and begin a new chapter.

[85] For what is known of Oedipus' story after the self-blinding, see *RE* suppl. VII 779–84. Most scholars now agree that Oedipus' connection with Colonus predates both *Phoenissae* and *Oedipus at Colonus*. See Mastronarde (1994) 24–5.

CHAPTER 5

THE CHORUS: SHARED SURVIVAL

INTRODUCTION

Through its characteristic way of communicating, I have argued in the four preceding chapters, Sophoclean language can give spectators the sense of having something in front of them, something that is 'there', as I put it, something around which to gather. The sentences suggest a world beyond themselves, and entities such as myth, prophecies, characters and gods may seem as real as they are invisible. The language of Sophocles gives spectators something to share, getting them all involved, each in his or her own way. This is what I have called communality among the different.

A corresponding situation to that which I have tried to describe in those chapters can be found in the tragedies themselves. As the group that is the audience gathers around something that is there in the plays, so the group that is the chorus confronts the individual characters with whom they share the stage. All ancient Greek drama presents such a model of communal response. The model is particularly pronounced in tragedy, where the named characters are set against choruses formed by anonymous *choreutai*.[1] These anonymous choruses are present during most of the action of the plays, watching, and to a degree interacting with, the individual characters. With few exceptions they speak and sing with one voice, whether as a choir in unison or represented by the *coryphaeus*.[2]

Choruses and the model of communal response they present will be my theme in this last chapter. They will provide a

---

[1] This is not always the case in comedy. In Aristophanes' *Birds* (267–304) all birds that form the chorus are introduced individually. For further examples of individualised comic choruses, not all of them certain, see Wilson (1977).

[2] The only certain exception in the surviving plays of Sophocles is *Aj.* 866–78.

suitable conclusion to the book since they will allow me to discuss communality among the different not only as communality of shared involvement but, more specifically, as communality of shared involvement *as part of a group*. In other words, the term 'communality', which I have used loosely until now for the fact that many different people in many different ways are all at times captivated by the way Sophoclean language communicates, will now be more narrowly focused as I discuss what might more properly be called a group experience.[3] My guiding question is how the chorus, responding as a group to the individual characters as they do, may engage spectators who are themselves members of a group.

A first answer, one that has proved fruitful over the years, goes back all the way to the *Problems* which antiquity attributed to Aristotle:[4] the individual characters, 'Aristotle' says, 'enact the heroes (ἥρωες); among the ancients only the leaders were heroes, the army (λαοί) ordinary humans (ἄνθρωποι). The latter form the chorus.' 'Aristotle's' theory has become influential in this century when Vernant glossed ἄνθρωποι by 'civic community':[5] 'thus the tragic technique exploits a polarity between two of its elements: on the one hand the chorus, an anonymous and collective being whose role is to express, through its fears, hopes, and judgements, the feelings of the spectators who make up the civic community; on the other the individualized figure whose action forms the center of the drama and who is seen as a hero from another age, always more or less alien to the ordinary condition of citizen'. Vernant, then, points to one way in which the chorus offer at least Athenian spectators as members of a group a way into the play: the spectators belong to the 'civic community' and can thus engage with the action of the 'heroes' as they see them-

---

[3] As a result, what I say about spectators in this chapter is probably less easily extended to readers than most of what I have said about them in previous chapters.

[4] *Problems* XIX 48.922b. The discussion over the authorship of *Problems* is summarised on pp. xxiii–xxx of the introduction to Louis's edition.

[5] Vernant (1988a) 24.

selves represented by the chorus. This is a powerful model, and one that will be fundamental to this chapter.

As it stands, however, it is too imprecise. No chorus in surviving Greek tragedy have the exact identity of the 'civic community'; most of them portray groups, such as women, foreigners or old men, which historians regard as marginal to Athenian society because they are marked off against the norm of the citizen, who is an adult male.[6] Moreover, it seems restrictive to say that spectators regard the characters in Greek tragedy as ἥρωες or as 'heroes from another age'. In some ways characters certainly are removed in time, but in others spectators can treat them as contemporary. The division into 'civic community' and 'heroes' does not work.[7]

More recent criticism has therefore abandoned attempts to match the chorus or any other character in Greek tragedy directly with the 'civic community' of the fifth century. Particularly relevant is the work of Mark Griffith. Drawing on narratological theory, Griffith suggests in a recent article[8] that 'in the absence of an external narrator, our point of view shifts incessantly and unpredictably back and forth with the different "focalizers" of the action'. Applying this framework to the *Oresteia* and in particular to Orestes' killing of Clytemnestra and Aegisthus, he explores ways in which tragedy appeals to both 'lower-class' and 'elite' spectators. More recently still,[9] Griffith has adopted a similar, if less strongly narratological, approach for investigating the role of kings and fathers in Greek tragedy. Using Aeschylus' *Persae* and Sophocles' *Antigone* as his examples, he suggests that spectators can criticise certain rulers in Greek tragedy and at the same time derive pleasure from, as it were, subjecting themselves to their rule. Griffith does not extensively discuss the role of the chorus as one particular focaliser, but, by implication, he suggests one

---

[6] As I will go on to argue, choruses are not always and not in equal degrees marked off against the civic community.

[7] For criticism of Vernant see Goldhill (1986) 267–8 and Gould (1996).

[8] Griffith (1995) 72.

[9] Griffith (1998).

way in which 'Aristotle's' and Vernant's statements can be adapted: by avoiding the glosses 'civic community' for the chorus and 'heroes from another age' for the individual characters, and instead discussing various ways in which various spectators can look at the action, he presents a generally persuasive model of audience involvement.

Criticism of Griffith's approach has concentrated on the way in which (at least in the earlier article) he differentiates between 'elite' and 'lower-class' interests. Nothing, for instance, would stop the 'lower-class' spectators using kings on stage as their 'focalisers'.[10] And inversely, as Simon Goldhill[11] puts it, one might 'hesitate before [Griffith's] image of the polis where the ordinary citizen "looks up to his 'betters' for protection, supervision, representation and direction"'. Yet with such modifications most critics writing on the political aspects of Greek tragedy, I believe, would accept Griffith's central suggestion that there is more than one way in which spectators can find access to the interaction of groups and their leaders. Goldhill himself, for instance, expresses this flexibility by using the term 'ideology'. 'There is necessarily', he writes,[12] 'a complex *dynamic* of contest and competition *within* what I have been calling civic ideology. On the one hand, the projection of other positions, the recognition of transgression, the expectation of competing arguments is part and parcel of democratic ideology. On the other hand, the power of ideological argument is precisely to frame and recoup difference in terms of itself.' 'Ideology', as Goldhill uses the term, provides enough space for each spectator to choose to react to a play from a particular political standpoint on one occasion, and at another time (or even at the same time) to adopt the opposing standpoint.

P. E. Easterling arrives at a comparable position by a different route.[13] She points out that many of the political terms

---

[10] Easterling (1997a) 24–5.
[11] Goldhill (unpublished).
[12] Goldhill (unpublished), his italics; cf. Pelling (1997) 224–35. In Goldhill (1990a) 'ideology' has still less room for contradiction.
[13] Easterling (1997a). The quotation is taken from p. 25. Cf. Easterling (1997c).

in tragedy are too vague to suggest rigid associations with contemporary politics, and terms this 'heroic vagueness'. Like Griffith and Goldhill, she highlights individual choice. Greek tragedy, she says, offers 'something for everyone in the audience. The fact that political, legal, and social issues are dealt with in language carefully integrated into the heroic setting enables problematic questions to be addressed without overt divisiveness and thus to be open from the start to different interpretations.'

The stress that Griffith, Goldhill, Easterling and others put on flexibility is instructive and helps to explain how tragedy can let spectators with differing political views all engage with controversial problems without threatening political stability in Athens. All these critics' suggestions will therefore provide building-blocks for my discussion in this chapter, and in particular Easterling's emphasis on the ways in which language creates 'vagueness' will be a recurring theme. More immediately, however, I notice that by trying to remove shortcomings from 'Aristotle's' and Vernant's model of the tragic chorus, I have gone further and further away from my original question: how do the chorus as a group engage spectators who are themselves members of a group? In the articles that I cited Griffith, Goldhill and Easterling, who set themselves different questions, give only partial answers. In the context of those questions, the chorus is not so much a group as one of the characters.[14] Moreover, I have so far focused on the fifth century and said hardly anything about the *modern* spectators' potential for involvement. And finally, I have not talked so far about the topic of this book: the language of Sophocles. I therefore restate my original question with more precision and ask again how the language used of and by the group that is the Sophoclean chorus may engage the members of the group that is the spectators – both in classical Athens and in contemporary Europe (and elsewhere).

I begin with a negative point. For many people today,

---

[14] The chorus's identity as a group has been stressed recently by Goldhill (1986) 268–70 and Gardiner (1987) 191, among others.

choruses are probably one of the most alien aspects of Greek tragedy. Many directors find them an embarrassment and spectators who are used only to a theatre of individuals find it difficult to engage with the songs and dances of the chorus. There is a good reason for this: modern spectators and directors are not familiar with choruses. Choruses are one of those elements of Greek tragedy which strongly point back to fifth-century Athens. Here choruses of all kinds were a prominent part of almost everybody's life. Most of all, they were part of young people's upbringing. 'Shall we assume, then, that people without education (ὁ μὲν ἀπαίδευτός) are people without choir-training (ἀχόρευτος), and that people with education (τὸν δὲ πεπαιδευμένον) are people with proper choir-training (ἱκανῶς κεχορευκότα)?', Plato makes the Athenian Stranger ask in the Laws.[15] A wide variety of male and female choruses drawn from different age groups performed at many festivals all over ancient Greece and were an important aspect of public life.[16] Particularly prominent at Athens were the dithyrambic performances by ten choirs of fifty boys and ten choirs of fifty men and, of course, the choruses of tragedy and comedy.[17] Participation in these choruses was subject to *polis* legislation, and the task of funding a chorus, the *chorēgia*, was a high-profile liturgy.[18]

This is why I begin with a negative point. Choruses will never have the same kind of attraction for modern spectators as they did for ancient ones. They will never be the same kind of focal point. Here, if anywhere, cultural differences bite. In this chapter, if in any, therefore, everything I say will need to be granted a large margin of flexibility.

And yet, if this margin is granted, there is again plenty of room for communality among ancient and modern spectators. Cultural context is not everything. There is much also in

[15] *Laws* II 654a9–b1.
[16] See Calame (1997), Herington (1985) and Stehle (1997).
[17] Dithyramb: Pickard-Cambridge (1968) 75–7 (esp. p. 75 n. 1, which quotes schol. Aesch. *In Tim.* 10); tragedy and comedy: Pickard-Cambridge (1968) 232–62 and Csapo and Slater (1994) 349–68.
[18] Legislation: MacDowell (1989); *chorēgia*: Wilson (1993).

Sophocles' choruses themselves, particularly in the language that is used by and of them, that can engage spectators – and engage not only ancient spectators but also modern ones. Sophoclean language has the power to convey the sense of communality that is embodied in the chorus not just to spectators for whom the choruses are part of their world. They can do the same, if inevitably with less intensity, for those to whom choruses are rather alien. The language that Sophocles' choruses use and that is used of them, I will argue, can prompt not only ancient but also modern spectators to use the chorus as one of their ways into a play, to use them, in Griffith's words, as their focaliser – to use them, in more traditional terminology, as a group with which they, members of a group themselves, can identify and sympathise or whose perspective they can adopt.[19]

In particular, I will put forward two arguments, both of which I will outline briefly straightaway. The first centres on the large off-stage group which is, I suggest, implied in all surviving plays of Sophocles. This large group, I will argue, has complex connections with the chorus. While never being the large group's straightforward representatives, the chorus are always in some ways part of it. *Oedipus at Colonus* will illustrate what I mean. Here the large group is the city of Athens, which is always in the background. The Chorus are introduced as old men (πορεύονται γὰρ οἵδε δή τινες | χρόνῳ παλαιοί, 'here come some men advanced in age', 111–12), and later their old age becomes manifest especially when they are unable to protect Oedipus and his daughters from Creon and his men (814–86). They belong therefore to a particular category of citizen, rather than being representatives of all citizens. Moreover the Chorus are characterised as locals of Colonus. They refer to Oedipus as πλανάτας | ... οὐδ' ἔγχωρος ('a wanderer ... not a local', 122–5) and try to remove him from ἐμᾶς χθονός ('my country', 234). Oedipus addresses them as τῆσδ' ἔφοροι χώρας ('guardians of this land', 145) and

---

[19] Recent literature on the Sophoclean chorus in general includes Burton (1980), Gardiner (1987), Rosenmeyer (1993), Esposito (1996), Scott (1996). The approach adopted in this chapter is closest to that of Gardiner.

Creon as τῆσδε τῆς ἐγχώριοι ('locals of this land', 871). They are thus inhabitants of a rural deme rather than of the city of Athens itself. A few times it is made clear that Colonus is distinct from Athens, where the Chorus send for advice.[20]

But there are not only contrasts. While being citizens of a particular kind, the old men are still citizens, speaking for all other citizens. They protect the shrine of the Furies, instruct Oedipus and his daughters how to pour libation, and value Oedipus' offer of a gift to Colonus.[21] And the differences between Athens and Colonus, as Easterling points out, developing her argument about 'heroic vagueness',[22] are blurred at least as often as they are emphasised. Theseus is ruler over both, the Chorus appear to respond to Oedipus' arguments about the reputation of Athens as a home for suppliants, and they divide the so-called Colonus ode equally between Colonus and Athens, without presenting the two parts as separate.[23] In this context it becomes obvious that many of the expressions that I just cited as establishing the Chorus's connections with Colonus do not in the least exclude Athens. There is, for instance, no reason why ἔγχωρος ('local') should not cover Athenians. Similarly, ἐμὴ χθών and ἥδε χθών ('my' and 'this land') are not necessarily confined to Colonus. Antigone once even calls them ἄστοι ('townsmen', 171), a term which points to Athens if anywhere. Much more could be said about the large group and the Chorus in *Oedipus at Colonus*, but even this short paragraph should be able to give an impression of the kind of thing I shall be interested in. A number of factors, and language is a particularly prominent one, conspire to keep Chorus and large group continuous in some ways, despite marking them off from one another in others.

It is this partial continuity that is central to my argument. There are three reasons, I suggest, why continuity with the large group may prompt spectators to adopt the perspective

---

[20] 292–307; cf. 67 and 77–80.
[21] Protection of the shrine: 118–236. Libation: 461–509. Interest in Oedipus' gift: 292–5, 461–4, 629–30, 1496–9.
[22] Easterling (1997a) 34 with note 51; in more detail Easterling (1997c).
[23] Theseus: 67, 294–5. Athens and suppliants: 258–95. Colonus ode: 668–719.

the Chorus offer them. First, the large group is the only conspicuous group in the play. There is some talk of Thebes, but
that city never assumes a dominant role. On the contrary,
Theseus takes great trouble to sever links between Creon,
ruler of Thebes and prominent in the central scenes of the
play, and his city (911–23). In so far as they are part of the
only conspicuous group, the Chorus do not, either as friends
or as enemies, interact with any other groups. There is therefore no other group perspective offered to the spectators. The
Chorus have no rival for the attention spectators may pay
them as a group. They are part of the only group that there is
to identify with.

Secondly, the large group resembles the audience in so far
as it is too large to be counted. There are innumerable Athenians as there are (almost) innumerable spectators. To the
degree that the city of Athens (partially fused with Colonus) is
perceived as standing behind the chorus, the chorus are not
just fifteen individuals dancing on stage but belong, like the
spectators, to a multitude. This similarity may prompt involvement. The chorus are an obvious group for the audience
to identify with.

For ancient spectators, and this is the third reason I wish to
point to, there is also the question of the chorus's identity. As I
noted earlier, Vernant's gloss 'civic community' for the chorus
is too imprecise to be generally valid. Yet in plays like *Oedipus
at Colonus* the large group lends at least some support to
Vernant's case. The chorus are formed by old men of Colonus
rather than ordinary citizens but, as I have noted, they are at
the same time part of the large group and speak for the city of
Athens. It is more than likely that their links with Athens were
a reason for Athenian spectators to adopt their perspective.

The first, then, of my two central arguments is this: *Oedipus
at Colonus* is not exceptional. Not least because of the language that they use and that is used of them, the choruses of
all surviving Sophoclean tragedies are to a degree continuous
with the large group. Since this large group resembles the
audience as a multitude, as the only group in the play and as a
group whose identity brings it close to the Athenian citizen

body, it may help to make the chorus's perspective an attractive one for both ancient and modern spectators to adopt.[24]

Details of course vary. The precise identity of the large group and the nature of its relationship with the chorus vary from play to play. The body of this chapter will therefore be taken up by detailed discussions of the language used by and of the chorus in a number of individual plays. Yet before embarking on this discussion, I will briefly introduce my second argument. I began this chapter by drawing attention to the model of communal response on stage: the chorus as a group look at individual characters. Since then I have been concentrating on the chorus side of the model. Now it is time to give some thought to the other side. If my first argument suggests reasons why Sophocles' spectators might look together with the chorus and the large group at the individual characters, I ask now what they come to look for. What kind of perspective do the chorus and the large group have on the individual characters' action? Here Richard Seaford's recent *Reciprocity and ritual* [25] is instructive.

Seaford argues in great detail that 'the cult of Dionysos ... transmitted a pattern of action to tragedy: the self-destruction of the ruling family, expressed in the perversion of ritual, ends in benefit, and in particular in the foundation of cult, for the whole polis'.[26] There is much in both this claim and in the book as a whole that would repay extensive discussion. Most

---

[24] As elsewhere in this book, my aim is to say something positive about Sophocles rather than something negative about Aeschylus and Euripides (see the Introduction, p. 17). None the less, a brief look at their choruses is instructive. Some Aeschylean and Euripidean choruses are contrasted or even opposed to other groups, often groups that are close to the adult male citizen of Athens: Aeschylus, *Persae* (Persian elders – Greek army), *Supplices* (daughters of Danaus – sons of Aegyptus – Argives), *Eumenides* (Furies – Athenians); Euripides, *Hecuba* (female Trojan captives – Greek army), *Troades* (female Trojan captives – Greek army), *Supplices* (mothers of killed Argives – Athenians), *Iphigenia at Aulis* (women of Chalcis – Greek army) and, less clearly, *Bacchae* (foreign women following Dionysus – Theban citizens). In other plays the chorus, while not *set off* against other groups, are still not *part* of a prominent large group: *Prometheus Bound*, *Iphigenia in Tauris*, *Helen*, *Ion*. Needless to say, all these Aeschylean and Euripidean choruses can be as engaging as those of Sophocles. This engagement, however, will be of a different kind.

[25] Seaford (1994) 235–405.

[26] Seaford (1994) xix.

important in the context of this chapter is what Seaford says about groups. Like Vernant's suggestions about the chorus and the 'civic community', Seaford's argument does not fit all plays equally well. The dominant group is not in all plays a *polis*, and it is not in all plays benefited by the 'self-destruction of the ruling family'. Due attention needs to be given both to the ways groups are presented in each play and to the ways in which they gain or do not gain from the sufferings of the individual characters, but with this *proviso*, Seaford's attention to the pattern of individuals suffering and groups profiting brings out something that is characteristic of Sophocles, something in fact that is arguably more characteristic of Sophocles than of Aeschylus or Euripides.

As my first argument, therefore, is indebted especially to Easterling, so the second is an adaptation from Seaford. All of Sophocles' surviving plays, I will suggest, putting the emphasis on the groups' survival rather than the 'foundation of cult', give a certain degree of prominence to groups who are first under threat but ultimately safe, with individuals, who often suffer, playing an important role in the process. This suggestion is rather vague. Who are the groups? What does 'prominence' mean? What do 'under threat' and 'safe' mean? And what is the part of the individuals? Once again there are no universal answers. The second argument, just like the first, will need to be elaborated separately for each play. And just like the first, it will demand close attention to the language of the play in question. Yet what I want to stress straightaway is the great scope for involvement. Through its concern both with groups in danger and with groups in safety, Sophoclean tragedy has the potential of capturing the attention of many spectators. Spectators vary in their interests, their judgements and much else, but almost all of them, I believe, share a desire for safety and survival.[27]

---

[27] Again a brief look at Aeschylus and Euripides will help to bring out what is characteristic of Sophocles. In many of their plays the well-being of groups is no issue. In the two *Supplices* plays, *Heraclidae* and to some degree *Eumenides*, in all of which it is an issue, the groups under threat, unlike their Sophoclean counterparts, are contrasted with further, civic, groups. In two of the plays, moreover, in

With these preliminary remarks, I will now begin detailed discussions of the language of three plays. The plays that I have chosen are *Oedipus Rex*, *Ajax* and *Electra*.

OEDIPUS REX

Oedipus Rex opens with a silent crowd sitting on stage and wreathed with suppliants' branches (3).[28] Oedipus addresses the crowd as ὦ τέκνα, Κάδμου τοῦ πάλαι νέα τροπή ('children, latest to be reared from the stock of Cadmus', 1) and relates its supplication to the incense-burning, the performance of paeans and the lamenting that are going on in the *polis* (4–5): the stage crowd represents the large group that are the suffering Thebans. One man, the priest of Zeus, speaks up for the silent rest (9–10, 15). He describes the destruction the plague has brought on land and people and implores Oedipus to help them (40–2):

> νῦν δ', ὦ κράτιστον πᾶσιν Οἰδίπου κάρα,
> ἱκετεύομέν σε πάντες οἵδε πρόστροποι
> ἀλκήν τιν' εὑρεῖν ἡμίν ...

But now, Oedipus, mightiest man in the sight of all, all we suppliants implore you to find some protection for us ...

The Priest closes the scene with a prayer to Apollo (149–50):

> Φοῖβος δ' ὁ πέμψας τάσδε μαντείας ἅμα
> σωτήρ θ' ἵκοιτο καὶ νόσου παυστήριος.

And may Phoebus, who sent these prophecies, come to preserve us and to put a stop to the plague!

The Priest is taken up directly by the Chorus, who also pray for the large group. Incorporating elements of a paean, they

which questions over the safety of the group are particularly prominent, the group is destroyed rather than saved: *Persae* and *Troades*. The closest equivalent to Sophoclean stories is found in *Septem*, but even here much is made of the contrast between the women of the Chorus and the citizens of Thebes. In general terms, the 'security of cities' as a predominant theme of many tragedies is highlighted by Ley (1986).

[28] On the tableau at the opening of the play see Burian (1977) 83 and 91–4, and Seale (1982) 215–16.

sing (151–4):

> ὦ Διὸς ἀδυεπὲς φάτι, τίς ποτε τᾶς πολυχρύσου
> Πυθῶνος ἀγλαὰς ἔβας
> Θήβας; ἐκτέταμαι φοβερὰν φρένα δείματι πάλλων,
> ἰήιε Δάλιε Παιάν ...

Sweet-speaking message of Zeus, what are you that have come from Pytho rich in gold to glorious Thebes? I am prostrated, my mind is shaken by terror, Delian healer invoked with cries ...

As the silent crowd and the Priest leave, the Chorus enter to take over as the voice of the large group.[29]

Oedipus accepts the group's request (58–64):

> ὦ παῖδες οἰκτροί, γνωτὰ κοὐκ ἄγνωτά μοι
> προσήλθεθ᾿ ἱμείροντες, εὖ γὰρ οἶδ᾿ ὅτι
> νοσεῖτε πάντες· καὶ νοσοῦντες, ὡς ἐγὼ
> οὐκ ἔστιν ὑμῶν ὅστις ἐξ ἴσου νοσεῖ.
> τὸ μὲν γὰρ ὑμῶν ἄλγος εἰς ἕν᾿ ἔρχεται
> μόνον καθ᾿ αὑτὸν κοὐδέν᾿ ἄλλον, ἡ δ᾿ ἐμὴ
> ψυχὴ πόλιν τε κἀμὲ καὶ σ᾿ ὁμοῦ στένει.

Children, I pity you! I know, I am not ignorant of the desires with which you have come; yes, I know that you are all sick, and, sick as you are, *none of you is as sick as I*. Your pain comes upon each by himself and upon no other; but my soul mourns equally *for the polis and for myself and for you*.

Oedipus declares that he suffers as much as the suppliants before him, lamenting the *polis*, himself and them alike. More passages[30] could be quoted in which Oedipus' perspective and that of the large group are identical. There is only one communal wish: that the *polis* be saved. As Oedipus continues, it becomes clear that he does not confine himself to lamentation. After giving the matter much thought, he says, he has sent Creon to Delphi to inquire what Oedipus can do to protect the *polis* (ἐρυσαίμην πόλιν, 72). Oedipus has taken on the task of saving the large group.

Oedipus Rex, it seems, provides an open-and-shut case for my two arguments. The Chorus represent the large group

---

[29] Cf. 168–70, 190–4.
[30] See especially Oedipus' first speech to Tiresias (300–15) and compare 326–7.

which is a *polis* and thus close to the norm of the Athenian citizen body. This large group looks to Oedipus for rescue, and Oedipus has set out to do what he is asked to do. No tragedy survives in which spectators are given more clearly the perspective of a group under threat and, to judge from Oedipus' response, a group that is about to be safe. Yet even in *Oedipus Rex* there is much that complicates this perspective. Discussion of these complications will bring out in more detail what kind of group the large group is, and what kind of group-perspective spectators are offered, and what contributions Sophoclean language makes to all this.

Oedipus and the large group

The chief complication is Oedipus. As the play goes on, Oedipus gradually ceases to regard himself, and to be regarded, as the saviour of the large group. The development leaves its earliest traces when Oedipus declares his determination to find the person whose expulsion Apollo demanded. He adds (139–41):

> ὅστις γὰρ ἦν ἐκεῖνον ὁ κτανὼν τάχ' ἂν
> κἄμ' ἂν τοιαύτῃ χειρὶ τιμωρεῖν θέλοι.
> κείνῳ προσαρκῶν οὖν ἐμαυτὸν ὠφελῶ.

Whoever killed him may well wish to turn the same violence against me, so that in defending him I am helping myself.

Oedipus still does everything in his power to save the group, but he considers the implications for himself: Laius' killer might want to kill him, too.[31] Somewhat later, he accuses Tiresias of wanting to harm him (374–5, 399–400), and the victory over the Sphinx, which in the prologue was an act of delivering the large group (35–6, 47–8, and perhaps 104), becomes a contest with the prophet (390–400). Finally in the Jocasta scene Oedipus seems to have stopped thinking about

---

[31] Oedipus stresses his own perspective while still keeping it aligned with the large group's also at 252–63.

the large group's safety and is interested solely in his own identity. Three examples will serve to illustrate how this growing unconcern for the safety of the large group is brought out in the characters' language: the house, the changed usage of *polis* and the description of Oedipus as *turannos*.

At the beginning of the play the house is little distinguished from the large group. I have already quoted Oedipus' opening address ὦ τέκνα, Κάδμου τοῦ πάλαι νέα τροφή ('children, latest to be reared from the stock of Cadmus'): right from the start Oedipus regards the Thebans as his children, and as if to confirm this relationship, he uses a similarly familial expression at the beginning of his second speech (ὦ παῖδες οἰκτροί, 'O pitiable children', 58). Between the two speeches falls the long appeal by the Priest. Speaking of the plague, he says (27-9):

> ἐν δ' ὁ πύρφορος θεὸς
> σκήψας ἐλαύνει, λοιμὸς ἔχθιστος, πόλιν,
> ὑφ' οὗ κενοῦται δῶμα Καδμεῖον.

... the fire-bearing god, hateful Pestilence, has swooped upon the *polis* and harries it, emptying the *house* of Cadmus.

In this sentence it is hardly possible to distinguish between the *polis* and the Cadmeian house. For all the spectators know, the house out of which Oedipus stepped is the palace from which he rules over Thebes, and as his children all Thebans belong to this house.

This happy symbiosis does not remain undisturbed. Already at 223 and 273 the phrases 'all Cadmeians' and 'the rest of the Cadmeians' drop Oedipus as the father of his people and leave only Cadmus. More significantly, Oedipus gets a house of his own; he both establishes who the members of his family are and collects them on stage. The Priest and the silent crowd go, Tiresias leaves soon after, allowing Jocasta to fill his place, and Creon, who was a child of Menoeceus at 85, becomes the brother of Jocasta at 639. The Chorus on stage are the only remaining representatives of the large group. Now words meaning 'house' no longer have anything to do with the large group but refer to Oedipus' private house.[32] Jocasta and Oedipus go ἐς δόμους ('into the house', 861) as a couple, and while the δῶμα Καδμεῖον ('house of Cadmus') in the prologue included the citizens of Thebes, the Second Messenger now introduces his report of Jocasta's suicide and Oedipus' self-blinding by lamenting the Λαβδακεῖα ... δώματα ('house of the Labdakids', 1226, cf. 1228), the house of Oedipus' ancestors. Oedipus' house is finally cut off from the large group as Creon admonishes him near the end of the play (1429–31):

> ἀλλ' ὡς τάχιστ' ἐς οἶκον ἐσκομίζετε·
> τοῖς ἐν γένει γὰρ τἀγγενῆ μάλισθ'[33] ὁρᾶν
> μόνοις τ' ἀκούειν εὐσεβῶς ἔχει κακά.

Take him at once into the house! It is most in keeping with propriety that only kinsmen see and hear the sorrows of their kin.

Oedipus enters his house at 1523 to leave the stage to the Chorus for a tailpiece which was possibly addressed to the inhabitants of Thebes.[34]

As the play goes on, the 'house' changes from something closely associated with the large group into Oedipus' private domain. To have a house of one's own is not to be opposed to saving the large group, but it is to be more than a function of the large group and its safety. It is to have a life of one's own. My other two examples, *polis* and *turannos*, will add to this point.

At the beginning of the play the word *polis* refers to the group that needs to be saved, both from the Sphinx in the past and from the plague now: 'the *polis* is tossed by storms' (πόλις ... σαλεύει: the Priest at 22–3), 'raise up the *polis*' (ἀνόρθωσον πόλιν: the Priest at 46 and 51), '[how] I may protect the *polis*' (ἐρυσαίμην πόλιν: Oedipus at 72), 'this bloodshed that has brought the storm upon the *polis*' (τόδ' αἷμα χειμάζον πόλιν:

---

[32] Apart from the lines cited in this paragraph see 249, 434, 533, 637, 925, 927, 951, 1262, 1447, 1515. There are also references to Tiresias', Creon's and Laius' houses, as well as to Oedipus' home in Corinth.

[33] Lloyd-Jones and Wilson print Pflugk's μόνοις θ'.

[34] Following the scholiast on 1523, various scholars have attacked lines 1524–30. Dawe (1973) 266–73 makes a strong case for deletion (although his arguments about the references to the inhabitants of Thebes are unconvincing). *Contra*: Lloyd-Jones and Wilson (1990) 113–14.

Creon at 101), 'the *polis* is perishing' (πόλις ... ὄλλυται: the Chorus at 179), 'the nature of the sickness that besets the *polis*' (πόλιν ... οἵα νόσῳ σύνεστιν: Oedipus, 302–3), 'save the *polis*' (ῥῦσαι ... πόλιν: Oedipus at 312), 'destroy the *polis*' (καταφθεῖραι τόλιν: Oedipus at 331), and so on.[35] The first to use *polis* in a different way is Oedipus at the beginning of the Tiresias scene.

Tiresias enters at 300. Rather than fitting himself into everybody's save-the-group perspective, he demands to be sent home (320–1):

> ἄφες μ' ἐς οἴκους· ῥᾷστα γὰρ τὸ σόν τε σὺ
> κἀγὼ διοίσω τοὐμόν, ἢν ἐμοὶ πίθῃ.

Let me go home! You will find it easier to bear your fate and I mine, if you do as I say.

One of the things Tiresias does is to speak of Oedipus', rather than the group's, affairs (τὸ σόν; cf. 329 τὰ σά ... κακά). This distinction reverberates in Oedipus' reply (322–3):

> οὔτ' ἔννομ' εἶπας οὔτε προσφιλῆ πόλει
> τῇδ', ἥ σ' ἔθρεψε, τήνδ' ἀποστερῶν φάτιν.

What you say is neither lawful nor friendly to this *polis*, which reared you, since you are withholding this message.

Already, Oedipus' perspective on the group begins to change slightly. This is the first time that *polis* is not the group that needs to be saved but appears to exist without specific needs. It is not difficult to conjecture that Oedipus' statement is prompted by his wish to avert the plague, but rather than saying what he will do to save the *polis*, he uses the word in order to criticise a third party.

This becomes more obvious as anger comes into play (337–40):

> Τε. ὀργὴν ἐμέμψω τὴν ἐμήν, τὴν σὴν δ' ὁμοῦ
> ναίουσαν οὐ κατεῖδες, ἀλλ' ἐμὲ ψέγεις.
> Οι. τίς γὰρ τοιαῦτ' ἂν οὐκ ἂν ὀργίζοιτ' ἔπη
> κλύων, ἃ νῦν σὺ τήνδ' ἀτιμάζεις πόλιν;

---

[35] Cf., less pronounced, 4, 28, 64, 165.

Teir.   You find fault with my *temper*, but you have not seen your own that lives with you, and you blame me.

Oed.   Why, who would not *lose his temper*, hearing such words as those with which *you now show disrespect for this* polis.

Oedipus' claim that Tiresias fails to honour the *polis may* imply the claim that he fails to save it. But more immediately, it serves as an explanation for Oedipus' temper. His wish to save the *polis* disappears behind his anger. After these lines Oedipus never again speaks of the *polis* as something threatened or something to be saved. The one time he does, he refers to what he did in the past: 'I preserved this *polis*' (443).

The last passage in which Oedipus uses the word *polis* is perhaps the most remarkable. His quarrel with Creon, which ultimately provokes Jocasta's intervention, culminates as follows (628–30):

> Κρ.   εἰ δὲ ξυνίης μηδέν;   Οι. ἀρκτέον γ' ὅμως.
> Κρ.   οὔτοι κακῶς γ' ἄρχοντος.   Οι. ὦ πόλις πόλις.
> Κρ.   κἀμοὶ πόλεως μέτεστιν, οὐχὶ σοὶ μόνῳ.

Creon   But if you understand nothing?   Oed. None the less, I have to rule!
Creon   Not if you rule badly!   Oed. *O polis, polis!*
Creon   But I too have a share in the *polis*, and not you alone.

Oedipus' expostulation can be taken in a number of ways. Creon appears to link it with Oedipus' insistence on his rule (ἀρχή) in the previous line. He thus evokes a moment in the exchange with Tiresias when Oedipus stressed that the *polis* put the rule into his hands without him asking for it (383–4). Oedipus has gone a long way from seeing the *polis* as the group he tries to save. Rather, he now sees it as a group over which he can rule. Alternatively, Oedipus' exclamation might be interpreted as a call for protection by the *polis*, as what is generally known as βοή.[36] As Creon implies that Oedipus is a bad ruler and therefore has no right to rule, Oedipus feels threatened and turns to the *polis* for help. Finally, there is a

---

[36] This is the most likely reading of Oedipus' 'O *polis*' at *OC* 834 (also in a dispute with Creon). In that play the development is reversed. Oedipus originally seeks the protection of the *polis*, and increasingly emerges as its saviour. He himself is saved more by Theseus than by the group. The classic discussion of βοή is Schulze (1966).

third way of understanding the line. Creon's implicit refusal to accept Oedipus as king might be a sign of *stasis*. In invoking the *polis* Oedipus might therefore plausibly be regarded as lamenting its dissolution.[37] All these ways of binding 'O *polis, polis*' into its context are possible. Rather than trying to decide which is the best of them, I wish to stress something that they have in common: Oedipus has stopped looking for good at the *polis* as its potential saviour.

In *Oedipus Rex* the word *polis* is a gauge of a character's relation with the large group. The Chorus, as part of the large group, always use *polis* of the group that wants to be saved. Jocasta and Creon, by contrast, never do so. For them the well-being of the large group is a lesser concern.[38] For Oedipus the *polis* needs saving at the beginning of the play, but not at the end. He is a saviour, if a problematic one. Michel Woronoff,[39] in an article that tries to classify all Sophoclean instances of *polis*, says that 'by preference, Sophocles uses *polis* when the city is defined as an entity viewed from the outside, *which is attacked or defended*, regarded as something that is alive, *capable of suffering and complaining*'. This generalisation suggests that it would be an interesting project to look at *all* Sophoclean plays, taking the usage of the beginning of *Oedipus Rex* as the unmarked way of employing *polis*, and marking off all others against this norm. Such a study, I think, would both show that no other Sophoclean character complies with the large group's wish to be delivered in the same way as Oedipus at the beginning of *Oedipus Rex*, and make it possible to investigate the kind of things that happen when an individual's perspective differs from that of the large group. But as I am here concerned not so much with comparing Oedipus to other Sophoclean characters as with tracing

---

[37] For 'O *polis, polis*', lamenting the state of the city, see Aristoph. *Ach.* 27 and Eupolis fr. 219.2 K–A.

[38] Chorus 165, 179 and (less clearly) 880; Creon: 521, 630; Jocasta: 737, 850.

[39] Woronoff (1983) 90; my translation and emphasis ('entity viewed from the outside' translates 'entité extérieure à soi'). Many studies are available which try to elucidate the word *polis*; see Sakellariou (1989), Hansen (1993), Hansen (1995), Hansen (1996).

how the interest he takes in the large group's survival gradually fades, I turn to my third and last example, the word *turannos* and its cognates.

Oedipus uses a *turannos* word for the first time at 380–1:

ὦ πλοῦτε καὶ τυραννὶ καὶ τέχνη τέχνης
ὑπερφέρουσα τῷ πολυζήλῳ βίῳ ...

O riches and *turannis* and surpassing skill in a life much-envied ...

and later on he calls Creon a 'would-be robber of my *turannis*' (ληστής ... τῆς ἐμῆς τυραννίδος, 535) who tries to 'steal a *turannis*' (τυραννίδα | θηρᾶν, 541–2; cf. Creon at 588 in defence). Other characters refer to Oedipus as a *turannos* no less than six times.[40] These occurrences of *turannos* words make Oedipus stand out both from *Oedipus Rex* and from Sophoclean tragedy in general. Clearly, something is said about Oedipus as a ruler. But what is it?

It is impossible to determine one precise meaning of *turannos* or of *turannis*, the rule of the *turannos*. These are of course the terms that give us 'tyrant' and 'tyranny', but Greek *turannos* words have a far greater range of connotations than their modern successors. Often many of these connotations are present together in the same passage. This is also the case in *Oedipus Rex*. Critics have stressed a number of associations that may all be appropriate here. *Turannoi* are known, for instance, to be given to violence and hubris, and they often come to power as outsiders rather than by inheritance. There are moreover various parallels between the stories of Oedipus and those of a particular *turannos*: Periander.[41] At the same time, other scholars object to giving the word connotations which are too specific. They regard it as interchangeable with

---

[40] 408, 514, 873 (Oedipus not named: see below), 925, 939 (at Corinth) and 1095.

[41] Violence and *hubris*: Scodel (1982), Podlecki (1993). Outsiders: Knox (1957) 53–6, Carey (1986) 175–6 with a more wide-ranging and more nuanced discussion. Periander: Gentili (1986), Vernant (1988e). O'Neil (1986) lists various connotations of *turannos* words in archaic and classical literature, and gives references to further treatments. Parker (1998) traces a development in the meaning of *turannos* and tries to account for it. See also Nagy (1990) 274–313 for simultaneous eulogistic and pejorative connotations, and McGlew (1993) for a study of the 'discourse of tyranny'.

basileus ('king') in many of its fifth-century attestations, especially those in tragedy, and do not detect much more than a colourless 'ruler' where it is used in *Oedipus Rex*.[42]

There can be little doubt, then, that different spectators understand, and have understood, *turannos* words in *Oedipus Rex* in different ways. What I wish to do here is emphasise yet another aspect of the meaning of those words, an aspect, I hasten to add, which does not conflict with any of those that I have just mentioned. One of the first to formulate it was Aristotle when he wrote about *turannis* in its relation to other forms of government:[43] 'the best of these [*basileia, aristokratia* and *timokratia*; roughly 'monarchy', 'aristocracy' and 'timocracy'] is *basileia*, the worst is *timokratia*. The deviant form of *basileia* is *turannis*, in both of them power is in the hands of one man, but there is a great difference: *the* turannos *is interested in his own advantage, the* basileus *in the advantage of his subjects* (ὁ μὲν γὰρ τύραννος τὸ αὑτῷ συμφέρον σκοπεῖ, ὁ δὲ βασιλεὺς τὸ τῶν ἀρχομένων)' (my emphasis). For Aristotle, a *turannos* is a ruler who governs for his own sake, while a *basileus* governs for the benefit of his people.

One implication of this definition is that *turannos* words are not as such pejorative, but vary in their tone from speaker to speaker. A *turannos* himself may take a very different view of the benefits of *turannis* from those his subjects may hold: for him, after all, it is an advantage, for them it is not. As W. R. Connor says,[44]

[*sc.* in the Archaic and Classical periods] tyranny is commonly represented as a deplorable system of government which the citizens are advised to avoid. But tyranny can be viewed in a different perspective, from the point of view not of those ruled, but of the tyrant or aspiring tyrant himself. Greek literature does occasionally adopt this perspective. And when it does so, tyranny can appear in a favorable light.

---

[42] Burton (1980) 161, Winnington-Ingram (1980) 191–2. For the indifferent use of *turannos* and *basileus* in general see Andrewes (1956) 20–30.

[43] *NE* 1160a35–b2. Cf. 1134ab, *Politics* 1276a, 1279b, 1295a and Isoc. 8.91, all cited by Tuplin (1985) 356.

[44] Connor (1977) 98–9. He discusses *OT* briefly on p. 102. Carey (1986) 175–6 and Podlecki (1993) are in some respects comparable.

A few examples will serve to illustrate Aristotle's and Connor's observations. In one of the two earliest attestations of a *turannos* word the speaker of Archilochus 19W denies being interested in having a *turannis*:

> οὐ μοι τὰ Γύγεω τοῦ πολυχρύσου μέλει,
> οὐδ' εἶλέ πώ με ζῆλος, οὐδ' ἀγαίομαι
> θεῶν ἔργα, μεγάλης δ' οὐκ ἐρέω τυραννίδος·
> ἀπόπροθεν γάρ ἐστιν ὀφθαλμῶν ἐμῶν.

I do not care for Gyges and his gold, I have no envy, nor am I jealous of what the gods give, and I am not in love with a great *turannis*. For this is far away from my eyes.

Apparently a *turannis*, like the riches of Gyges and the gift of the gods, could serve as an example of something that everybody might be expected to want. Similarly, Solon makes an opponent mock him for not wishing to rule (33.5–7W):

> ἤθελον[45] γάρ κεν κρατήσας, πλοῦτον ἄφθονον λαβὼν
> καὶ τυραννεύσας Ἀθηνέων μοῦνον ἡμέρην μίαν,
> ἀσκὸς ὕστερον δεδάρθαι κἀπιτετρίφθαι γένος.

I wish I had ruled, acquiring immense wealth and being *turannos* over the Athenians for only one day. After that I would have been happy to be flayed into a wineskin and to have my family wiped out.

Many further passages in archaic and classical literature take the viewpoint of the *turannos* or of somebody who imagines being a *turannos*, and stress the advantage, financial and otherwise, of this position.[46]

Correspondingly, it can become quite clear that a *turannos* does not rule for the benefit of his subjects. Often *turannos* words are used by subjects who reject their ruler. Calling him *turannos*, they imply that he is self-seeking and therefore unacceptable. Particularly interesting for *Oedipus Rex* is a passage from Solon (32W) in which it is the prospective *turannos*

---

[45] Xylander's emendation of the MSS' ἤθελεν.
[46] E.g. Dion. Tyr. 2W, *PMG* 584 (Sim.), Pind. *Pyth.* 3.85, Thuc. 6.85.1, Eur. *Hec.* 809, *Ion* 626, *Phoen.* 506. Connor himself discusses (apart from various passages in Thucydides which are the subject of his article) the following passages as supporting his views: Arch. 19W, Arch. 23.17–21W (the other of the two earliest attestations), Sol. 33.5–7W, Aristoph. *Equ.* 1111–14, Soph. *Ant.* 506–7, Eur. *Phoen.* 521–5 and Pl. *Rep.* I 344b and x 619bc.

himself who adopts the subjects' viewpoint and rejects a *turannis*:

εἰ δὲ γῆς ἐφεισάμην
πατρίδος, τυραννίδος δὲ καὶ βίης ἀμειλίχου
οὐ καθηψάμην μιάνας καὶ καταισχύνας κλέος,
οὐδὲν αἰδέομαι· πλέον γὰρ ὧδε νικήσειν δοκέω
πάντας ἀνθρώπους.

If I spared the earth of my country, did not seize a *turannis* or use harsh force, thus staining and disgracing my name, I am not ashamed. For I believe that this way I shall win a greater victory over all men.

To seize a *turannis*, Solon implies, would be to use 'harsh force' and would be irreconcilable with 'sparing the earth of my country'. This passage brings out very well the fact that *turannos* words change their tone depending on the speaker's viewpoint. While Solon rejects becoming a *turannos* because of the harm this would do to the community, he implicitly acknowledges that it is generally regarded as advantageous for the ruler in the way he defends his decision to reject it: no, he says, 'I am *not* ashamed' (οὐδὲν αἰδέομαι) of refusing a *turannis* (as one might think he should be). For by refusing, he adds, he won a *greater* (πλέον) victory (than he would have done by becoming a *turannos*). Solon imagines the benefits a *turannis* might have brought him (victory and whatever is the opposite of shame[47]), but then adopts the community's viewpoint and rejects them.[48]

It goes without saying that not all cases are as clear as those quoted and cited above. Especially where the speaker does not adopt the viewpoint of either tyrant or subjects (as for example in much of the narrative of Herodotus) it is often difficult

---

[47] And, as E. Irwin points out to me, glory, if μιάνας καὶ καταισχύνας κλέος ('thus staining and disgracing my name') is taken with οὐ καθηψάμην, that is to say if Solon's *avoidance* of *turannis* and force, rather than his imaginary *desire* for them, is envisaged as a danger to his reputation.

[48] For further instances of *turannos* words where rulers are rejected by their subjects or by somebody adopting the perspective of their subjects see Xen. 3.2W, *PMG* 893, 895, 896 (all *skolia*), Aesch. *Ag.* 1355, 1365, *Ch.* 973, Eur. *Suppl.* 404, 429, *Hel.* 395, Hdt. 5.92.1, Thuc. 1.20.2, 1.222.3, 1.124.3. By contrast, *praises* of one's ruler are addressed to the *basileus* (e.g. Ion 27.1W, Tyrt. 5.1W). Zeus, who accounts for most occurrences of *basileus* in lyric, elegiac and iambic poetry, is polemically called *turannos* throughout *PV*.

to distinguish between *turannos* and *basileus*. Even such passages, however, do not usually *contradict* the stress on the *turannos*'s advantage which was first formulated by Aristotle and which has been elaborated by Connor as depending for its tone on the speaker's viewpoint.

Aristotle's and Connor's suggestions are borne out also by many of the Sophoclean passages in which *turannos* words occur. Again a *turannos* is rich (*Ant.* 1169, cf. *El.* 664), again he has a pleasant life (*Ant.* 506, *OC* 1338), and again he seeks personal gain (*Aj.* 1350, *Ant.* 1056). The *turannos*'s interest in his rule is particularly clear in two passages in which the old Oedipus uses *turannos* words when he criticises his sons' preference for their position over looking after him (τυραννίδα at *OC* 419 and τυραννεύειν at *OC* 449). In all these instances of *turannos* words[49] there is emphasis on the ruler's advantage. Depending on the speaker's perspective, this advantage is presented as desirable or deplorable.

What, then, about the Oedipus of *Oedipus Rex*? For him, too, I suggest, Aristotle's definition makes much sense. Oedipus is called *turannos* when his own advantage, rather than that of the large group, becomes the centre of attention. Again it is important to realise with Connor that the precise tone depends on the speaker's perspective. None of the speakers – Tiresias, Creon, the Chorus, the Messenger (or of course Oedipus himself) – look at Oedipus as a bad ruler who needs to be deposed. As critics have pointed out, there is no obvious pejorative connotation in the context of any of the instances. None of the passages attack Oedipus. Rather, what they do is draw attention to Oedipus' growing unconcern for the large group's safety. Solon uses *turannis* in order to stress that his perspective is that of the community. He imagines the advantage of the *turannos* but chooses that of the land and rejects

---

[49] The other Sophoclean instances are *Aj.* 749 (τυραννικὸς κύκλος, 'the *turannos*'s circle', presumably of the Atridae and Odysseus), *El.* 661 (the Paedagogus of Aegisthus; the choice of word may, but need not, be linked to the plot against the rulers), *Ant.* 60 (Ismene of Aegisthus, again with a possible hint at rejection of the ruler), *Tr.* 217 (of the god dominating the chorus), *Tr.* 316 (of Iole's father, when Deianira is interested in Iole's high station) and *OC* 851 (Creon of himself, stressing his decision-making power).

the *turannis*. In *Oedipus Rex*, by contrast, *turannos* words have almost the opposite effect. They start appearing (as I noted, in v. 380) at a time when Oedipus is a man who is more concerned with himself than with the large group, at a time when he sees himself as a ruler under threat, as an individual with an uncertain past and as much else, but not as a saviour.

The Chorus

The use of the words meaning house, the use of *polis* and that of *turannos* are all indicative of an Oedipus who is increasingly concerned with himself rather than Thebes. It would be possible now to think about reasons and ultimately even to ask in what way, if any, Oedipus may be regarded as responsible for the change he undergoes. But the subject of this chapter is the chorus and it is therefore to them that I now turn. Are they still the voice of the large group when Oedipus changes? Do they remind him of his original promise and beseech a chosen saviour who is reluctant to save them? In short, can spectators engage with the perspective of a group that wants to be saved when the saviour has abandoned his task?

When the Chorus first come on stage, I noted, they establish themselves as the voice of the large group with the paean-like opening of the parodos. They do not beseech Oedipus as the Priest did in the prologue, but, like the Priest, they make it clear that the *polis* needs protection when they pray to various gods. Then there follows the scene in which Oedipus quarrels with Tiresias and begins to develop a perspective in which the large group does not feature. Thebes, and its survival, is no longer the unrivalled centre of attention. At this point, the Chorus sing their first stasimon (463–511). Notably, they are no longer able to express their wish to be saved by a prayer: they profess that they 'cannot tell what to say' (ὅ τι λέξω δ' ἀπορῶ, 486). Accusations have been levelled against the man whom they know as a saviour and as being 'dear to the *polis*' (ἡδύπολις, 510) in the past. As the large group's wish to be saved by Oedipus has become problematic, the Chorus stop singing about the plague and instead ponder at some length the identity and whereabouts of the man whom Apollo pointed out, and debate what they should believe about Oedipus.

As a result, it has become more difficult to assume that the Chorus say everything they say on behalf of the large group. In their worry about the accusations they partially reflect Oedipus' changed perspective, and with an interest in the killer which is so intense that it silences talk about the plague they anticipate his increasingly self-absorbed murder inquiry. At the same time their worry is about the saviour of the *polis* and their interest in the killer is an interest in Apollo's oracle about the pollution of the *polis*; in these respects the Chorus still clearly represent the large group that wants to be saved. The ode joins Oedipus' and the large group's viewpoints and brings out some of the intertwining between them. There is no longer the unified perspective from the beginning of the play, when Oedipus, the *polis* and the stage crowd suffered alike, but the Chorus, here and, as will become clear, elsewhere, play an important role in holding together as much as can be held together. If they were to insist that Tiresias' accusations needed urgent pursuing in order to secure the large group's safety, Oedipus' position would become considerably more difficult. Through the Chorus, the large group's viewpoint moves to some degree along with Oedipus and holds on to him as the potential saviour.

In the first *kommos* (649–96) the Chorus face much the same problems as in the first stasimon, but the confrontation with Oedipus in dialogue makes differences of perspective more explicit. Oedipus glosses their request to spare Creon as the wish to kill or exile him (658–9). The Chorus show their concern for him when they express their horror at this supposition (660–4), but go on to worry about themselves and about the land (665–6, cf. 685, 694):

> ἀλλά μοι δυσμόρῳ γᾶ φθίνου-
> σα τρύχει †ψυχάν†.

But alas for me, the land (*gē*) that is wasting away tears my †soul†.

The interests of Oedipus and the large group are juxtaposed and separated by a 'but' (ἀλλά, 665). The prologue, in which everybody was concerned with the safety of the group, seems far away.

But Oedipus gives in, abandoning his threats against Creon ('well, let him go', 669), and thus continues to be amenable to the large group's demands. The voice of the large group and that of Oedipus are closer together again, and by the end of the *kommos* the Chorus are able to move from expressing support for Oedipus to demanding to be saved without a contrasting 'but' intervening (690–6).

Like the first stasimon, the *kommos* holds together the perspectives of Oedipus and the large group that wants to be saved. The reconciliation is made possible by Oedipus, who allows himself to be persuaded by the Chorus. Yet even so a return to the prologue's undistracted communal interest in the large group's safety is no longer on the cards. The Chorus speak for the large group that wants to be saved when they express their worry for the 'land (*gē*) that is wasting away' (γᾶ φθίνου|σα, 665–6) and when they end the *kommos* by recalling the help that Oedipus brought to the land (*gē*, 694) in the past, adding the wish 'now again may you waft it to safety' (696).[50] Oedipus does not decline their wish, but neither does he promise to fulfil it. What is more he does not even take over the word *gē* at any point in the *kommos* (let alone speak of *polis* as he did at the beginning of the play). Rather, he draws attention to the men on stage when he promises to let Creon off not for the sake of the large group in general, but out of pity for the Chorus in particular: 'it is your pathetic words [literally "mouth"] ... that rouse my pity' (671–2). As important, therefore, as Oedipus' openness to argument is the flexibility of the Chorus, who both speak for the large group and are an identifiable small group in the play. This distinction will become more pronounced later. For now it is enough to note that, as in the first stasimon, the Chorus are not just the voice of the large group.

---

[50] The text is uncertain at the end of the line.

The ensuing scene between Jocasta and Oedipus centres on Oedipus' identity, closing with confidence pending the Shepherd's testimony. When Jocasta and Oedipus have entered the house, the Chorus sing the famous second stasimon (863–910).[51] How can the large group make itself heard in this situation? The Chorus sing at some length about the threats it faces. They mention the *turannos* who is bred by hubris (873)[52] and say they prefer the kind of wrestling that is good for the *polis*. In strophe b they go on to ask why they should dance if a man who transgresses what is right in all kinds of ways is honoured. They do not speak of *polis* or *gē* in this stanza, but what they describe is the dissolution of much that the large group needs for its well-being. No longer, they complain, is there right and wrong and no longer are rites observed. Finally they conclude the song with ἔρρει δὲ τὰ θεῖα: 'the divine is gone'. The Chorus do not speak for the large group *that wants to be saved* any more but, in various ways, they can still be understood as the voice of the large group *under threat*, now lamenting its own dissolution.

'Lament', however, is insufficient as a description of this song. Almost everything the Chorus say is conditional; six times they use the word εἰ. Dissolution is only a threat. Possibly ('if...') it will happen, possibly not. There is still room for action. In various ways the Chorus recreate the enfeebled group. First, they pray: μοι ξυνείη ... μοῖρα ('may such a destiny abide with me...', 863), κακά νιν ἕλοιτο μοῖρα ('may an evil fate take him', 887), Ζεῦ ... μὴ λάθοι | σέ ('Zeus, may this not escape you', 904–5). To the degree that the Chorus pray they give the lie to their own diagnosis that 'the divine is gone'. Secondly, they sing and dance. As they perform the ode, they take the sting, or at least the poison, out of their question why they should dance.[53] Only when they stop

---

[51] On the second stasimon see especially Hölscher (1975) and Winnington-Ingram (1980) 184–200, and more recently Carey (1986) and Sidwell (1992).

[52] Thus the MSS. For present purposes Blaydes's ὕβριν φυτεύει τυραννίς makes little difference. See further Carey (1986) 176 with nn. 8 and 9 and Podlecki (1993) 9–18 with further references.

[53] On this question see Henrichs (1994/5) 65–71.

dancing is it all over and 'the divine gone'. Thirdly, the Chorus make normative decisions about who is in the group and who is not. So they expel the man who poses a threat to the group because he acts without regard for Justice and the seats of the gods: 'may an evil fate take him' (887). In the parodos the threat to the group was such that the group could not ward it off without help. Now they need again to pray and they end in despair, but in so far as the threat is that the gods have vanished, that the large group will dissolve and that it will lose its voice, the Chorus's song is at least a temporary cure. The Chorus sing about the threat to the group, but at the same time do much to avert this threat themselves. This self-help becomes important when one asks what the ode has to say about Oedipus, the man whom the group under threat once chose as its saviour.

The Chorus may be understood to concentrate once again on Oedipus as they make their normative statement about the offender against Justice and the seats of the gods, praying for his undoing. Much that they say applies to him: Oedipus has been called *turannos* by other characters. Especially in the preceding scene he has shown no concern for the group. And it is Oedipus' inquiry that has made belief in gods and oracles infinitely more complex than it was at the beginning of the play. The group, it seems, recovers its voice and recreates itself partly by abandoning its saviour, regarding him now as the man who threatens them. At last the Chorus seem to have stopped representing Oedipus' interests and to speak solely for a group that has turned against him.

Yet true as it is that Oedipus will eventually suffer to the advantage of the group's well-being,[54] it would be imprecise to say that in the second stasimon the Chorus give a voice to a group whose wish to be saved clashes with Oedipus' self-interest. The first thing to note is the fact that they do not name him. They speak about some man who threatens them

---

[54] Parallels between the plot of *OT* and scapegoat rituals and myths were pointed out long ago by Girard (1977) 68–88 and Vernant (1988c) 125–38; more recently see Foley (1993) and, for criticism, Griffith (1993) 96–101.

and who *may* be Oedipus. In fact the association of this man with Oedipus is difficult in many respects. Even if the *turannos* is identified with Oedipus, did Oedipus not 'wrestle for the *polis*'? Indeed for all that has happened in the play, it would be very harsh on Oedipus to accuse him of everything the Chorus are mentioning in the stasimon. In many ways, the group's re-creation is at the expense of a rather imaginary victim.[55] There is no overt clash between the interests of Oedipus and the large group.

On the contrary, in some ways the Chorus come close to sharing Oedipus' perspective at the same time as they are concerned with the threat to the large group. *Hubris*, they sing, begets the *turannos*. The word *hubris* is then glossed as, among other things, being too full, walking too high and 'rushing into necessity' (ὤρουσεν εἰς ἀνάγκαν, 877). Somewhere in the chain of events that produces a *turannos*, the Chorus suggest, there is compulsion in conjunction with an exposed position. Applied to Oedipus, this is a meditation on why the highly honoured king became a man more concerned with himself than the group: perhaps at one level it was inevitable (ἀνάγκαν, 'necessity'). Arguably, this is a feasible interpretation of much that went before. Be that as it may, the important thing to note is that the Chorus are thinking not only about the threat the *turannos* poses to the group, but also about what makes a *turannos*. And this question is at least as close to Oedipus' question of who he is as it is to the large group's fear of dissolution.

As in the first stasimon, then, the Chorus sometimes have a rather flexible vantage-point and thus are able to move along with many of Oedipus' concerns at the same time as giving a voice to the large group under threat. What I wish to point out is the fact that they do so partly by stressing that they are a chorus. Both when they draw attention to their dancing (896) and when they pray for 'purity in all words and deeds' (863–5), they point at themselves as a chorus. They do so not to the exclusion of the large group – neither dancing nor ref-

---

[55] This is the central thesis of Carey (1986) among others.

erences to auspicious speech are limited to tragic performances – but they none the less give much emphasis to the
fifteen performers on stage that they are. *Qua* generic chorus,
they ensure that, at least for the moment, the group keeps a
voice despite the threat of dissolution. And *qua* generic chorus, they also have the freedom to follow some of Oedipus'
lonely paths at a time when much points towards a clash
of interests between Oedipus and the large group. Like the
kommos, the second stasimon keeps together the perspectives
of Oedipus and the large group under threat and, like the
kommos, it does so partly by suggesting that the Chorus are
not only representatives of the large group: they are also a
chorus.

The rise of the Chorus's own *persona* continues when they
refer to their dancing again in the third stasimon (1092–5). As
before, the emphasis they put on their identity as a chorus by
no means prevents them from speaking for the large group,
whose members may also dance at festivals, but it is notable
that along with this emphasis there comes a disregard for the
large group's safety. More clearly than in the second stasimon, the Chorus's concerns are those of Oedipus. They let
themselves be infected by the enthusiastic confidence Oedipus
displayed when he portrayed himself as the son of Fortune
immediately before their ode, they sing about Kithairon, and
they wonder about his parents' identity. He is their *turannos*
(τοῖς ἐμοῖς τυράννοις) to whom they want to 'do kindness'
(1094–5) and, in a striking reversal of the parodos, they sing a
paean-like prayer which on this occasion is not for the large
group but for Oedipus (1096–7).

The further Oedipus moves away from the deliverance of
the large group and becomes involved in questions about his
identity, the more difficult it becomes for the Chorus to hold
together his perspective and that of the large group that wants
to be saved. They increasingly express the former and give less
and less room to the latter. At the same time, they put less and
less emphasis on their identity as citizens of Thebes, drawing
attention to themselves as a small group on stage instead.
Other characters contribute to the effect when they address

the Chorus. Earlier in the play the Chorus were included among the 'Cadmeians' (273) and 'men of the *polis*' (ἄνδρες πολῖται, 513). After the second stasimon, during which they recreated the group's voice, Jocasta has called them 'lords of the land' (χώρας ἄνακτες, 911), thus differentiating, at least to a degree, between them and the rest of the large group. Now this distance is increased further as Oedipus addresses them as 'elders' (πρέσβεις, 1111).[56] The Chorus are not just Thebans, but, more particularly, old men. Oedipus is stressing the Chorus's familiarity with the Shepherd, who quit service a long time ago (cf. 1117), but this particular identity which he attributes to the Chorus has a further effect: it allows them to turn their attention to Oedipus' well-being although it is now largely divorced from that of Thebes.

Concern for Oedipus' well-being also dominates the fourth stasimon (1186–1222), and the voice of threatened Thebes is again rather faint. Oedipus now serves as a paradigm (παράδειγμα, 1193) of the changeability of human fortune, and in strophe b (1204–12), again coming close to his own viewpoint, the Chorus sing about his misery and ask how he came to sleep with his mother. Intermittently (1200–3) they still call him 'a wall for my country, keeping off death' (θανάτων . . . ἐμᾷ χώρᾳ πύργος) and 'my *basileus*', and in that respect they might seem to represent the needs of the large group. But most of the verbs in that stanza are in a past tense (ἐκράτησας, 'you won a success', at 1197; ἀνέστας, 'you stood up', at 1201; ἐτιμάθης, 'you were honoured', at 1203; against καλῇ, 'you are called', at 1202), and past is also the perspective on Oedipus the saviour at the end of the ode (1221–2):

ἀνέπνευσά τ' ἐκ σέθεν
καὶ κατεκοίμησα τοὐμὸν ὄμμα.

. . . you restored me to life and you lulled my eyes in death.

As for the present, the Chorus wish they had never seen Oedipus and lament his plight (1217–20). Is this what the large

---

[56] Some manuscripts have the singular. See Renehan (1992) 361 for a brief discussion.

group says about Oedipus as they now look at him? Perhaps: the whole of Thebes, one might say, is mourning, wishing Oedipus had never set foot in the city. But if this is the large group's voice, then the large group has lost or forgotten the need to be saved. What makes it easier for spectators to accept this attack of amnesia is the recent stress on the Chorus as a small group on stage. The Chorus are no longer part of the large group in the same way they were at the beginning of the play. The emphasis on their specific identity as a chorus in the previous two songs and as old men in the previous scene (the latter is recalled by 'ah, generations of mortals' at the beginning of the ode) helps to suggest that the eyes that do not want to see (εἰδόμαν, 1217) and the mouths that lament (στομάτων, 1220) are in the first place those of the fifteen men on stage.

The longer the play goes on, the more rarely the Chorus appear to speak for the large group under threat. Increasingly they go along with Oedipus' quest for his own identity. Some spectators may draw the conclusion that the large group has been saved, but the end of the plague is never mentioned in the play.[57] There is no communal celebration of the kind that there is at the end of many comedies or even of the kind that there is at the end of Aeschylus' *Eumenides*. One of the contributors to this lack of finality is the Chorus's identity. The language they have used and that has been used of them has turned them, little by little, into old men and a generic chorus who dance and sing. When they are in the end more interested in the story of Oedipus than in that of the large group, who are they speaking for? The large group? Themselves? And who are they?

The audience and the large group

Let me begin with the large group. It is clear at the end that there is no longer a group that wants to be saved as there was

---

[57] Stressed most recently by Foley (1993).

for long stretches of the play, nor is there one that has been saved. Is there, one may wonder, *any* group beyond the Chorus? I will end this section by suggesting that there is, and that the group in question is all humankind, including the spectators. Unlike the Thebans at the beginning of the play, this group is not one that wants to be saved, but one that watches Oedipus.

Oedipus Rex is a play firmly set in the *polis* from the prologue on. But as it proceeds, it gains a further dimension and increasingly opens out to all humankind and thus to the spectators. In the Jocasta scene Oedipus declares that he would rather disappear unseen 'from among mortals' (ἐκ βροτῶν 831) than be found a parricide.[58] The Chorus demand in the second stasimon that the validity of oracles be shown 'to all mortals' (πᾶσιν ... βροτοῖς, 903), and in the fourth they address the 'generations of mortals' (γενεαὶ βροτῶν, 1186; cf. 1195) and make Oedipus their paradigm. In keeping with their stance as old men and as a generic chorus, both identities which make them appropriate commentators on human affairs, the Chorus widen the frame of reference more and more to humans in general. Membership in the large off-stage group is no longer restricted to the Thebans, but opened up to humankind at large.

This change has two notable effects. First, it does much to make the increasing concentration on Oedipus the man possible. For Thebes Oedipus is a saviour or a threat, for humans in general he is a paradigm whose thoughts and feelings may be of as much interest as his saving powers. Secondly, the widening of the large group draws in spectators. Any large group, I have suggested, invites spectators as members of a group to adopt its perspective. The difference at the end of this play is that the large group includes the spectators, whether ancient or modern, almost explicitly: they are as human as anybody.[59] Put together, this is to say that the

---

[58] 'Cf. 791–2: 'that I was destined ... to show to mortals a brood they could not bear to look on'.

[59] For the inclusion of the spectators in Oedipus' audience at the end of the play see Segal (1993) 27–9.

widening out of the large group at the end of *Oedipus Rex* involves an appeal to spectators *qua* humans to look at Oedipus the paradigm.

The Thebans, I hasten to add, are of course still part of the large group. In the third stasimon the Chorus invoke Kithairon, Thebes' local mountain, and in the fourth stasimon they sing of those happy times in the past when Oedipus was honoured, 'ruling in mighty Thebes' (1203–4). More explicit[60] is something Oedipus says after all has been discovered and after he has blinded himself. As the Second Messenger reports, he requests to be shown to 'all the Cadmeians' (1287–8):

> βοᾷ διοίγειν κλῇθρα καὶ δηλοῦν τινα
> τοῖς πᾶσι Καδμείοισι ...

He is crying for someone to unbar the gates and show to all the Cadmeians...

Clearly, Thebes is still there. But as the Second Messenger goes on, he reaches out further (1294–6):

> δείξει δὲ καὶ σοί. κλῇθρα γὰρ πυλῶν τάδε
> διοίγεται· θέαμα δ᾽ εἰσόψῃ τάχα
> τοιοῦτον οἷον καὶ στυγοῦντ᾽ ἐποικτίσαι.

But he will display it to you also; for the bars of the gates are being opened, and you shall soon see such a sight as would drive to pity even one who hates him.

Spectators can refer the two addresses in these lines to themselves as much as to the Chorus or anybody else. For them, too, Oedipus is a 'sight' (θέαμα). And immediately after, the Chorus take up the Second Messenger with 'O grief terrible for humans to see' (ὦ δεινὸν ἰδεῖν πάθος ἀνθρώποις, 1297), now explicitly reaching beyond 'the Cadmeians'. Similarly, Oedipus laments somewhat later that he is called husband of his mother by all 'mortals' (βροτοῖς, 1359) and wishes he had never shown himself to 'humans' (ἀνθρώποισιν, 1393; cf. 1408 ἐν ἀνθρώποισιν). The Thebans merge with humankind at large.

---

[60] Note also the tailpiece which is addressed to the 'dwellers in our native land of Thebes' (1524). There is, however, a strong possibility that these lines are spurious: p. 210, n. 34 above.

Throughout *Oedipus Rex* the Chorus offer spectators the perspective of the large group. For the most part this is the perspective of a group that is under threat and needs to be saved. None the less, the play does not tell the story of a group that is saved. Rather it tells the story of Oedipus, the chosen rescuer who gradually sheds his appointed role as he becomes caught up in the quest for his own past. Surprisingly perhaps, the result is not an open clash of interests. When Oedipus, who has effectively brought the plague upon Thebes, ends the play in misery, asking to be exiled, the Chorus are not triumphant. Throughout the play they move along with Oedipus. In the end the large group is widened out so as to include all humans as well as the Thebans, and Oedipus looked at as a paradigm and spectacle. The group that is saved never gets a voice. Until the end the fate of Thebes remains unresolved. The changing perspective of the Chorus is one of the reasons why there are many questions to be asked about what has happened and what will happen to both Oedipus and Thebes at all points of the play, and even when it is over.

But despite the questions with which spectators are confronted, the ending of *Oedipus Rex* also yields a strange kind of comfort. Here it should become clear why I say that Sophoclean tragedy gives prominence to groups under threat but ultimately *safe*, rather than *saved*. Thebes, I just noted, is never explicitly saved, but spectators who in the beginning adopted the perspective of the group under threat can none the less feel safe now. Partly, they can feel safe because the plague, while not declared to have stopped, is at least no longer mentioned. Partly, however, they can feel safe also because almost imperceptibly the perspective of the large group has shifted. Oedipus is now a paradigm more than he is a saviour, and the large group is no longer just Thebes but incorporates all humans. Spectators watching a play are always safe in so far as they are not part of the action. They can always suffer with the characters and still retain a certain distance from their suffering. The end of *Oedipus Rex* highlights this distance and reinforces the spectators' sense of security when the perspective of the large group shifts from that of Theban citizens under threat to that of on-lookers onto a spectacle. Of course the shift is never complete. The Chorus never lose their Theban connections, just as the plague is never said to abate. But this is exactly what makes this ending so effective. Spectators, both ancient and modern, are made to ask questions at the same time as they are transported from danger to safety.

When Max Reinhardt staged *Oedipus Rex* at Covent Garden in 1912, critics discussed, among other things, the enormous stage crowd that he used in order to extend the Chorus and the ways in which he made the audience part of the play, not least when Oedipus left the stage through the auditorium at the end of the play. One of the more hostile critics adapted Bentley's jibe at Pope's *Homer* to fit Reinhardt's production: 'It is a pretty performance, Herr Reinhardt, but you must not call it Sophocles.'[61] I hope that the preceding pages have gone some way towards suggesting that it may have been *both* a pretty performance *and* deserving of the name Sophocles.

AJAX

No other Sophoclean play opens with a group under threat in the same way as *Oedipus Rex* does, but *Ajax* comes close. After Ajax, Odysseus and Athena have left the stage, the Chorus enter and address the absent Ajax (137–40):

> σὲ δ' ὅταν πληγὴ Διὸς ἢ ζαμενὴς
> λόγος ἐκ Δαναῶν κακόθρους ἐπιβῇ,
> μέγαν ὄκνον ἔχω καὶ πεφόβημαι
> πτηνῆς ὡς ὄμμα πελείας.

But when the stroke of Zeus assails you, or a quick-spreading rumour voiced by evil tongues comes from the Danaans, I am greatly anxious and am fearful, like the troubled glance of the winged dove.

Repeatedly throughout the play the Chorus make it clear that their happiness and safety depend on Ajax.[62] As in *Oedipus*

---

[61] On Reinhardt's Covent Garden *Oedipus* and the critics' reaction see Styan (1982) 80–5 (my source for the quotation: p. 84).

[62] 164–6, 193–200, 229, 583, 900–2, 1211–15.

Rex, the chorus are under threat and, as in *Oedipus Rex*, they turn to an individual to be saved.

The Chorus are formed by Ajax's men (201), and as such they are part of the Greek army at Troy. The model for a sub-group of the army which has its own leader without being cut off from the whole is provided by the Myrmidons in the *Iliad*, who have a catalogue of their own after they have been armed by Achilles, while also figuring as an entry in the catalogue of the whole army (16.168–97 and 2.681–94). In this respect the Chorus represent the large group.

What is more, the Chorus come close to the Athenian citizen body. They are soldiers and thus citizens, and are in fact not just soldiers but sailors, the kind of soldiers that are immediately associated with Athens. Most importantly, they are Salaminians (596–608; cf. 134–5, 201–2, 1216–22). Their Salaminian origin not only almost makes them Athenians but evokes fifth-century ritual practice. At 565ff. Ajax gives the Chorus a role in conveying Eurysakes home. As many critics have pointed out, Ajax and Eurysakes received cult in Athens and on Salamis.[63] For all these reasons the Chorus's identity brings them as close to Athenian spectators as any chorus in surviving Greek tragedy. Were it not for the temporally and geographically distant setting, they might indeed be dangerously close to home.

The deadlock

The beginning of *Ajax*, then, appears to resemble that of *Oedipus Rex*. There is only one group: the Chorus-*cum*-large-group. This one group bears a certain resemblance to the Athenian citizen body, and it looks to its leader for protection. Yet it is obvious that things are not quite so simple. There are two problems: the large group and Ajax. I will begin

[63] On Ajax and Eurysakes in Athens and Salamis see Kearns (1989) 80–2, 141–2 and 164 with further references, March (1991–3) 3–4, and pp. 5–6 of Garvie's edition. On allusions to hero cult in the play see Burian (1972) and Henrichs (1993). Athenian features in general have been stressed most recently by Rose (1995).

with the first. Although the Chorus are part of the Greek army, they are not as unproblematically so as the Myrmidons in the *Iliad*. Ajax, their leader, is the army's enemy. Because he was not awarded Achilles' arms, he has slaughtered some of the army's cattle in an attempt to kill the Atridae, Odysseus and other soldiers. Even when the madness that Athena sent him has abated, Ajax calls upon the Erinyes not to spare the army (μὴ φείδεσθε πανδήμου στρατοῦ, 844). And the army, Ajax imagines, hates him (μισεῖ δέ μ' Ἑλλήνων στρατός, 458). The enmity between Ajax and the army is a recurrent theme.[64]

As a result, the loyal Chorus also draw a line between themselves and the army. They do not use words which plainly mean 'army', but when they speak with various degrees of enmity of the 'Danaans' (138), 'each hearer' (of Odysseus' report about mad Ajax) (151), 'fools' (162), 'such men' (164), 'Argives' (186) or 'enemies' (196), they clearly distance themselves from the army at large. Because of their affiliation with Ajax they (and, supposedly, the rest of Ajax's contingent) even feel under threat. At the end of the parodos they sing of their wish to escape because they fear stoning (245–56). The first problem, then, is that Ajax's men are continuous with the large group only in theory.[65]

The second problem is that Ajax is in no state to act as saviour. Unlike Oedipus, he never agrees to look after the Chorus. Far from being able to help them, he needs support himself. After he realises that he has killed cattle rather than men, he falls into gloom. Rather than being recognised as an outstanding fighter, he senses, he has become a laughing stock (364–7):

> ὁρᾷς τὸν θρασύν, τὸν εὐκάρδιον,
> τὸν ἐν δαΐοις ἄτρεστον μάχας,
> ἐν ἀφόβοις με θηρσὶ δεινὸν χέρας;
> οἴμοι γέλωτος· οἷον ὑβρίσθην ἄρα.

---

[64] Apart from the quotations in this paragraph note the following passages. Ajax hostile towards the army: 44–5, 175, 1055–6. Army hostile towards Ajax: 151–3 (Chorus speaking), 196–9 (Chorus), 409 (Ajax), 560–1 (Ajax speaking about Eurysakes); note also the army's threats against Teucer, as reported by the Messenger 719–34.

[65] Compare Vidal-Naquet (1988) 478–86, who asks 'où se trouve la cité?' and argues that there are no easy answers.

Do you see that I, the bold, the valiant, the one who never trembled in battle among enemies, have done mighty deeds among beasts that frightened no one? Ah, the mockery! What an insult I have suffered!

These lines contain much of Ajax's problem. Throughout the play he wants to be looked at[66] and is looked at,[67] but at this point the Chorus are alone in seeing him as the man he wants to be seen as, rather than cheering at his misery (ὁρᾷς, 'do you see. . .?'). They still rely on him and regard him as able to protect them. Their estimation of Ajax is unchanged and they go along with his condemnation of his enemies.[68] So it is unsurprising that Ajax calls them (349–50; cf. 359–60):

> φίλοι ναυβάται, μόνοι ἐμῶν φίλων
> μόνοι ἔτ' ἐμμένοντες ὀρθῷ νόμῳ . . .

Dear sailors, the only ones among my friends who still abide by the rule of loyalty.

In their rather different ways Ajax and the Chorus need each other, he in order to be looked at in the right way, and they in order to be protected. As the Chorus said themselves earlier on (158–61), the great need the small, just as the small need the great. As long as this symbiosis was working, the one's advantage was difficult to distinguish from that of the other.

Now, however, it no longer works, and Ajax calls on the Chorus to kill him (361). He does not give a reason, but about a hundred lines later he says the following (479–80; cf. 473, 505):

> ἀλλ' ἢ καλῶς ζῆν ἢ καλῶς τεθνηκέναι
> τὸν εὐγενῆ χρή.

The noble man must live with honour (lit. 'beautifully') or be honourably (lit. 'beautifully') dead.

---

[66] 351, 364, 379, 425, 462, 471.

[67] 66, 81, 218–20, 229–30, 346–7, 915–19, 992–3, and see below for the end of the play. Cf. Segal (1989–90) = Segal (1995) 16–25, who explores the different perspectives different characters have on Ajax. More generally, dramatic characters as the object of the spectators' and other characters' gaze have increasingly interested critics; most recently Hawley (1998).

[68] 150–7, 167–71, 196–9.

Ajax wants a life or a death that is beautiful. To judge from these lines, Ajax kills himself because he cannot have a beautiful life.[69] He is suffering from the discontinuity between Chorus and large group. Everybody looks at him, but only some look at him in the right way, and this is no basis for a beautiful life. For Ajax the judgement of arms continues. Then as now, the army does not see him the way he wants to be seen. Once he fought for the army,[70] but now he fails to fight even for his own men. The play opens with a deadlock: the Chorus are part of the large group only in theory; Ajax is not looked at as he wants to be; Ajax's men need, but do not have, a saviour. These are three aspects of one problem.

As a result, the spectators are offered on the one hand the perspective of a group that wants to be saved. On the other hand, the perspective is not as clear as that at the beginning of *Oedipus Rex*. The saviour shows little interest in saving and the Chorus are a problematic group. They are part of the large group but are opposed to the rest of it. Athenian spectators will notice that as armies, Salaminian or Greek, *both* sides have distinct civic affiliations, and all spectators will notice that the other side is in many ways justified in its hostility towards the Chorus.

Concord restored: (1) Chorus and individuals

Much of the play is taken up by moves towards breaking the deadlock and creating a clearer group perspective. In the rest of the section on *Ajax* I will argue that the Chorus, who at the beginning of the play seem to stand alone with their views on Ajax, are less and less isolated as the play goes on. They are both joined by individuals who, like them, are *philoi* ('friends',

---

[69] Whether or not his *death* is beautiful is of course a matter of debate. The notion of a 'beautiful death' carries strong connotations concerning the role of the warrior in epic, archaic and classical literature. See Loraux (1986) 98–118, Loraux (1982) and Vernant (1991c).

[70] 1266–87, also 617–20, 636–7, and (in a different way) the *Iliad*.

'relatives') of Ajax, and liberated from the hostility of the large group.

I begin with the individuals. Since the subject of this chapter is choruses, discussion can be swift.[71] First of all there is Tecmessa, who enters immediately after the parodos. She both cares for Ajax's well-being[72] and makes it clear that she cannot live without him.[73] As a result, she and the Chorus sometimes seem to speak with one voice.[74] Next, in the Messenger scene (719–865) the world at large intrudes into the small circle of Ajax's *philoi*. The Messenger gives instructions designed to ensure Ajax's survival, and he does so by quoting the seer Calchas and passing on orders given by Teucer. They all want to save Ajax.[75] Demands for Ajax's protection are growing increasingly rare, but a sense of dependency on the part of Tecmessa and the Chorus remains.[76] They still need him.

Both their hope to be saved by him, however, and their hope to save him are disappointed: Ajax commits suicide. From now on the focus is on the burial that Ajax has demanded, which Agamemnon and Menelaus try to prevent. Ajax has not stayed alive to secure the safety of his *philoi*, but in a different sense, he is still a source of strength for them. Between Menelaus' and Agamemnon's appearances Teucer sets up a tableau with Eurysakes, Tecmessa and Ajax, handing Eurysakes a lock of his own hair to be held along with locks of Tecmessa's and Eurysakes' own and admonishing the Chorus to support them (1171–84).[77] Ajax's dead body becomes the object of his *philoi*'s supplication (ἱκέτης, 1172,

---

[71] See Easterling (1993a) 9–17 for more; also Segal (1981) 142–51 on the reintegration of Ajax.

[72] See especially the discussion of Tecmessa's, Ajax's and the Chorus's happiness in vv. 257–83. Also 205–7, 323–30.

[73] 392–3, 496–9, 518–19, 585–95.

[74] 216–17, 263–81.

[75] Especially 778–9, 811–14.

[76] 791. Compare the Messenger at 737 and Tecmessa's and the Chorus's lament after Ajax's death: 891–960.

[77] On this passage see Burian (1972) and Henrichs (1993) 166–8, and see below. The paradox of Ajax's support for his *philoi* despite his lack of concern for them is elaborated, with a more psychological emphasis, by Taplin (1979).

ἰκτήριον, 1175). The danger has not yet abated[78] but, in complying with Ajax's commands, the Chorus, Tecmessa, Eurysakes and Teucer are able both to continue to look to him for protection, and to do so as a close-knit unit. Clearly, the Chorus are not alone: never before have they been so visibly part of a group.

Finally even the danger abates when the group of Ajax's *philoi* gains a further member. Odysseus re-enters near the end of the play and guarantees Ajax's burial (1332–5). As he makes Agamemnon leave the stage, the last dissenting voice is silenced and Ajax's corpse is surrounded only by *philoi*. At 1376–7 Odysseus declares to Teucer that he will in future be a friend (*philos*), just as he was once an enemy (*echthros*).

Even now, it is worth stressing, not all is harmony. Agamenon and Menelaus remain enemies. Menelaus indeed has left the stage with thinly veiled threats of further action (1159–60) and Teucer curses both of the Atridae at 1389–92. Even Odysseus is excluded from the burial itself. Teucer says to him (1396–9):

> τὰ δ' ἄλλα καὶ ξύμπρασσε, κεἴ τινα στρατοῦ
> θέλεις κομίζειν, οὐδὲν ἄλγος ἕξομεν.
> ἐγὼ δὲ τἄλλα πάντα πορσυνῶ· σὺ δὲ
> ἀνὴρ καθ' ἡμᾶς ἐσθλὸς ὢν ἐπίστασο.

But for the rest do you help us, and if you like to bring any other man from the army, we shall not be aggrieved. I will see to all the rest; but do you know that in your dealings with us you have been noble!

Clearly, some divisions remain. However, the predominant atmosphere in the final episode is one of concord. Menelaus never comes back to make true what he has threatened, Agamemnon who appears after him, yields to Odysseus with bad grace but without threats, and Odysseus, while excluded from the burial is invited to participate in the funeral ('but for the rest do you help us...'). Divisions remain, but they are carefully contained.

One indication of this newly found concord is an equally new consensus in the evaluation of Ajax. No longer are there

---

[78] In this passage: 1175–6.

two camps. Ajax is at last recognised by everybody as an outstanding man. Odysseus calls him 'best of the Argives' (ἄριστον Ἀργείων, 1340) and includes him among 'the best men' (τοῖς ἀρίστοις ἀνδράσιν, 1380), and Teucer speaks of 'the man ... in all things excellent' (τῷδ' ἀνδρὶ ... τῷ πάντ' ἀγαθῷ, 1415). Comparison with the language that Ajax used earlier in the play suggests that ἄριστος ('the best') is very much his kind of word: Achilles, he claimed, would have awarded him the κράτος ἀριστείας, 'prize of valour' (443), in the contest for the arms, and he added that without this prize, ἀριστείων ἄτερ (464), he did not dare to face his father. Ajax is at last called what he always wanted to be called.

Concord restored: (2) Chorus and large group

As various individuals keep joining the Chorus to form a group of Ajax's *philoi*, Ajax is in the end recognised as the man he believed he was. His *philoi* have for a long time been threatened by the army and especially by Menelaus and Aga-memnon, but finally, it seems, the threats vanish. At least in part, the deadlock is broken. With this provisional conclusion I return to the relationship between the Chorus and the large group. In the beginning, the Chorus, consisting of Ajax's Salaminian sailors, were opposed by the army at large. Are they still at the end of the play, or is Odysseus' support for Ajax part of a general melt-down? Is the deadlock broken completely?

The first thing to note is that the Chorus are never simply subsumed in the army. They always retain their identity as Salaminians and, like Achilles' Myrmidons in the *Iliad*, are thus singled out from the army at large. As late as the third stasimon, they show their affiliations to Attica when they pronounce the wish to be near Cape Sunium and Athens (1216–22). Moreover, the repeated and much-discussed evo-cations of Ajax the fifth-century cult hero recall Salamis as the centre of his cult. As Ajax gives his *philoi* instructions about his burial (1171–84; see pp. 236–7 above), as the Chorus speak about his 'occupying the dark tomb that shall ever be remembered' (1166–7; see pp. 242–3 below) and at many other moments of the play[79] ancient spectators will have been reminded of just how closely Ajax and hence his men were associated with Athens and Salamis. There can be no doubt, therefore, that the Chorus remain divided off from the army at large.

However, as I will argue, the dividing-line becomes increasingly blurry as the play goes on. In particular there are two developments I wish to point to. The first is the gradual disappearance of the hostility that separates Chorus and army. Unlike Achilles' Myrmidons, Ajax's Salaminians were once the army's enemies. This changes as the play goes on. The first sign is an ambiguity as early as the prologue. The Chorus sing (185–6):

> ἥκοι γὰρ ἂν θεία νόσος· ἀλλ' ἀπερύκοι
> καὶ Ζεὺς κακὰν καὶ Φοῖβος Ἀργείων φάτιν.

A godsent sickness must have come upon you; but may Zeus and Phoebus avert the evil rumour of the Argives!

These lines can be taken together with other passages in which the Chorus seem concerned with the hostility of the army. Looked at in this context, the Chorus are praying to Zeus and Phoebus to ward off the adverse rumours the Greeks spread about Ajax, just as they showed themselves worried about the λόγος ἐκ Δαναῶν (the 'rumour coming from the Danaans', 138) a little earlier. There is another way, however, of construing the genitive Ἀργείων ('Argives'). Rather than taking it with φάτιν ('avert the evil rumour of the Argives', as in the translation I print), one may regard it as dependent on ἀπερύκοι ('avert the evil rumour *from* the Argives'). On this interpretation the rumours are detrimental to all, as is the divine disease. The scene of general suffering that is described corresponds to that in *Iliad* 1, where it is also a divine disease that kills the cattle and leads to a quarrel between leaders and to inactivity on the part of the most important fighter. At least

---

[79] See above p. 232, n. 63 for references to recent discussions.

at one level the Chorus represent the interests of the large group already early in the play.

Later the large group's enmity vanishes not just through the ambiguity of a small phrase. The Chorus, who in the parodos appeared to speak of the army as separate from themselves and to speak of it as an enemy, afterwards never again hint at the existence of a group other than themselves, let alone one that is hostile towards them. Ajax himself curses the army as late as 843–4, but the Chorus say nothing about this hostility after the parodos. Instead it is always the Atridae and Odysseus whom they regard as threatening them or as opponents of Ajax.[80] Separating off Atridae and Odysseus from the large group, the Chorus make the way free for a solution that moves them closer towards the large group at the expense of the Atridae. The Chorus's move is the less visible for the great emphasis that Ajax himself and other characters put on the Atridae and Odysseus (rather than the army) as Ajax's special enemies throughout the play. Ajax sometimes speaks as though there were no army surrounding them. So he asks (460–1):

πότερα πρὸς οἴκους, ναυλόχους λιπὼν ἕδρας
μόνους τ' Ἀτρείδας, πέλαγος Αἰγαῖον περῶ;

Shall I cross the Aegean sea, leaving behind the station of the ships and the sons of Atreus, and go home?

In this passage and elsewhere[81] the Atridae or Odysseus help to take the enmity out of the army. The Chorus still have a clear identity as Salaminian sailors, but there are no longer two opposed groups.

When Menelaus and Agamemnon come on stage near the end of the play, the Chorus end their hostility towards even the individual representatives of the army. That they would commend moderation to the Atridae (1091–2, 1264–5) was to be expected from them as followers of Ajax, but that they are equally critical of Teucer (1118–19), perhaps less so. Of course choruses are often impartial in discussions and censure

---

[80] 616–20, 715–18, 927–33, 946–8, 955–60, 1042–3.
[81] 57, 97–113, 301–4, 380, 387–91, 838, 1134, 1356, 1372–3, 1383–8.

all kinds of strong statements. None the less, it is noteworthy that the criticism here follows a speech in which Teucer claims that Menelaus' command does not extend to Ajax and his men (especially 1100–6), thus rejecting the idea of the 'entire army' (στρατὸς ξύμπας, 1055) that Menelaus put forward, and it is also noteworthy that they welcome Odysseus after Teucer's angry rejoinder to Agamemnon with words stressing reconciliation (1316–17):

> ἄναξ Ὀδυσσεῦ, καιρὸν ἴσθ' ἐληλυθώς,
> εἰ μὴ ξυνάψων, ἀλλὰ συλλύσων πάρει.

Lord Odysseus, know that you have come at the right moment, if you have come not to help make the tangle worse but to help untie it.

Rather than lining up a pro-Ajax against an anti-Ajax party, the Chorus try increasingly to make the latter disappear.

Their efforts are rewarded when not only Agamemnon and Menelaus leave the play but Odysseus joins Ajax's *philoi*. In lines which I have quoted already, Teucer now invites both Odysseus and the army to participate in all the rites apart from the burial proper (1396–7):[82]

> τὰ δ' ἄλλα καὶ ξύμπρασσε, κεἴ τινα στρατοῦ
> θέλεις κομίζειν, οὐδὲν ἄλγος ἕξομεν.

But for the rest do you help us, and if you like to bring *any other man from the army*, we shall not be aggrieved.

All enmity has gone, and Teucer can issue a second, general, invitation (1413–14):

> ἀλλ' ἄγε πᾶς, φίλος ὅστις ἀνὴρ
> φησὶ παρεῖναι, σούσθω, βάτω ...

Come, let *every man* who claims to be here as a *philos* make haste, and set forth ...

Finally all hostility between Chorus and large group has disappeared. In Teucer's invitation the members of the army have become *philoi* along with Odysseus. The deadlock is finally broken. This is the first of two developments that soften the divisions between Chorus and large group.

---

[82] Dawe unnecessarily revives Schneidewin's deletion.

The audience and the large group

The second development which I will point to turns on the Chorus's identity. As I have stressed repeatedly, the Chorus consist of Salaminians. At the same time as moving closer towards the army, however, they do something else: they widen the horizon beyond both the men of Ajax and the army, bringing in the Greeks and, as in *Oedipus Rex*, humanity in general near the end of the play.

A first hint at this development comes as early as the first stasimon, when the Chorus sing that Ajax came to Troy as the best of the much-enduring Achaeans (πολυπόνων Ἀχαιῶν),[83] but it is not until the later parts of the play that such references become frequent. One of the most striking examples occurs in the anapaests at 1163–7, in which the Chorus urge Teucer to take action:

> ἔσται μεγάλης ἔριδός τις ἀγών.
> ἀλλ' ὡς δύνασαι, Τεῦκρε, ταχύνας
> σπεῦσον κοίλην κάπετόν τιν' ἰδεῖν[84]
> τῷδ', ἔνθα βροτοῖς τὸν ἀείμνηστον
> τάφον εὐρώεντα καθέξει.

There will be a struggle arising from a great dispute! Come, as quickly as you can, Teucer, hasten to find a hollow trench for this man, where he shall occupy the dank tomb that shall ever be remembered by *mortals*.

As so often before, Ajax is seen as the object of many people's interest: the Chorus imagine that his grave will be remembered by 'mortals' (βροτοί), a term that can include not only the Chorus themselves, but also the army, Teucer, Menelaus and Agamemnon alike. More than that, however, the term 'mortals' reaches out to all humankind, and first of all, therefore, to the audience. This appeal to the spectators is supported by the language of the passage in general. κοίλην κάπετον ('a hollow trench') is a quotation from the burial of Hector in the *Iliad* (24.797) and thus pointedly introduces a further frame of reference on which spectators can draw.

---

[83] 637. The exact text is uncertain.
[84] ἰδεῖν is possibly corrupt. See Renehan (1992) 352 for a defence.

More obviously, both the future καθέξει ('he shall occupy')
with overtones of hero cult and ἀείμνηστον ('that shall ever be
remembered') with its claim to eternity bring in the audience
by placing Ajax's grave in the time of the performance as
much as that of the play.[85]

A little later the Chorus sing again of Greeks and humans
(1192–8):

> ὄφελε πρότερον αἰθέρα δῦ-
> ναι μέγαν ἢ τὸν πολύκοινον Ἅιδαν
> κεῖνος ἀνήρ, ὃς στυγερῶν ἔδειξεν ὅ-
> πλων Ἕλλασιν κοινὸν Ἄρη
> ὢ πόνοι πρόγονοι πόνων·
> κεῖνος γὰρ ἔπερσεν ἀνθρώπους.

That man should first have entered the mighty sky or Hades, common to all,
who first showed to *the Greeks* how to league in war with hateful weapons!
O sorrows progenitors of sorrows! For he was the ruin of *humankind*.

The lines form part of the third stasimon and are sandwiched
between stanzas which complain about the misery that war
inflicts on the Chorus. Again the Chorus see themselves not
only as Ajax's men or as part of the Greek army, but also, it
seems, as Greeks and humans. Spectators are not appealed to
as directly as in the anapaests, but again have all reason to
find themselves included.

Odysseus and Teucer, I noted earlier, use words such as
ἄριστος ('the best') to describe Ajax. They too can now be seen
as widening the frame of reference to the Greeks (ἄριστον
Ἀργείων, 'best of the Argives', 1340) and humans (†κοὐδενί
πω λῴονι θνητῶν†, 'never yet ... a nobler among humans',
1416).[86] Finally, the Chorus, too, make their contribution
when they chant the tailpiece (1418–20):[87]

> ἦ πολλὰ βροτοῖς ἔστιν ἰδοῦσιν
> γνῶναι· πρὶν ἰδεῖν δ' οὐδεὶς μάντις
> τῶν μελλόντων ὅ τι πράξει.

---

[85] κοίλην κάπετον: Easterling (1993a) 11; καθέξει: Henrichs (1993) 171–5; ἀείμνηστον: Segal (1981) 144.

[86] For humans (and Greeks) at large see also 836, 1191, 1266, 1358 and 1363.

[87] Dawe (1973) 174–5 supports Ritter's (rather weak) case for deletion.

Mortals can *learn* many things by *seeing*, but, before he *sees*, no man can prophesy what his fortune shall be in the future.

The parallels with *Oedipus Rex* are obvious. Where Oedipus becomes a paradigm and a spectacle, Ajax is (as he always was) the object of the communal gaze (ἰδοῦσιν, ἰδεῖν), and (what he was not before) a lesson: there is something to be learned (γνῶναι) from looking at him. As in *Oedipus Rex*, moreover, this new way of looking at the former saviour is made possible by a change in the group the Chorus are speaking for. It is 'mortals' (βροτοῖς), not just his men or the army, who look at Ajax now. A development has found its conclusion. Extending the large group, the Chorus have at last become its unquestioned representatives. Spectators could not desire a more explicit invitation to adopt a group perspective: the Chorus speak for the large group, and the large group almost explicitly reaches out to the spectators.

Thus the play moves from division and danger towards concord and safety. The opposed perspectives of the Salaminian sailors and the large group are brought together; and superimposed there is the viewpoint of humans and Greeks at large. In their different ways, spectators can adopt and combine these various perspectives and, without a sense of threat, look at Ajax the cult-hero and Ajax the lesson.

What makes this concord at the end of *Ajax* particularly attractive is the fact that it is not facile. Divisions are not just wished away; rather, they are still there but safely contained. Spectators can probe the gaps that there inevitably are between the various perspectives and can ask questions that arise from these gaps. Is the large group that is safe really the one that was threatened in the beginning? How 'Salaminian', how 'Greek', and how generally 'human' are the Chorus in the end? Are the threats with which Menelaus left the stage cancelled by Odysseus' support for Ajax and his *philoi*? How much weight should be given to the exclusion of Odysseus from Ajax's burial? Will the army follow Odysseus' and Teucer's lead and leave the Atridae out in the cold, or are matters more complex than that? *Ajax*, and especially its language, allows spectators to pursue all these questions and many more, and at the same time to get involved in the sense of celebration that pervades its climactic moments.

ELECTRA

This chapter suggests two reasons why Sophoclean choruses can engage different spectators in communality. In accordance with the subject of this book, the discussion focuses on language, but, as in previous chapters, it inevitably also involves non-linguistic features. Thanks not least to the language that Sophoclean choruses use and that is used of them, I argue that they offer spectators the perspective of what I call the large group and that this is, at least in some ways, first the perspective of a group under threat and then of a group that is safe. These arguments are obviously generalisations which fail to express many of the differences between the various surviving plays. For a more complete account, it would be necessary to discuss how the Chorus of *Philoctetes* partially represent the Greek army, which needs Philoctetes to sack Troy, and how through their compassion they go some way towards reconciling Philoctetes, whose hatred concentrates like Ajax's on the Atridae and Odysseus, with this army. It would be necessary further to see how the Chorus of *Oedipus at Colonus*, who (as I noted) are at the same time old men of Colonus and citizens of Athens, both feel threatened by Oedipus and are eager to secure for their *polis* the gift that he promises.

Even further removed from *Oedipus Rex* and *Ajax* are the plays that centre on women, and which therefore cannot tell the story of a saviour like Oedipus or Ajax. Antigone, facing a chorus of Theban citizens, never meets a group that demands she act on its behalf. The civic community's support for her action is audible only in allusions and in reports of the citizens' grumbling (289–94, 692–700, 733), and it is unclear how the Chorus relate to these alleged citizens. Only when she is dead does Tiresias report that the *polis* is suffering from Creon's failure to have Polynices' corpse buried (1015) and, in consequence, do the Chorus pray for the delivery of the *polis*

(1115–54). Saviour and group, as it were, miss each other almost completely (with 940–3 providing minimal overlap). *Trachiniae*, one of two plays with a female chorus, displays a different pattern yet again: as women, the Chorus share Deianira's anxieties of a wife left at home by her husband in a way a male chorus would not be able to. But in their hopes for Heracles' return they also speak for the *polis* (646, 657). When Heracles' arrival fulfils these hopes, and Deianira drops out of the play, the Chorus increasingly widen out the horizon from Deianira's household to all of Greece (1112, cf. 1011, 1079). All these choruses and their perspectives deserve discussion. For reasons of space, however, I will confine myself to *Electra* as the play which may be seen as the one that is most distinct from *Oedipus Rex* in various respects.

The house

Electra has *both* a female leading character like *Antigone* and a female Chorus like *Trachiniae*. Moreover, unlike *Antigone* and more emphatically than *Trachiniae*, it is set predominantly around the house. The play opens with the Paedagogus pointing out at a distance the landmarks of Argos and then turning to the place where they stand (8–10):

οἷ δ' ἱκάνομεν,
φάσκειν Μυκήνας τὰς πολυχρύσους ὁρᾶν,
πολύφθορόν τε δῶμα Πελοπιδῶν τόδε, ...

... and at the place where we have arrived, you may say that you see *Mycenae*, rich in gold, and the *house* of the sons of Pelops here ...

From the brief mention of Mycenae the sentence shifts to the house of the Pelopids, and there the play will stay for a long time. Orestes ends his reply to the Paedagogus with an address to the 'house of his father' (69; cf. 72) which he hopes to regain. As the two men leave, the scene is firmly fixed outside the royal palace. Electra, a female chorus, Chrysothemis, Clytemnestra and (much later) Aegisthus dominate the play and receive Orestes and the Paedagogus as they come to the house from outside.

Anybody looking for a group in need of rescue will therefore have to begin with the house.[88] And indeed, he or she has to wait no longer than until Orestes' prayer in verses 67-72:

> ἀλλ', ὦ πατρῷα γῆ θεοί τ' ἐγχώριοι,
> δέξασθέ μ' εὐτυχοῦντα ταῖσδε ταῖς ὁδοῖς,
> σύ τ', ὦ πατρῷον δῶμα· σοῦ γὰρ ἔρχομαι
> δίκη <u>καθαρτὴς πρὸς θεῶν</u> ὡρμημένος·
> καὶ μή μ' ἄτιμον τῆσδ' ἀποστείλητε γῆς,
> ἀλλ' ἀρχέπλουτον καὶ <u>καταστάτην</u> δόμων.

But do you, my native land and you, gods of the place, receive me in good fortune on this mission, and you, *house of my fathers!* For I come in justice to *cleanse* you, sped on my way by the gods. And do not send me from the land dishonoured, but let me control my riches and *set the house upon its feet!*

Orestes hopes to 'cleanse' and to 'set upon its feet' the house of his fathers. Welcome as these statements are, they beg some questions. What does 'cleansing' and 'setting upon its feet' mean in this context? And, more urgently, what does 'house' mean in this play? Is it the large group of *Electra*, as the *polis* of Thebes is that of *Oedipus Rex*?

Unlike the *polis* of Thebes, the house is first of all a building. Even when *domos*, *oikos* and other such words are translated as 'family', the building remains part of the concept. In many performances of many tragedies, including *Electra*, the stage-building acts as a constant reminder of the physical connotations of 'house'. In fact, the inhabitants of the house, Electra, Chrysothemis, Clytemnestra and Aegisthus, hardly ever see it as *anything other than* a building. Rather than saying (as Orestes and other outsiders sometimes do[89]) what is done to the house or what the house does, they only speak of

---

[88] The importance of the house in Greek tragedy was first elaborated in detail for *Agamemnon* by Jones (1962) 82–111. Most recently see Wiles (1997) 161–74 with further bibliography. On the house in *Electra* see especially Segal (1981) 249–62.

[89] Orestes: 69, 72 and 1290. Paedagogus: 10. Chorus (not in every way outsiders: see pp. 251–6 below): 514 and 1070.

movement into and out of the house, or something or somebody being in it or away from it.[90]

One way of accounting for the inhabitants' concentration
on the house as a building is to link it to the disruption of the
house as a group. Many scholars have discussed how in *Electra* the group the house ought to be is in many ways dysfunc-
tional. In particular it has been pointed out that insiders and
outsiders are partially exchanged. Clytemnestra, for instance,
rules together with her lover Aegisthus after killing Agamemnon, the proper head of the household, and Orestes,
Agamemnon's son, is away from the house as an 'exile'
(1136). As a group, the house, unlike the anonymous *polis* and
army, is to a large degree defined by its members. It is therefore perhaps unsurprising that the house has lost many of the
connotations that extend beyond its physical building for
those living in it. At a time when it is difficult to tell who is a
member and who ought to be one, the inhabitants of the
house find difficulty in regarding it as a group. Most of all, for
them there is no longer a family. Only those who, like Orestes,
look at the house from outside, and perhaps from memory,
still imagine it as a group.

The struggle that insiders have with the uncertainty of who
is part of the house and who is not can best be seen in Electra's efforts to establish a normative list of its members. Included is first of all Orestes, whose return Electra desires
throughout the play and whose alleged death throws her into
despair. He is for her not only the man who will change her
miserable life,[91] but also the man whom she saved as a child
and about whose well-being and proper burial she is concerned.[92] The second member of Electra's re-established
house is Agamemnon. He is of course dead, but Electra has

---

[90] Into the house: 574, 1165, 1386, 1392, 1493. Out of the house: 324, 1130. In the
house: 93 (lit. the beds *of* the house know), 262, 282, 651 (δόμους ... ἀμφέπειν
suggests both living in and looking after the house), 1308, 1309, 1404 (the house is
empty of Clytemnestra's friends). Away from the house: 311, 912, 1136, 1325.
There are three exceptions (978, 1354, 1497), all of which will be discussed below.
[91] 118–20, 164–72, 303–4, 453–8, 603–4, 807–16, 1149–70.
[92] 321, 601–2, 865–70, 1126–48.

never come to terms with his death, lamenting it incessantly,[93] and still holding it against Clytemnestra.[94]

Electra's efforts to found a house different from the one she lives in are particularly obvious in cases where she excludes rather than includes. Clytemnestra is as emphatically not part of it as Orestes and Agamemnon are part of it. This is obvious for the first time when Electra accuses Chrysothemis of acting as Clytemnestra's mouthpiece and forgetting that she is her 'father's child' (341–4). Chrysothemis, according to Electra, fails to support her when she herself does the utmost to avenge Agamemnon (349–50), and finally rules (365–8):

νῦν δ᾽ ἐξὸν πατρὸς
πάντων ἀρίστου παῖδα κεκλῆσθαι, καλοῦ
τῆς μητρός. οὕτω γὰρ φανῇ πλείστοις κακή,
θανόντα πατέρα καὶ φίλους προδοῦσα σούς.

But as things are, when you could be called the daughter of the noblest of men, be called the child of your mother! In that way you will seem to most people a traitor, who have betrayed your dead father and your *philoi*.

She herself, Electra implies, is most of all her father's daughter. She adds the complementary claim that she is not her mother's daughter, when she later says to Clytemnestra (597–8):

καί σ᾽ ἔγωγε δεσπότιν
ἢ μητέρ᾽ οὐκ ἔλασσον εἰς ἡμᾶς νέμω, ...

I think you more a despot than a mother towards us ...

Later Electra contests Clytemnestra's position as mother also of Orestes. Addressing the urn that she believes contains his ashes, she says (1145–6):

οὔτε γάρ ποτε
μητρὸς σύ γ᾽ ἦσθα μᾶλλον ἢ κἀμοῦ φίλος, ...

You were never your mother's *philos* more than you were mine ...

Clytemnestra is excluded. And as Electra continues, it becomes clear that Agamemnon and Orestes are included (Chry-

---

249

sothemis is less prominent) (1150–2):

> πάντα γὰρ συναρπάσας,
> θύελλ' ὅπως, βέβηκας. οἴχεται πατήρ·
> τέθνηκ' ἐγὼ σοί· φροῦδος αὐτὸς εἶ θανών.

Like a whirlwind, you have gone, carrying off everything. My father is gone; you have killed me; you yourself are dead and gone.

Electra, like the other inhabitants of the house, does not speak of the house as a group. Instead she tries to assemble her own group, by including some and excluding others.

The difference between those who regard the house as a functional group and those who can only see individuals is further illustrated by the speech in which Electra tries to persuade her sister to help her avenge Agamemnon, now that Orestes is known to be dead (947–89). Towards the end Electra quotes the praise that she imagines 'all humans' (πᾶς τις ... βροτῶν, 984) will bestow on the sisters (977–83):

> ἴδεσθε τώδε τὼ κασιγνήτω, φίλοι,
> ὣ τὸν πατρῷον οἶκον ἐξεσωσάτην,
> ὣ τοῖσιν ἐχθροῖς εὖ βεβηκόσιν ποτὲ
> ψυχῆς ἀφειδήσαντε προὐστήτην φόνου.
> τούτω φιλεῖν χρή, τώδε χρὴ πάντας σέβειν·
> τώδ' ἔν θ' ἑορταῖς ἔν τε πανδήμῳ πόλει
> τιμᾶν ἅπαντας οὕνεκ' ἀνδρείας χρέων.

Look on these sisters, *philoi*, who preserved their father's house, who when their enemies were firmly based took no thought of their lives, but stood forth to avenge murder! All should love them, all should reverence them; all should honour them for their manliness at feasts and when the whole *polis* is assembled.

Taking over the role of her dead brother (951–7), Electra imagines herself and Chrysothemis celebrated in the *polis* for saving their father's house. πατρῷον οἶκον takes up Orestes' πατρῷον δῶμα (both mean 'house of my father' or 'of my fathers') from the prologue (69). This is the first time that Electra speaks of saving the house, and significantly she does so only in an imaginary quotation.[95] In the rest of the speech

---

[95] There is much else that is imaginary about the speech. As Juffras (1991) points out, Electra's stance is almost that of a tyrannicide who is honoured with a statue

she speaks, here as elsewhere, of individual people's interests. So she puts it to Chrysothemis that acting themselves is the only hope left to them (958–9). Otherwise they will never enjoy their father's wealth or marry, since Aegisthus will never let their children come into being (σόν ποτ' ἢ κἀμὸν γένος | βλαστεῖν, 965–6). Electra closes her speech with an exhortation to help Agamemnon, Orestes, Electra and herself (986–9). *In propria persona* she still assembles a group of individuals rather than speaking of rescuing the house. The inhabitant of the house, painfully aware of Orestes' death and Clytemnestra's and Aegisthus' rule over the house, does not conceive of the house as a group, while those outside it, who look at it moreover once it has been saved, can speak of the rescue of the house. Under present circumstances the house is a group only for those who do not live in it.

The house of *Electra*, then, is highly problematic as a group. Its inhabitants imagine it only as a building, and there is considerable disagreement over who ought to live in it. Like all houses, moreover, it is more distant from a fifth-century audience than a *polis* or an army in so far as theatre-going was a political rather than a private activity. All this seems almost certainly to disqualify the house as the large group of the play. Before passing final judgement, however, I wish to look at the Chorus. It is they after all who, according to the first of my two arguments, are the (at least partial) representatives of the large group. I will begin with the episodes before the recognition.

The Chorus

Near the beginning of the parodos, when the Chorus respond to Electra's lament, they describe Agamemnon as follows (124–6):

> τὸν πάλαι ἐκ δολερᾶς ἀθεώτατα
> ματρὸς ἁλόντ' ἀπάταις Ἀγαμέμνονα
> κακᾷ τε χειρὶ πρόδοτον.

and worshipped by the *polis*. It is difficult to gauge how these overtones would affect Electra's credibility in the eyes of ancient spectators.

Agamemnon, long since brought down in unholy fashion by a plot through your mother's cunning, and sent to his doom by her cruel hand.

They go on (126–7):

> ὡς ὁ τάδε πορὼν
> ὄλοιτ', εἴ μοι θέμις τάδ' αὐδᾶν.

May he who has done this perish, if it is right for me to speak this word!

Like Electra, the Chorus condemn the murder of Agamemnon and desire vengeance. Later they express their pity for Agamemnon (193–200), show interest in Orestes (160–3, 317–18), make Justice and revenge their concern (472–503) and after the Paedagogus's false messenger speech lament the catastrophe of the γένος ('race', 764–5). After the parodos they declare that they have come καὶ τὸ σὸν σπεύδουσ' ἅμα | καὶ τοὐμὸν αὐτῆς ('in your interest and also in my own', 251–2). Repeatedly the Chorus share Electra's viewpoint. At times it is as though there were sixteen, rather than one, Electras on stage.

And yet, the Chorus are of course not just a multiplied Electra. Throughout the play they are sympathetic to her, but retain a certain distance. They advise her to stop lamenting, comfort her, encourage her and wish her well.[96] So who are they? In the parodos Electra addresses them as γενέθλα γενναίων ('race of noble ones', 129) and φιλία γενέθλα ('friendly race', 226). Both these terms of address, and passages that have a bearing on them, point in various directions. On the one hand, the adjective γενναῖος ('noble') establishes a link between the Chorus and Electra, who later stresses her nobility with εὐγενής and καλῶς πεφυκόσιν (257 and 989, both meaning 'nobly born'). The link between the Chorus and Electra is further emphasised when Electra describes the 'race' as 'friendly' (φιλία, the adjective with *philos*), and when the Chorus address her as 'child' (ὦ παῖ παῖ, 121) and claim they speak to her 'like a mother' (μάτηρ ὡσεί, 234).

The noun γενέθλα, on the other hand, makes it clear that the Chorus are local noble-women and places them in the context of a larger and more political community. This asso-

---

[96] 137–44, 153–63, 173–84, 213–20, 233–5, 322, 473–86, 823–70, 1070–97, 1171–3.

ciation is reflected in the Chorus's references to *gē* ('land'). Pelops, they sing, came to 'this land' (504–7), and already in the parodos they describe Orestes as follows (160–3):

> ... ὃν ά κλεινὰ
> γᾶ ποτε Μυκηναίων
> δέξεται εὐπατρίδαν, Διὸς εὔφρονι
> βήματι μολόντα τάνδε γᾶν ᾿Ορέσταν.

... he whom the famous land (*gē*) of the Mycenaeans shall receive, the *eupatridēs*, when he comes to this land, brought by the kindly aid of Zeus.

While being closely associated with Electra, the Chorus also bring in the wider perspective of 'the land' and 'the land of Mycenae'.[97] The flexibility is encapsulated by the word *eupatridēs*, which they here apply to Orestes. In an instance of what Easterling calls 'heroic vagueness', it both describes Orestes as a partisan of his father (*eu-patridēs* = 'good to his father'; cf. *eupatris* at 1081) and, since *hoi Eupatrides* can refer to the aristocrats of early Athens ('of good fathers'),[98] puts him into a political context.

Flexible as it is, the Chorus's perspective bridges the gap between Electra and the civic community (as I shall gloss the 'land', the 'Myceneans' and, later, the '*polis*' with some inevitable imprecision). By speaking sometimes as though they were fifteen Electras, the Chorus make Electra's perspective to some degree the perspective of a group. And the group, although formed by women and although closely associated with a woman, is not opposed to a male group. The continuity between this Chorus and the community of Mycenae is of course not as strong as that between the Chorus and the Thebans in *Oedipus Rex*, but continuity there is. This continuity is important for the spectators' involvement in the play. For modern spectators it makes the Chorus the representatives of the large off-stage group. For ancient spectators it does even more than that. It moves the Chorus, women though they are, closer to the Athenian citizen body of which they themselves

---

[97] See also vv. 310–11, which make it clear that the Chorus are not part of the house.
[98] See LSJ *s.v.* εὐπατρίδης II. Both connotations are conceivably present again at 856 (where there is uncertainty over the text).

are part. Both modern and ancient spectatators, then, have good reason to adopt the Chorus's perspective.

If they do, what they adopt is the perspective of a group which longs for change, particularly for retribution, that is, without stretching the usual meaning of the words too much, a group under threat. The chorus of *Electra*, unlike those of *Ajax* and *Oedipus Rex*, do not fear for their lives, but they, too, are strongly dissatisfied with things as they are.

The last two or three pages have suggested, I hope, both that there is a large group in *Electra* and that it is represented by the Chorus. This large group, however, is the civic community. What, then, about the house? How does it relate to the large group? I will argue that, while not by itself qualifying as the large group, the house still has a connection with it. This connection is the Chorus. They speak not only for the civic community but also, perhaps surprisingly, for the house. Possibly because they are both close to Electra, who lives inside the house and suffers from its disruption, and still have the distance that allows them to look at the house without immediately beginning to discuss its individual members, the Chorus come as close as anybody to giving the house a voice. Not only do they describe Agamemnon's death in pitiful terms as though they had been present in the house at the time (193–200), but they also speak about the sufferings of the house in a way no other character does.

After Pelops' chariot race, they sing (513–15):

> ... οὔ τί πω
> ἔλιπεν ἐκ τοῦδ' οἴκου[99]
> πολύπονος αἰκεία.

... never yet has the torment of many troubles departed from *this house.*

Once again the house is a building: somebody does not leave it. But the somebody is 'the torment of many troubles' and the house therefore more than a building. The image of torment as a permanent dweller in the house conjures up the disgrace-

---

[99] Some editors print the variant οἴκους; see Lloyd-Jones and Wilson (1990) 52. The choice of reading does not affect my discussion here.

ful acts and sufferings of its members. The house, the Chorus suggest, is disrupted.

More obviously still, the Chorus speak of the sufferings of the house in the second stasimon, when they pray (1066–73):

> ὦ χθονία βροτοῖσι φάμα,
> κατά μοι βόασον οἰκτρὰν
> ὄπα τοῖς ἔνερθ' Ἀτρείδαις,
> ἀχόρευτα φέρουσ' ὀνείδη.
>
> [new stanza]
>
> ὅτι σφὶν ἤδη τὰ μὲν ἐκ δόμων νοσεῖται,[100]
> τὰ δὲ πρὸς τέκνων διπλῆ φύ-
> λοπις οὐκέτ' ἐξισοῦται
> φιλοτασίῳ διαίτα.

O voice that for mortals travels below the earth, cry out a sad message to the Atridae below *for me*, carrying a joyless message of dishonour! Tell them that *their house* [*lit. 'the matters that come out of the house'*] *is sick*, and that the strife between their children is no longer levelled out in loving life together.

ἐκ ('out of') suggests that the house is a building even here, but the expression as a whole calls the house sick and thus makes the house a group of people. Unlike Electra or any other inhabitant of the house, the Chorus address what many critics find a central theme of the play: the disruption of the house. Since they moreover make it clear that they have an interest in setting things right (μοι, 'for me'), they almost lend their voice to the house.

All this is not to say that the Chorus are part of the house. What it *is* to say is that the Chorus are a link between Electra, the house and the civic community. The three differ greatly, one a person, one a (debated) set of persons, and one an anonymous group. But for all their differences, they are never opposed to one another. There are no conflicts between them. This co-existence is emphasised by the Chorus, who speak about the concerns of all three. Because of the Chorus's fluid perspective it is difficult at times to tell apart the interests of

---

[100] νοσεῖται is in only one of the MSS. The majority have the metrically deficient νοσεῖ. Various emendations are possible.

any one of the three from those of the other two. Through the Chorus, Electra, the house and the civic community almost become an interest group.

This has effects for the large group. Strictly speaking, the large group in this play is the civic community that is there faintly in the background. But the Chorus with their flexible perspective come close to making the house part of this large group and to giving it a voice, disrupted and problematic group though it is.[101] In *Electra* the large group is both polymorphous and vague. At no point is there the kind of clear demarcation that there is at least at the beginning of *Oedipus Rex*. But it is precisely thanks to this vagueness that spectators are offered at the same time something like the perspective of both the civic community and the house. And this is, as at the beginning of *Oedipus Rex*, the perspective of a group that, at least in a manner of speaking, is under threat.

The saving of the group

The obvious next question is whether the perspective of a group under threat ever turns into that of a group which is safe. The answer will be similar to that given for *Oedipus Rex* and *Ajax*: yes, spectators are given the perspective of a group that is safe at the end of the tragedy, but there are various complications. The 'yes' is in some ways obvious: Orestes, with the help of Electra, kills Clytemnestra and at the end of the play is about to kill Aegisthus. As he returns to the house, order is restored. Orestes is its saviour. I therefore move straightaway on to the complications, returning to the 'yes' later.

The first complication concerns the saviour. Rather than concentrating on one saviour like Oedipus or Ajax, the play offers several.[102] In the prologue *Orestes* expresses his hope of saving the house; after Orestes' alleged death *Electra* adopts

---

[101] The difficulty of making a house speak is made explicit at Aesch. *Ag.* 37–8 and Eur. *Hipp.* 1074–6.

[102] Cf. Sommerstein (1997), who points out that during much of the play it is unclear both who will be killed and who will kill.

his role and imagines how she and Chrysothemis will be celebrated as saviours of the house; after the recognition Electra is
convinced that Orestes' return means the restoration of the
house and calls the *Paedagogus*, as Orestes' saviour, also the
'only saviour of the house of Agamemnon' (μόνος σωτὴρ
δόμων | Ἀγαμέμνονος, 1354-5). Only later on, as I will go on
to say, will Orestes take centre stage again.

A second and related complication is that there is little indication of the group – house, Mycenaeans or otherwise –
desiring any of these various saviours. The Chorus give no
time at all to the Paedagogus and where they mention Orestes
in the part of the play that I have discussed so far, they simply
speak of his coming and never make it clear that they need
him. Their extensive treatment of vengeance and justice does
not focus on a particular avenger. In fact, where they speak
about the house, they confine themselves to lamenting its suffering, without articulating any particular kind of change they
desire. In the prayer that I quoted above (1066-73), for instance, they turn directly to 'Atridae' with a rather vague wish
for intervention. Unlike Orestes, Electra has much of their
attention, but although they support many of her hopes, they
never see her as a saviour. The large group that the Chorus
represent is a group that wants change and a group, as I put
it, that is under threat, but not a group that turns to an individual to deliver them from the threat.

The third and last complication I wish to draw attention to
is one which is already familiar: who is the large group? Until
now I have confined myself to the Chorus's statements before
the recognition. Discussion of the later scenes will suggest that
the group represented by the Chorus, which has never been
straightforward, becomes even more problematic as the play
goes on. It will also put the two complications that I have
already mentioned into a wider context.

The recognition scene ends with the following exchange
between Electra and the Chorus (1227-31):

Ελ. ὦ φίλταται γυναῖκες, ὦ πολίτιδες,
     ὁρᾶτ' Ὀρέστην τόνδε, μηχαναῖσι μὲν
     θανόντα, νῦν δὲ μηχαναῖς σεσωμένον.

257

Χο. ὁρῶμεν, ὦ παῖ, κἀπὶ συμφοραῖσί μοι
γεγηθὸς ἕρπει δάκρυον ὀμμάτων ἄπο.

El. *Dearest women, O politides*, you see here Orestes, dead by a stratagem,
and now by a stratagem preserved!
Chorus   We see him, daughter, *and a tear of rejoicing at your fortune comes
from our eyes!*

The Chorus are overjoyed to see Orestes alive before them.
They do not declare him with hindsight their desired saviour,
but with their tears they express their happiness at his return
more strongly than they have ever previously expressed their
wish for his return. It is as though they had been waiting for a
long time.

Who, then, is it that has been waiting? As before, the Chorus are close associates of Electra ('dearest women'). Perhaps
they are, as one puts it, 'glad for Electra' that Orestes has
come. The second half of the address, 'O *politides*', can be
translated 'O women of the *polis*' and then recalls the local
noblewomen of the prologue. But *politides* has further connotations. This is only the second time after Electra's imaginary quotation that *polis* and its derivatives appear in the
play, and *politides*, which may also be translated 'female citizens', is a concept that has no parallel in Athenian society.[103]
The word is therefore likely to have been noted by many at
least of the ancient spectators. It is impossible to tell how
precisely they would have reacted, but one thing is clear.
Electra's address not only re-emphasises the close bond that
there is between her and the Chorus but also moves the Chorus further towards the community of Mycenae than they
have been before. They are made 'female citizens'.

This passage, then, brings two new kinds of emphasis: the
Chorus's attachment to Orestes and their links to the *polis*.
Perhaps the two are unrelated, but perhaps they are not. Of all
group terms that appear in the play *polis* is most markedly
distinct from *doma*, *oikos* and other words for 'house'. Both

---

[103] Unsurprisingly the word is rare: LSJ *s.v.* The common expressions are αἱ Ἀττικαί
('women of Attica') and αἱ ἀσταί ('townswomen'). See Loraux (1993) 111–23,
Mossé (1985) and especially Patterson (1986).

'land' and 'Mycenaeans' suggest the civic community, but neither term does so as emphatically as *polis*. Neither of them, moreover, has been used in addresses. The Chorus *speak about*, and perhaps *for*, the 'land' and the 'Mycenaeans', but now they *are* (in some sense) 'female citizens'. Close though they remain to Electra, the house is rather distant. Now, the house, I noted, is a deeply problematic group, if only because it is a matter of debate who its members are. Unsurprisingly, therefore, the voice that the Chorus have at times given the house has never been very articulate in its desires. What I wish to point out in this passage is the coinciding of the Chorus's clearly voiced attachment to Orestes and the emphasis on a *persona* that removes them from the rather inarticulate house. Perhaps their coinciding is a matter of chance, perhaps it is not. Be that as it may, the coinciding marks the beginning of a development which I am going to trace: as the play goes on, a group is saved by Orestes. But as it is saved, the emphasis turns out to be on the civic community rather than the house.

This development, it is worth emphasising, never removes all the multi-facetedness of the Chorus. No matter how much stress is put on their civic associations, they remain Electra's close associates. After the third stasimon she still addresses them as 'dearest women' (1398) and *philai* (1406), and immediately before Clytemnestra is killed they exclaim (1413–14):

ὦ πόλις, ὦ γενεὰ τάλαινα, νῦν σοι
μοῖρα καθημερία φθίνει φθίνει.

O *polis*, O unhappy race (*geneā*), now the fate that was yours from day to day is decaying decaying!

Once more the Chorus are concerned with both public and private. I suggested earlier that they represent the polymorphous large group when they speak for both house and civic community. So, too, they may now again be seen as the voice of this large group when they say that both *polis* and 'race' (*geneā*) have been saved. But as in the previous passage there is more to be said. 'Public and private' does not catch all the nuances of the passage. First, *polis* is again not just any word for the public in this play, but one that is much more emphatic than *gē* ('land') or suchlike would be. The language the Chorus choose puts considerable stress on the civic community. Secondly, 'private' is a gloss for *geneā* which conceals as much as it expresses. Unlike the house, the race has not been prominent in the play,[104] and, more importantly, it seems distinct from the house. While the Chorus say that the 'race' has been saved, Clytemnestra has just been stressing that the 'house' (στέγαι) is 'empty of friends but full of killers' (1404–5). The house in this context can only be regarded as saved if Clytemnestra, who would at this point certainly not call it saved, is not one of its members. Unsurprisingly the Chorus choose a word that need not include her. Thirdly, a wedge, small as it may be, is driven between *polis* and *geneā* by the reiterated φθίνει ('is decaying').[105] To say, as I just did, that the Chorus are celebrating that *polis* and race have been saved is grossly imprecise. 'Decay' suggests anything other than safety. The Chorus's statement leaves much room for thought. What I want to suggest at least tentatively is that it does so especially for the second of the two subjects. *geneā*, linked as it is to *gignesthai* ('to come into being'), is a word that stresses procreation. Perhaps even more than *polis*, therefore, it is affected by the metaphor of decay.

The Chorus's exclamation celebrates the rescue of the polymorphous large group. But at the same time it raises questions. What does it mean for the celebrations that the verb which describes the fate of the *polis* is φθίνει ('is decaying')? Even more disconcertingly, what does it mean that the verb which describes the fate of the race is also φθίνει? And what about the house, which has been so prominent throughout the play? I have already noted that the *polis* is more vocal than the house in its attachment to Orestes. Now I add that when Orestes, together with Electra, kills Clytemnestra, there are some moves towards separating the consequences for the house, the race and the *polis*. Is the large group perhaps not just polymorphous but too polymorphous?

---

[104] 706 (a charioteer of the 'Aenian race'), 765, 1010, 1121.
[105] For a brief discussion of the metaphor see Segal (1981) 255.

The process of separation becomes more obvious as the episode develops. The setting, which throughout the play has been around the house, now shifts to a *polis* context. Aegisthus arrives from the suburbs (ἐκ προαστίου, 1431). When he understands from Electra that Orestes has been killed, he orders the display of his body (1458–63):

> † σιγᾶν ἄνωγα κἀναδεικνύναι πύλας †[106]
> πᾶσιν Μυκηναίοισιν Ἀργείοις θ᾽ ὁρᾶν,
> ὡς εἴ τις αὐτῶν ἐλπίσιν κεναῖς πάρος
> ἐξῆρετ᾽ ἀνδρὸς τοῦδε, νῦν ὁρῶν νεκρὸν
> στόμια δέχηται τἀμά, μηδὲ πρὸς βίαν
> ἐμοῦ κολαστοῦ προστυχὼν φύσῃ φρένας.

†I tell you to be silent and to reveal what is behind the doors† *for all the Mycenaeans and the Argives to see*, so that *if anyone was previously buoyed up by vain hopes centred on this man*, he may now see him a corpse and accept my bridle, and not need violent chastisement from me to teach him sense.

This passage does what comparable passages near the end of *Oedipus Rex* and *Ajax* do: it draws in the audience. As the *ekkyklema* is rolled out, the body (not of Orestes but of Clytemnestra) is presented to them as much as to any off-stage Mycenaean and Argive. Spectators, whether citizens of the Athenian *polis* or of a modern state, are merged with the inhabitants of Mycenae-Argos. As Mark Ringer puts it, this 'is a strong moment of unity between the stage and the audience space'.[107] Spectators are given a distinct group perspective.

But what kind of a group perspective is this? More than anything else, it is the perspective of the civic community which is saved. Aegisthus' little speech is the culmination of the development that I have been tracing in the last few pages. In the last part of *Electra* there has been a growing emphasis on the *polis* as the large group of the play, and increasingly there has been a sense that the *polis* is saved. First Electra imagined being celebrated by the *polis*, then the Chorus, addressed as *politides*, wept in joy over Orestes' return, and later

---

[106] The line is probably corrupt. See Jebb's appendix *ad* 1458f., Lloyd-Jones and Wilson (1990) 75, and Dawe (1973) 201 for possible emendations.
[107] Ringer (1998) 205.

they were elated by the 'decay' of the 'day-to-day fate' of *polis* and race. Now finally Aegisthus, trapped in Orestes' deception ploy, addresses 'all the Mycenaeans and Argives' who were 'previously buoyed up by vain hopes centred on' Orestes.

Of course all this could be clearer. In the last episode, the Chorus, who have done so much to shift the emphasis towards the civic community as the large group, are silent apart from a brief tailpiece. What is more the various references to the *polis* are not easy to interpret. Electra was imagining something which did not happen in the event, *politides* is a difficult word and the metaphor of 'decay' is no easier. However, for all these uncertainties, there is no doubt about the safety of the civic community. The body is not that of Clytemnestra; Aegisthus will have little time to apply his bridle.

By contrast, the group (if it ever was a group) about whose safety there *is* doubt is the house. It is markedly absent from Aegisthus' address to the Mycenaeans and Argives. House and civic community are finally coming apart. Long stretches of the play were dominated by the house – building, disrupted group, and group with a weak voice that it is. And for a long time it seemed as though the Chorus's flexible perspective made the house part of the large group. When towards the end the emphasis is on the civic community as the large group that is saved, the question arises what happens to the house.

A good starting-point for answering this question is provided by the Chorus's tailpiece (1508–10):[108]

> ὦ σπέρμ' Ἀτρέως, ὡς πολλὰ παθὸν
> δι' ἐλευθερίας μόλις ἐξῆλθες
> τῇ νῦν ὁρμῇ τελεωθέν.

Seed of Atreus, after many sufferings you have at last emerged in freedom, made complete by this day's enterprise.

This is as close as anybody comes to saying that the house has been saved. But firstly words like τελεωθέν ('made complete') that try to establish finality may throw doubt on this very

---

[108] Dawe accepts Ritter's deletion, but offers little substantial argument: Dawe (1973) 204.

finality at the same time.[109] Secondly and more importantly, the 'seed of Atreus', like the 'race', is not the same as the house. The seed of Atreus includes Orestes, Electra and Chrysothemis (in so far as she still has any significance), but not Clytemnestra and Aegisthus. It is therefore true that, at least for the moment, suffering has ended and freedom has come at last for the 'seed of Atreus'. As in the Chorus's exclamation about *polis* and 'race', a more or less reassuring statement about the safety of Atreus' line is made while nothing is said about the safety of the house.

But what is said about the house itself? Electra and Orestes famously have the following exchange (1424–5):

> Ηλ. 'Ορέστα, πῶς κυρεῖ τάδ';[110]   Op. ἐν δόμοισι μὲν
> καλῶς, 'Απόλλων εἰ καλῶς ἐθέσπισεν.

El. Orestes, how is it with you? Or. In the house all is well, if Apollo prophesied well (*kalōs*).

It has often been remarked that Orestes attaches an unverifiable condition to his statement that all is well in the house.[111] In the light of the previous discussion it is notable moreover that Orestes makes a statement only about what happens *inside* the house. The house is once again a building rather than something he has saved, as he proposed to do in the prologue.

The last character to speak of the house is Aegisthus. When Orestes orders him to go inside, he replies (1493–4):

> τί δ' ἐς δόμους ἄγεις με; πῶς, τόδ' εἰ καλὸν
> τοὔργον, σκότου δεῖ, κοὐ πρόχειρος εἶ κτανεῖν;

Why do you force me into the house? If this act is good (*kalon*), why must it be in darkness, and why are you not ready to kill me?

Again the house is a building rather than a group that has been saved. What is more, Aegisthus' question is disconcerting. As in the previous passage, the conditional 'if' raises doubts about whether Orestes' action is 'good' (*kalon*). The

---

[109] Winnington-Ingram (1980) 226.
[110] There is uncertainty about the precise text.
[111] Among the first: Bowra (1944) 252–3 and Friis Johansen (1964) 27.

house, he suggests, has become a means of concealing shady deeds.

Finally the house becomes more than a building and is invested with vision. Aegisthus asks (1497–8):

ἦ πᾶσ' ἀνάγκη τήνδε τὴν στέγην ἰδεῖν
τά τ' ὄντα καὶ μέλλοντα Πελοπιδῶν κακά;

Is it needful that his house should witness the present and the future woes of the Pelopids?

The house has learned to see. But all it gets to see is the sufferings of the Pelopids. At the end of the first stasimon the Chorus sang that ever since Pelops' chariot race, 'the torment of many troubles' has not left the house (513–15). If Aegisthus' assessment is correct, the house is still in the same trouble as before.

I began this section by pointing out that *Electra* of all surviving Sophoclean tragedies is the most familial and hence the one that is furthest removed from any large group. I have discussed it, therefore, as what one might call a limiting case for the two arguments that I am putting forward in this chapter. What results, then, has this discussion yielded? A convenient way of answering this question is a brief comparison with the two surviving plays that dramatise the same story: Aeschylus' *Choephori* and Euripides' *Electra*.[112]

Like Sophocles' *Electra*, *Choephori* is a play which makes reference to the civic community here and there despite a predominantly domestic setting. Most significantly, the Chorus seem to be praying for the good of the *polis* in the second stasimon and seem to anticipate Orestes' rule over it in the anapaests soon after.[113] Orestes himself, moreover, begins his triumphant speech over the corpses of Clytemnestra and Aegisthus with an address that resembles Aegisthus' short speech in Sophocles' *Electra* in the way it draws in the spectators:

---

[112] Some such comparison would no doubt suggest itself also to many spectators – but possibly not at the first performance: the relative dating of Sophocles' and Euripides' *Electra* is notoriously difficult.

[113] πόλει τάδ' εὖ (824) and ἀρχάς τε πολισσονόμους (864). The text is most uncertain in both passages: Garvie *ad loc*. See also 55–60, 188, 289, 302, 431.

ἴδεσθε χώρας τὴν διπλῆν τυραννίδα | πατροκτόνους τε δωμάτων πορθήτορας ('you see the two *turannoi*, parricides and destroyers of the house', 973–4; cf. 1040). And a little later the Chorus praise Orestes as follows: ἠλευθέρωσας πᾶσαν Ἀργείων πόλιν | δυοῖν δρακόντοιν εὐπετῶς τεμὼν κάρα ('You have freed the entire city of Argos, easily cutting off the heads of the two serpents', 1046–7). Next, in the second half of *Eumenides*, the play that follows *Choephori* in the *Oresteia* trilogy, what are only a few lonely references in *Choephori* become a central part of the dramaturgy when the setting shifts to Athens. To give just the most obvious examples, the extended aetiology of the Areopagus, the on-stage presence of silent jurors, and the procession at the end of the play which evokes that of the Panathenaia all place the play firmly in a *polis* context.

In its own way, Euripides' *Electra* also intermittently introduces a civic community, which welcomes Orestes and benefits from the killing of Aegisthus and Clytemnestra, into a play which is set in the countryside and centres on domestic affairs. In a brief song after the recognition the Chorus pray that Orestes' arrival in the *polis* be accompanied by good fortune (593–5), and after the Messenger has reported the death of Aegisthus, they call the killing 'just' and refer to the former regime as a *turannis* (877). The report itself is introduced by the Messenger with words that seem to link the country-women who form the Chorus to the town of Mycenae: 'Ο young women of Mycenae, glorious in victory (ὦ καλλίνικοι παρθένοι Μυκηνίδες), I report Orestes' victory to all *philoi*' (761–2). Similarly, Electra bids farewell at the end of the play to the *polis* and (the only other instance of the word in tragedy) its *politides* (1334–5). Imitating *Eumenides*, moreover, Euripides' *Electra* makes reference to Athens near the end. Speaking as *deus ex machina*, Castor tells Orestes in some detail that he should go to Athens and escape the Furies by clasping the statue of Athena and being tried on the hill of Ares (1254–75).

Compared to these plays, it is notable that Sophocles' *Electra* does not make any mention of Athens, the *polis* of

Sophocles' first spectators. Compared to *Eumenides*, moreover, Sophocles does not even remotely give the prominence to the civic community that he could have done. On the other hand, however, it is obvious that Sophocles *does* give a *certain* prominence to the civic community and that he does so especially through the Chorus. Like Aeschylus' and Euripides' choruses, Sophocles' has distinct civic connections, and in some ways perhaps even more so.

As I just noted, the Chorus of *Choephori* take some interest in the fortunes of the civic community but in one important respect they are more removed from the *polis* than their counterparts in Sophocles: as early as the parodos, it is established unequivocally that they belong to the household ('I come out of the house...', 22–3) and, what is more, that they are slavewomen (75–81). This distinctly uncivic identity focuses them on the house. By comparison, the Chorus of Euripides' *Electra*, free women that they are, are potentially closer to the civic community. Euripides uses this potential when he has them addressed as 'women of Mycenae' and *politides*. Like Sophocles' chorus, that of Euripides has the kind of vague identity that allows them both to speak as young women to the young woman Electra and still to have civic associations. However, the vagueness of their identity has a larger gap to bridge than is the case in Sophocles' play. Despite the two civic addresses, the Chorus are emphatically countrywomen. 'Far away from town', they say, 'I don't know the *polis*' (298–9). And it is, I think, worth pointing out that they reply to neither of the two addresses that I just quoted. Euripides seems less at pains than Sophocles to weld the various parts of his chorus's identity into a homogeneous whole. Different again is *Eumenides*. The play ends with the Eumenides praying extensively for the good of the *polis* and (probably) with a supplementary chorus accompanying the procession off-stage. Sophocles' *Electra* does not imitate this heavy emphasis on the civic. None the less, it is worth noting that even after being assuaged by Athena the Eumenides always remain dangerous goddesses. They are never as close to the Athenian citizen body as the chorus of Sophocles.

This brief comparison of the various Electra plays helps to put my discussion of Sophocles' *Electra* into perspective. First of all it confirms what I stressed at the outset: *Electra* is a play in which the large group that is the civic community plays a far smaller role than it might have done. Secondly, however, something else has become clear. Thanks not least to the Chorus, the large group does have its place.

Looked at, therefore, in the context of my two general arguments about the large group in Sophocles, *Electra* does indeed turn out to be a limiting case. It is a play that differs strongly from the other two Sophoclean plays I have discussed in this chapter (and indeed from the four plays for which there was not enough space), but many of the differences are quantitative rather than qualitative. Most importantly, in all three plays the chorus represent the large group. In *Electra* this large group is not under threat to the same degree as it is in *Oedipus Rex* and *Ajax*, but here, too, the large group strongly desires change from early on. The large group of *Electra* does not look at one individual in the way those of *Oedipus Rex* and *Ajax* do, but, as the play goes on, it increasingly focuses on Orestes as the man who will bring change, and in the end it is not disappointed in its hopes. As in the other two plays, its precise identity is vague, perhaps in fact even more so. At its centre there is the civic community of Mycenae-Argos, but for a long time the house seems to have its place too. Once again the Chorus with their flexible perspective are crucial. They speak about the concerns of both the house and the civic community, thus doing their best to give the house a voice and to make it part of the large group. As a result, even the most female, domestic and familial of Sophoclean tragedies offers spectators more than negligible involvement in the plight of a large group, a large group, moreover, which is surprisingly close to the Athenian citizen body.

As in *Oedipus Rex* and *Ajax* the large group undergoes change, if change of a different nature. The large group in *Electra* is too polymorphous to last. In the end it is only the civic community that is saved. Nothing is said about the well-being of the house. What is more, spectators are given various hints which suggest that the house, which has always been in trouble, is still not safe when the play is over. Orestes' coming, it seems, will save the civic community and, at least for the moment, Orestes and Electra, but it does not seem to help the house. The references to the community that are scattered through the play, difficult to interpret as some of them are, are ultimately a source of comfort when the large group seems to benefit from Orestes' and Electra's revenge. However, there is at least as much discomforting as comforting at the end of *Electra*. Many questions remain open. Not the least disturbing among them is that of the fate of the house. As the definition of the house has become no easier than it was for long stretches of the play, one way of talking about it is to fall back again, as Electra always does, on individuals in a building and put the question like this: what kind of lives will Orestes and Electra lead in a house in which both their parents have been murdered by kin?

CONCLUSION

Choirs, I noted near the beginning of this chapter, had their very specific place in ancient Greek culture, singing and dancing as they did at a wide variety of festivals. Ancient spectators, therefore, will have got involved in the performances of Sophoclean choruses in ways that are barred to their modern successors. However, I went on to argue, cultural context is not the only factor that has a bearing on the way spectators engage with the choruses. In keeping with the subject of this book, I concentrated instead on the language that they use and that is used of them. I suggested that there is much in the language that can communicate to the spectators the group experience that is enacted on stage. In the first place of course, this is true for performances in ancient Greece but, so I claimed, to a lesser degree it is also true for the modern world. I hope that my discussion of *Oedipus Rex*, *Ajax* and *Electra* has justified this claim.

Most of what I have said relates to two main arguments. The first turns on what I referred to as the large group. The language which is used of and by Sophoclean choruses gives them a vague continuity with large off-stage groups which, like the audience itself, are uncountable multitudes, are the only such multitudes in their respective plays, and, important especially for ancient spectators, resemble civic communities. Because of this vague continuity, I suggested, Sophoclean choruses offer a group perspective that can be an attractive one to adopt, for spectators in ancient Athens but also for their modern successors.

Following on from there, my second central argument was that in so far as spectators adopt this group perspective they are at first threatened and in need of a saviour, but find themselves ending the play in safety. As I noted repeatedly, details vary greatly. Neither of the two arguments applies to all plays in the same way. The large group, its relation with the chorus, the saviour and the large group's eventual safety differ both in kind and in prominence from one play to the next, just as spectators no doubt differ in the way they respond to all these matters. But despite all such differences, it is (I think) fair to say that in all of Sophocles' extant plays the chorus and the language used by and of them provide much scope for many different spectators to engage with a group that is in danger but ultimately survives. I will conclude with a few remarks about both of the two arguments, beginning with the second.

The focus on the safety of groups is one of many features of Sophoclean tragedy which justify Sophocles' title the 'tragic Homer'.[114] An all-pervasive concern of both *Iliad* and *Odyssey* is the threat posed to cities, to armies, to comrades, to suitors and to other groups. Yet this similarity highlights an equally central difference. While in Homer many groups are destroyed, Sophoclean groups survive. Iliadic Troy is sacked but Sophocles' Thebes survives the plague.[115] Further work

---

[114] Attributed to Polemo: Diog. Laert. 4.20.

[115] Unfortunately there is only little evidence for Sophocles' *Troy*. Its destruction is likely to have had a place in *Ajax Lokros*, *Polyxena* and *Laocoon*, but hardly anything is known about the way it was treated; see Anderson (1997) 174–6. It is noteworthy that in the Sophoclean tragedies that survive, the fall of Troy plays a much smaller role than in various Euripidean ones (especially *Andromache*, *Hecuba* and *Troades*).

on this recurrent deviation from Homeric stories would be likely to throw new light on the meaning of both Homer and tragedy in fifth-century Athens.

All I want to do here is recall the article by Robert Parker to which I referred in the previous chapter.[116] Parker begins an investigation into similarities and differences between civic and tragic gods by pointing to a commonplace that is frequent in Athenian civic discourse: the gods are not to be blamed for the misfortunes of the *polis*. Tragic gods, Parker goes on to argue, may be different, but they are so to a much lesser degree than has often been assumed. In the previous chapter I concentrated on the notion of divine responsibility that is implied in the civic commonplace which Parker discusses, and found myself agreeing with Parker's emphasis on similarities between civic and not generally tragic but more particularly Sophoclean gods. This chapter, which has been concerned with choruses and groups rather than gods, now confirms a further aspect of the similarity Parker describes: Sophoclean gods let the group survive. The link between gods and the group's survival is not as direct as in the civic commonplace but it is still noticeable. Gods, I argued in the previous chapter, make individuals act and give them stories. These stories, I now add, often include a threat to, and the ultimate safety of, the group. While the limelight falls on the individuals, the beneficiaries in their shadow are the cities and armies: Sophocles' groups survive.

With this conclusion the chapter could end. Yet one of the words in the last sentence prompts continuation, and this word is 'shadow'. It suggests that spectators who want to watch Sophoclean groups survive have to strain their eyes. The question arises just how much they can see. This question brings me back for a last time to the chorus. This chapter has in some ways moved away from the concerns of those preceding it. Most notably perhaps, I have said nothing about the involvement created by simultaneous knowledge and igno-

---

[116] Parker (1997). See chapter 4, pp. 185–6.

rance. As a result, I also seem to have said more about *what* Sophoclean language communicates (the choruses' vague continuity with the large group and the large group's move from danger to safety) than about *how* it communicates it. But as I arrive at the end of the chapter, it becomes clear that I have not moved away as far from my original programme as it might at first have seemed. Vagueness and hovering between certainty and uncertainty have again played a large role, if not the same one as before. Again it has been obvious that Sophoclean language often communicates by leaving much unsaid and much unclarified. A recurrent theme of my discussion has been the flexibility of Sophoclean choruses. The language that both the choruses and other characters use often makes it difficult to know what kind of group a chorus represent. It is clear that this particular aspect of the characteristic elusiveness in the way Sophoclean language communicates is rather different from those which I presented in earlier chapters. Yet even so it, too, makes its own significant contributions to the spectators' potential involvement in the plays.[117]

Spectators who adopt the perspectives which choruses offer them get to see the play from a variety of angles. As the threatened *polis* of Thebes, they can look at Oedipus the chosen saviour; as humans and spectators, they can look at Oedipus the paradigm. They may worry with Ajax's men about the Greek army and think as Greeks about the terrors of war. They may long for the return of Orestes perhaps not only as the civic community of Mycenae-Argos but also as the house of Atreus. Plays differ in the way perspectives change, are combined and separated. But at least in all three plays that I discussed, the perspective at the end is no longer that of the beginning. Both

---

[117] I should stress that what I have described for Sophocles is certainly not unheard of in Aeschylus or Euripides either. The choruses of Aeschylus' *Eumenides* and Euripides' *Hippolytus, Phoenissae, Electra* and *Medea*, to name just a few, all share with their Sophoclean counterparts a certain vagueness of outlook and identity which lends them both civic and distinctly uncivic features (cf. the remarks in Gould (1996) 224–33). However, to judge from the surviving tragedies, the identity of Sophoclean choruses is more elusive more often. Cf. also above, p. 204, n. 24 and p. 205, n. 27.

Thebans and Ajax's men are still there but have to share their place with humans at large, and the house of *Electra* has been completely dropped from the Chorus's concerns.

This elusiveness of Sophocles' chorus has two rather different but connected effects on the way spectators may perceive the saving of the group. On the one hand, it is difficult to follow the continuous story of a particular group that is first threatened and then saved. The group behind the chorus is too fluid to make it sustain such a narrative. Assessment of what happens to it is bound to vary from spectator to spectator and from play to play. Some may assume that the group that was threatened is eventually saved, while others may have doubts. Some may be confident in *this* play and others in *that* play.

On the other hand, at the end of all extant plays all spectators are offered *a* perspective of a group that is safe. Thanks to the same fluidity of the large group, even spectators who are worried when they cannot follow the story of a group that is threatened and saved, can detect behind every Sophoclean chorus first *a* group that is in one way or another threatened and then *a* group that is safe. Although little is seen of the large group, it undergoes manifest development. Something that gives Sophoclean tragedies an almost consolatory power despite the terrible suffering and the disconcerting questions with which they confront spectators is the fact that spectators, then and now, and with all their individual differences, not only suffer and not only look for answers but can also have themselves collectively transported from danger to safety. Sophoclean choruses and the large group that is somewhere behind them provide a degree of permanence and stability in a world of death, despair and destruction.

SHORT TITLES OF EDITIONS AND WORKS
OF REFERENCE

Allen	T. W. Allen, *Homeri opera*, vol. v. Oxford 1909
Barrett	W. S. Barrett, *Euripides: Hippolytos*. Oxford 1964
Buchheim	T. Buchheim, *Gorgias: Reden, Fragmente und Testimonien*. Hamburg 1989
Campbell	L. Campbell, *Sophocles: the plays and fragments*, 2 vols. Oxford 1871–81
Davies	M. Davies, *Sophocles: Trachiniae*. Oxford 1991
Dawe	R. D. Dawe, *Sophocles*, third edn. Stuttgart and Leipzig 1996
Dawe	R. D. Dawe, *Sophocles: Oedipus Rex*. Cambridge 1982
Dover	K. J. Dover, *Aristophanes: Clouds*. Oxford 1968
Easterling	P. E. Easterling, *Sophocles: Trachiniae*. Cambridge 1982
Ellendt	F. Ellendt, *Lexicon Sophocleum*, second edn. Berlin 1872
Fraenkel	E. Fraenkel, *Aeschylus: Agamemnon*, 3 vols. Oxford 1950
Garvie	A. F. Garvie, *Sophocles: Ajax*. Warminster 1998
Garvie	A. F. Garvie, *Aeschylus: Choephori*. Oxford 1986
Greene	W. C. Greene, *Scholia Platonica*. Haverford, PA, 1938
Jebb	R. C. Jebb, *Sophocles: the plays and fragments with critical notes, commentary, and translation in English prose*, 7 vols. Cambridge 1883–96
K–A	R. Kassel and C. Austin, *Poetae comici Graeci*, vol. v. Berlin and New York 1986
Kamerbeek	J. C. Kamerbeek, *The plays of Sophocles: commentaries*, 7 vols. Leiden 1963–84
Kells	J. H. Kells, *Sophocles: Electra*. Cambridge 1973
K–G	R. Kühner and B. Gerth, *Ausführliche Grammatik der griechischen Sprache: zweiter Teil: Satzlehre*, third edn. Hanover and Leipzig 1898–1904

LIMC	*Lexicon iconographicum mythologiae classicae*, 8 vols. Zurich and Munich 1981–97
Lloyd-Jones	H. Lloyd-Jones, *Sophocles*, Loeb, 2 vols. Cambridge, MA, and London 1994
Lloyd-Jones and Wilson	H. Lloyd-Jones and N. G. Wilson, *Sophoclis fabulae*, reprinted with corrections. Oxford 1992
Louis	P. Louis, *Aristote: Problèmes*, 3 vols. Paris 1991–4
LSJ	H. G. Liddell, R. Scott, H. Stuart Jones, R. McKenzie, *A Greek–English lexicon*, ninth edn. Oxford 1940
N	A. Nauck, *Tragicorum Graecorum fragmenta*, second edn. Leipzig 1926
Pearson	A. C. Pearson, *The fragments of Sophocles*, 3 vols. Cambridge 1917
Pearson	A. C. Pearson, *Sophoclis fabulae*, reprinted with corrections. Oxford 1928
PMG	D. L. Page, *Poetae Melici Graeci*. Oxford 1962
Radt	S. Radt, *Tragicorum Graecorum fragmenta: vol. 3: Aeschylus*. Göttingen 1985
Radt	S. Radt, *Tragicorum Graecorum fragmenta: vol. 4: Sophocles*. Göttingen 1977; 'Addenda et corrigenda' in *Tragicorum Graecorum fragmenta: vol. 3: Aeschylus*. Göttingen 1985, 561–92
RE	G. Wissowa *et al.*, *Pauly's Realencyclopädie der classischen Altertumswissenschaft: neue Bearbeitung*, 83 vols. Stuttgart and Munich 1893–1978
Schwyzer	E. Schwyzer, *Griechische Grammatik*, 2 vols. Munich 1939–71
Stanford	W. B. Stanford, *Sophocles: Ajax*. London and New York 1963
Ussher	R. G. Ussher, *Sophocles: Philoctetes* (Φιλοκτήτης). Warminster 1990
Webster	T. B. L. Webster, *Sophocles: Philoctetes*. Cambridge 1970
West	M. L. West, *Iambi et elegi Graeci*, 2 vols., second edn. Oxford 1989–92

BIBLIOGRAPHY

Adams, S. M. (1957) *Sophocles the playwright.* Toronto
Anderson, M. J. (1997) *The fall of Troy in early Greek poetry and art.* Oxford
Andrewes, A. (1956) *The Greek tyrants.* London
Åzelius, I. E. (1897) *De assimilatione syntactica apud Sophoclem.* Upsala
Bakker, E. J. (ed.) (1997) *Grammar as interpretation: Greek literature in its linguistic contexts.* Leiden, New York and Cologne
Bauer, B. L. M. (1995) *The emergence and development of SVO patterning in Latin and French: diachronic and psycholinguistic perspectives.* New York and Oxford
Beckerman, B. (1970) *Dynamics of drama: theory and method of analysis.* New York
Bennett, S. (1990) *Theatre audiences: a theory of production and reception.* London and New York
Bers, V. (1994) 'Tragedy and rhetoric', in Worthington (1994) 176–95
Beye, C. R. (1970) 'Sophocles' *Philoctetes* and the Homeric embassy', *TAPA* 101: 63–75
Bierl, A. and P. von Möllendorff (eds.) (1994) *Orchestra: Drama, Mythos, Bühne.* Stuttgart and Leipzig
Bilde, P. *et al.* (eds.) (1997) *Conventional values of the Hellenistic Greeks.* Aarhus
Blau, H. (1983) 'Universals of performance; or, amortizing play', *SubStance* 37/8: 140–61
  (1990) *The audience.* Baltimore
Bowersock, G. W. *et al.* (eds.) (1979) *Arktouros: Hellenic studies presented to Bernard M. W. Knox on the occasion of his 65th birthday.* Berlin and New York
Bowra, C. M. (1944) *Sophoclean tragedy.* Oxford
Bruhn, E. (1899) *Sophokles: erklärt von F. W. Schneidewin und A. Nauck: achtes Bändchen: Anhang.* Berlin
Bulman, J. C. (ed.) (1996) *Shakespeare, theory, and performance.* London
Burian, P. (1972) 'Supplication and hero cult in Sophocles' *Ajax*', *GRBS* 13: 151–6
  (1977) 'The play before the prologue: initial tableaux on the Greek stage', in D'Arms and Eadie (1977) 79–94

Burkert, W. (1985a) 'Opferritual bei Sophokles: Pragmatik – Symbolik – Theater', *AU* 28: 5–20

(1985b [1977]) *Greek religion: archaic and classical*, trans. John Raffan. Oxford

Burton, R. W. B. (1980) *The chorus in Sophocles' tragedies*. Oxford

Buxton, R. G. A. (1982) *Persuasion in Greek tragedy: a study of peitho.* Cambridge

(1987) 'The gods in Sophocles', in Nearchou (1987) 9–14

(1988) 'Bafflement in Greek tragedy', *Metis* 3: 41–51

Calame, C. (1997 [1977]) *Choruses of young women in ancient Greece (their morphology, religious role, and social functions)*, trans. D. Collins and J. Orion. Lanham

Calder, W. M. III (1971) 'Sophoclean apologia: *Philoctetes*', *GRBS* 12: 153–74

Cameron, A. (1968) *The identity of Oedipus the King: five essays on the Oedipus Tyrannus*. New York and London

Campbell, L. (1871) 'Introductory essay on the language of Sophocles', in *Sophocles: the plays and fragments*, vol. I, 1–98. Oxford (this work is cited by paragraph numbers, which, unlike the page numbers, are identical in various editions)

Carey, C. (1986) 'The second stasimon of Sophocles' *Oedipus Tyrannus*', *JHS* 106: 175–9

Carlson, M. (1990a) *Theatre semiotics: signs of life*, Bloomington and Indianapolis

(1990b [1986]) 'Psychic polyphony', in Carlson (1990a) 95–109

(1990c [1989]) 'Theatre audiences and the reading of performance', in Carlson (1990a), 10–25

(1993) *Theories of the theatre: a historical and critical survey from the Greeks to the present*, expanded edition. Ithaca and London

Cartledge, P. and F. D. Harvey (eds.) (1985) *Crux: essays in Greek history presented to G. E. M. de Ste Croix on his 75th birthday*. London

Comrie, B. (1989) *Language universals and linguistic typology: syntax and morphology*, second edn. Oxford

Connolly, A. (1998) 'Was Sophocles heroised as Dexion', *JHS* 118: 1–21

Connor, W. R. (1977) 'Tyrannis polis', in D'Arms and Eadie (1977) 95–109

Cook, A. B. (1914–40) *Zeus: a study in ancient religion*, 3 vols. Cambridge

Coray, M. (1993) *Wissen und Erkennen bei Sophokles*. Basel and Berlin = *Schweizerische Beiträge zur Altertumswissenschaft* 24

Costanza, S. *et al.* (eds.) (1972) *Studi classici in onore di Quintino Cataudella*, vol. I. Catania

Craik, E. M. (ed.) (1990) *'Owls to Athens': essays on classical subjects presented to Sir Kenneth Dover*. Oxford

Cropp, M. (1997) 'Antigone's final speech (Sophocles, *Antigone* 891–928)', *G & R* 44: 137–60

Csapo, E. and W. J. Slater (1994) *The context of ancient drama*. Ann Arbor

D'Arms, J. H. and J. W. Eadie (eds.) (1977) *Ancient and modern: essays in honor of Gerald F. Else*. Ann Arbor

Davidson, J. F. (1987) 'Sophocles, *Trachiniae* 497: μέγα τι σθένος ἁ Κύπρις ἐκφέρεται νίκας ἀεί', *PP* 42: 286–90

   (1995) 'Homer and Sophocles' *Philoctetes*', in Griffiths (1995) 25–35

Davies, M. (1991) 'The end of Sophocles' *O.T.* revisited', *Prometheus* 17: 1–18

Dawe, R. D. (1973) *Studies on the text of Sophocles: volume I: the manuscripts and the text*. Leiden

   (1978) *Studies on the text of Sophocles: volume III: Women of Trachis – Antigone – Philoctetes – Oedipus at Colonus*. Leiden

De Grouchy, G. A. (1985) 'Proverbial and gnomic material in Greek tragedy', unpublished Ph.D. thesis. Cambridge

De Jong, I. J. F. (1987) *Narrators and focalizers: the presentation of the story in the Iliad*. Amsterdam

De Marinis, M. (1987) 'Dramaturgy of the spectator', *TDR* 31.2: 100–14

   (1993 [1992]) *The semiotics of performance*, trans. Aine O'Healy. Bloomington and Indianapolis

Denniston, J. D. (1952) *Greek prose style*. Oxford

Diggle, J. (1981) *Studies on the text of Euripides: Supplices, Electra, Heracles, Troades, Iphigenia in Tauris, Ion*. Oxford

Dolan, J. (1988) *The feminist spectator as critic*. Ann Arbor and London

Dover, K. (1997) *The evolution of Greek prose style*. Oxford

Duchemin, J. (1945) *L'agon dans la tragédie grecque*. Paris

Earp, F. R. (1944) *The style of Sophocles*. Cambridge

Easterling, P. E. (1977) 'Character in Sophocles', *G & R* 24: 121–9

   (1978) '*Philoctetes* and modern criticism', *ICS* 3: 27–39

   (1990) 'Constructing character in Greek tragedy', in Pelling (1990) 83–99

   (1993a) 'Tragedy and ritual', in Scodel (1993) 7–23

   (1993b) 'Gods on stage in Greek tragedy', *Grazer Beiträge* Suppl. V: 77–86

   (1997a) 'Constructing the heroic', in Pelling (ed.) (1997) 21–37

   (1997b) 'Form and performance', in Easterling (ed.) (1997) 151–77

   (1997c) 'The language of the *polis* in *Oedipus at Colonus*', in Papademetriou (1997) 273–82

   (ed.) (1997) *The Cambridge companion to Greek tragedy*. Cambridge

Easterling, P. E. and J. V. Muir (eds.) (1985) *Greek religion and society*. Cambridge

Eckermann, J. P. (1971 [1836]) *Conversations with Goethe*, trans. J. Oxenford, ed. J. K. Moorhead. London

Edmunds, L. and R. W. Wallace (eds.) (1997) *Poet, public, and performance in ancient Greece*. Baltimore and London

Elam, K. (1980) *The semiotics of theatre and drama*. London and New York

Ellis, J. (1992) *Visible fictions: cinema: television: video*, revised edition. London and New York

Esposito, S. (1996) 'The changing roles of the Sophoclean chorus', *Arion* 4.1: 85–114

Euben, J. P. (ed.) (1986) *Greek tragedy and political theory*. Berkeley, Los Angeles and London

Falkner, T. (1998) 'Containing tragedy: rhetoric and self-representation in Sophocles' *Philoctetes*', *Classical Antiquity* 17: 25–58

Ferrari, F. (1983) *Ricerche sul testo di Sofocle*. Pisa

Finkelberg, M. (1996) 'The second stasimon of the *Trachiniae* and Heracles' Festival on Mount Oeta', *Mnemosyne* 49: 129–43

Fischer-Lichte, E. (1992 [1983]) *The semiotics of theater*, trans. Jeremy Gaines and Doris L. Jones. Bloomington and Indianapolis

Flashar, H. (ed.) (1997) *Tragödie: Idee und Transformation*. Stuttgart and Leipzig

Foley, H. P. (1993) 'Oedipus as *Pharmakos*', in Rosen and Farrell (1993) 525–38

Forster, E. M. (1993 [1927]) *Aspects of the novel*. London

Foxhall, L. and J. Salmon (eds.) (1998) *Thinking men: masculinity and its self-representation in the classical tradition*. London

Fraenkel, E. (1977) *Due seminari romani: Aiace e Filottete di Sofocle*, eds. L. E. Rossi *et al.* Rome

Friis Johansen, H. (1954) 'Some features of sentence-structure in Aeschylus' *Suppliants*', *C & M* 15: 1–59

  (1962) 'Sophocles 1939–1959', *Lustrum* 7: 94–288

  (1964) 'Die Elektra des Sophokles: Versuch einer neuen Deutung', *C & M* 25: 8–32

Fuqua, C. (1976) 'Studies in the use of myth in Sophocles' "Philoctetes" and the "Orestes" of Euripides', *Traditio* 32: 29–95

Gardiner, C. P. (1987) *The Sophoclean chorus: a study of character and function*. Iowa City

Garner, R. (1990) *From Homer to tragedy: the art of allusion in Greek poetry*. London and New York

Garvie, A. F. (1972) 'Deceit, violence, and persuasion in the *Philoctetes*', in Costanza *et al.* (1972) 213–26

Gellie, G. (1986) 'The last scene of the *Oedipus Tyrannus*', *Ramus* 15: 35–42

Genette, G. (1980 [1972]) *Narrative discourse*, trans. Jane E. Lewin. Oxford

Gentili, B. (1986) 'Il tiranno, l'eroe e la dimensione tragica', in Gentili and Pretagostini (1986) 117–23

Gentili, B. and R. Pretagostini (eds.) (1986) *Edipo: il teatro greco e la cultura europea: Atti del convegno internazionale (Urbino 15–19 novembre 1982)*. Rome

Gill, C. (1986) 'The question of character and personality in Greek tragedy', *Poetics today* 7: 251–73

(1990) 'The character–personality distinction', in Pelling (1990) 1–31

(1996) *Personality in Greek epic, tragedy, and philosophy: the self in dialogue.* Oxford

Girard, R. (1977 [1972]) *Violence and the sacred*, trans. Patrick Gregory. Baltimore

Gnoli, G. and J.-P. Vernant (eds.) (1982) *La mort, les morts dans les sociétés anciennes.* Cambridge and Paris

Goff, B. (ed.) (1995) *History, tragedy, theory: dialogues on Athenian drama.* Austin

Goheen, R. F. (1951) *The imagery of Sophocles'* Antigone: *a study of poetic language and structure.* Princeton

Goldhill, S. (1986) *Reading Greek tragedy.* Cambridge

(1990a) 'The Great Dionysia and civic ideology', in Winkler and Zeitlin (1990) 97–129

(1990b) 'Character and action, representation and reading: Greek tragedy and its critics', in Pelling (1990) 100–27

(1997a) 'The language of tragedy: rhetoric and communication', in Easterling (ed.) (1997) 127–150

(1997b) 'The audience of Athenian tragedy', in Easterling (ed.) (1997) 54–68

(unpublished) 'Power and politics in the *Oresteia*'

Gould, J. (1978) 'Dramatic character and "human intelligibility" in Greek tragedy', *PCPS* 24: 43–67

(1985) 'On making sense of Greek religion', in Easterling and Muir (1985) 1–33

(1996) 'Tragedy and collective experience', in Silk (1996) 217–43

Griffith, M. (1995) 'Brilliant dynasts', *CA* 14: 62–129

(1998) 'The king and eye: the rule of the father in Greek tragedy', *PCPS* 44: 20–84

Griffith, R. D. (1992) 'Asserting eternal providence: theodicy in Sophocles' *Oedipus the King*', *ICS* 17: 193–211

(1993) 'Oedipus *Pharmakos*?: alleged scapegoating in Sophocles' *Oedipus the King*', *Phoenix* 47: 95–114

Griffiths, A. (ed.) (1995) *Stage directions: essays in ancient drama in honour of E. W. Handley*, London = *BICS* Supplement 66

Haberlandt, O. (1897) *De figurae quae vocatur etymologica usu Sophocleo.* Freienwalde

Hall, E. (1995) 'Lawcourt dramas: the power of performance in Greek forensic oratory', *BICS* 40: 39–58

(1997) 'The sociology of Athenian tragedy', in Easterling (ed.) (1997) 93–126

Hamilton, R. (1975) 'Neoptolemos' story in the *Philoctetes*', *AJPh* 96: 131–7

Hancock, J. L. (1917) *Studies in stichomythia.* Chicago

Hansen, M. H. (ed.) (1993) *The ancient Greek city-state: Symposium on the occasion of the 250th anniversary of The Royal Danish Academy of*

Sciences and Letters July 1–4 1992. Copenhagen = *Acts of the Co-penhagen Polis Centre* vol. I

(ed.) (1995) *Sources for the ancient Greek city state: Symposium August 24–27 1994*. Copenhagen = *Acts of the Copenhagen Polis Centre* vol. II

(ed.) (1996) *Introduction to an inventory of poleis: Symposium August 23–26 1995*. Copenhagen = *Acts of the Copenhagen Polis Centre* vol. III

Hawley, R. (1998) 'The male body as spectacle in Attic drama', in Foxhall and Salmon (1998) 83–99

Hay, J. *et al.* (eds.) (1996) *The audience and its landscape*. Boulder, CO, and Oxford

Heiden, B. (1989) *Tragic rhetoric: an interpretation of Sophocles'* Trachiniae. New York

Henrichs, A. (1984) 'Loss of self, suffering, violence: the modern view of Dionysus from Nietzsche to Girard', *HSCP* 88: 205–40

(1993) 'The tomb of Aias and the prospect of hero cult in Sophokles', *CA* 12: 165–80

(1994/5) '"Why should I dance?": choral self-referentiality in Greek tragedy', *Arion* 3.1: 56–111

Herington, J. (1985) *Poetry into drama: early tragedy and the Greek poetic tradition*. Berkeley

Hester, D. (1984) 'The banishment of Oedipus: a neglected theory on the end of the *Oedipus Rex*', *Antichthon* 18: 13–23

(1986) 'The central character(s) of the *Antigone* and their relationship to the chorus', *Ramus* 15: 74–81

Hodgdon, B. (1996) 'Looking for Mr. Shakespeare after "the revolution": Robert Lepage's intercultural *Dream* machine', in Bulman (1996) 68–91

Hölscher, U. (1975) 'Wie soll ich noch tanzen?: Über ein Wort des sopho-kleischen Chores', in Köhler (1975) 376–93

Holt, P. (1989) 'The end of the *Trachiniai* and the fate of Herakles', *JHS* 109: 69–80

Hoppin, M. C. (1981) 'What happens in Sophocles' *Philoctetes?*', *Traditio* 37: 1–30

(1990), 'Metrical effects, dramatic illusion, and the two endings of Sophocles' *Philoctetes*', *Arethusa* 23: 141–82

Horrocks, G. (1997) *Greek: a history of the language and its speakers*. London and New York

Ingarden, R. (1973 [1937]) *The cognition of the literary work of art*, trans. Ann Crowley and Kenneth R. Olson. Evanston

Iser, W. (1976) *Der Akt des Lesens: Theorie ästhetischer Wirkung*. Munich

Jörgensen, O. (1904) 'Das Auftreten der Götter in den Büchern ι–μ der Odyssee', *Hermes* 39: 357–82

Jones, J. (1962) *On Aristotle and Greek tragedy*. London

Jordan, B. (1979) *Servants of the gods: a study in the religion, history and literature of fifth-century Athens*. Göttingen = *Hypomnemata* 55

Juffras, D. M. (1991) 'Sophocles' *Electra* 973–85 and tyrannicide', *TAPA* 121: 99–108

Kearns, E. (1989) *The heroes of Attica*. London = *Bulletin of the Institute of Classical Studies* Suppl. 57

Kempson, R. M. (1977) *Semantic theory*. Cambridge

Kennedy, G. A. (1994) *A new history of classical rhetoric*. Princeton

Kip, M. M. van E. T. (1990) *Reader and spectator: problems in the interpretation of Greek tragedy*. Amsterdam

Kirkwood, G. M. (1994a [1958]) *A study of Sophoclean drama*. Ithaca
(1994b) 'Persuasion and allusion in Sophocles' "Philoctetes"', *Hermes* 122: 425–36

Kittmer, J. (1995) 'Sophoclean sophistics: a reading of *Philoktetes*', *MD* 34: 9–35

Kitto, H. D. F. (1958) *Sophocles: dramatist and philosopher*. London, New York and Toronto

Kitzinger, R. (1991) 'Why mourning becomes Elektra', *ClAnt* 10: 298–327
(1993) 'What do you know? the end of Oedipus', in Rosen and Farrell (1993) 539–56

Knox, B. M. W. (1957) *Oedipus at Thebes*. London and New Haven
(1964) *The heroic temper: studies in Sophoclean tragedy*. Berkeley, Los Angeles and London

Köhler, E. (ed.) (1975) *Sprachen der Lyrik: Festschrift für Hugo Friedrich zum 70. Geburtstag*. Frankfurt

Kugler, L. G. E. (1905) *De Sophoclis quae vocantur abusionibus*. Göttingen

Lada, I. (1996) '"Weeping for Hecuba": is it a "Brechtian" act?', *Arethusa* 29: 87–124
(1997) (Lada-Richards) '"Estrangement" or "reincarnation"?: performers and performance on the classical Athenian stage', *Arion* 5.2: 66–107

Lanza, L. and L. Fort (1991) *Sofocle: problemi di tradizione indiretta*. Padua

Lardinois, A. (1997) 'Modern paroemiology and the use of gnomai in Homer's *Iliad*', *CPh* 92: 213–34

Lattimore, R. (1958) *The poetry of Greek tragedy*. Baltimore and London

Lefèvre, E. (1987) 'Die Unfähigkeit, sich zu erkennen: unzeitgemäße Bemerkungen zu Sophokles' *Oidipus Tyrannos*', *WJb* 13: 37–58

Lesky, A. (1972) *Die tragische Dichtung der Hellenen*, third edn. Göttingen

Ley, G. (1986) 'On the pressure of circumstance in Greek tragedy', *Ramus* 15: 43–51

Lloyd, A. B. (ed.) (1997) *What is a god?: studies in the nature of Greek divinity*. London

Lloyd, M. (1992) *The agon in Euripides*. Oxford

Lloyd-Jones, H. and N. G. Wilson (1990) *Sophoclea: studies on the text of Sophocles*. Oxford
(1997) *Sophocles: second thoughts*. Göttingen

Long, A. A. (1968) *Language and thought in Sophocles: a study of abstract nouns and poetic technique.* London

Loraux, N. (1982) 'Mourir devant Troie, tomber pour Athènes: de la gloire du héros à l'idée de la cité', in Gnoli and Vernant (1982) 27–43

(1993 [1984]) *The children of Athena: Athenian ideas about citizenship and the division between the sexes,* trans. C. Levine. Princeton

(1986 [1981]) *The invention of Athens: the funeral oration in the classical city,* trans. Alan Sheridan. Cambridge, MA, and London

McDevitt, A. S. (1982) 'The first Kommos of Sophocles' *Antigone* (806–882)', *Ramus* 11: 134–44

MacDowell, D. M. (1989) 'Athenian laws about choruses', in Nieto (1989) 65–77

McGlew, J. F. (1993) *Tyranny and political culture in ancient Greece.* Ithaca and London

Mackail, J. W. (1910) *Lectures on Greek poetry.* London, New York, Bombay and Calcutta

Mandel, O. (1981) *Philoctetes and the fall of Troy: plays, documents, iconography, interpretations.* Lincoln, NE and London

Manuwald, B. (1992) 'Oidipus und Adrastos: Bemerkungen zur neueren Diskussion um die Schuldfrage in Sophokles' "König Oidipus"', *RhM* 135: 1–43

March, J. R. (1991–3) 'Sophocles' *Ajax*: the death and burial of a hero', *BICS* 38: 1–36

Mastronarde, D. J. (1990) 'Actors on high: the skene roof, the crane, and the gods in Attic drama', *CA* 9: 247–94

(1994) *Euripides: Phoenissae.* Cambridge

Matthews, P. H. (1981) *Syntax.* Cambridge

Mikalson, J. D. (1983) *Athenian popular religion.* Chapel Hill and London

(1991) *Honor thy gods: popular religion in Greek tragedy.* Chapel Hill and London

Moorhouse, A. C. (1982) *The syntax of Sophocles.* Leiden

Morley, D. (1996) 'The geography of television: ethnography, communications, and community', in Hay *et al.* (1996) 317–42

Mossé, C. (1985) ''Αστὴ καὶ πολῖτις: la dénomination de la femme athénienne dans les plaidoyers démosthéniens', *Ktéma* 10: 77–9

Muecke, D. C. (1969) *The compass of irony.* London

Müller, C. W. (1997) *Philoktet: Beiträge zur Wiedergewinnung einer Tragödie des Euripides aus der Geschichte ihrer Rezeption.* Stuttgart and Leipzig

Nagy, G. (1990) *Pindar's Homer: the lyric possession of an epic past.* Baltimore and London

Nearchou, P. (ed.) (1987) *International meeting of ancient Greek drama Delphi 8–12 April 1984, Delphi 4–25 June 1985.* Athens

Nieto, F. J. F. (ed.) (1989) *Symposion 1982: Vorträge zur griechischen und hellenistischen Rechtsgeschichte (Santander, 1.–4. September 1982).* Cologne and Vienna

Norden, E. (1898) *Die antike Kunstprosa vom VI. Jahrhundert v. Chr. bis in die Zeit der Renaissance*, 2 vols. Leipzig
  (1913) *Agnostos theos: Untersuchungen zur Formengeschichte religiöser Rede*. Leipzig
North, H. F. (1966) *Sophrosyne: self-knowledge and self-restraint in Greek literature*. Ithaca
  (1979) *From myth to icon: reflections of Greek ethical doctrine in literature and art*. Ithaca
Nuchelmans, J. C. F. (1949) *Die Nomina des sophokleischen Wortschatzes: Vorarbeiten zu einer sprachgeschichtlichen und stilistischen Analyse*. Nijmegen
Nussbaum, M. C. (1986) *The fragility of goodness: luck and ethics in Greek tragedy and philosophy*. Cambridge
Ober, J. and B. Strauss (1990) 'Drama, political rhetoric, and the discourse of Athenian democracy', in Winkler and Zeitlin (1990) 237–70
O'Higgins, D. (1991) 'Narrators and narrative in the *Philoctetes* of Sophocles', *Ramus* 20: 37–52
O'Neil, J. L. (1986) 'The semantic usage of *tyrannos* and related words', *Antichthon* 20: 26–40
Osborne, R. and S. Hornblower (eds.) (1994) *Ritual, finance, politics: Athenian democratic accounts presented to David Lewis*. Oxford
Østerud, S. (1973) 'The intermezzo with the false merchant in Sophocles' Philoctetes (542–627)', *C & M* Dissertationes 9: 10–26
Panhuis, D. (1984) 'Prolepsis in Greek as a discourse strategy', *Glotta* 62: 26–39
Papademetriou, J.-Th. A. (ed.) (1997) *First panhellenic and international conference on ancient Greek literature: Acta*. Athens
Parke, H. W. and D. E. W. Wormell (1956) *The Delphic oracle*, 2 vols. Oxford
Parker, R. (1997) 'Gods cruel and kind: tragic and civic theology', in Pelling (ed.) (1997) 143–60
Parker, V. (1998) 'Τύραννος: the semantics of a political concept from Archilochus to Aristotle', *Hermes* 126: 145–72
Patterson, C. (1986) '*Hai Attikai*: the other Athenians', *Helios* 13: 49–67
Pavis, P. (ed.) (1996) *The intercultural performance reader*. London and New York
Pelling, C. (1997) 'Conclusion', in Pelling (ed.) (1997) 213–35
  (ed.) (1990) *Characterization and individualization in Greek literature*. Oxford
  (ed.) (1997) *Tragedy and the historian*. Oxford
Peradotto, J. (1992) 'Disauthorizing prophecy: the ideological mapping of *Oedipus Tyrannus*', *TAPA* 122: 1–15
Perlman, S. (1964) 'Quotations from poetry in the Attic orators of the fourth century B.C.', *AJPh* 85: 155–72

Perysinakis, I. N. (1992) 'Sophocles' *Philoctetes* and the Homeric epics', ΔΩΔΩΝΗ, 21: 79–120

   (1994–5) 'Sophocles' *Philoctetes* and the Homeric epics: an anthropological approach', *Maia* 9–10: 377–89

Pickard-Cambridge, A. (1968) *The dramatic festivals of Athens*, second edn, revised by J. Gould and D. M. Lewis. Oxford

Pinker, S. (1995 [1994]) *The language instinct: the new science of language and mind*. Harmondsworth

Pinnoy, M. (1984) 'Plutarch's comment on Sophocles' style', *QUCC* 45: 159–64

Podlecki, A. J. (1966a) 'Creon and Herodotus', *TAPA* 97: 359–71

   (1966b) 'The power of the word in Sophocles' *Philoctetes*', *GRBS* 7: 233–50

   (1980) 'Ajax's gods and the gods of Sophocles', *AC* 49: 45–86

   (1989) 'Another look at character in Sophocles', in Sutton (1989) 279–94

   (1993) 'The hybris of Oedipus: Sophocles, *Oed. Tyr.* 873 and the genealogy of tyranny', *Eirene* 29: 7–30

Poe, J. P. (1974) *Heroism and divine justice in Sophocles' Philoctetes*. Leiden

Pucci, P. (1988) 'Reading the riddles of *Oedipus Rex*', in Pucci (ed.) (1988) 131–54

   (1991) 'The endless end of the *Oedipus Rex*', *Ramus* 20: 3–15

   (1992) *Oedipus and the fabrication of the father: Oedipus Tyrannus in modern criticism and philosophy*. Baltimore and London

   (ed.) (1988) *Language and the tragic hero: essays on Greek tragedy in honor of Gordon M. Kirkwood*. Atlanta

Pulleyn, S. (1997) *Prayer in Greek religion*. Oxford

Reckford, K. J. (1987) *Aristophanes' old-and-new comedy: six essays in perspective*. Chapel Hill and London

Reeve, M. D. (1973) 'Interpolation in Greek tragedy, III', *GRBS* 14: 145–71

Reinhard, L. (1920) *Die Anakoluthe bei Platon*. Berlin

Reinhardt, K. (1979 [1947]) *Sophocles*, trans. Hazel Harvey and David Harvey. Oxford

Renehan, R. (1992) 'The new Oxford Sophocles', *CPh* 87: 335–75

Riemer, P. (1991) *Sophokles, Antigone – Götterwille und menschliche Freiheit*. Stuttgart = *Abh. d. geistes- u. sozialwiss. Klasse, Akademie der Wissenschaften und der Lit.* Jahrgang 1991.12

Ringer M. (1998) *Electra and the empty urn: metatheater and role playing in Sophocles*. Chapel Hill and London

Robinson, D. B. (1969) 'Topics in Sophocles' *Philoctetes*', *CQ* 19: 34–56

Romilly, J. de (1968) *Time in Greek tragedy*. Ithaca

Rose, P. W. (1995) 'Historicizing Sophocles' *Ajax*', in Goff (1995) 59–90

Rosen, R. M. and J. Farrell (eds.) (1993) *Nomodeiktes: Greek studies in honor of Martin Ostwald*. Ann Arbor

Rosenmeyer, T. G. (1993) 'Elusory voices: thoughts about the Sophoclean chorus', in Rosen and Farrell (1993) 557–71

(1996) 'Ironies in serious drama', in Silk (1996) 497–519

Russo, J. (1997) 'Prose genres for the performance of traditional wisdom in ancient Greece: proverb, maxim, apothegm', in Edmunds and Wallace (1997) 49–64

Sakellariou, M. B. (1989) *The polis-state: definition and origin.* Athens

Schein, S. L. (1997) 'Divinity and moral agency in Sophoclean tragedy', in Lloyd (1997) 123–38

Schlesier, R. (1983) 'Daimon und daimones bei Euripides', *Saeculum* 34: 267–79

Schlesinger, E. (1968) 'Die Intrige im Aufbau von Sophokles' Philoktet', *RhM* 111: 97–156

Schmid, W. (1934) 'Sophokles', in W. Schmid and O. Stählin, *Geschichte der griechischen Literatur*, Munich, 1.2.309–514

Schmitt, A. (1997) 'Wesenszüge der griechischen Tragödie: Schicksal, Schuld, Tragik', in Flashar (1997) 5–49

Schnebele, A. (1988) *Die epischen Quellen des sophokleischen Philoktet: die Postiliaca im frühgriechischen Epos.* Karlsruhe

Schulze, W. (1966 [1918]) 'Beiträge zur Wort- und Sittengeschichte II', in *Kleine Schriften*, ed. W. Wissmann, second edn, Göttingen, 160–89

Schwartz, J. D. (1986) 'Human action and political action in *Oedipus Tyrannos*', in Euben (1986) 183–209

Scodel, R. (1982) 'Hybris in the second stasimon of the *Oedipus Rex*', *CPh* 77: 214–23

(ed.) (1993) *Theater and society in the classical world.* Ann Arbor

Scott, W. C. (1996) *Musical design in Sophoclean theater.* Hanover, NH, and London

Seaford, R. (1994) *Reciprocity and ritual: Homer and tragedy in the developing city-state.* Oxford

Seale, D. (1982) *Vision and stagecraft in Sophocles.* London and Canberra

Segal, C. P. (1977) 'Philoctetes and the imperishable piety', *Hermes* 105: 133–58, reprinted in Segal (1995) 95–118

(1981) *Tragedy and civilization: an interpretation of Sophocles.* Cambridge, MA, and London

(1989–90) 'Drama, narrative, and perspective in Sophocles' *Ajax*', *Sacris Erudiri: Jaarboek voor Godsdienstwetenschappen* 31: 395–404, reprinted in Segal (1995) 16–25

(1993) *Euripides and the poetics of sorrow: art, gender, and commemoration in Alcestis, Hippolytus, and Hecuba.* Durham, NC, and London

(1995) *Sophocles' tragic world: divinity, nature, society.* Cambridge, MA, and London

Seidensticker, B. (1994) 'Beobachtungen zur sophokleischen Kunst der Charakterzeichnung', in Bierl and Möllendorff (1994) 276–88

Sfameni Gasparro, G. (1997) '*Daimōn* and *tychē* in the Hellenistic religious experience', in Bilde *et al.* (1997) 67–109

Sheppard, J. T. (1927) '*Electra*: a defence of Sophocles' and '*Electra* again', *CR* 41: 2–9 and 163–5

Sidwell, K. (1992) 'The argument of the second stasimon of *Oedipus Tyrannus*', *JHS* 112: 106–22

Silk, M. S. (ed.) (1996) *Tragedy and the tragic: Greek theatre and beyond.* Oxford

Slings, S. R. (1992) 'Written and spoken language: an exercise in the pragmatics of the Greek sentence', *CPh* 87: 95–109

(1997) 'Figures of speech and their lookalikes: two further exercises in the pragmatics of the Greek sentence', in Bakker (1997) 169–214

Sommerstein, A. H. (1997) 'Alternative scenarios in Sophocles' *Electra*', *Prometheus* 23: 193–214

Sommerstein, A. H. *et al.* (eds.) (1993) *Tragedy, comedy and the polis: papers from the Greek drama conference, Nottingham, 18–20 July 1990.* Bari

Sourvinou-Inwood, C. (1994) 'Something to do with Athens: tragedy and ritual', in Osborne and Hornblower (1994) 269–90

(1997) 'Tragedy and religion: constructs and readings', in Pelling (ed.) (1997) 161–86

Stanford, W. B. (1954) *The Ulysses theme: a study in the adaptability of a traditional hero.* Oxford

Stehle, E. (1997) *Performance and gender in ancient Greece: nondramatic poetry in its setting.* Princeton

Steiner, G. (1984) *Antigones.* Oxford

Stephanus, H. (1568) *De Sophoclea imitatione Homeri, seu de Sophoclis locis imitationem Homeri habentibus, dissertatio*, printed as pp. 86–95 in the author's *Annotationes in Sophoclem et Euripidem.* No place of publication

Stevens, P. T. (1945) 'Colloquial expressions in Aeschylus and Sophocles', *CQ* 39: 95–105

Stinton, T. C. W. (1990a) *Collected papers on Greek tragedy*, ed. Hugh Lloyd-Jones. Oxford

(1990b [1976]) 'Notes on Greek tragedy, I', in Stinton (1990a), 197–235

Styan, J. L. (1982) *Max Reinhardt.* Cambridge

Sutton, R. F. (ed.) (1989) *Daidalikon: studies in memory of Raymond V. Schoder, S.J.* Wanconda, IL

Taplin, O. (1978) *Greek tragedy in action.* London

(1979) 'Yielding to forethought: Sophocles' *Ajax*', in Bowersock *et al.* (1979) 122–9

(1983) 'Sophocles in his theatre', Fondation Hardt, *Entretiens* 29: 155–83

(1987) 'The mapping of Sophocles' *Philoctetes*', *BICS* 34, 69–77

(1995) 'Opening performance: closing texts?', in *Essays in criticism* 45: 93–120

(forthcoming) 'Spreading the word through performance'

Thummer, E. (1981) 'Der Bogen und das Leid. Zu Sophokles' *Philoktetes*', Ἀρχαιογνωσία 2: 1–8

Tsitsoni, E. (1963) *Untersuchungen der EK-Verbal-Komposita bei Sophokles.* Kallmünz

Tuplin, C. (1985) 'Imperial tyranny: some reflections on a classical Greek political metaphor', in Cartledge and Harvey (1985) 348–75

Turner, V. W. (1982) *From ritual to theatre: the human seriousness of play.* New York

Ubersfeld, A. (1978) *Lire le théâtre.* Paris

(1996 [1981]) *Lire le théâtre II: l'école du spectateur.* Paris

Usener, H. (1896) *Götternamen: Versuch einer Lehre von der religiösen Begriffsbildung.* Bonn

Vernant, J.-P. (1988a [1968]) 'The historical moment of tragedy in Greece: some of the social and psychological conditions', in Vernant and Vidal-Naquet (1988) 23–28

(1988b [1969]) 'Tensions and ambiguities in Greek tragedy', in Vernant and Vidal-Naquet (1988) 29–48

(1988c [1970]) 'Ambiguity and reversal: on the enigmatic structure of *Oedipus Rex*', in Vernant and Vidal-Naquet (1988) 113–40

(1988d [1972]) 'Intimations of the will in Greek tragedy', in Vernant and Vidal-Naquet (1988) 49–84

(1988e [1981]) 'The lame tyrant: from Oedipus to Periander', in Vernant and Vidal-Naquet (1988) 207–36

(1991a) *Mortals and immortals: collected essays*, ed. Froma I. Zeitlin. Princeton

(1991b [1974]) 'Speech and mute signs', in Vernant (1991a) 303–17

(1991c [1982]) 'A "beautiful death" and the disfigured corpse in Homeric epic', in Vernant (1991a) 50–74

Vernant, J.-P. and P. Vidal-Naquet (1988) *Myth and tragedy in ancient Greece*, trans. Janet Lloyd. New York

Vidal-Naquet, P. (1988) 'Ajax ou la mort du héros', *BAB* 74, 463–86

Wallace, R. W. (1997) 'Poet, public, and "theatrocracy": audience performance in classical Athens', in Edmunds and Wallace (1997) 97–111

Wardy, R. (1996) *The birth of rhetoric: Gorgias, Plato and their successors.* London and New York

Webster, T. B. L. (1969 [1936]) *An introduction to Sophocles*, second edn. London

West, M. L. (1978) 'Tragica II', *BICS* 25: 106–22

(1990) 'Colloquialism and naïve style in Aeschylus', in Craik (1990) 3–12

Whitby, M. (1996) 'Telemachus transformed?: the origins of Neoptolemus in *Philoctetes*', *G & R* 43: 31–42

Wilamowitz-Moellendorff, T. von (1969 [1917]) *Die dramatische Technik des Sophokles*, unchanged reprint. Zurich

Wilamowitz-Moellendorff, U. von (1921) *Griechische Verskunst.* Berlin

Wiles, D. (1997) *Tragedy in Athens: performance space and theatrical meaning*. Cambridge

Williams, B. (1993) *Shame and necessity*. Berkeley, Los Angeles and Oxford

Wilson, A. M. (1977) 'The individualized chorus in Old Comedy', *CQ* 27: 278–83

Wilson, P. J. (1993) 'The representation and rhetoric of the collective: Athenian ragic choroi in their social context'. Diss. Cambridge

(1996) 'Tragic rhetoric: the use of tragedy and the tragic in the fourth century', in Silk (1996) 310–31

Winkler, J. J. and F. I. Zeitlin (eds.) (1990) *Nothing to do with Dionysos?: Athenian drama in its social context*. Princeton

Winnington-Ingram, R. P. (1948) *Euripides and Dionysus: an interpretation of the Bacchae*. Cambridge

(1969) 'Tragica', *BICS* 16: 44–54

(1980) *Sophocles: an interpretation*. Cambridge

Woronoff, M. (1983) 'Ville natale et cité chez Sophocle', *Ktéma* 8: 85–94

Worthington, I. (ed.) (1994) *Persuasion: Greek rhetoric in action*. London and New York

Zak, W. F. (1995) *The polis and the divine order: the* Oresteia, *Sophocles, and the defense of democracy*. Lewisburg and London

Zeitlin, F. I. (1982) *Under the sign of the shield: semiotics and Aeschylus'* Seven Against Thebes. Rome

Zielinski, T. (1924) 'De Sophoclis fabula ignota', *Eos* 27: 59–73

GENERAL INDEX

Aeschylus
  different from Sophocles 17–18, 89,
    153 n. 36, 204 n. 24, 205 n. 27,
    264–7
  Philoctetes 96–7, 99, 111, 271 n. 117
agōn scenes 66–74
Ajax
  A. and the chorus 231–5
  A. evaluated 40–2, 233–8
  A.'s *philoi* 235–8
  chorus 231–45
  chorus and army: 232–3, 238–45
  continues after A.'s death 192–3
  gods 144–8, 182–5, 189, 192–3
  see also Athena
ambiguity *see* Sophoclean language
anacolouthon 49–50 n. 41
Antigone
  A. perceived as more central than
    Creon 78, 189–90
  chorus 245–6
  Creon as a character 75–7
  responsibility for A.'s suffering 175–80
Apollo
  in *Electra* 152–3, 180–2, 188–9
  in *OT* 137, 171–5
Aristotle 215–19
Athena 144–8, 182–5, 189
audience *see* spectators

Bowra, C. M. 119–20, 135–6
Bruhn, E. 1, 27–8
Burkert, W. 144, 147, 152–3

Campbell, L. 1, 19, 20, 27–8
characters
  asking questions 70–1
  dramatic irony 80–7
  emphasis on emotions 83
  have depth 61–91
  perspective 90–1
  using argument from *eikos* 71–4
  using general statements or *gnōmai*
    67–8, 71–80

  using logical argument 69–71
  using personal phrasing 67–8, 72, 76,
    83
  using personification 79–80, 84
  using verbal themes 73–6, 79
  vs. singular 'character' 61–2
  see also Antigone, Electra, Oedipus
    Rex and Oedipus at Colonus
chorus
  Ajax 231–45
  Antigone 175–80
  cultural context 199–201
  Electra 245–68
  flexible 201–2, 219–31, 238–45, 251–
    64, 271–2
  in danger and safe 195–272, esp.
    205–6
  model of spectators' communal
    response 195–6
  opening out to Greeks and humans in
    general 227–31, 242–5, 261–2
  OT 171–2, 206–31
  part of 'the large group' 195–272, esp.
    201–5
  representing civic community 195–
    272, esp. 196–8, 203–5
  Trachiniae 169–71
communality 7–17 and *passim*
communication 8–9, 15–17 and *passim*
complement *see* head, governing

daimōn 143–54, 166–8, 177
diptych plays 192–4
dramatic irony *see* 'characters'

Easterling, P. E. 62–3, 198–9
eikos 71–4
Electra
  agōn 66–71
  chorus 245–68
  civic community 251–68
  Clytemnestra as a character 66–71,
    83–5

Clytemnestra's prayer to Apollo 152–3
dramatic irony 80–7
E. as a character 82–7
E. constructing a family 248–51
gods doubtful near the end 180–2
house 246–68
oracle 180–2, 188
ellipse *see* sentences *and* Sophoclean
    language
Euripides
different from Sophocles 17–18, 68,
    78, 89, 153 n. 36, 204 n. 24, 205 n.
    27, 264–7, 269 n. 115, 271 n. 117
Philoctetes 96–7, 99, 111

focus (pragmatic role) 32–3, 37

general statements *see* characters
genitive, in need of governing head 36–8
Gill, C. 89–90
gnōmai see 'characters'
gods
and the *polis* 270
as possible supplement in elliptic
    phrases 52–4
central yet inscrutable 133–9
difficult to hold responsible 168–87
dual motivation 173–5
epithets: 154–68
initiate action 187–94
named and unnamed 139–68
oracles 109–30, 187–9
power brought out in the phrasing
    (Aphrodite) 45–7
scholarship 134–8
see also Ajax, Apollo, Athena,
    daimōn, prophetic language and
    Zeus
Goldhill, S. 73–4, 198–9
Gorgias 12, 24–7, 58–9, 169
Griffith, M. 197–9
groups
and individuals 195–272
threatened and safe 195–272
see also 'chorus'

head, governing
complement transferred from one to
    another 49 n. 41
definition 24–6
followed unexpectedly by complement
    49 n. 41

separated from modifier / specifier 34–
    40
historic present 102
historic specificity 5–6, 10–13, 199–200
Homer 166, 269–70
hyperbaton 34–42, 49 n. 41

involvement 7–18 and *passim*

language *see* Sophoclean language
Long, A. A. 2–3, 6, 19, 27

metre 127–8
Moorhouse, A. C. 2, 19, 27–8
myth, innovations reflected in the
    language 93–108

names
gods named and unnamed 139–68
Oedipus unnamed at the end of *OC*
    42–5
nominativus pendens 47–9

Oedipus at Colonus
chorus and large group 201–3
O. as a character 78–80
O. transformed at the end 42–5
time 78–80
Zeus and *daimōn* 149–52
Oedipus Rex
chorus 206–31
continues after self-blinding 193–4
Creon as a character 71–4
house 209–10
O. and the *polis* 208–19
O. as *turannos* 214–19
responsibility for O.'s suffering 171–5
Tiresias 55–7
see also Apollo

Parker, R. 185–6
Peradotto, J. 137, 174
personal phrasing *see* characters
personification *see* characters
perspective 90–1, 201–72
Philoctetes
ending 107–8, 128–30
False Merchant scene 54–5, 98–100,
    113–23
Helenus' prophecy 109–30, 187–8
Lemnos uninhabited 97–8
Neoptolemus 96, 100–13, 127–30
Odysseus 95–100, 109–27

Philoctetes 106–8, 125
use of myth 93–108
polis 198, 200, 205–31, 245–51, 258–68, 270–1
prolepsis 31–3
prophetic language 55–7, 109–30

readers *see* spectators and readers
repetition 42–5, 84, 115
reported speech 44, 114

Seaford, R. 204–5
sentences
  ambiguous or elliptic 50–7
  change direction 40–50
  flow interrupted 31–40
  Sophoclean unlike Gorgianic 23–31, 58–60
  unpredictable yet clear 22–60
Sophoclean language
  ambiguous, elliptic or vague 4, 6–7, 50–7, 109–30, 167–8, 185–7, 271–2
  clarity 27–60
  creates trust in something that is there 57–60, 87–91, 130–2, 186–7, 195
  engages through blend of certainty and uncertainty 10–12 and *passim*
  evokes situations 51–7
  scholarship 1–7
  studied on small and large scale 17, 19, 92
Sourvinou-Inwood, C. 137–8, 157
specifier *see* head, governing
spectators
  and choruses 195–206

and readers 13–16, 196 n. 3
differences between 7–17 and *passim*
expectations, knowledge 10–13, 22–30
involvement *see* 'involvement'
make judgements about characters 61–91
sun-compounds 53 n. 43, 54 n. 44
syntax *see* sentences

text uncertain 31 n. 12, 34 n. 19, 38 n. 23, 45–7, 85 n. 34, 116 n. 34, 160 n. 43, 162 n. 46, 177 n. 61, 184 n. 72, 210 n. 34, 222 n. 52, 226 n. 56, 242 n. 84, 254 n. 99, 255 n. 100, 261 n. 106, 263 n. 110
theatre *see* spectators
themes, verbal 3–4, 31–4, 36–8, 47–8, 73–4
topic (pragmatic role) 32–3, 37, 48–9
Trachiniae
  chorus 246
  Lichas 162–6
  Zeus 154–66, 169–71
translation 8, 18
turannos 214–19, 222–5

Vernant, J.-P. 196–9, 203

Wilamowitz, T. v. 114–15, 119–23
word order *see* sentences

questions *see* characters

Zeus 148–68, 181–2

INDEX OF PASSAGES DISCUSSED

Major discussions are indicated in **bold** type

AESCHYLUS
Ag. 37–8: 256 n. 101
  884–5: 41
Ch. 22–3: 266
  75–81: 266
  824: 264 n. 113
  849: 45
  864: 264 n. 113
  973–4: 265
  1046–7: 265
Pe. 620–1: 153 n. 36

ARCHILOCHUS
19: 216

ARISTOPHANES
Av. 544–5: 144

ARISTOTLE
AP 1460a11–17: 12 n. 28
  1460b32–5: 88
NE 1160a35–b2: 215
Probl. XIX 48.922b: 196–7

CYPRIA
p. 104, 23: 102 n. 17

DEMOSTHENES
19.246: 76–7

DIO CHRYSOSTOMOS
52.2: 99 n. 11, 111 n. 28
52.7–8: 97
52.9: 96
52.14: 99 n. 11
59.2: 111 n. 27
59.3: 96

EURIPIDES
Ba. 22: 153 n. 36
  474–5: 12 n. 28

El. 298–9: 266
  593–5: 265
  761–2: 265
  877: 265
  958: 46 n. 35
  1072–3: 48 n. 39
  1254–75: 265
  1334–5: 265
Hip. 1074–6: 256 n. 101
fr. 898.6: 45

GORGIAS
Hel. 3: **24–7**
  5: 12
  21: **24–7**
fr. 1: 12 n. 26
fr. 3.1: 12
fr. 23: 12 n. 28
fr. 26: 12
fr. 28: 12 n. 26

HERODOTUS
1.53: 50–1
1.55: 123–4
1.91: 124
6.138: 97
7.141: 124

HOMER
Il. 1.590–4: 97
  2.681–94: 232
  2.722: 102 n. 17
  16.168–97: 232
  18.606: 45
  19.86–7: 163 n. 47
  21.40: 97
  21.195: 45
  24.797: 242

LIFE OF SOPHOCLES
12: 135

LITTLE ILIAD
p. 106, 20–3: 101
p. 106, 23–5: 110–11
p. 106, 25: 96, 99
p. 106, 29–30: 100

PINDAR
Ol. 6.22–3: 46

PLATO
Apol. 21d: 11
Laws II 654a9–b1: 200
   III 700c–701b: 14
Rep. x 606b: 14
   x 617e4–5: 185–6
schol. vet. *Hipp. Mai.* 288b: 56 n. 46

PLUTARCH
De profectibus in virtute 7.79b: 1
Sol. 21.1: 41

SEMONIDES
fr. 2: 41

SOLON
32: 216–17
33.5–7: 216

SOPHOCLES
Aj. 14: 145, 182
  25–7: 39 n. 24
  41: 37 n. 22
  51–65: 145
  74: 182
  91: 145, 182
  132–3: 184–5
  137–40: 231–3, 239
  151: 233
  158–61: 234
  162–6: 233
  185–6: 233, 239
  196: 233
  201: 232
  243–4: **144–5**
  245–56: 233
  263–4: **51–2**
  301: 182
  311–27: 185
  331–2: 34 n. 19
  334–5: 39 n. 24
  349–50: 234
  361: 54 n. 44, 234
  364–7: 233–4

383: 182
401–2: 182
443: 238
450: 182
454–5: 49 n. 41
458: 233
460–1: 240
464: 238
479–80: 234
504: **145–6**
534: **145–6**
541–2: 39 n. 24
545–82: 192
556–7: 39 n. 24
565–73: 232
574–6: **34–5**
596–608: 232
656: 182, 192
738–9: 39 n. 24
756–7: 143, 182, 192
770–3: 34 n. 19
770: 36 n. 21
771: 182
778–9: 192
824: 192
843–4: 233, 240
946–7: 38 n. 22
953–4: 142, **183–4**
955–70: 184, 192
988–9: 41, 49 n. 41
1040–1: 49 n. 41
1055: 241
1057: 183
1060: 183
1071–83: 78 n. 23
1091–2: 240
1100–6: 241
1118–19: 240
1128: 183
1130: 147 n. 28
1159–60: 237
1163–7: 43 n. 30, **242–3**
1171–84: 236–8
1192–8: 243
1214–15: 147
1216–22: 238
1244–5: 49 n. 41
1264–5: 240
1266–7: 38 n. 22
1266–70: 39 n. 24
1316–17: 54 n. 44, 241
1332–5: 237
1340: 238, 243

SOPHOCLES (continued)
1342–5: **40–2**
1348–9: 41
1350: 218
1363: 49 n. 41
1376–7: 237
1380: 237
1389–99: 237
1413–14: 241
1415: 238
1416: 243
1418–20: 243–4
Ant. 1–3: 49 n. 41
74–7: 175
175–84: **75–7**
278: 179 n. 63
289–94: 245
298–9: 49 n. 41
450–5: 49 n. 41, 175
458–60: **36–8**
506: 218
519: 141
523: 54 n. 44
542: 141
570: 57 n. 48
594–5: 39 n. 24
692–700: 245
733: 245–6
799–800: 57 n. 48
810–943: **176–9**
891–4: 49 n. 41
940–3: 246
944–87: 142
1015: 245
1056: 218
1074–5: 38 n. 22, 143
1115–39: 159
1115–54: 142, 246
1169: 218
1199–1202: 39 n. 24
1312–13: 39 n. 24, 180 n. 68
1319–20: 180 n. 68
1339: 180 n. 68
El. 8–10: 246
32–7: 188
67–72: 247, 250
78–9: 39 n. 24
121: 252
124–7: 251–2
129: 252
153–63: 39 n. 24, 49 n. 41, 252–3
171–2: 57 n. 48
193–200: 252, 254
226: 252

234: 252
251–2: 252
257: 252
303–4: 39 n. 24
317–18: 252
341–4: 249
349–50: 249
365–8: 249
431–2: 39 n. 24
417–19: 49 n. 41
472–507: 252–3
513–15: 254, 264
525–6: 39 n. 24
528–48: **67–71**
563–76: 142
597–8: 249
637–59: 142
655–9: **152–3**
709–11: 39 n. 24
743–8: 49 n. 41
764–5: 252
788–96: **82–5**
809–12: 39 n. 24
817–22: 85–6
856: 253 n. 98
881–2: 49 n. 41
947: 57 n. 48
947–89: 250
954–7: 39 n. 24
958–66: 251
977–83: **250–1**
984: 250
986–9: 25–2
1015–16: 39 n. 24
1027: 37 n. 22
1063–5: 57 n. 48
1066–73: 255, 257
1081: 253
1136–7: 49 n. 41, 248
1145–52: 268–9
1153–6: 38 n. 22
1227–31: **257–9**
1251–2: 57 n. 48
1253–5: 39 n. 24
1260–1: **38–9**
1264–70: 188
1344: 57 n. 48
1354–5: 257
1372–5: 39 n. 24
1376–83: 142
1398: 259
1404–5: 260
1406: 259
1413–14: **259–60**

SOPHOCLES (continued)

1424–5: 85, 141, 181, 263
1431: 261
1458–63: 261
1466–7: 57 n. 48, 181
1493–8: 263–4
1505–7: 39 n. 24
1508–10: 262–3
OC 47–8: 49 n. 41
62–3: **52–4**
67: 202
84–93: 49 n. 41
101–5: 39 n. 24
111–12: 201
122–5: 201–2
145: 201–2
171: 202
292–307: 202
410: 54 n. 44
419: 218
440–4: 39 n. 24
449: 218
555–9: 49 n. 41
607–15: **78–80**
647: 53
691–3: 141
727: 45
814–86: 201
834: 212 n. 36
871: 202
911–23: 203
939–43: 49 n. 41
944–6: 49 n. 41
978–80: 49 n. 41
1150–2: **47**
1161–2: 39 n. 24
1173–4: 38 n. 22
1338: 218
1360–1: 49 n. 41
1448–50: 57 n. 48
1480–5: 150
1526–7: 49 n. 41
1540–1: 39 n. 24
1615–16: 39 n. 24
1748–50: 150–1
1760–3: **42–5**
OT 1–13: 206, 209–10
6–8: 49 n. 41
9–11: 57 n. 48
22–3: 210
27–9: 209
35–6: 208
35–9: 49 n. 41
40–2: 206

46: 210
47–8: 208
51: 210
56–7: 49 n. 41
58–64: 207, 209
60–1: 49 n. 41
72: 207, 210
85: 209
87–8: 57 n. 47
93–4: 49 n. 41
101: 210–11
110–11: 57 n. 47
139–41: 208
149–54: 206–7
151–215: 142
159–63: 49 n. 41
179: 211
220–1: 54 n. 44
223: 209
264–8: 81
273: 209, 226
302–3: 211
310–13: 49 n. 41
312: 211
320–1: 211
325: 57 n. 47
328–9: 57 n. 47
331: 211
337–40: 211–12
339–41: 20–1, **55–7**
362: 57 n. 47
366–7: 57 n. 47
369: 45
372–3: 57 n. 47
374–5: 208
376–7: 143
379: 57 n. 47
380–1: **214–19**
383–4: 212
390–400: 208
399–400: 208
408–9: 57 n. 48
412–25: 57 n. 47
438: 57 n. 47
443: 212
463–511: 219–20
498–9: 141
513: 226
523–4: 57 n. 48
527: 57 n. 48
535: 214
541–2: 214
583–615: **71–4**
628–30: **212–13**

SOPHOCLES (continued)
639: 209
646–96: **220–1**
676–7: 57 n. 48
681–2: 57 n. 48
707–19: 153 n. 37
711: 57 n. 47
713: 57 n. 47
739–41: **31–4**
758–62: 49 n. 41
786: 57 n. 48
791–2: 228 n. 58
800–4: 39 n. 24
831: 228
857–8: 38 n. 22
861: 210
863–910: **222–5**
897–902: 57 n. 48
903: 228
906–9: 57 n. 48
911: 226
936: 48 n. 39
953: 57 n. 47
1011: 57 n. 47
1084: 57 n. 47
1086–1109: 225–6
1111: 226
1173: 57 n. 48
1175: 57 n. 48
1177: 57 n. 48
1186–1222: 226–9
1226: 210
1287–8: 229
1294–6: 229
1297: 229
1327–32: 49 n. 41, 142, **172–3**
1349–55: 173
1359: 229
1360: 173
1391–408: 173, 229
1429–31: 210
1432: 193
1438–9: 193
1524: 229 n. 60
Ph. 1–2: **97**
3–4: 96, 104–5
6: 102
8–11: 49 n. 41, 98
14: 96
15: 96
50–3: 57 n. 48
68–78: 110–11
88–91: 111–12
101–3: 112, 114, 121

113–15: 112
106: 57 n. 48
119: 105 n. 18
126–9: **54–5**, 98
192–200: 39 n. 24, 113
236–7: 39 n. 24
271–5: 49 n. 41
314–16: 107
343–7: 39 n. 24
343–460: **100–6**
352–3: 57 n. 48
380–1: 39 n. 24
391–402: 49 n. 41
410–42: **103–6**
497–9: 49 n. 41
519–21: 54 n. 44
533: 115
547–52: 49 n. 41
554–6: 99
561–97: 98
567: 99
591–7: **117–18**, 121
598–602: 116
610–13: 113–14, **119–23**, 129
614–19: 118, 121, 126
618–19: 38 n. 22
622–30: 125
635–7: 115
799–803: 107–8
839–42: 127
989–90: 163 n. 47
1016–18: 49 n. 41
1054–62: 126
1128–39: 49 n. 41
1270: 57 n. 48
1314–47: **128–30**
1362–6: 101
1395–6: 49 n. 41
1415: 149, 188
1464–8: **148–50**
Tr. 1–3: 49 n. 41
19: 156
26–7: 156, 161
49–51: 39 n. 24
73–9: 188
127–8: 156, 161
139–40: 155, 161
200–1: 156, 161
238: 162
250–1: **162–5**
275: 162
278–9: 162
288: 162
303–5: 156, 161

351–7: 143, 164
399: 162
441–2: 141
479–83: 102
490–6: 102
497: 141
499: 156, 161
507–13: 39 n. 24
513: 155
515–16: 142
566: 156
644: 155
646: 246
653–4: 57 n. 48
657: 246
750–4: 155
786–7: 49 n. 41, 54 n. 44
826: 155
896–7: 54 n. 44
956: 155
983–4: 160

993–1003: **160–1**
1022: 161
1042: 159
1048: 159
1055–9: 108
1086: 159
1088: 159
1106: 159
1112: 246
1122–3: 38 n. 22
1148–9: 159
1164–73: 121
1185: 159
1222–4: 39 n. 24
1238–9: 49 n. 41
1264–74: **170–1**
1278: 148, 161, **169–71**
fr. 555.2: 146 n. 27
fr. 939: 45
schol. on *El.* 1260–1: 38
schol. on *Ph.* 1468: 149